STATE PARKS *of the* MIDWEST

A Guide to Camping, Fishing, Hiking, & Sightseeing

Vici DeHaan

A Cordillera Press Guidebook
Johnson Books: Boulder

Library of Congress Cataloging-in-Publication Data
DeHaan, Vici
    State parks of the Midwest: America's heartland: a guide to camping,
fishing, hiking & sightseeing / Vici DeHaan. –1st ed.
    p.   cm
    ISBN 1-55566-109-2 : $16.95
    1. Middle West—Guidebooks.   2. Parks—Middle West—Guidebooks.
I. Title.
F351.D35   1993
917.704'33—dc20
                                   92-42539
                                      CIP

Front Cover Photograph
   Fall colors in the Midwest ERIC J. WUNROW

Back Cover Photographs
   Marblehead Lighthouse, Sailboats, Crane ERIC J. WUNROW
   Riverboats ROBERTS RIVER RIDES, DUBUQUE, IOWA
   Bicyclists MACKINAC ISLAND STATE HISTORIC PARKS
   Re-enactment ILLINOIS DEPARTMENT OF CONSERVATION

Cover Design ERIC J. WUNROW

First Edition
1 2 3 4 5 6 7 8 9

Printed in the United States of America by
Johnson Printing Company
1880 South 57th Court
Boulder, Colorado 80301

Printed on recycled paper with soy ink to conserve America's resources.

Contents

AMERICA'S HEARTLAND

Take a tour through America's Heartland: Michigan, Wisconsin, Iowa, Indiana, South Dakota, North Dakota, Nebraska, Missouri, Minnesota, Kansas, Ohio and Illinois. Leave the interstate highways and explore the back roads. Stroll through the town square, and stop for a meal where you can chat with the locals. As you traverse the wide open prairies, passing countless fields of wheat and corn, you can't help but be struck by the vastness found in this section of the country.

While I was researching many of the state parks in the Midwest, I found that they had their own distinctive characteristics. Instead of the mountainous terrain more prevalent in the West, I discovered a land full of many lakes, large flowing rivers, and thick forests providing the perfect opportunity to escape from the challenges of everyday life.

Many travelers are attuned to visiting the various national parks as they cross the country. They know that these parks were established to preserve a special natural or historic feature, and that most provide accommodations for staying overnight, either in a campground or in a lodge with individual cabins.

I, too, have toured a large number of the national parks while researching two earlier books, but I often encountered crowded conditions, particularly while traveling during the summer months. Then, I began spending time in the various state parks, and I discovered places I believe are just as beautiful, but generally much less crowded, besides offering many of the same amenities found in the national parks.

Like the national parks, many state parks have visitor centers where you can watch slides, attend naturalist-led activities, and listen to entertaining campfire programs complete with fascinating stories about the local area. Sometimes you can even take a step back in time and join in a living history presentation .

Whether you visit state parks as an overnight stop while en route to another destination or make them your choice for a vacation spot, you'll find much to keep you entertained. Since the majority of them are located near a body of water, you can enjoy fishing, boating, and swimming, and if your timing is right, participate in a fishing derby or sailing regatta.

As an avid hiker, I'm always on the lookout for new trails to explore and have spent many delightful hours tracking the numerous paths that wind through the Midwest state parks. Many trails traverse deep woods, which, although beautiful during the summer, promise an exceptionally colorful fall display.

The "rails to trails" program adopted by many of the states has provided bikers and hikers with some wonderful trails to follow. Since these routes follow former railroad beds, the grades are usually very gradual.

Much of my traveling was done while pulling a travel trailer, so I have included the kind of information I needed when searching for an overnight campsite. Since the Midwest can be hot and muggy during the summer, I usually searched for campsites with electrical hookups for running the air conditioner. I found that many state parks provide this convenience in at least part of their campsites, whereas national parks usually do not.

As a pilot, I've flown to some of the state park areas in a private plane. Sometimes I had my touring bicycle inside the plane to provide the necessary transportation to town or to the nearby state park. At other times, I needed a rental car in order to explore. For others who also fly in small planes, this book includes the names of airports located close to the parks whenever rental cars were available at the strip.

While visiting many of the state parks, I also found nearby attractions that added an extra element of excitement to my explorations. While some of the parks are themselves historic in nature, others are located near historic towns which you can tour on your own or with a guide. Sometimes you'll find yourself in town in time to watch their local parade and to participate in their various holiday celebrations. You'll often be treated to a glimpse into the various cultures that have led to the richness of life we enjoy today.

I hope that you can also enjoy some of the fun that goes along with poking into some new and different places scattered across America's Heartland. It makes each day an adventure as you wander into spots you might have overlooked before.

The Illinois and Michigan Canal stretches 61.6 miles from Lake Michigan to the town of Peru in La Salle County. This corridor contains 11 state parks and 37 natural areas, including Lockport, where these youngsters are exploring.

ILLINOIS

Illinois is bordered by the Mississippi, Ohio and Wabash rivers and Lake Michigan, and is one of the most level of all the prairie states. Like many of the states, it has joined in preserving our national heritage. As you travel throughout Illinois, you'll have the opportunity to attend many festivities celebrating our heritage including fairs, parades, re-enactments of historical events, and arts and crafts of the past.

You also will be struck by the impact that geological forces have had on the state that was once covered by an extensive inland sea which left behind many feet of sedimentary layers. This was followed by the Ice Age when sheets of ice moved across much of the state, leaving their imprint on the landscape. Part of the state is in the "driftless" zone that escaped the glaciers, and as a result, you'll encounter different terrain from that found where the land was crushed beneath the grinding ice.

The Indian heritage dates back to 6,000 B.C. to 1,000 B.C. when these early inhabitants passed through here hunting food. Gradually, they became settled, relying more on agriculture. We can see their artifacts and mounds in various parts of the state. They were eventually displaced by the early explorers, and later by the settlers who began moving here.

APPLE RIVER CANYON STATE PARK
1

LOCATION - The park is nine miles northwest of Stockton. It can be reached by going two miles west of Stockton on U.S. 20 and then six miles north on Illinois 10.

FEATURES - The Apple River has cut through layers of limestone, dolomite and shale, leaving behind sheer vertical cliffs, some rising 250 feet above the stream.

The old village of Millville was established in the 1830s, and boasted 330 inhabitants, sawmills, grist mills, and other shops. The dam above Millville

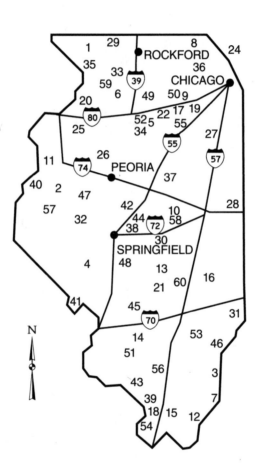

N

broke in the 1870s, and the town was washed away. Today, you can still see a plaque on the side of a boulder commemorating its earlier presence.

ACTIVITIES - Enjoy a picnic at one of four picnic areas, camp in one of 50 campsites without electrical hookups, or in a rent-a-camp.

Fish the Apple River for bass, sunfish, crappie and carp. Trout are stocked in the river in April, but their season is brief since they can't survive the hot summers.

The park has five hiking trails: Pine Ridge, Tower Rock, River Route, Sunset and Primrose Lane. Purchase snacks from the concession stand.

In nearby Galena, tour private homes open for viewing during the second weekend in June, and again the last weekend in September. Tour the Belvedere Mansion and Gardens, a 22-room mansion built in 1857, the Dowling House, Galena's oldest house built in 1826, and the Ulysses S. Grant Home State Historic Site with his pre–Civil War home.

For a narrated trolley tour of Galena with seven historic stops, contact Galena Trolley Tours: 815-777-1248 or 777-1251.

The Old Stockade, which originally served as protection against Indians for the early settlers, has been converted to a museum, and is open May 1–November 1. For information, call 815-777-1646.

Six miles north of Galena is the old Vinegar Hill Lead Mine, one of the most famous mines operating in the 19th century. Tours are available April 15–November 15 for a small fee. The tours last 30-45 minutes. Information: 815-777-0855.

INFORMATION
Apple River Canyon State Park
Apple River, Illinois 61001
815-745-3302

ARGYLE LAKE STATE PARK
2

LOCATION - The park is in western Illinois, seven miles west of Macomb and two miles north of Colchester off U.S. 136.

FEATURES - The lake occupies the area that was formerly part of the old stagecoach route that went northwest from Beardstown to Galena.

ACTIVITIES - Rent a boat or canoe and go fishing for bluegill, catfish, bass, crappie, muskie and trout. The lake has a boat launch and has a motor limit of 10 horsepower. Campers may select from 246 sites with electrical hookups and a dump station.

A concession stand is located near the boat dock and has boat and canoe rentals, refreshments, hot meals and bait.

Equestrians have a campground and a rugged seven-mile trail to explore.

A rugged five-mile hiking trail circles Argyle Lake. During the winter, come to cross-country ski, or snowmobile along a 7.5-mile trail.

Over the Labor Day weekend, attend the annual Argyle Antique Gas Engine show to observe many crafts from the past. Watch demonstrations of wheat threshing, sorghum making, and whittling, or wander through the antique auto displays. Watch the hot air balloon launch or the "slo-tractor" races. A tractor and auto/truck parade is offered at 12:30 each day.

INFORMATION
Argyle Lake State Park
R. R. 2
Colchester, Illinois 62326
309-776-3422

BEALL WOODS NATURE PRESERVE AND STATE PARK
3

LOCATION - The preserve and park are six miles south of Mt. Carmel near Keensburg off Illinois 1.

FEATURES - Beall Woods contains the largest single tract of original deciduous forests still standing in the U.S. Approximately 64 species of trees have been identified here.

ACTIVITIES - You can enjoy a picnic here, but no camping is available. Go boating from the boat launch.

The White Oak Trail, 1.7 miles, offers you the greatest variety of forestlands. Sweet Gum Trail, 1.5 miles, goes across the bottom-land forest, and follows Coffee Creek. During rainy times, the small creeks create waterfalls.

Two other trails include Tulip Tree Trail, 1.5 miles, and Ridgeway Trail, 1.75 miles long. Be sure to remain on the trails and stay alert for poison ivy. Insect repellent is highly recommended.

INFORMATION
Beall Woods Nature Preserve and State Park
R. R. 2
Mt. Carmel, Illinois 62863
618-298-2442

BEAVER DAM STATE PARK
4

LOCATION - The dam is seven miles south of Carlinville.

FEATURES - The park includes upland and bottomland woods. Watch for their white squirrels, which aren't albinos, but are instead a white phase of the gray squirrel.

ACTIVITIES - Go camping in the campground with electricity and a dump station. A concession stand is open from April through September, and provides picnic supplies, boat rentals and fishing licenses.

The lake has 1.7 miles of shoreline, and is stocked with bass, bluegill, and catfish. A boat launch and dock are available.

Seven miles of hiking trails circle the lake.

INFORMATION
Beaver Dam State Park
Box 127
Plainview, Illinois 62676
217-854-8020

BUFFALO ROCK STATE PARK
5

See under ILLINOIS AND MICHIGAN CANAL

CASTLE ROCK STATE PARK
6

See under WHITE PINES FOREST STATE PARK

CAVE-IN-ROCK STATE PARK
7

LOCATION - The park is a half-mile northeast of the village Cave-in-Rock off Illinois 1, and borders the Ohio River for nearly a mile.

FEATURES - The most prominent feature of the park is its large cave. When the river is lower, the cave's mouth is approximately 30 feet from the river's edge, but in the spring, the water is higher and the cave may be entered by boat. The cavern extends back horizontally for about 160 feet.

The cave has a notorious history from its use by outlaws and river pirates who attacked Ohio riverboats. By 1834, however, the last outlaws were gone, and it was often used as a shelter by early pioneers en route to Illinois.

ACTIVITIES - Visitors can enjoy picnicking, and dining in the restaurant.

The campground has 35 campsites with full hookups and a trailer dump facility. Limited groceries are available. You can also stay in one of the Cave-in-Rock cabins located along the river front. For reservations, call 618-289-4545.

Hikers have a couple of established trails to explore: Hickory Ridge and Pirates Bluff, both of moderate difficulty.

Go fishing in the Ohio River, or in the trout pond. Boaters have two launching ramps located on the western boundary of the park. A ferry operates to Kentucky daily from 6–6.

If you're here the third weekend of July, attend the Frontier Days celebration.

Bicyclists traveling along U.S. Bike Route 76 can travel east to the park for an overnight.

If you enjoy spectacular rock formations, visit nearby Garden of the Gods, ten miles southeast of Harrisburg between Illinois 1 and Illinois 34, to see the many shapes erosion has sculpted in the 300-million-year-old sandstone. See Camel Rock, Fat Man's Squeeze and other unusual formations. The area has a campground and eight miles of hiking trails.

INFORMATION
Cave-In-Rock State Park
P.O. Box 338, #1 New State Park Road
Cave-in-Rock, Illinois 62919
618-289-4325

CHAIN O' LAKES STATE PARK
8

LOCATION - The park is in northeastern Illinois 20 miles west of Lake Michigan and four miles south of the Illinois-Wisconsin border. It's three miles east of Spring Grove off U.S. 12.

FEATURES - These ten lakes were linked by the Fox River, and together they have 180 miles of shoreline. The state park borders three of the ten lakes in the Fox Chain O' Lakes: Grass, Marie and Bluff. The other seven lakes include the Fox, Pistake, Channel, Petite, Catherine, Nippersink and the Redhead, but these are all outside of the state park boundary.

The Fox River continues south from the Chain providing additional miles of boating to the Mississippi River.

ACTIVITIES - Picnic in one of the seven picnic areas. A concession stand has food, boat and canoe rentals, plus fishing and camping supplies.

Fish for bluegill, walleye, crappie, bass, northern pike, catfish and bullhead in the river or in the lakes. Fishing piers and launching ramps are provided. No motors are allowed on Turner Lake, but canoes and inflatable boats are allowed. No swimming is allowed in the park.

Camp in a rent-a-camp, or in the campground with 206 sites, all with electrical hookups and a trailer dump station.

Hike the 2.25-mile Nature's Way Trail that begins in the Oak Grove picnic area. An eight-mile horse trail is located in the park, and doubles as a winter cross-country ski trail. If you bring your own horse, park in the lot off Wilmot Road. Horse rentals are available May–October, one mile west of the Deerpath picnic area. For information, call 815-675-6532.

On July 4th, Fox Lake holds an aquatic parade featuring decorated boats. Call 312-395-7900 for details.

For a boat ride, contact the Island Queen Boat Rides on Fox Lake at 312-587-2222. For a float trip, contact Fox Floats in Carpentersville at 312-428-6811.

INFORMATION
Chain O' Lakes State Park
33947 North State Park Road
Spring Grove, Illinois 60081
312-587-5512

CHANNAHON STATE PARK
9

See under ILLINOIS AND MICHIGAN CANAL

CLINTON LAKE STATE RECREATION AREA
WELDON SPRINGS STATE RECREATION AREA
10

LOCATION - Clinton Lake is located in central Illinois eight miles east of the city of Clinton on Illinois 54.

Weldon Springs is three miles southeast of Clinton off Illinois 10 and east of U.S. 51.

FEATURES - From 1901–1920, Weldon's park grounds were used by a chautauqua when a large tent was erected to house lecturers, entertainers and educational programs. By 1904, the crowds had become so large that a 4,500-person auditorium was constructed.

Some of the speakers included William Jennings Bryan, William Howard Taft, Carrie Nation and Helen Keller. When motion pictures and the automobile became more prevalent, the chautauquas lost their audience.

ACTIVITIES - WELDON SPRINGS LAKE is stocked with crappie, bass, catfish and bullhead. Boat rentals and a boat launch ramp are available. No gas motors are permitted.

Weldon Springs Campground has rent-a-camp facilities, and 78 sites with electrical hookups and a trailer dump station. Backpackers can hike to a primitive campsite.

Hikers can explore Lakeside Trail, a two-mile self-guided trail. You can also hike the 3.5-mile trail north of the beach, or a 12-mile trail that extends from the North Fork boat access area to the North Fork canoe access area and back. During the winter, ski three miles of trails along the frozen creek.

July 4th features an afternoon's entertainment followed by evening fireworks over the lake. The last weekend in July, attend Chautauqua Days and enjoy a horseshoe tournament, canoe rides, car show, fishing derby and a three-mile race.

CLINTON LAKE STATE PARK has a shoreline of 130 miles, five boat ramps, and a marina with full boating services and concessions. Boats have no horsepower limits. Fish for bass, crappie, bluegill, walleye, catfish, muskie and bass.

Go swimming from the beach located in the Mascoutin area, or water-skiing between the Illinois 48 bridge and the Illinois 54 bridge by the Illinois Power Visitor Center.

Campers can select from 154 units located in the Mascoutin area with water, but no electrical hookups, and a trailer dump station.

Clinton is home to the Revere Copper and Brass Manufacturers. To tour the shop, call 217-935-3822 for information.

INFORMATION

Weldon Springs State Recreation Area	Clinton Lake State Recreation Area
R. R. 2	R. R. 1, Box 4
Clinton, Illinois 61727	Dewitt, Illinois 61735
217-935-2644	217-935-8722

DELABAR STATE PARK
11

LOCATION - The park is on the Mississippi River 1.5 miles north of Oquawka near Illinois 164.

ACTIVITIES - The park has three picnic areas. Camp in one of the 124 campsites, all with electrical hookups. Hike two miles of wooded trails.

Fishing is available either in the Mississippi River, or in nearby Gladstone Lake. Access to the river is via a launching ramp at the south end of the park. No boat rentals are available, but a marina is close by.

INFORMATION

Delabar State Park	Big River Complex: 309-374-2496
R. R. 2	
Oquawka, Illinois 61469	
309-867-3671	

DIXON SPRINGS STATE PARK
12

LOCATION - The park is in the Shawnee Hills of the Ozark Mountains at Dixon Springs, six miles northeast of Reevesville near the junction of Illinois 145 and 146. The park is ten miles west of Golconda on Illinois 146.

FEATURES - Dixon Springs was a favorite for the Algonquin Indians who enjoyed camping here. They called the springs "Kitchie Mus Ke Neebe" meaning "Medicine Water." Later, its 19th century health spa attracted many visitors to relax in the seven mineral-enriched springs.

ACTIVITIES - Camp in the campground on the summit of the Ozarks with 40 campsites with electrical hookups and a dump station.You can also backpack to their primitive campground.

The park still has the bathhouse. Go swimming in the pool with its 45-foot water slide. Concessions are sold near the pool.

Hike the self-guided 1.7-mile-long nature trail. Some nearby rock formations to visit include "The Devil's Workshop," "Honeycomb Rock," "The Canyon," "Ghost Dance," and "Balanced Rock."

Bird watchers will find a large variety of birds here with over 300 species spotted.

INFORMATION
Dixon Springs State Park
R. R. 2
Golconda, Illinois 62938
618-949-3394

EAGLE CREEK STATE PARK
13

See under WOLF CREEK STATE RECREATION AREA

ELDON HAZLET STATE PARK
SOUTH SHORE STATE PARK
14

LOCATION - The park is four miles north of Carlyle on Illinois 127, and then two more miles east.

FEATURES - Carlyle Reservoir is the largest man-made lake in Illinois.

ACTIVITIES - Eldon Hazlet State Park has ten miles of roads winding through it. Hike three mile-long trails overlooking the lake, and into the historic cemetery.

The lake is five miles across and 18 miles long, and offers great boating and sailing. It has a launching ramp for small boats. No horsepower limit is observed on the lake, and boat rentals aren't available. Go fishing for bass, walleye, bluegill, crappie and catfish.

The campground has rent-a-camp facilities, 36 tent pads, and can accommodate 336 trailers with electrical hookups.

For additional camping and boating ramps, go to SOUTH SHORE STATE PARK, located two miles east of Carlyle on U.S. 50. Boat rentals are available at the Patoka Access Area on the east side, or at the Tamalco Access Area on the west side.

INFORMATION

Eldon Hazlet State Park
R. R. 3
Carlyle, Illinois 62231
618-594-3015

South Shore State Park
R. R. 2
Carlyle, Illinois 62231
618-594-3015

FERNE CLYFFE STATE PARK
15

LOCATION - The park is on Illinois 37, one mile south of Goreville, and 12 miles south of Marion. It's accessible from either I-57 or I-24. The Ferne Clyffe exits are well marked.

FEATURES - The park is well known for its unique rock formations including Hawks' Cave and the 100-foot waterfall that flows intermittently.

ACTIVITIES - Ferne Clyffe Lake has a hiking trail around its one-mile shoreline, and is open to bank fishing for bass, bluegill and catfish. Twice a year, the lake is stocked with 10-inch rainbow trout.

Camp in rent-a-camp facilities, or in Deer Ridge campground with electrical hookups. Turkey Ridge has 20 walk-in campsites, and equestrians have their own campground.

Hikers will find ten trails covering 15 miles. These range in length from the .25-mile Rebman Trail to Happy Hollow Trail which is 5.5 miles long. Happy Hollow Trail is also used by equestrians.

Round Bluff Nature Preserve, located south of the Lakeview picnic shelter, is known for its unusual plants and ferns that are generally found in southern Illinois.

No boating or swimming is permitted in the lake.

INFORMATION
Ferne Clyffe State Park
Box 120
Goreville, Illinois 62939
618-995-2411

FOX RIDGE STATE PARK
16

LOCATION - The park is eight miles south of Charleston in east-central Illinois. Illinois 130 passes the park.

FEATURES - Most of the park is heavily forested with steep ravines below ridges that were carved by the last glacier that occupied Wisconsin 16,000 years ago.

ACTIVITIES - Hikers can hike along ten miles of trails that criss-cross the ridgetops and ravines. The trail system has nine wooden stairways climbing 1,200 feet and 18 wooden bridges.

Its campground has 40 year-round sites, rent-a-camp facilities, and a trailer dump site.

An interesting feature of the park is its Teams Challenge Trail including the "meat grinder," "wild woosey," "the wall," and "the giant ladder."

Even though the Embarras River flows past Fox Ridge, only hard-core canoeists come here to the take-out point, since it's 300 yards to the nearest parking lot, and during the summer, the water may be too shallow.

Fishing is allowed by reservation only April–October. Contact the I.N.H.S. laboratory at the lake: 217-345-6490. The lake contains bluegill, bass and catfish. Fishing boats are available at no charge at the lake. River fishing is available to anyone willing to descend the steep slopes to reach the Embarras River. Lake Charleston, four miles from the park, is recommended for your fishing expedition.

INFORMATION
Fox Ridge State Park
R. R. 1, Box 234
Charleston, Illinois 61920

GEBHARD WOODS STATE PARK
17

See under ILLINOIS AND MICHIGAN CANAL

GIANT CITY STATE PARK
MURPHYSBORO STATE PARK
18

LOCATION - Giant City is 12 miles south of Carbondale off U.S. 51, or 2.5 miles from Makanda.

Murphysboro State Park is 3.6 miles west of Murphysboro off Illinois 149.

FEATURES - Artifacts left behind by Indians living here as early as 400 B.C. have been found in the shelter bluffs. The park was named for the large cube blocks of stone located in the canyons.

ACTIVITIES - The best time of year to visit Giant City is in the spring when almost 170 kinds of flowers are in bloom. For a unique hike, go to Fern Rock Nature Preserve south of the main entrance, and hike Trilium Trail to see such rare plants as French's shooting stars and large flowering mints.

Hiking trails include Post Oak, Devil's Standtable, Giant City, Stonefort and Indian Creek Shelter. Backpackers will find a 16-mile trail with a primitive campground. Climb the spiral staircase of the 82-foot water tower. Equestrians have their own trails with rental horses available.

Go fishing for bass, bluegill and crappie in the lake, or in the smaller fishing ponds scattered throughout the park. You can go boating and canoeing from launching ramps on the Little Grassy Lake. The lake has 30 miles of shoreline, and its boat dock has boat rentals available.

The campground has rent-a-camp facilities, and 125 campsites have electrical hookups and a trailer dumping station. Equestrians have their own campground; backpackers have access to 14 campsites in the park's south end.

If you prefer not to "rough it," stay in the lodge or in one of the 34 cabins open from March through mid-December. For information, call 618-457-4921. The lodge is a National Register Historic Site.

The Carbondale/Murphysboro Airport is located four miles northwest of Murphysboro. Rental cars are available.

Bike Route #76 passes near here, entering the Shawnee National Forest at Illinois 51 south of Carbondale, and continuing east to Cave-in-Rock State Park.

For a glimpse into the "Little Grand Canyon," go northwest from the park to Murphysboro. Then take 20th Street south out of town for about 1.5 miles and turn left onto Hickory Ridge Road. Continue for three miles until reaching the first main intersection. Turn right and follow this road for another three miles until you reach the sign for the Little Grand Canyon. The hike down into the canyon is a 3.6-mile loop. .

MURPHYSBORO STATE PARK, 3.5 miles west of town, has 54 campsites with electrical hookups, hiking trails, bass fishing and boating in the lake. Boats are limited to ten horsepower and rentals are available. A concession stand is located near the boat docks.

If you want access to an even larger lake near Murphysboro, go to Lake Kinkaid northwest of town on Illinois 149, with 82 miles of shoreline, where you can fish for bass, bluegill, catfish, walleye and trout. Marinas are located at both ends of the lake. The best fishing is in April and May.

Hike the Kinkaid Lake Hiking Trail located in the Shawnee National Forest. Backpack in to one of the campsites in the Johnson Creek Recreation Area. The campground has 77 campsites.

In mid-September, attend the Murphysboro Apple Festival. Since the town is known as the "Apple Capital of the Southern Illinois Ozarks," you'll be in time for their "Olympic" events complete with the firemen's water fight, racing pigs, pie eating contest, a 10-kilometer race and concerts. For information, call 618-684-3200 or 684-6421.

Bald Knob Cross, America's tallest Christian monument at 111 feet, is located on top of Bald Knob Mountain. It's reached by taking Illinois 127 to Alto Pass and following the signs. Passion plays are presented here during the summer months. Southern Illinois University has an environmental center here, and offers recreational programs and a unique buffalo cookout. For information, call 618-529-4161.

INFORMATION

Giant City State Park
P.O. Box 70
Makanda, Illinois 62958
618-457-4836

Lake Murphysboro State Park
R. R. 4
Murphysboro 62966
618-684-2867

Kinkaid Lake Marina
Southern Illinois Recreation Center
Route 4
Murphysboro, Illinois 62966
618-687-4914

GOOSE LAKE PRAIRIE STATE NATURAL AREA
19

LOCATION - Two miles south of the Illinois River, and southeast of Morris on Pine Bluff Lorenzo Road, midway between Illinois 47 and I-55.

FEATURES - Goose Lake Prairie is the largest remnant of prairie left in Illinois, known as the "Prairie State." Goose Lake was once so covered with ducks and geese that you couldn't see the water, thus giving the lake its name. Tribes of the early mound-building Indians lived here, and 19 of their mounds have been uncovered.

A replica of Cragg's Cabin originally built in 1834 is in the area. It once served as a station on the underground railroad.

ACTIVITIES - Visit the large visitor center. Check the schedule for ongoing events and hikes. Picnic in one of the two areas.

The Tallgrass Nature Trail is 1.5 miles long, and winds through the prairie. Cross-country skiers come here to ski on 12.5 miles of trails during the winter, and to warm up in the visitor center.

Heidecke State Fish and Wildlife Area is adjacent to Goose Lake, where only gas-powered boats used for fishing or duck hunting are permitted. No water-skiing, swimming, sailing or wading is allowed. A concession stand is near the boat launching area and has rental boats.

The lake is stocked with walleye, bass, muskellunge, and catfish. Fishing season runs from April 1 until two weeks before duck hunting season.

The area has no campground facilities, but is near Kankakee River State Park or Gebhard Woods State Park that have camping available.

Special programs include a demonstration prairie burn in the spring, a cabin festival in the fall, and hunting and fishing seminars held before their respective seasons begin.

Bird watchers can pick up a checklist for the approximately 130 species of birds that have been spotted here.

INFORMATION

Goose Lake Prairie State Natural Area
5010 North Jugtown Road
Morris, Illinois 60450
815-942-2899

Heidecke State Fish
and Wildlife Area
815-942-6352

HENNEPIN CANAL PARKWAY STATE PARK
20

LOCATION - The parkway is 96 miles long, and extends from the great bend in the Illinois River to the Mississippi River west of Milan. Its northernmost area is at Lake Sinnissippi. From this lake, a feeder canal goes south for 29.3 miles. Then north of I-80, midway between Illinois 78 and 88, this feeder line intersects the main canal. Now the parkway turns southwest for 46.9 miles before reaching the Mississippi River near Rock Island, and southeast for 28.4 miles until it reaches the Illinois River near Hennepin.

The western feeder line has two sections: an area running from the feeder basin to the Rock River west of Greenrock, and a 4.5-mile-long section that bypasses the lower rapids of the Rock River at Milan. This feeder connects with the main line between Sheffield and Mineral.

FEATURES - Originally the canal was constructed for use by boats traveling between the Illinois and Mississippi rivers. It was begun in 1890, and was the first American canal to be built of concrete without using stone cut facings. It was used as a commercial waterway from 1907 until 1951 when it was closed to navigation. It was later reopened to the public in the 1970s.

ACTIVITIES - Tour the visitor center northeast of Sheffield at the junction of Illinois 88 and 6, visit the waterfowl observation area, and boat from launching ramp and marina. One of the remaining overseers' houses is a short distance west of the visitor center on County Road 645E, north of Sheffield.

Boating is allowed anywhere on the canal with boats limited to ten horsepower except between Bridge 37 and Lock 24, where horsepower is unlimited. Additional launching ramps are at Lock 21, Illinois 82 north of Geneseo; Illinois 92, Illinois 78 north of Annawan, Bridge 39, Bridge 28 and Bridge 45.

Fishing is available all along the canal for bass, crappie, catfish, bluegill, walleye and pike.

Hikers and bikers can explore the entire length of the canal. Mountain bikes are recommended rather than touring bicycles. Hikers can also explore a 1.5-mile interpretive trail at Wyanet Prairie, located on the north side of the canal between Locks 18 and 19.

You can ride horseback all along the trail except in the day-use areas, or along the towpath from Bridge 43 to Bridge 45.

Primitive camping is available along the western line between Sheffield and Mineral. This site also has a day-use area and a boat launching ramp. Another camping area is located on the south canal bank off Illinois 78 immediately north of Annawan.

Primitive camping is available at Lock 22, one mile west of the basin at County 1750E and 300E, and at Lock 23, accessible from either Illinois 78 or County Road 2200E north of Atkinson. You can also camp near Lock 26, approximately 1.5 miles north of U.S. 6, accessible via County Road 900E, School Road.

At Lock 21, east of U.S. 6 and Illinois 34, you'll find additional primitive camping, and a boat launch ramp. Another primitive campground is at Lock 17, reached from County road 1550E, and at Lock 11, north of Tiskilwa, and at Lock 6, accessible from County road 2160E.

To camp in an equipped campground, go to nearby Johnson Sauk Trail State Park.

During the winter, snowmobilers can follow a 78-mile trail that parallels the feeder section from Rock Falls. Cross-country skiers have 4.5 miles of marked trails beginning at the visitor center.

INFORMATION
Hennepin Canal Parkway State Park
R. R. 2
Sheffield, Illinois 61361
815-454-2328

HIDDEN SPRINGS STATE FOREST
21

LOCATION - The forest is seven miles southwest of Strasburg, and ten miles southeast of Shelbyville.

FEATURES - The park was named because of the seven known springs located on the property that were used for drinking water by both the Indians and the early settlers. However, over time, these springs filled in with vegetation and became "hidden." You can still access Rocky Spring and Quicksand Spring by trail.

ACTIVITIES - Camp in the 28-site Possom Creek Campground with a trailer dump station. Picnic in one of three picnic areas.

Go fishing on one of four fishing ponds, one accessible by vehicle, and the others on foot only. The ponds are stocked with bass, bluegill and catfish.

Hike the .75-mile-long, self-guided Possom Hollow Nature Trail, or the Big Tree Trail that features a 78-inch sycamore, estimated to be 300 years old.

Rocky Spring Trail is three miles long. The forest has 25 additional miles of fire lanes that provide access for backpackers searching for remote campsites.

INFORMATION
Hidden Springs State Forest
Box 200, R. R. 1
Strasburg, Illinois 62465
217-644-3091

ILLINI STATE PARK
22

See under ILLINOIS AND MICHIGAN CANAL

ILLINOIS AND MICHIGAN CANAL
CHANNAHON STATE PARK
GEBHARD WOODS STATE PARK
W. G. STRATTON STATE PARK
ILLINI STATE PARK
BUFFALO ROCK STATE PARK

STARVED ROCK STATE PARK
MATHIESSEN STATE PARK
23

LOCATION - This 61.6-mile-long canal route stretches from Lake Michigan on the east to the town of Peru in La Salle County on the west. Along this corridor are 11 state parks and 37 natural areas including Goose Lake Prairie, the largest tallgrass prairie in Illinois.

FEATURES - The original canal initially stretched 96 miles, linking Lake Michigan with the Illinois River at La Salle.

As you traverse the canal route, watch for evidence of the presence of the continental glaciers that invaded Illinois repeatedly during the Ice Age. The last major ice sheet occurred during the Wisconsin Glacial period from 75,000 to 10,000 years ago. Around 20,000 years ago, when the glacier had reached its southernmost limit, the ice measured a mile thick at Chicago.

ACTIVITIES - Approximately 55.5 miles of the trail are open for hiking. Bicycling is also available along parts of this trail, but not all of the canal has been finished to accommodate bikes. For up-to-date maps for either bicycling or hiking, contact the Illinois-Michigan Canal park headquarters.

Fish in Nettle Creek or the canal for bass, crappie, bluegill, catfish, and bullhead.

Backpacking camping is available at Channahon, and Gebhard Woods. Obtain a permit from the park offices first. Trailer camping is provided at the Starved Rock and Illini state parks.

Canoeists will find approximately 28 miles of the canal suitable for canoeing. Launch facilities are provided at Channahon, Aux-Sable, Gebhard Woods and at La Salle.

Throughout the summer, a multi-media exhibition entitled "Harvesting the River," travels from state park to state park. Check with the one you visit to see when it arrives there.

CHANNAHON STATE PARK is at 2 West Story Street in Channahon. Walk along the canal towpath once followed by the mules who towed the heavy barges and canal boats through here. The park is the site of the DuPage River Dam, Locks 6 and 7, and a restored lock tender's house.

The park has picnic shelters, tent camping, boating and fishing in the Du Page River and in the I&M Canal adjacent to the park, where you can catch bass, bluegill, crappie, bullhead and catfish. The I&M Canal towpath goes from here to Gebhard Woods, 15 miles away, and is an excellent bird watching area.

Channahon Mound is located between Joliet and Morris, and is set aside as part of the Illinois and Michigan Canal National Heritage Corridor. It's a remnant of a sand and gravel terrace that was deposited here by the melt water coming from the retreating Wisconsin glacier.

GEBHARD WOODS STATE PARK is located on the west edge of Morris, and serves as the headquarters for the Department of Conservation's Illinois and Michigan Canal State Trail.

One of the main features of the park is the eastern cottonwood, the biggest tree found in Illinois. It's one mile west of the park on the south side of the canal, and soars 120 feet, with a circumference of 32 feet.

The park has a campground, picnicking area, hiking, fishing, and bicycling along the canal. In December, attend "Christmas in the Woods," a re-creation of 1830s holiday activities.

W. G. STRATTON STATE PARK is located below the Illinois River bridge in Morris, and has four launching ramps on the Illinois River. Visitors can go river fishing, hiking, water-skiing, and bicycling along the 15-mile stretch of trail that extends from Channahon to here.

The Grundy County Corn Festival is held in Morris in late September or early October, and is one of the largest of its kind in the state. There are parades, concerts, and paddle wheel boat excursions along the Illinois River. For information, call 815-942-CORN.

ILLINI STATE PARK is four miles south of Marseilles near Illinois 6, and boasts a beautiful view overlooking the Illinois River. Here boats pass through the Illinois River Marseilles Lock.

Its campground has 95 sites with electrical hookups and a trailer dump station. Enjoy fishing for crappie, bullhead and catfish, hiking on their three trails ranging in length from .5-mile to the two-mile-long Chassagoac Trail. Also enjoy flying model airplanes and kites and enjoy biking and boating from the ramp with no horsepower restrictions.

BUFFALO ROCK STATE PARK and Effigy Tumuli are located two miles west of Ottawa on Dee Bennett Road on a sandstone bluff overlooking the Illinois River Valley. The Effigy Tumuli Sculpture is one of the largest earth sculptures ever built. In 1985, a combined reclamation and land sculpture resulted in the creation of five large effigies. These earthen figures were shaped to represent native aquatic animals, and were constructed in memory of the earlier prehistoric Indians who had lived here over 3,000 years ago.

In September, attend the I&M Canal Music Fest, a festival of bluegrass, clogging, gospel music and traditional music. For information, call 815-942-0796.

STARVED ROCK STATE PARK is five miles east of La Salle on the south side of the Illinois River off Illinois 71. It's also one mile south of Utica, midway between the cities of La Salle, Peru and Ottawa.

During spring, when the snow melts and frequent rain falls, waterfalls stream down the heads of 18 canyons. The most spectacular are in St. Louis, French, La Salle and Ottawa canyons.

Watch for Council Overhang located in the east end of the park. Its roof is strong enough to support Illinois 71 that passes almost directly overhead. Because of its size, the Native Americans used the area for their gatherings for approximately 12,000 years.

La Salle built Fort St. Louis here in 1682, but the French abandoned the fort after La Salle was murdered. Then, in 1769, a band of Illini Indians hid on the rock's summit where they were surrounded by their enemy and starved to death, giving the rock its name.

Tour the Illinois Waterway Visitor Center to see the exhibit on the I&M Canal and the 20th century waterway system. Information: 815-667-4054.

The park has a 75-room lodge, 12 cabins and a dining room. It's open year-round. For reservations, call 815-667-4211.

The campground, open most of the year, has 133 sites with electrical hookups and a trailer dump station. Besides camping, you can fish the Illinois River, go boating from the ramp, or participate in the year-round interpretive program.

Horseback riders have their own campground and riding trails along Illinois 71 in the far western section of the park. Horse rentals are available on weekends on Illinois 71, .5-mile west of Illinois 178.

.Starved Rock has 15.3 miles of well-marked hiking trails that are open year-round. No horses or bikes are allowed on the trails. Trails range in length from the .3-mile trail to Starved Rock to the longer 4.7-mile hike to Illinois Canyon.

Absolutely no swimming is permitted in the river due to its extremely hazardous undertows. Boats aren't permitted to be within 600 feet above or below the dam. A ramp is located at the west end of the park.

Fishermen must also stay 600 feet away from the dam. Fishing is generally good for channel catfish, bullhead, bass, walleye and carp. Fishing tournaments begin here in March with the Wallython Fishing Tournament that runs from the end of March until mid-May. This is overlapped in mid-May with the White Bass Fishing Tournament. Then in June, the park holds the state fishing championships with both a pro division and a family derby held at Lake De Pue.

In September, come for the "Fall Colors Weekend," and enjoy a colorful guided nature hike among the hardwoods. This month has a "Turn of the Century Celebration" when you can observe arts and crafts of the late 1800s, and watch a hot air balloon ascension.

Tour the visitor center generally open on weekend afternoons in peak season.

Take a Starved Rock Heritage Cruise starting from the riverfront in Peoria. Overnight in the Starved Rock State Park lodge before returning to Peoria. Reservations are required. Call 309-673-2628 or 1-800-383-2618.

MATTHIESSEN STATE PARK NATURE AREA is seven miles south of La Salle off Illinois 178, three miles south of Utica, and three miles east of Oglesby. The geology of the park is similar to Starved Rock, and its main canyon features both an Upper Dells and a Lower Dells. The Upper Dells has a wildlife habitat, and 25 miles of horse and cross-country skiing trails. The Lower Dells has concessions, a small fort and stockade, picnic area, and a hiking trail to Cascade Falls.

The park has seven miles of well-marked, well-surfaced hiking trails. Hikers should remain on these trails since there are steep cliffs in the park. The upper area and bluff tops provide the easiest hiking, while the trails into the interior of the two Dells are more difficult.

The Illinois and Michigan Canal Visitor Center is located in Lockport, 35 miles southwest of Chicago. It's open Tuesday through Sunday from 10–5. For information, call 815-838-4830.

INFORMATION

Channahon State Park
Box 636
Channahon, Illinois 60410
815-467-4271

Gebhard Woods State Park
Box 272
Morris, Illinois 60450
815-942-0796

William Stratton State Park
c/o Gebhard Woods State Park
Illini State Park
R. R. 1, Box 60
Marseilles, Illinois 61341
815-795-2448

Buffalo Rock State Park and
  Effigy Tumuli
Box 39
Ottawa, Illinois 61350
815-433-2220

Starved Rock State Park
Box 116
Utica, Illinois 61373
815-667-4726

Matthiesen State Park
Box 381
Utica, Illinois 61373
815-667-4868

Illinois and Michigan Canal State Trail
Box 272
Morris, Illinois 60450
815-942-0796

I & M Canal State Trail
Gebhard Woods Access
Ottawa Street, south of Route 47
Morris, Illinois 60450
815-942-0796

ILLINOIS BEACH STATE PARK
24

LOCATION - The beach lies 6.5 miles along the shores of Lake Michigan, and four miles north of Waukegan on Illinois 42.

FEATURES - The Lake Michigan Dunes running through the park contain the only natural beach and dunes in Illinois. During the Ice Age, this entire area was buried. As the glacier melted, Lake Michigan's water level was 640 feet higher. Gradually the water level dropped, leaving behind many ridges of former beaches and sand deposits. As these deposits eroded, they formed the current dunes.

The area was once inhabited by the Algonquin and Potawatomi Indians who left behind many arrowheads and other artifacts.

Camp Logan was originally used as a Union prisoner-of-war camp during the Civil War, and later as an Army basic training center during both world wars.

ACTIVITIES - Camp in the campground with 244 sites, all with electrical hookups, and a dump station. A concession stand is located in the southern unit. If camping doesn't appeal to you, overnight in their lodge with 106 guest rooms. The lodge is close to Waukegan's airport where arriving pilots and their passengers can be met by the lodge's station wagon.

Go fishing along the beach, or in Sand Lake in the northern park unit. Kellog Creek, within Camp Logan, is closed to fishing September 1–December 15 because of its salmon operations.

Swimming from the 1,000-foot beach is popular during the summer.

Go hiking or bicycling on five miles of trails. A park interpreter leads year-round hikes. During the winter, 10 miles of trails are open for cross-country skiing.

Golfers have access to an 18-hole golf course near the park. To reserve a tee-off time, call 312-249-2100.

INFORMATION
Illinois Beach State Park
Lake Front
Zion, Illinois 60099
312-662-4811

JOHNSON SAUK TRAIL STATE PARK
25

LOCATION - The park is in north-central Illinois off Illinois 78, five miles north of Kewanee and six miles south of I-80.

FEATURES - The trail is considered to be one of the most concentrated wildlife habitats in the center of North America. Its marshland is known as the "Great Willow Swamp."

The lake has a shoreline of 2.3 miles.

ACTIVITIES - Visitors can camp in trailers or tents. Electrical hookups are available.

Fishermen can catch a variety of fish including largemouth bass, bluegill, crappie, northern pike and channel catfish.

Rental boats are available, and a launching ramp is provided. Gas motors aren't permitted, and only electric trolling boats are allowed.

Hike the trails that wind through the park, many of them through the woods. During the winter, cross-country ski along ten miles of designated roads and trails. Thaw out in the warming house where concessions are sold.

INFORMATION
Johnson Sauk Trail State Park
R. R. 3
Kewanee, Illinois 61443
309-853-5589

JUBILEE COLLEGE STATE PARK
26

LOCATION - The college is 14 miles west of Peoria off U.S. 150.

FEATURES - Originally the college was founded by the first Episcopal Bishop of Illinois, Philander Chase, and was built in 1839. Unfortunately, the college closed a decade following the Bishop's death in 1852.

ACTIVITIES - Enjoy camping in rent-a-camp facilities, or in campsites either with or without electrical hookups. From November 15–April 15, camping is restricted to walk-in camping only.

An equestrian campground is in the north end of the park where 25 miles of trails converge. No horse rentals are available, however.

You can do limited fishing in Jubilee Creek or in four of the ponds. Three miles of hiking trails are open year-round. Go snowmobiling and cross-country skiing along 14 miles of trails.

The Olde English Faire is held annually the last weekend in June when a 15th-century English fair is presented. Enjoy medieval-style food, music and roving entertainment.

INFORMATION
Jubilee College State Park
R. R. 2, Box 72
Brimfield, Illinois 61517
309-243-7683

KANKAKEE RIVER STATE PARK
27

LOCATION - This park is located along the Kankakee River between Kankakee and Wilmington, eight miles northwest of Kankakee on Illinois 102, and 60 miles south of Chicago.

FEATURES - The Kankakee River passes through this park. Rock Creek, a tributary, is nestled in a deeply carved limestone canyon. Its name is "Illiniwek" meaning "beautiful river."

The last known Indians to inhabit the area were the Potawatomi. Their Indian Chief, Shaw-waw-nas-see, is buried in the park.

ACTIVITIES - For a look back at history, stroll through the old Smith Cemetery located just inside the main entrance.

The park has two boat ramps, but caution should be exercised when boating since much of the river is hazardous because of shallow water and rocks. Canoe rentals are provided at the concession stand. Only experienced canoeists should enter the river from the park.

Anglers can try for bass, pike, catfish and walleye. Each year, starting on July 4th, and continuing for nine days, dozens of tagged fish are released into the water for the fishing derby. Each fish is redeemed for money or merchandise. Pre-registration is required. For information, call 815-935-7390, or in Illinois, 1-800-892-6450.

Campers in both the Potawatomi and Chippewa campgrounds have boat access to the river. The campgrounds are open year-round, and have 500 sites.

Equestrians can go to the Kankakee River riding stable where horse rentals are available. For information, call 815-939-0309.

A concession stand sells camping supplies and rents canoes and bicycles. For information, contact them at 815-932-0488.

Bike the 3.5-mile loop Kankakee River Bike Trail. Hike or cross-country ski along 12 miles of trails. During the winter, you can stop in their warming house and pavilion.

INFORMATION
Kankakee River State Park
P.O. Box 37
Bourbonnais, Illinois 60914
815-933-1383

KICKAPOO STATE PARK
28

LOCATION - The park is six miles west of Danville.

FEATURES - The Middle Fork River eroded through the deep glacial deposits, leaving behind steep valley slopes and high bluffs. This river became the state's first state scenic river. Prehistoric man occupied a village along the Middle Fork River a few miles north of the present park between A.D. 500 and 1500

Later, the park was strip-mined for coal. Gradually the ridges were recovered with trees, and the stagnant mine pools were reclaimed for fishing ponds.

ACTIVITIES - Camp in a rent-a-camp facility, or in the campground with electrical hookups and a trailer dump station. Attend interpretive summer campfire programs and nature tours. A concession stand is open summer weekends.

The lakes and the Vermilion River offer visitors the opportunity to fish for bass, channel catfish, bluegill, crappie, sunfish and rainbow trout.

Boaters will find 12 launching ramps. Only electric motors are permitted on the area's lakes. There are five canoe access areas along the Middle Fork River's 14 miles.

Boat and canoe rentals are available for Long Pond, and canoe rental and shuttle services are available for the Middle Fork River. For information, call 217-443-4939.

An unusual feature of this park is its 8.5-mile off-road recreation vehicle trail. It's only open on weekends from Memorial Day to the last weekend in September. Riders must register before using this trail.

Hikers and runners are treated to a 7.6-mile-long trail accessible from the parking lot near the office at 2400N off Newton Road.

Scuba divers enjoy diving in the waters of Inland Sea and Sportsman's Lake.

The Middle Fork facility, five miles north of the park, and eight miles north of I-74 at Oakwood, contains the Collins Archeological District, a late Woodland Indian ceremonial site. The Windfall Prairie Nature Preserve and the Horseshoe Bottoms Nature Preserve are also located here.

INFORMATION
Kickapoo State Park
R. R. 1, Box 374
Oakwood, Illinois 61858
217-442-4915

LAKE LE-AQUA-NA STATE PARK
29

LOCATION - The park is in northwestern Illinois—four miles north of Lena off Illinois 73, and six miles south of the Illinois-Wisconsin state line.

FEATURES - The park got its name from combining the names of the nearby town of Lena and aqua.

ACTIVITIES - The park has three campgrounds with rent-a-camp facilities, and over 200 campsites with electricity and a trailer dump station. Equestrians have their own campground.

The lake is stocked with walleye, northern pike and channel catfish. Bass, bluegill, crappie and bullhead may also be caught.

Rent a boat and go boating. Only electric motors are permitted on the lake. The concession stand has camping supplies and boat rentals. It's open May 1– September 15. A naturalist is on duty year-round.

Travel along the historic Stagecoach Trail that goes from Lena to Galena. This trail traces the actual route stagecoaches followed from Galena to Chicago.

In Lena, tour the Kolb-Lena Cheese Company that produces a wide variety of cheeses.

During August in Freeport, attend the Tutty Baker Days Festival that offers carriage and train rides, special shows and tours. In October, you can tour some historic homes including Louella Parson's home, a restored 1840 Shaker home, and the childhood home of Jane Addams, located in Cedarville.

INFORMATION
Lake Le-Aqua-Na State Park
8542 North Lake Road
Lena, Illinois 61048
815-369-4282

LINCOLN TRAIL HOMESTEAD STATE PARK
30

LOCATION - To reach the park, go ten miles west of Decatur on U.S. 36, and then turn south onto Illinois 27.

FEATURES - This park is the site of the Lincoln family's first home in Illinois built along the Sangamon River in 1830.

ACTIVITIES - Lake Decatur has a 12-mile-long shoreline. If you're in the area on Memorial Day weekend, attend the powerboat races.

To see the historic buildings, pick up a self-guided brochure at the visitor center in the Transfer House, 1 Central Park East.

INFORMATION
Lincoln Trail Homestead State Park
Box 705
Mt. Zion, Illinois 62549
217-963-2729

LINCOLN TRAIL STATE RECREATION AREA
31

LOCATION - The area is two miles south of Marshall and one mile west of Illinois 1.

FEATURES - This entire area was originally inhabited by several Indian tribes, the Delaware, Potawatomi and Miami, who ceded their claims to the U.S. in a treaty.

The Lincoln family passed through here en route from Indiana to Macon County in 1830.

ACTIVITIES - The Lincoln Trail Recreation Site surrounds a lake in the south-western corner of the park. Visitors can go fishing, and boating from the ramp where rentals are available. Outboard motors are limited to ten horsepower.

The park has a total of 208 campsites. Two campgrounds, Plainview and Lakeside, have electrical hookups and a dumping station. A tent camping site is located within the Lakeside Campground. Go hiking on their nature trails: Sand Ford and Beech Tree Trail. The latter goes through a thick forest of beech-maple trees, and the preserve looks much as it did when the early pioneers passed through here.

INFORMATION
Lincoln Trail State Park
R. R. 1
Marshall, Illinois 62441
217-826-2222

LINCOLN'S NEW SALEM STATE HISTORIC SITE
32

LOCATION - The site is two miles south of Petersburg and 20 miles north-west of Springfield on Illinois 97.

FEATURES - The village is a reconstruction of a village in the 1830s when Abraham Lincoln lived here while co-piloting a flatboat down the Sangamon, Illinois and Mississippi waterways. While here, he studied law by candlelight.

ACTIVITIES - Take a self-guided tour of the village, open year-round. As you wander through the area, you'll encounter interpretive staff dressed in period costume. Tour the museum to see articles actually owned by Lincoln and his neighbors.

Campers will find rent-a-camp facilities, and 100 sites with electrical hookups, and 90 non-electrical sites. The campground is open March 15–December 15. Four concession stands are located in the park.

Hikers can explore the .75-mile Mentor Graham Trail that goes past the cemetery where Lincoln's first love, Ann Rutledge, is buried. Hike the 10-kilometer trail sanctioned by the American Volksport Association.

Take a riverboat ride aboard the "Talisman" when the river is up. For information, call 217-632-2219, or 217-632-7681.

Special events held annually include a quilt show in June; in July, the village features a re-enactment of a typical Illinois summer day in the early 1830s; a storytelling festival occurs in August; a traditional music and bluegrass festival is in September.

During the summer in Petersburg, you can attend the Great American People Show presenting "Your Obedient Servant, A. Lincoln." Performances are given

Tuesday through Sunday at 8 p.m. For information, call 217-367-1900, September through May, or 217-632-7755 June through August.

INFORMATION
Lincoln's New Salem State Historic Site
R. R. 1, Box 244-A
Petersburg, Illinois 62675
217-632-7953

LOWDEN STATE PARK
33

See under WHITE PINES FOREST STATE PARK

MATHIESSEN STATE PARK
34

See under ILLINOIS AND MICHIGAN CANAL

MISSISSIPPI PALISADES STATE PARK
35

LOCATION - The park is located near the confluence of the Apple and Mississippi rivers in northwestern Illinois. It's four miles north of Savanna on Illinois 84.

FEATURES - The park is in the "driftless" zone which was left untouched by the glaciers during the Ice Age. Watch for some unusual rock formations such as "Indian Head" that resembles the face of a Native American, and "Twin Sisters," two columns that resemble two humans.

ACTIVITIES - The campground has two dump stations, rent-a-camp sites, an equestrian campground, and 241 campsites, 105 with electrical hookups. A concession stand is located near the park office.

Boaters have access to launch ramps on the Mississippi River. Rental boats may be obtained from private concessionaires. Fish in the river for bluegill, crappie, bass, walleye and pike.

Eight miles of well-marked trails lead from the river to the top of the palisades. Lookout Point is an observation point on top of the bluffs. It's accessible either by car or on foot. In the wintertime, these trails offer good intermediate cross-country skiing.

INFORMATION
Mississippi Palisades State Park
4577 Route 84 North
Savanna, Illinois 61074
815-273-2731

MORAINE HILLS STATE PARK
36

LOCATION - The park is in the northeast corner of Illinois, three miles south of McHenry. The park entrance is off River Road, and is between Illinois 176 and 120. The Fox River runs through the western part of the park.

McHenry Dam controls the water level in the Chain O'Lakes, and the adjoining locks permit pleasure boats to navigate around the dam to get from the Chain O'Lakes to Algonquin.

FEATURES - Lake Defiance, a 160-foot deep glacial lake called a "kettle hole," was created from a large block of ice that melted after it became separated from the Wisconsin Glacier that occupied the area approximately 15,000 years ago. There are three other lakes within the park: Warrior, Tomahawk, and Wilderness lakes.

Artifacts found in the park show man has inhabited the region since 4000 B.C.

ACTIVITIES - Go fishing in Lake Defiance. No bank fishing is permitted because of the peat shoreline, so you'll need a boat to access the lake. No private boats are allowed on Lake Defiance, but rental boats are available at the McHenry Dam and Lake Defiance concession stands.

Private boats may only be brought into the park on top of your car, and may only be used on the Fox River and on the northern lakes.

Access to the Fox River fishing area is located at the north end of the McHenry Dam. Try your skill at landing bass, pike, catfish, carp and perch. The northern lakes, Wilderness and Tomahawk, have bass, bluegill and bullhead.

Enjoy picnicking in one of the ten picnic sites. Concessions are sold at McHenry Dam, and in the lower level of the park office building, both open mid-April through mid-October.

Bicyclists and hikers have access to 10.2 miles of trails surfaced with crushed limestone. You can also explore a couple of nature trails: Lake Defiance, .5-mile-long, and Pike Marsh Nature Trail that has a 1,300-foot floating boardwalk that takes you into the marsh environment.

During the winter, go cross-country skiing through the frozen marsh and woodland. Ski clinics, rentals, a concession stand and warming house pavilion are available.

To learn more about the park, visit the interpretive center located in the park office building to watch their slide show and view various displays.

The park has no camping or overnight accommodations; however, you can stay at nearby Chain O'Lakes State Park on Fox Lake.

INFORMATION
Moraine Hills State Park
914 South River Road
McHenry, Illinois 60050
815-385-1624

MORAINE VIEW STATE RECREATION AREA
37

LOCATION - The park is accessible from U.S. 150 or I-74 to LeRoy. Go north on the LeRoy-Lexington blacktop for five miles to reach the park entrance. You can also go 12 miles east of Bloomington on Illinois 9 to the LeRoy-Lexington road, and then continue south for 4.5 miles to reach the park entrance.

FEATURES - The Bloomington Moraine, one of the state's largest, was formed around 15,000 years ago when the Wisconsin glacier advanced into the area, pushing rock and earth up into long ridges.

ACTIVITIES - Dawson Lake has over five miles of shoreline, and is stocked with bass, bluegill, crappie, catfish and pike. Sailboats and boats with motors of ten horsepower or less are allowed. A concession stand is located near the boat docks and has rental boats, fishing tackle, refreshments and other supplies.

Swim near the Black Locust picnic area from Memorial Day to Labor Day.

Ten miles of bridle paths wind along the Timber Line Ridge Trail. Rent a horse at the "Lazy H" riding stable. These trails are used for intermediate cross-country skiing during the winter when a warming house is open.

The campground has rent-a-camp facilities, a separate equestrian campground, primitive backpacking campsites, 207 sites with electrical hookups, a trailer dump station, and its own boat launch and dock.

INFORMATION
Moraine View State Recreation Area
R. R. 2
LeRoy, Illinois 61752
309-724-8032

MT. PULASKI COURTHOUSE STATE HISTORIC SITE
38

See under RAILSPLITTER STATE PARK

MURPHYSBORO STATE PARK
39
See under GIANT CITY STATE PARK

NAUVOO STATE PARK
40

LOCATION - The park is on Illinois 96 on the southern edge of Nauvoo. From Illinois 96 and U.S. 136, drive north 13 miles on 96.

FEATURES - Nauvoo was named by the Mormons who came here after they were driven out of Missouri. It means "beautiful place," or "pleasant place."

While here, their leader, Joseph Smith, began erecting a great temple, but after his death, it was never completed. In 1848, it burned down, but a sunstone from one of the pilasters can be seen in the park.

ACTIVITIES - The Rheinberger home, originally built by the Mormons, was later taken over by the Icarians who experimented with a communistic colony and introduced the grape vineyards and the making of wine. This home, now restored, was the site of one of the first wine cellars in the community. A pageant is celebrated over Labor Day weekend when the grapes ripen. In December, the Nauvoo State Park Museum is decorated in the traditional Christmas custom of a different country.

Enjoy a picnic at one of the picnic facilities. Go fishing in the lake that is stocked with bass, channel catfish and bluegill. The park has a boat launch, but no boat docks or rentals; no motor boats are permitted. You can also fish in the Mississippi River. Hikers can tramp around the lake and through the woods.

There are three campgrounds with 150 sites equipped with electrical hookups and a trailer dump station.

To learn more about the history of Nauvoo, stop in town and pick up a walking tour map at the Nauvoo Visitor Center at Main and Young streets. For information, call 217-453-2237.

INFORMATION
Nauvoo State Park   217-453-2512
Box 337
Nauvoo, Illinois 62354

PERE MARQUETTE STATE PARK
41

LOCATION - Pere Marquette is located on bluffs that overlook the Illinois River five miles west of Grafton on Illinois 100, and approximately 25 miles northwest of Alton.

FEATURES - The park was named in honor of Father Jacques Marquette, who with Louis Jolliet, were the first Europeans to enter Illinois in 1673.

The park has 18 sites where a prehistoric Indian village was located on the site of the current lodge.

Pere Marquette is also site of the famous McAdams Peak Hill Prairie, a 54-acre natural area with many native grasses.

ACTIVITIES - Stay in the Pere Marquette Lodge with 50 rooms, or in one of the seven stone guest houses nearby. For lodge reservations, call 618-786-3351.

Chess players will enjoy seeing what is believed to be the world's largest chess set with figures larger than an average six-year old.

Go boating from one of the launching ramps. A concession stand is available by the dock where you can rent pontoon and power boats. For reservations, call the Harbor Concession at 618-786-3546.

Camp in a rent-a-camp, or in one of the 85 sites with electrical hookups and a dump station. It has water, but no individual water hookups.

Equestrians will find 12 miles of trails, but you need to provide your own horse. Make prior arrangements with the park supervisor before coming to the park to ride. Stables are located two miles north of Grafton on Illinois 100, or two miles south of the lodge. For information, call 618-786-2156.

Enjoy fishing in the Illinois River, or hiking along 15 miles of trails winding through the wooded bluffs.

The visitor center is northwest of the lodge where you can check the schedule of guided hikes. The park offers 15 miles of hiking trails ranging in length from .5 miles to 2.25 miles long.

Bicyclists can enjoy bicycling along the 14-mile Senator Sam Vadalabene Bike Trail that follows Lake Alton to Grafton. Watch for the Piasa Bird, a large pictograph of a dragonlike creature painted on the cliffs. For information, call the Alton Visitors Center: 618-465-6676.

Near the park on Illinois 100 is Brussels Ferry, one of the few ferries that still runs regularly. Call 618-786-3636 for information. After crossing the river, stop at the Wittmond Hotel, once a stagecoach stop and now a country inn with a restaurant. For information, call 618-883-2345.

INFORMATION
Pere Marquette State Park
P.O. Box 158
Grafton, Illinois 62037
618-786-3323

POSTVILLE COURTHOUSE STATE HISTORIC SITE
42

See under RAILSPLITTER STATE PARK

PYRAMID STATE PARK
43

LOCATION - The park is in southwest Illinois, six miles southwest of Pinckneyville.

FEATURES - It gets its name from the coal mine that was once located here.

ACTIVITIES - Enjoy a picnic in one of the small picnic sites. Hike or ride horseback along the 16.5 miles of trails. A rugged ten-mile trail circles much of the park.

Camp in one of the three campgrounds without hookups, or hike in to one of the backpack campsites by Hook Lake or sites located en route to Hidden and Blackberry Lakes.

There are several lakes in the park where fishing for bass and bluegill is available. Because of the rough terrain, canoes are a popular form of boating, although boats with ten horsepower are permitted. Some of the larger lakes have boat launches available.

INFORMATION
Pyramid State Park
R. R. 1
Box 115 A
Pinckneyville, Illinois 62274
618-357-2574

RAILSPLITTER STATE PARK
POSTVILLE COURTHOUSE STATE HISTORIC SITE
MT. PULASKI COURTHOUSE STATE HISTORIC SITE
44

LOCATION - Railsplitter State Park is located along Salt Creek on the south edge of Lincoln, and surrounds the Logan Correctional Center.

Postville Courthouse is in Lincoln. From I-55, take Lincoln Exit 126, Illinois 10. At the first stop light, turn south. At the next stop light, 5th Street, turn east and continue east five more blocks.

Mt. Pulaski Courthouse is in Pulaski on the town square. From Illinois 54, exit right on Illinois 121. Watch for the historic marker at DeKalb Street. Turn left on DeKalb and go four blocks to Vine Street. Turn left and continue two blocks to Jefferson. Turn right and continue two more blocks to reach City Square.

ACTIVITIES - RAILSPLITTER STATE PARK is open for day-use only, where you can enjoy a picnic, go fishing in Salt Creek for bass, bluegill, crappie, catfish, bullhead and carp. An annual National Railsplitting Festival is held each September.

The POSTVILLE COURTHOUSE that you visit is a reproduction. The original structure was purchased by Henry Ford in 1929, and he moved it to his Greenfield Village in Dearborn, Michigan. Furnishings in the court are authentic period pieces. The second floor houses a courtroom and county office furnished in the 1840s period. In the courthouse, you'll also see exhibits of some of early Illinois's judicial practices.

Abraham Lincoln visited the courthouse twice a year as he traveled on the Eighth Circuit full time for 12 years. Then, a judge traveled from county to county where he held court for as long as six weeks at a time.

The Postville Courthouse is open from 9–5 daily except holidays. Admission is free. It was the oldest courthouse on the circuit. The Lincoln Arts Festival and Watermelon Days are held annually each August.

Visit the large museum in the Lincoln College McKinstry Memorial Library with 2,000 Lincoln volumes, plus other historical items. A second museum, the Museum of Presidents, contains documents signed by every president.

Lincoln also has a community theater that operates during the summer, and its music society presents seasonal concerts. For information, contact the Abraham Lincoln Tourism Bureau: 217-735-2385.

The MT. PULASKI COURTHOUSE was also part of the Eighth Circuit where Lincoln worked. This courthouse, too, is open daily from 9–5 and is free.

INFORMATION

Railsplitter State Park
R. R. 3
Lincoln, Illinois 62656
217-735-2424

Mt. Pulaski Courthouse State Historic Site
Postville Courthouse State Historic Site
c/o Illinois State Historic Sites
Department of Conservation
405 East Washington
Springfield, Illinois 62706

RAMSEY LAKE STATE PARK
45

LOCATION - The lake is one mile northwest of Ramsey.

FEATURES - Ramsey Lake has a timbered shoreline of four miles.

ACTIVITIES - White Oak Campground has 95 campsites with electrical hookups and a dump station. Hickory Grove has 75 campsites without hookups.

Hikers have access to a one-mile-long trail plus several additional miles of unmarked fire lanes to explore. Equestrians have 13 miles of trails plus a small horse campground.

The lake is stocked with fish including bass, catfish and crappie. Fishing is also permitted on several ponds in the park.

Boaters can rent boats and launch them from the ramp. Gas motors aren't allowed, and only electric trolling motors are permissible.

A concession stand has boat rentals, food, camping and fishing supplies available during the summer season.

An August summer festival is held in the park. For information, call the park headquarters.

During winter, eight miles of unplowed roads are available for snowmobiling.

INFORMATION

Ramsey Lake State Park   618-423-2215
P.O. Box 97
Ramsey, Illinois 62080

RED HILLS STATE PARK
46

LOCATION - Red Hills is one mile northeast of Sumner between Olney and Lawrenceville. It's also nine miles west of Lawrenceville on U.S. 50 that divides the park into sections.

FEATURES - Red Hill is the highest point along the B&O Railroad route between Cincinnati and St. Louis, and its peak gave this park its name.

Red Hill has a tower and a cross with a "little tabernacle" constructed at the base of the cross for use on special occasions.

ACTIVITIES - Have a picnic on either side of the road. Picnic grounds are on the south side of the lake.

You can drive around the lake's 2.5 miles of shoreline. Go bank fishing for bass, catfish, bluegill and bullhead.

You can launch your boat from the ramp. Only electric motors are permitted; no gas motors are allowed. A bait shop and rental boat concession are operated during the summer.

The campground, located in the south section of the park, has 120 sites with electrical hookups and a trailer dump station.

A dining room remains open most of the year, and park naturalists conduct summer recreational programs.

Horseback riders will find a 2.5-mile trail for riding on the south side of the road. On the north side are several hiking trails ranging in length from one mile to the Valley Springs Trail that is 2.5 miles long.

Old Settlers' Days are held in late April. The festivities include a recreation of pioneer arts, crafts, music, dance, games and customs from 1820–1850.

The park has a 2,400-foot grass landing strip for private planes right next to the campground, so you can fly in and camp quite easily.

INFORMATION
Red Hills State Park
R. R. 2
Sumner, Illinois 62466
618-936-2469

SAND RIDGE STATE FOREST
47

LOCATION - Sand Ridge is Illinois's largest state forest, and is about 25 miles southwest of Peoria. To reach the park, go north for five miles on Forest City Road to Sand Ridge Road from the intersection of U.S. 136 and Forest City Road. Continue west for three more miles on Sand Ridge Road.

FEATURES - Around 15,000 years ago, during the time of the last Ice Age, glacial melt unleashed a torrent of waters called the "Kankakee Torrent." Later, the area became extremely dry and desert-like, and sand dunes as high as 100 feet were formed. These dunes are still apparent under the wooded ridges for which the forest is named.

ACTIVITIES - Family camping is available at the Pine Campground where you'll find 27 sites without electricity, and a trailer dump station.

Horseman's Park offers equestrian camping and access to Oak Trail that begins on Pine Valley Drive. Sand Ridge Trail on Pine Valley Drive has a 2.2-mile loop. The area also has 120 miles of fire roads to explore. Snowmobilers have access to 22 miles of trails.

INFORMATION
Sand Ridge State Forest
P.O. Box 111
Forest City, Illinois 61532
309-597-2212

SANGCHRIS LAKE STATE PARK
48

LOCATION - The lake is 11 miles southeast of Springfield near Rochester, four miles southeast of New City, and seven miles northwest of Bulpitt.

ACTIVITIES - The lake has three arms, 120 miles of shoreline, and offers anglers good fishing for bass, bluegill, crappie, catfish and bullhead.

Boating is available from a ramp on either the east or west side of the lake, and the park has a 25-horsepower motor limit. No sailboats are permitted.

Campers have access to Deer Run Campground located on the north end of the lake with approximately 135 sites with electrical hookups and a dump station. Hickory Point Campground is located at the east boat dock area, and has 19 sites without electricity.

Hikers have three miles of nature trails around the campgrounds. Snowmobilers have access to 11 miles of trails, and cross-country skiers have 8–10 miles of trails.

INFORMATION
Sangchris Lake State Park
R. R. 1
Rochester, Illinois 62563
217-498-9208

SHABBONA LAKE STATE RECREATION AREA
49

LOCATION - The lake is a quarter-mile south of the village of Shabbona, near U.S. 30, approximately 20 minutes west of the Sugar Grove exit on I-80.

FEATURES - The park was originally inhabited by the Winnebago Indians whose most famous leader was Chief Shabbona. His tribe was very friendly with the early settlers, and when Chief Black Hawk crossed the Mississippi, Chief Shabbona rode three horses to death warning the settlers of his arrival. As a result, he was allowed to enter any store, hotel or business and help himself without cost.

ACTIVITIES - The Upland fishing area provides a spot for observing wildlife, fishing, and also boating with rowboats, canoes or electric trolling motors.

The refuge area has been set aside for waterfowl. During the fall migration period, lasting from October 1 through when the lake freezes, boat access and bank fishing are prohibited. The rest of the year, bank fishing and boating is allowed.

The lake is stocked with game fish such as bass, bluegill, crappie, bullhead and catfish. Access to the lake is available from a launching ramp, or from the lake bank at any time.

Camping in the park is available in 50 sites equipped with electricity and a trailer dumping station. In addition, there are 100 other sites without electricity. The campground may be closed during spring thaw because of road conditions. For information, call 815-824-2565. Concession facilities provide boat rentals and snacks on a seasonal basis.

Hikers and cross-country skiers will find 4.5 miles of trails along steep glacial slopes and bottom land, or have access to open snow fields, plus a seven-mile snowmobile trail.

INFORMATION
Shabbona Lake State Park
Route #1, Box 120
Shabbona, Illinois 60550
815-824-2106

SILVER SPRINGS FISH AND WILDLIFE AREA
50

LOCATION - Five miles west of Yorkville off Illinois 47.

FEATURES - The park was named for the small pool of water that is constantly bubbling and never freezes over—regardless of how cold it becomes.

ACTIVITIES - Go fishing in one of the two small lakes for catfish, bass, bluegill and crappie. You can go boating on Loon Lake where gasoline motors are prohibited.

You can also fish in the Fox River from either the river bank or from a small boat. Because of the shallowness of the water, large boats aren't recommended on the river. A concession stand with canoe rentals and refreshments is located near the Fox River Bridge, and is open weekends and holidays from May through September.

Hikers can explore a 3.5-mile nature trail along the lake and through the surrounding woods. Equestrians have access to a seven-mile trail. Cross-country skiers can ski 5.5 miles of trails.

Cross-country skiers have 15 kilometers of trails to explore in wintertime.

INFORMATION
Silver Springs Fish and Wildlife Area
R. R. 1 Box 318
Yorkville, Illinois 60560
312-553-6297

SOUTH SHORE STATE PARK
51

See under ELDON HAZLET STATE PARK

STARVED ROCK STATE PARK
52

See under ILLINOIS AND MICHIGAN CANAL

STEPHEN A. FORBES STATE FISH AND WILDLIFE AREA
53

LOCATION - It's located 14 miles northeast of Salem.

FEATURES - The lake has a maximum depth of 28 feet and 48 miles of shoreline.

ACTIVITIES - A Fisheries Research Center was built here in 1966 where a variety of aquatic experiments are conducted throughout the year. The lab is open for tours Monday through Friday from 7–4. To arrange for a tour, call 618-245-6348.

The lake is stocked with bass, bluegill, crappie and catfish. Besides fishing in the lake, you can also fish Boston or Morlow Ponds. Unlimited horsepowered boats are permitted year-round, and boat rentals are available at the concession stand. A swimming beach is located at Rocky Point, and water-skiing is available near the dam on the southern half of the lake.

Camp in Oak Ridge campground with 115 campsites with electricity and a dump station.

Hike one of their three nature trails. The Heneman Trail takes you along the .5-mile walk to their early settlement cemetery.

Equestrians will find 15 miles of trail plus an equestrian campground. Both are located one mile east of Omega.

INFORMATION
Stephen A. Forbes State Fish and Wildlife Area
R. R. 1
Kinmundy, Illinois 62854
618-547-3381

TRAIL OF TEARS STATE FOREST
54

LOCATION - The forest is five miles northwest of Jonesboro and 20 miles south of Carbondale. It's easily reached via Illinois 127 on one side and Illinois 3 on the west.

FEATURES - Ten thousand Cherokee Indians were forced to move 800 miles from the Great Smokies to a reservation in Oklahoma in the winter of 1838–39.

They had to pause south of the state forest because of floating ice on the Mississippi River. That winter was unusually severe, and their camps weren't able to sustain them against the weather, causing many deaths.

ACTIVITIES - This is a hiker's paradise with 45 miles of fire and horse trails to explore. Picnickers have two picnic shelters. Camping is without electrical hookups.

INFORMATION
Trail of Tears State Forest
R. R. 1, Box 1331
Jonesboro, Illinois 62952
618-833-4910

W. G. STRATTON STATE PARK
55

See under ILLINOIS AND MICHIGAN CANAL

WAYNE FITZGERRELL STATE RECREATION AREA
56

LOCATION - The recreation area is located on the shore of Rend Lake, which is 13 miles long, and has 162 miles of shoreline. It is six miles north of Benton, west of I-57 and on both sides of Illinois 154.

ACTIVITIES - Because of its location, the area is popular for water sports including fishing, boating, water-skiing and swimming. Go fishing for crappie, bass, bluegill and catfish. The area has two marinas, one on each side of the lake.

Campers have access to rent-a-camp facilities, 245 trailer sites with electrical hookups, and a trailer dump station.

Nine miles of bridle trails circle the wildlife field trial area, closed from September 15–April 15 when designated field trials and hunting season occur. You can also hike and bike in the area.

The Rend Lake Visitor Center is open April through October, and features exhibits, live wildlife displays and slide presentations. Attend naturalist programs during the regular season.

The lake also has an 18-hole championship golf course, tennis courts, a 10-station championship style trap and skeet range, and a restaurant. To reserve a golf tee-off time, call 618-629-2353. For information on the trap range, call 618-629-9920.

Private pilots can arrive near the lake by using the Mount Vernon-Outland Airport located three miles south of town. Benton also has an airport one mile west of town. Both airports have rental cars available.

INFORMATION

Wayne Fitzgerrell State Rec. Area
P.O. Box 68, Rural Route 4
Benton, Illinois 62812
618-629-2320

Rend Lake Management Office
R. R. 3
Benton, Illinois 62812
618-724-2493
Visitor center: 618-439-7430
Recreation information:
618-724-4089

WEINBERG-KING STATE PARK
57

LOCATION - The park is in Schuyler County, three miles east of Augusta and north of Illinois 101.

FEATURES - The park is in an area of rolling hills with a creek and farm pond. Before the state took over the park, its previous owner operated a commercial poultry cannery.

ACTIVITIES - Picnic at one of the picnic areas. Go fishing in William Creek for bluegill, bullhead, catfish and bass.

Camp in the grassy campground with 50 spots with water but no electricity, and a trailer dump station.

A wildlife viewing platform is located on one of the nature trails, providing a scenic view of a log cabin.

Enjoy hiking, horseback riding, or snowmobiling along 18 miles of wooded trails. The trails begin from the main office.

INFORMATION

Weinberg-King State Park
P.O. Box 203
Augusta, Illinois 62311
217-392-2345

WELDON SPRINGS STATE RECREATION AREA
58

See under CLINTON LAKE STATE RECREATION AREA

WHITE PINES FOREST STATE PARK
LOWDEN STATE PARK
CASTLE ROCK STATE PARK
59

LOCATION - White Pines Forest is in northwestern Illinois about eight miles west of Oregon, and 12 miles north of Dixon.

Lowden State park is two miles north of Ogden on Illinois 64 on the east side of Rock River.

Castle Rock State Park is three miles south of Oregon on Illinois 2, along the west bank of the Rock River.

FEATURES - White Pines Forest State Park was set aside to protect Illinois's last stand of white pines that once dominated vast areas of the U.S.

ACTIVITIES - The WHITE PINES FOREST campground has 107 grassy sites, and a dumping station. You can also stay in the lodge April 1–November 1, in one of 13 log cabins. Reservations: 815-946-3817.

Go hiking or biking through the white pines and along the crest of the bluff located in the west end of the park. Two trails, Cathedral Corridor and Spring Creek Pass, offer 7.2 kilometers of intermediate cross-country skiing during the winter.

Anglers can try their skill at landing catfish from the stream.

If you arrive during rainy weather, fords rather than bridges have been constructed along the road because of the turbulent water conditions. High water and soft ground may cause campground closure, so check with the park.

Nearby LOWDEN STATE PARK, located on a bluff 12 miles northeast of White Pines Forest, features a giant, monolithic reinforced concrete figure of an American Indian standing 230 feet above the Rock River. The figure weighs approximately 100 tons, and is believed to be the second largest concrete monolithic statue in the world. The park has 130 campsites with 80 equipped with electrical hookups and a trailer dump station.

Adjacent to this park, boaters will find a launching ramp, and anglers can fish for bass, bluegill, crappie and pike.

A park naturalist offers recreational programs during the summer. The park has approximately four miles of hiking trails, some rather steep. During the winter, cross-country ski along 2.5 miles of trails.

CASTLE ROCK STATE PARK offers hiking along six miles of marked hiking trails. The south trails are closed September 15–December 31.

You can go fishing along Rock River's 1.5 miles of river bank for catfish, bass, walleye and crappie. Canoeists also have their own campsite available along the river.

INFORMATION

White Pines Forest State Park
R. R. 2
Oregon, Illinois 61061
815-946-3717

Lowden State Park
R. R. 2
Oregon, Illinois 61061
815-732-6828

Castle Rock State Park
R. R. 2
Oregon, Illinois 61061
815-732-7329

WOLF CREEK STATE RECREATION AREA
EAGLE CREEK STATE PARK
60

LOCATION - Wolf Creek Park is located eight miles northwest of Windsor, and Eagle Creek is three miles southeast of Findlay.

FEATURES - Lake Shelbyville is .5-mile east of downtown Shelbyville, and has 250 miles of shoreline. Eagle Creek State Recreation Area is on the west side of the lake, and Wolf Creek State Recreation Area is on its east side. Both parks are similar in their design and facilities.

ACTIVITIES - WOLF CREEK STATE PARK offers picnic facilities, and hiking along seven hiking trails. Equestrians have a 15-mile trail, and in the winter, snowmobiles have access to a 16.5-mile trail.

Go boating from the ramp, water-ski, or fish for pike, crappie, bass, walleye, catfish and bluegill. Rental boats are available from the marinas.

The campgrounds have 435 campsites with electrical hookups, rent-a-camp facilities, and an equestrian campground.

Park naturalists conduct recreational programs mid-June through Labor Day.

EAGLE CREEK STATE PARK also has fishing, boating, and water-skiing; however, no rental boats are available. The campground has 160 campsites with electrical hookups. Hikers have access to three hiking trails, a 15-mile backpack trail, and an eight-mile cross-country ski trail.

Nearby is Shelbyville Fish and Wildlife Area, located on the northern end of Lake Shelbyville, where you can go hiking, boating or fishing. You can also fish in five nearby ponds for bass, bluegill, bullhead and catfish.

Lake Shelbyville has a visitor center located in the Dam East Recreation Area, one mile east of Shelbyville, off Illinois 16. Tour the exhibit area, attend an interpretive program in the theater, and take a tour offered weekly. It's open from Memorial Day through Labor Day.

INFORMATION

Wolf Creek State Recreation Area
Rt. 1, Box 99
Windsor, Illinois 61957
217-459-2831 (May–October)
217-756-8260 (January–April)

Rent-a-camp: Wolf Creek
Rt. 1, Box 198A
Findley, Illinois 62534
217-459-2871 (May–October)

Eagle Creek State Park
Findlay, Illinois
217-756-8260

Shelbyville Fish and Wildlife Area
R. R. 1, Box 42A
Bethany, Illinois 61914
217-665-3112

Lake Shelbyville Office
Rt. 16 East, P.O. Drawer 126
Shelbyville, Illinois 61914
217-774-3951
Lake information recording:
217-774-2020

*Young visitors eagerly inspect the paddle boats at
Pokagon State Park in Angola, Indiana.*

POKAGON STATE PARK

INDIANA

Indiana is often referred to as the "Hoosier" state. The state has three geographic sections resulting from the glaciers that passed through here. If you visit the northern part of the state, you find moraines, lakes, and Lake Michigan. The central section consists of plains and shallow river valleys. The prettiest part in the eyes of many visitors is found in the southern part of the state which offers the foothills, valleys and ridges of the Cumberland Mountains.

Many visitors come to enjoy water sports on the various lakes, especially on Lake Michigan, which is lined with beaches and resorts. Also bicyclists will enjoy the wonderful Hoosier Bikeway System that utilizes lightly traveled roads and passes through many of Indiana's state parks. You can do a loop starting at Harmonie State Park, cycle through Lincoln State Park, continue northeast to St. Meinrad and then on to the Patoka Reservoir. From here, ride to Spring Mill State Park and turn northeast to ride to Starve Hollow Beach State Recreation Area. At this point, you can do a loop north to Brown County State Park and up to Indianapolis. From here, ride east to Richmond, and then turn south to ride through Whitewater Memorial State Park, Versailles State Park, and then to Clifty Falls State Park, returning to Starve Hollow Beach State Recreation Area.

A second long route begins at Eagle Creek Park, and goes northwest to Shades State Park, with a side trip to Turkey Run State Park. From Shades, ride northwest to Commandant's Home Historic Site, then to Tippecanoe Battle State Memorial, and on to Misssissinewa Lake, Salamonie Lake, Huntington Lake, and end up at Fox Island County Park.

To get a copy of the bicycling guidebook, contact Publications, Indiana State Parks, 616 State Office Building, Indianapolis, Indiana 46204. Canoeists can get an Indiana Canoeing Guide from the same place.

Runners can participate in the AUL/Governor's Cup Series that is held at five race sites. The race has an eight-kilometer run, a five-kilometer walking division, and a .5-kilometer PeeWee race for youngsters. The series begins in McCormick's Creek State Park in March, goes to Brown County State Park in April, then on to Mounds State Park in May, Pokagon State Park in August,

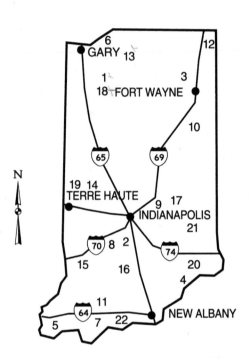

N

Potato Creek State Park in September, and culminates in the AUL/Governor's Cup Race in Indianapolis in late September.

Three parks have volksmarch courses, measuring 6.2 miles, and are laid out along trails where you can walk or jog at your own pace. The courses are located in Potato Creek State Park, Spring Mill State Park, and Turkey Run State Park. For information, call 1-800-622-4931 in Indiana, or 317-232-4124.

BASS LAKE STATE PARK x
1

LOCATION - The park is twelve miles north of Winamac on U.S. 35.

FEATURES - The Miami and Potawatomi Indians called the lake "Wincheton-qua," meaning "beautiful waters."

ACTIVITIES - Bass Lake is the state's fourth largest, with 11 miles of shoreline and a .5-mile-long beach open from Memorial Day to Labor Day. Swim with supervision, and go boating and water-skiing. Fish for bass, catfish and panfish.

The campground has 60 sites with electricity, and a trailer dump station.

Bass Lake is five miles from Tippecanoe River State Park where campers from Bass Lake can swim free if you bring along your receipt.

Visit nearby Culver Military Academy, home of the famous Black Horse Troop that has appeared in many presidential inaugural parades.

Kankakee State Fish and Wildlife area is one mile north on U.S. 35, and then five miles west on Missouri 8. The area lies along both sides of the Kankakee River, and offers fishing, canoeing, and boating. You can also enjoy a picnic, and go berry picking. For information, call 219-896-3522.

INFORMATION
Bass Lake State Park
Route 5
Knox, Indiana 46534
219-772-3382 (summer); 219-946-3213 (winter)

BROWN COUNTY STATE PARK
2

LOCATION - The park is two miles southeast of Nashville on Indiana 135.

ACTIVITIES - Drive across Indiana's oldest covered bridge to reach this park, famed for its fall foliage. From 13 viewpoints you can see for miles. A self-guided auto tour tape is available at the park office.

Brown County is Indiana's largest state park, and has a saddle barn, bridle trails, housekeeping cabins, 401 campsites with electrical hookups and 28 sites without. The campground is open year-round. Equestrians have a campground with 118 sites with electrical hookups, and 61 campsites without hookups. Horses may be rented at the saddle barn.

You can also stay in the inn and eat in its restaurant. For reservations in either the Abe Martin Lodge (open year-round) in one of the 56 cabins, or in one of the 22 housekeeping cabins, call 812-988-4418 or 988-7316.

Attend a cultural arts program, go fishing in two lakes for bass and bluegill, and hike on eight trails covering over ten miles. Swim in the pool open from Memorial Day to Labor Day, play tennis, and tour the nature center. Climb two lookout towers for an overlook of the surrounding area, and attend the naturalist-led activities. In the winter, cross-country ski along the trails.

Attend a country music show at the Little Nashville Opry, a cabaret-style puppet show at the Melchior Marionette Theater on South Van Buren Street, or ride aboard the Nashville Express Train for 2.5 miles for a narrated tour of town. Also, visitors can tour some of the historic homes located in Nashville.

INFORMATION
Brown County State Park
Box 608
Nashville, Indiana 47448
812-988-6406
812-988-4418 or 812-988-7316: Abe Martin Lodge

CHAIN O' LAKES STATE PARK
3

LOCATION - The park is six miles south of Albion on Indiana 9.

FEATURES - The ten kettle lakes, steeply rolling hills, and bogs were left behind by the massive ice sheets that once covered and then receded from this area near the end of the Pleistocene Epoch. The lakes range in depth from Dock Lake, 22 feet deep, to Bowen Lake, 65 feet deep.

ACTIVITIES - The lakes offer great boating and other water-based activities. You can paddle a canoe through the chain of lakes. Boats are restricted to electric trolling motors.

Hikers can get a good close-up view of the glacial features. Trails 1, 4, 5, 7, and 8 cross outwash deposits from the glacier. Trails 3 and 6 cross till, sediments that were once frozen in the ice and then transported here from as far away as Canada.

Some of the lakes have gradually filled with aquatic vegetation, and all you can see today are depressions filled with muck and peat. Trails 2, 6, and 9 will take you to some of these boggy, low-lying areas.

The campground has 333 campsites with electrical hookups, 49 without and 33 more primitive sites. It has a trailer dump station. You can also rent one of the 18 housekeeping cabins.

Pick up a schedule of summer events at the nature center located in the old two-room schoolhouse. Go hiking, fishing, or swimming from the beach.

During the winter, go cross-country skiing along two trails, one an easier .75-mile-long trail, and the other for intermediate skiers that's 2.75 miles long.

At nearby Rome City, visit the Gene Stratton-Porter Home, a State Historic Site. He wrote "Girls of the Limberlost," "Freckles," "Keeper of the Bees," and many other novels. It's one mile south of town on Indiana 9, and preserves the novelist's cabin. Since he was also a naturalist, the area was planted with over 3,000 trees, shrubs and wildflowers. Guided tours are offered. For information, call 219-854-3790.

Antique car lovers can go east to Auburn to see the Auburn-Cord-Duesenberg Museum at 1600 So. Wayne Street where over 130 antique and classic cars are kept. For information, call 219-925-1444.

INFORMATION
Chain O' Lakes State Park
2355 East 75 South
Albion, Indiana 46701
219-636-2654

CLIFTY FALLS STATE PARK
4

LOCATION - The park is one mile west of Madison on Indiana 56.

FEATURES - The park features the falls of Clifty Creek, Little Clifty Creek, and a deep canyon where the sun only shines at mid-day. You get some wonderful views of the Ohio River and Madison from a 400-foot cliff.

ACTIVITIES - Go hiking on the trails, visit the nature center, play tennis, or go for a swim in the Olympic-sized pool.

The campground has 106 campsites with electrical hookups, 59 sites without, and a trailer dump station. Stay at the inn and eat in its restaurant.

Go to nearby Madison to tour the mansion of frontier banker, James F. D. Lanier. It's located at 511 West First Street, and was completed in 1844. For information, call 812-265-3526.

If you're here in early July, attend the Governor's Cup Regatta hydroplane race. In late September, many Midwestern artists congregate at the annual Chautauqua of the Arts.

Take a beautiful drive up the Ohio River Valley.

Incoming pilots can land at the Madison Municipal Airport located four miles west of town. Rental cars are available.

INFORMATION
Clifty Falls State Park
1501 Green Road
Madison, Indiana 47250
812-265-1331

HARMONIE STATE PARK
5

LOCATION - The park is located on the banks of the Wabash River. It's four miles south of New Harmony on Indiana 69.

ACTIVITIES - The park offers six hiking trails, equestrian trails, and a three-mile-long biking trail. Bicycle rentals are available.

You can go fishing from the river bank, or boating on the Wabash River from the boat launching ramp.

Go swimming in the pool, tour the nature center where naturalist-led activities are available, and attend cultural arts programs. The campground has 199 campsites with electrical hookups, and a camp store.

The state park hosts an annual eight-kilometer road race. Contact the park authorities for the date.

Tour the historic New Harmony State Historic Site, originally established for experimental communal living during the 1800s, with restored buildings dating back to the Harmonist and Owen-Maclure periods. The site includes the Fauntleroy Home, Thrall's Opera House, the Harmonist Labyrinth, and the Harmonist Cemetery. The site is located at the intersection of Indiana 66 and 69, seven miles south of I-64. For information, call 812-682-3271.

You can combine this tour with the one for Atheneum, constructed as a monument to the explorations that were encouraged by the two communal societies. The Atheneum is located at North and Arthur Streets in New Harmony. For information, call 812-682-4474.

INFORMATION
Harmonie State Park
Route 1, Box 5A
New Harmony, Indiana 47631
812-682-4821

INDIANA DUNES STATE PARK
6

LOCATION - The park is three miles north of Chesterton on Indiana 49. The state park includes over three miles of Lake Michigan's southern shore.

FEATURES - The dunes were created by winds blowing off Lake Michigan. As the wind comes over the shore, plants, dunes and hills slow the wind so that it is forced to drop its load of sand, creating shoreline sand dunes.

As the level of the lake gradually dropped, the upper dunes became covered with vegetation, and then forested. Mt. Baldy is the largest dune on the National Lakeshore.

One of the more unusual features are the "blowouts" found among the dunes where, after many years, the sand was blown away, leaving behind dead stumps of what were once living trees.

The dunes are located along major Indian routes between the Great Lakes and the Mississippi River. The Miami and Potawatomi Indians hunted and gathered their food here through the warmer months.

ACTIVITIES - The park has three miles of shoreline along Lake Michigan. Trail #10 passes the tree graveyard in Big Blowout. Additional hiking trails may be found in Indiana Dunes National Lakeshore. Their many trails take you past historic structures, on trails through the woods, out into the wet prairie, across the dunes, and past ponds. Hike the .66-mile-long trail up Mt. Baldy.

Visitors can go swimming from the beach, where supervision is provided from Memorial Day to Labor Day, go fishing, and, of course, build sand castles.

While at the national lakeshore, explore evidence of Indian heritage at the Bailley Homestead, and see how pioneers harvested the land at the Chellberg Farm.

Bike along the 9.2-mile-long Calumet Trail, the state's first long distance trail built for bikers and hikers. This trail, adjacent to the park, is also used by cross-country skiers.

Camp in the campground, open all year, with 308 campsites, 121 with electrical hookups. A campground grocery store is open during the summer, and snacks are sold in the pavilion.

Tour the nature center where naturalists are on hand for various activities.

Arriving pilots can land on airstrips in Michigan City, Valparaiso and Gary. All three airstrips have rental cars available.

INFORMATION
Indiana Dunes State Park
1600 North 25 East
Chesterton, Indiana 46304
219-926-4520

LINCOLN STATE PARK
7

LOCATION - The park is one-half mile south of Lincoln City on Indiana 162. Take Exit 57 and follow the signs on I-64.

FEATURES - The Little Pigeon Primitive Baptist Church was built here on the site of an early building in which the Lincoln family worshipped. The church yard contains the graves of Sarah Lincoln Grigsby, Lincoln's only sister, and other pioneer settlers.

ACTIVITIES - During the summer, "Young Abe Lincoln," a musical outdoor drama, is given in the covered amphitheater. It's presented on Tuesday through Sunday evenings. For information, call 1-800-346-4665 in Indiana, or 812-937-4493.

The park's 58-acre Lincoln Lake is stocked with game fish including bass and bluegill. Boat rentals and docking facilities are adjacent to the swimming beach. Only electric trolling motors are permitted on the lake.

A snack shop and grocery store are located in the beach bathhouse, and are open daily from Memorial Day weekend to Labor Day weekend.

You can either stay in the campground with 270 campsites (150 with water and electrical hookups), in one of the 120 primitive sites, or in one of the 10 housekeeping cabins. The cabins are available from April through November. The park also has three rent-a-tents.

Hike 10 miles of trails ranging in length from 1.5 miles to 3.7 miles. The James Gentry Trail leads to the Gentry Store where Lincoln clerked as a young man. Another trail winds through Sarah Lincoln's Woods Nature Preserve, site of the state-endangered Butterfly Pea flower. Another trail goes from the north end of the park to the Lincoln Boyhood National Memorial.

Take the bike path to Weber Lake, or climb the fire tower for a panoramic view of the park. Visit the nature center open five days a week from Memorial Day to Labor Day. Go swimming from the beach—permitted only when a life-guard is on duty.

Pilots flying small planes can fly into the Tell City Airport or into Huntingburg Airport. Both provide courtesy car service, and Huntingburg has rental cars.

The Lincoln Boyhood National Memorial adjoins the state park. This site preserves the farm where Lincoln lived from 1816 to 1830, and has the reconstructed homestead, a visitor center, and his mother's burial site. The visitor center has a movie, "Here I Grew Up," telling about Lincoln's early years.

Tour the living historical farm, reached by trail or vehicle, to get an idea of Lincoln's early life. It contains reconstructed buildings, farm fields and a garden like those maintained in 1816. Costumed "pioneers" present family living and farming activities daily mid-April–October. For information, call 812-937-4757.

INFORMATION
Lincoln State Park
Box 216
Lincoln City, Indiana 47552
812-937-4710

McCORMICK'S CREEK STATE PARK
8

LOCATION - The park is two miles east of Spencer in south-central Indiana on Indiana 46.

FEATURES - The Miami Indians once hunted on the land now occupied by the park. It got its name from its first white settler, John McCormick, who homesteaded along the canyon by the waterfall.

ACTIVITIES - The park has eight trails leading into the 100-foot deep canyon, to a 90-foot fire tower, to Wolf Cave, and past giant sycamore trees. They range in length from .25-mile to three miles. Equestrians have their own bridle trail beginning at the saddle barn.

The recreation center is open May–October, and the nature center remains open year-round with naturalist-led activities. Attend cultural arts programs, rent horses at the saddle barn, fish in the creek, swim in the Olympic-sized pool, and play tennis.

You can stay in the campground with 325 campsites (189 with electrical hookups), in one of the 14 housekeeping cabins, or at the Canyon Inn with its own dining room. For inn reservations, call 812-829-4881.

INFORMATION
McCormick's Creek State Park
Route 5, Box 82
Spencer, Indiana 47460
812-829-2235

MOUNDS STATE PARK
9

LOCATION - The park is three miles east of Anderson on Indiana 32.

FEATURES - The park preserves ten mounds and earthworks believed to have been constructed around 150 B.C. by the Adena and Hopewell mound builders.

ACTIVITIES - If you hike Trail #1 to Great Mound, you'll see the largest and best preserved of the mounds in the park. The park has four miles of trails to explore, three of them beginning at the Pavilion.

Camp in the campground with 75 campsites, all with electrical hookups, and a trailer dump station.

Go canoeing on the White River. Canoe rentals and a canoe launch site are in the northwest corner of the park. Try your luck at fishing in the river for bass, bluegill and catfish.

Go swimming in the pool, open from the Saturday before Memorial Day through Labor Day. Concessions are sold at the pool.

Visit the nature center, located in the Bronnenburg House, considered the oldest building constructed as a dwelling in Madison County.

In 1991, the Adena-Hopewell Rendezvous was held in early June, and a living history program was presented in late June. Check with the park authorities for current information.

During winter, go cross-country skiing along trails, with ski rentals available.

In nearby Anderson, tour the Gruenewald House at 626 Main, which dates back to 1860. Tours are given by appointment. For information, call 317-646-5771.

INFORMATION
Mounds State Park
4306 Mounds Road
Anderson, Indiana 46017
317-642-6627

OUABACHE STATE PARK
10

LOCATION - The park is four miles east of Bluffton on Indiana 216.

FEATURES - Ouabache is the French Jesuit spelling of the Miami Indian pronunciation of "Wabash."

At one time, the park was known as the "Greatest Wildlife Laboratory in the U.S." because it was the largest producer of pheasant and quail chicks in the country. However, by the 1960s, the game-raising program was phased out. As you hike the trails, watch for remnants of some of the old pens.

ACTIVITIES - The park has five hiking trails, one six miles long, encircling the entire property.

You can go boating on Kunkel Lake where boat rentals are available. Only electric trolling motors are permitted. You can also fish for bass and bluegill.

The campground has 124 campsites with 77 offering electrical hookups. Equestrians have their own trails and campground with 45 campsites located near the Wabash River in the southeastern side of the park.

Swimmers have an Olympic-sized pool and bathhouse that opens the Saturday before Memorial Day and remains open through Labor Day.

Climb the 100-foot fire tower to get a good overlook of the entire park. Play tennis on the courts located in the north side of the park.

Work out on the one-mile-long exercise trail with 20 different stations. Attend one of their cultural arts programs.

INFORMATION
Ouabache State Park
6720 East 100 South
Bluffton, Indiana 46714
219-824-0926

PATOKA LAKE STATE RECREATION AREA
11

LOCATION - The park is south of Winslow off Indiana 61.

ACTIVITIES - Go swimming from the beach, water-skiing, and boating from nine launching ramps. Enjoy fishing, hiking, bicycling, working out on the fitness trail, and attend an interpretive program.

The campground has 455 campsites with electrical hookups, 96 primitive campsites, and a trailer dumping station.

INFORMATION
Patoka Lake State Recreation Area
R. R. 1
Birdseye, Indiana 47513
812-685-2464

POKAGON STATE PARK
12

LOCATION - The park is near Angola off I-69 on the shores of Lake James and Snow Lake.

ACTIVITIES - The park's two natural lakes offer good boating, swimming from the beach from Memorial Day to Labor Day, and fishing for bass, bluegill, crappie and catfish. Boat motors are permitted on the lakes, and rentals are available.

Rent horses from the saddle barn and explore the bridle trails. Go hiking along eight miles of trails, attend naturalist-sponsored activities, play tennis, or attend cultural arts programs.

The campground has 236 campsites with electrical hookups, 99 sites without, 102 primitive campsites, a trailer dump station, and a camp store.

If you prefer not to camp, stay at the Potawatomi Inn. The inn has 64 lodge rooms, 16 cabins and a dining room. For reservations, call 219-833-1077.

During the winter, experience thrills on the .25-mile-long toboggan track that enables you to reach speeds up 35 to 40 miles per hour. The toboggan operates weekends from Thanksgiving Day through February.

Incoming pilots can land at Tri-State Steuben County Airport located three miles west of town. A courtesy car is available.

INFORMATION
Pokagon State Park
1080 West Street Road 727
Angola, Indiana 46703
219-833-2102

POTATO CREEK STATE PARK
13

LOCATION - The park is two miles east of North Liberty on Indiana 4.

ACTIVITIES - The park offers two boat launching ramps, but boats are restricted to electric trolling motors only. Rental boats are available. You can go fishing for bass, bluegill, crappie and trout, or swimming from the beach in Lake Worster. Concessions are sold near the beach from the Saturday before Memorial Day to Labor Day.

Go horseback riding along the bridle trails, and hike the 11 miles of trails. Rent a bicycle to take a ride on the 3.2-mile bicycle trail, and take advantage of the naturalist's services by touring the visitor center. Go cross-country skiing on eight miles of groomed trails during the winter. Ski rentals are available.

The campground has 287 campsites with electrical hookups, a trailer dump station, and a camp store. You can also rent one of the 17 housekeeping cabins open year-round. The equestrian campground has 70 campsites.

INFORMATION
Potato Creek State Park
25601 State Road 4
North Liberty, Indiana 46554
219-656-8186

SHADES STATE PARK
14

LOCATION - The park is 17 miles southwest of Crawfordsville off I-74.

FEATURES - Originally the park was named "Shades of Death." One suggested reason is because of its nearly unbroken canopy of trees making the forest resemble a "black forest." Yet another story behind its name claims that a young settler's wife buried an ax in her wicked husband's head. Whatever the reason, "Shades of Death" was eventually changed to "The Shades."

The steep cliffs are formed of massive deposits of sandstone laid down hundreds of millions of years ago when this area was under the ocean. Look for fossils of plants and animals on the sandbars.

The hemlocks seen along the edges of the cliffs are remnants of an earlier forest that covered all of Indiana during the glacial period.

ACTIVITIES - Shades State Park is a favorite for hikers and canoeists who enjoy canoeing below the sandstone cliffs overlooking Sugar Creek. Deer's Mill Covered Bridge, located on Indiana 234, is maintained as a canoeists' public access to Sugar Creek.

No swimming is permitted in Sugar Creek since it is considered to be extremely hazardous.

The park has 10 trails covering 15 miles, taking you to breath-taking overlooks. Be sure to stop by Prospect Point, 210 feet above Sugar Creek, and by Lover's Leap. One of the more scenic trails, .75 miles long, begins at Devil's Punchbowl, goes through a ravine's creekbed to Silver Cascade Waterfall, then up to Inspiration Point and Prospect Point. Some of the trails may be impassable during high water.

Pick up a trail guide to the Pine Hills Nature Preserve, and take its .9-mile self-guided hike. Devil's Backbone area has several stone carvings including a bas-relief of the Devil, completed in 1910.

Try your luck at fishing for bass and bluegill, rent a bicycle at the gatehouse and go for a bike ride, or attend one of the cultural arts programs. Naturalists are on duty during the summer.

The campground has 105 campsites with water and a trailer dump station. Canoe campsites are also available.

Backpackers have a 2.5-mile-long trail that begins at the west end of the parking lot. The backpack camp is closed from November 1–March.

Pilots can land light aircrafts on Roscoe Turner Flight Strip located three miles northwest of Waveland. The strip has a 3,000-foot runway, and overnight parking is limited to people using accommodations either in the park or at nearby DNR properties. Transportation is available from the strip.

INFORMATION
Shades State Park
Route 1, Box 72
Waveland, Indiana 47989
317-435-2810

SHAKAMAK STATE PARK
15

LOCATION - The park is four miles west of Jasonville on Indiana 48.

ACTIVITIES - The campground has 122 campsites with electrical hookups, and .66 of the campsites are in the woods. It also has 74 primitive sites, and a trailer dump station. You can also rent one of the 29 family housekeeping cabins.

Launch your boat in one of the three man-made lakes. Rental boats are available. You can also go fishing, swimming, canoeing or sailing.

Rent a horse and go horseback riding, or play tennis on one of their courts.

Tour the nature center and take advantage of the naturalists' services. Check their schedule for cultural arts programs.

INFORMATION
Shakamak State Park
Route 2, Box 120
Jasonville, Indiana 47438
812-665-2158

SPRING MILL STATE PARK
16

LOCATION - The park is 3.25 miles east of Mitchell on Indiana 60 from Indiana 37.

ACTIVITIES - Tour Spring Mill Village, which flourished in the 1800s. Here, you can see the water-powered gristmill that still grinds corn on a daily basis to be sold in the village. You can also walk through several shops.

Stop by the Virgil I. Grissom Memorial Visitor Center to see his space suit, and "Molly Brown," his Gemini space capsule. One of the original seven astronauts, Grissom first made a sub-orbital flight in 1961, followed by three orbits of the earth in 1965. In 1966, while preparing to command Apollo's flight to the moon, he, along with Edward White and Roger Chaffee, was killed. Since he was from Mitchell, and had spent many hours fishing in the park, the memorial was constructed here.

Attend a performance at the Spring Mill Theater from June through August.

Rent a boat, or bring your own, to go boating on Spring Mill Lake. Go fishing for bass, bluegill and trout.

Camp in the campground with 220 campsites, 188 with electrical hookups. A camp store is open April–October. You can also stay overnight in the Spring Mill Inn open year-round. It has a restaurant. For reservations, call 812-849-4081.

Take a boat ride into Twin Caves April–October. The ride goes approximately 500 feet into the cave. Walking tours are offered into Bronson and Donaldson Caves. The dry side of Donaldson Cave may be explored on your own.

Naturalist programs are available year-round, and include hikes, cave tours, and evening programs.

Go for a trail ride or an evening hayride April–October. Inquire at the saddle barn.

Go swimming in the Olympic-sized pool, with a bathhouse opening the Saturday before Memorial Day, and remaining open until Labor Day. No swimming is permitted anywhere else in the park.

Several miles of hiking trails lace the park. If you take the long loop trail, you'll pass Donaldson Cave gorge, wander past some sink holes, pass Bronson Cave and Twin Caves, and go through a stand of virgin woods.

Festivals in the park include the Autumn Harvest Festival in mid-October, Haunted Village at Halloween, and a Winter Festival the end of December.

INFORMATION
Spring Mill State Park
Box 376
Mitchell, Indiana 47446
812-849-4129

SUMMIT LAKE STATE PARK
17

LOCATION - The park is ten miles south of Muncie off Indiana 3, near New Castle.

ACTIVITIES - The campground has 125 campsites with electrical hookups and a trailer dump station.

The large lake provides the opportunity to go boating from one of the three launching ramps, fishing for bass, crappie, perch and catfish, canoeing, or swimming from the beach open Memorial Day to Labor Day. Rental boats and concessions are available.

Go hiking along the trails, rent a bicycle and take a spin, check out activities of the naturalists, and attend cultural arts programs.

INFORMATION
Summit Lake State Park
5993 No. Messick Rd.
Route 4, Box 33C
New Castle, Indiana 47362
317-766-5873

TIPPECANOE RIVER STATE PARK
18

LOCATION - The park is six miles north of Winamac on U.S. 35.

ACTIVITIES - Canoeists particularly like to visit this park to float down the Tippecanoe River, which meanders seven miles along the eastern border of the park. A canoe campsite has ten tent sites.

The campground has 112 campsites with electrical hookups, and a dumping station. If you don't own camping equipment, rent one of their 12 rent-a-tents.

Go hiking along one of the 10 trails covering seven miles, or horseback riding along 13 miles of trails from the 60-site equestrian campground. Rent a bicycle and take a ride, attend a cultural arts program, and take advantage of the naturalists' services. You can also fish for bluegill and bass.

No swimming is permitted in Tippecanoe River because of its hazardous conditions; however, swimmers can go to Bass Lake State Beach to swim. Take along your gate or campground receipt for free admission.

Incoming pilots can land at Arens Airport, three miles north of Winamac. A courtesy car is available.

INFORMATION
Tippecanoe River State Park
Route 4, Box 95 A
Winamac, Indiana 46996
219-946-3213

TURKEY RUN STATE PARK
19

LOCATION - The park is 2.5 miles north of Marshall on Indiana 47.

ACTIVITIES - The park is known for its deep canyons and scenic gorges. Rent a canoe at Deer's Mills Covered Bridge from Clements Canoes, 12 miles from the park, from Sugar Valley Canoe Trips on Indiana 47 across from the Turkey Creek campground, or from Turkey Run Canoe Trips .5-mile north of the junction of 41 and 47 on Indiana 41, and paddle along Sugar Creek through the heart of covered bridge country.

Hike on one of the 10 trails going through the old forest and deep sandstone ravines. The longest trail, three miles long, begins by the Turkey Run Inn, and goes to a covered bridge.

If you hike into one of the ravines, you can see the sandstone gorges carved by Sugar Creek. As the glacier that covered the northern part of the park melted, some of the debris it collected was left behind, and was ground against the sandstone by the melt-water, gradually scouring out the streams and canyons found in Turkey Run.

Visit the Colonel Richard Lieber Cabin Memorial. You can also tour the Lusk home and mill site, built in 1841 by the first settlers to the area. It's open seasonally.

The log church near the inn was originally built in 1871, and was moved to the park in 1923. Non-denominational services are held during the warmer months on Sunday at 10:00 a.m.

Stop by the nature center with a Spitz-Nova star projection system in its planetarium.

The campground has 235 campsites with electrical hookups, or 29 without, a camp store, and a trailer dumping station. If you prefer not to camp, stay at the Turkey Run Inn that is open year-round. It has 52 lodge rooms, 21 sleeping cabins and a dining room. For reservations, call 317-597-2211.

Go swimming in the Olympic-sized pool, rent a bicycle or a horse at the saddle barn and go for a ride. Go fishing for bass and bluegill in the stream, attend a cultural arts program, and check out the naturalists' programs.

Tennis players have access to a tennis court, and horseback riders can rent horses at the saddle barn.

The nearby town of Marshall is known for its 34 covered bridges, and celebrates with a covered bridge festival in Rockville beginning the second Friday in October, and lasting for ten days.

INFORMATION
Turkey Run State Park
Route 1, Box 164
Marshall, Indiana 47859
317-597-2635

VERSAILLES STATE PARK
20

LOCATION - The park is one mile east of Versailles on U.S. 50.

ACTIVITIES - The lake has a boat launching ramp and rentals—only boats with electric trolling motors are permitted.

Try your luck at fishing, swim in the pool, hike the trails, attend a cultural arts program, or rent a horse and ride the bridle trails.

Bring your bicycle along to pedal the 27-mile Hoosier Hills Bicycle Route. This trail connects with the Whitewater Valley Route which adds an additional 66 miles to your riding options.

The campground has 226 campsites with electrical hookups, a camp store and a dump station.

INFORMATION
Versailles State Park
Box 205
Versailles, Indiana 47042
812-689-6424

WHITEWATER MEMORIAL STATE PARK
21

LOCATION - The park is three miles south of Liberty off Indiana 101.

FEATURES - The park was created to be a living memorial to those serving in World War II.

ACTIVITIES - Whitewater Lake has a boat ramp, rentals, fishing and swimming. The beach is open from Memorial Day through Labor Day. Brookville Reservoir has a boat launch at the Silver Creek Ramp. Fishing is excellent in both lakes for crappie, bluegill, bass and catfish.

Camp in the campground with 330 sites, 270 with electrical hookups, a trailer dump, and grocery store. You can also stay in one of the 20 housekeeping cabins. Equestrians have their own trail and campground. Hikers have access to eight miles of hiking trails.

The park is the gateway to the 66-mile-long Whitewater Valley Bicycle Route, and connects with the 27-mile-long Hoosier Hills Route that continues further south to Versailles State Park.

INFORMATION
Whitewater Memorial State Park
Route 2, Box 194
Liberty, Indiana 47353
317-458-5565

WYANDOTTE WOODS STATE RECREATION AREA
22

LOCATION - The area is five miles northeast of Leavenworth, and south of I-64.

FEATURES - Since prehistoric times, Indians have used the caves for shelter and burials.

ACTIVITIES - You can tour two caves: Little Wyandotte Cave that offers 30–45 minute guided tours, and Big Wyandotte Cave that requires at least a couple of hours to tour. The tour covers 1.5 miles, and features well-preserved helictites, rare twisted formations. Serious spelunkers can reserve tours lasting either five or eight hours, requiring several long crawls and some climbing. For information, call 812-738-2782.

The recreation area has 2,000 acres of forested hills that are traversed by bridle and hiking trails. The campground has 281 campsites with electrical hookups, and a 120-site equestrian campground.

Visitors can swim in an Olympic-sized pool, tour the nature center and fish either in the Blue River, Ohio River, or in the fishing pond.

To tour the Squire Boone Caverns and its village, go 13 miles south of Corydon and I-64 via Indiana 135, and then three more miles east on Squire Boone Caverns Road. The one-hour cave tour requires climbing a 73-step staircase. The village has craft demonstrations, and one of the largest collections of Indian relics in the Midwest. For information, call 812-732-4381.

INFORMATION

Wyandotte Woods State Rec. Area
7240 Old Forest Road
Corydon, Indiana 47112
812-738-8232

Wyandotte Caves
R. R. 1, Box 85
Leavenworth, Indiana 47137
812-738-2782

The Mississippi Belle *and the* Spirit of Dubuque *churn the Mississippi River near the town of Dubuque and Belleview State Park.*

IOWA

Iowa is bounded on the east by the Mississippi River, and on the western border by the Missouri and Big Sioux rivers. As you pass through the state, you can't help but notice that much of it is lush farmland. In fact, almost 95% of Iowa's land is cultivated, on which is raised 20% of all the corn grown in the U.S.

Iowa's state parks, recreation areas and state forests provide 58 campgrounds with 5,700 campsites; however, no campground reservations are accepted. Eight state parks have rental cabins: Backbone, Lacey-Keosauqua, Lake of Three Fires, Lake Wapello, Palisades-Kepler, Dolliver, Springbrook and Wilson Island.

Most state-owned lakes of 100 acres or larger allow any size boat as long as it's operated at a no-wake speed. If the lake is smaller, boats must use electric motors.

Iowa is well known for its annual bicycle ride sponsored by the Des Moines Register. The ride is called the RAGBRAI, "Register's Annual Great Bicycle Ride Across Iowa," and is held the last week in July. The ride takes seven days and covers approximately 500 miles. Iowa residents host the cyclists as they pass through their towns by providing food and entertainment for them. The number of participants varies from 8,000–9,000. Contact the newspaper for details: 515-284-8000.

AMBROSE CALL STATE PARK
1

LOCATION - The park is 1.5 miles southwest of Algona near the east fork of the Des Moines River in northern Iowa.

ACTIVITIES - Stay in the lodge or camp in the hills in one of their 20 campsites, 12 offering electrical hookups. Rent the log cabin-style lodge for group get-togethers.

Hike five miles of trails through the woods, down a ravine, and along a winding creek.

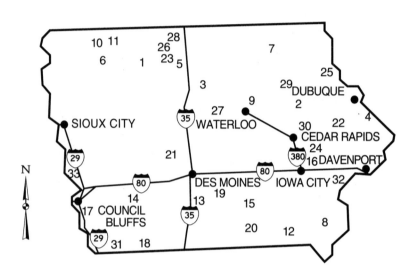

N

10 11 28
6   1 26 23 5

28
7

25

3   29 DUBUQUE
2

9
27
WATERLOO

SIOUX CITY

35

30 22
CEDAR RAPIDS
24

21   380 16 DAVENPORT

29
33

80   DES MOINES   80   IOWA CITY 32

14   13   19
17 COUNCIL   15
BLUFFS   35

29 31 18   20   12   8

INFORMATION
Ambrose Call State Park
2007 Call Park Drive
Algona, Iowa 50511
515-295-3669

BACKBONE STATE PARK
2

LOCATION - The park is four miles southwest of Strawberry Point.

FEATURES - The park has quite a few springs and caverns, an artificial lake, and some limestone bluffs that rise above the Maquoketa River. It was named for a high ridge of rock located in the center of the park.

ACTIVITIES - Hike along an extensive system of hiking trails, go swimming, trout fishing, and boating from the ramp or dock. Rent one of the cabins, or camp on one of 214 grassy sites, 32 with electrical hookups.

INFORMATION
Backbone State Park
Dundee, Iowa 52038
319-924-2527

BEEDS LAKE STATE PARK
3

LOCATION - The park is three miles northwest of Hampton.

FEATURES - In 1864, a pioneer settler, F. K. Hansberry, built a flour mill near Spring Creek, northwest of Hampton, and the west end of the lake was originally dammed to power his water wheel constructed to grind flour for his mill.

ACTIVITIES - Go camping in one of 144 campsites, with 70 electrical hookups. The campground has a dump station, and is open May 1–November 1. Overnight in one of the rooms in the lodge. Have a picnic, or go hiking along three miles of trails. Go swimming after changing in the bathhouse, or fishing for walleye, crappie, catfish, tiger muskie and bass. Go boating from the ramp, from which only boat motors up to ten horsepower may be launched.

Attend the annual Labor Day weekend celebration in town featuring music, a parade, and lots of good food. For information, call 515-456-5668.

INFORMATION
Beeds Lake State Park
Route 2, Box 37
Hampton, Iowa 50441
515-456-2047

BELLEVUE STATE PARK
4

LOCATION - The park is divided into two units. The Nelson Unit is on the south edge of Bellevue on top of a 300-foot limestone bluff. The Dyas Unit is two miles further south on U.S. 52.

ACTIVITIES - No camping is allowed at the Nelson Unit, but picnickers can enjoy a picnic under a shelter.

The South Bluff Nature Center is located in the Nelson Unit, and is open seasonally, offering a variety of summer programs. Walk through the nearby "Garden Sanctuary for Butterflies." Over 60 species of butterflies visit the garden throughout the year.

The park has five trails. One takes you to a scenic overlook of the lock, dam and historic mill. Another winds past three conical Indian burial mounds constructed by Woodland Culture Indians between 1000 B.C. and A.D. 1300 A third trail takes you through the "Garden Sanctuary for Butterflies."

In late July, the park features the Buckskinner Rendezvous that attracts frontier history enthusiasts to an encampment where early 1800s lifestyles are re-enacted. Learn to shoot a muzzle-loading rifle, throw a tomahawk and taste some early frontier cuisine. Watch period craftsmen work with scrimshaw, do quill work and start fires with flint and steel. Attend a live bluegrass musical concert on Saturday night.

The Dyas Unit has over nine miles of trails, a self-guided nature trail, and a stream with beaver dams. Bald eagles congregate here during the winter to feed below Lock and Dam 12. This unit has 52 campsites, 23 with electrical hookups, and a dump station. Go fishing for pike in the Mississippi River.

Bicyclists have four scenic loops that begin from Bellevue. The Highland Tour, 34.8 miles, takes you from the Mississippi River Valley to the ridgetop. The Ansel Briggs Tour, 27 miles, takes you past some National Register historic buildings.

The Central County Tour, 26 miles, offers you the opportunity to explore limestone caves, see a natural bridge and balancing rock at Maquoketa, or tour Iowa's largest antique store, Banowetz Antiques, also in Maquoketa.

The Great River Tour is 36.5 miles long, and passes the Green Island State Wildlife Refuge where you can watch canoeists gliding along the lakes, or go fishing in the backwater lakes for panfish and bass.

To get further details on the back country highways, call 319-652-3605 or 319-652-4782. To get a list of the sites on the National Register of Historic Places, call 319-652-2050.

While you're in Bellevue, take the Riverview boat ride on the Mississippi. For information, call 319-872-4729.

INFORMATION
Bellevue State Park
Route 3
Bellevue, Iowa 52031
319-872-4019

CLEAR LAKE STATE PARK
5

LOCATION - The park is two miles south of Clear Lake. Take Exit 193 from I-35. Go west for a mile on Iowa 106, then two miles south on Iowa 107, and then west .5 mile on B-35 to reach the park entrance.

FEATURES - The lake is spring fed, and was formed by glacial activity.

ACTIVITIES - Go camping in one of the state's most popular campgrounds with 215 campsites, 95 with electrical hookups. The campground has a dump station. Enjoy a picnic, biking the trail, and go swimming from the 900-foot sandy beach.

Go fishing from 24 public accesses along the lake for walleye, bass, crappie, northern pike, panfish and bullhead.

Visitors can also enjoy wind surfing, water-skiing, boating, sailing, tennis, golf or watching a sailing regatta.

Take a drive around the six-mile-long lake, or enjoy a cruise to see the many residences that surround the water.

Visit the Surf Ballroom where Buddy Holly performed his last concert before his fatal crash. Attend the Buddy Holly Memorial concert held in February. For information, call 515-357-2159.

Contact the Clear Lake Summer Theater at 515-357-3500 to obtain their performance schedule and information.

Annual events include a professional fishing tournament, "Welcome Back Summer" celebration, and a lake race in May. Summer concerts in the park and the F-100's Midwest camp-out occur in June. An antique and classic boat show is in July, and Governor's Days is in August. Go through the Halloween Fun House in October, and enjoy "Christmas in the Park" in December.

Woodford Island is a three-acre island acquired by the park from the Woodford family in 1971. The island is a wildlife habitat as well as an excellent fishing spot.

For a five-mile round trip on another nature trail, begin in Mason City at 14th Street N.E. and Elm Drive. The trail follows the banks of the Winnebago River, and passes through the original site of Masonic Grove and an historic mill site to the Lime Creek Nature Center.

While in Mason City, tour Van Horn's Antique Truck Museum on Iowa 65 North, to see one of the nation's largest collections of restored pre-1930s trucks including models by Nash, Sternberg, Acme and Packard. The museum operates from Memorial Day through Labor Day. For information, call 515-423-0550 or 423-0655 off-season.

INFORMATION
Clear Lake State Park
2730 South Lakeview Drive
Clear Lake, Iowa 50428
515-357-4212

EMERSON BAY STATE PARK
6

See under GULL POINT STATE PARK

FORT ATKINSON STATE PRESERVE
7

LOCATION - The preserve is next to Fort Atkinson and south of Decorah on Iowa 24 in northern Iowa.

FEATURES - The fort was established along the Turkey River in 1840 to protect the Winnebago Indians from attack by the hostile Sioux, Sac and Fox. Part of the original barracks has been converted into a museum with many items from the early days of military and pioneer life.

ACTIVITIES - Come the last weekend in September for the annual Fort Atkinson Rendezvous. This two-day pageant attracts buckskinners who re-create early frontier living in the upper Midwest from 1790 to 1840. A large encampment is set up on the parade ground where you can observe the art of wilderness skills including rope-making, weaving and shingle-splitting. Barter for trinkets such as clay pipes, and sample the frontier-style cooking of venison stew, Indian fried bread and apple cider.

Tour the fort that is open Tuesday through Sunday mid-May–mid-October. .

INFORMATION
Fort Atkinson State Preserve
c/o Volga River State Park
R. R. 1, Box 72
Fayette, Iowa 52124
515-281-3251

GEODE STATE PARK
8

LOCATION - The park is in southeast Iowa, near Middletown on Iowa 78, or you can access it from Lowell on County Road J-20.

FEATURES - Geodes are unusual rocks that have rough-looking exteriors, but contain beautiful crystal formations within their hollow cavities.

ACTIVITIES - The park has 200 campsites with 80 providing electrical hookups, and a dump station. The campground is open April 15–November 1.

Most visitors come to fish for bass, bluegill, crappie, catfish and tiger muskie in the 205-acre Lake Geode. You can also swim with supervision, purchase concessions and rent boats and canoes to launch from their boat ramp.

Hikers can explore the main trail that begins at the north end of the lake and goes to the dam. Another trail starts at the dam on the lake's west side and ends at a picnic shelter.

INFORMATION
Geode State Park
R. R. 2
Danville, Iowa 52623
319-392-4601

GEORGE WYTH MEMORIAL STATE PARK
9

LOCATION - The park is on the Cedar River in the Waterloo-Cedar Falls area.

ACTIVITIES - Visitors come here to go bird watching, lake and stream fishing, swimming, camping, picnicking, hiking, and to bike the five-mile-long trail that goes from the park into town. You can also enjoy mushroom hunting and boating.

The park has three water areas: Fisher Lake, the Cedar River, and George Wyth Lake, considered to be one of the best largemouth bass fishing lakes in the area. Fisherman may use only electric trolling motors. Boating ramps and rentals are available on the river and near the lakes.

The campground has 64 campsites, 43 with electrical hookups, and a dumping station. Visitors can also stay in the lodge.

A multi-use trail, the Cedar Valley Nature Trail, is 52 miles long, and extends from Waterloo to Cedar Rapids. For information, contact the Waterloo Chamber of Commerce at 319-233-8431.

Waterloo also is the southern end of the Star Clipper Dinner Train that follows the Cedar River to Glenville in southern Minnesota. This 52-mile round trip takes over three hours and features a four-course meal. It runs daily May 1–October 31, and weekends November–April. For information, call 319-232-7558.

INFORMATION

George Wyth Memorial State Park
Route 2
Waterloo, Iowa 50301
319-232-5505

GULL POINT STATE PARK
ISTHMUS ACCESS STATE RECREATION AREA
EMERSON BAY STATE PARK
10

LOCATION - Gull Point is located on the west side of West Okoboji Lake, three miles north of Milford on the northwestern border of Iowa. Emerson Bay is on the southwest shore of West Okoboji, 2.5 miles north of Milford on Iowa 32. Isthmus Access is on the north shore of East Okoboji Lake.

FEATURES - The lake is the country's only blue water lake and was created by glacial activity 14,000 years ago. It's fed by subterranean springs and its water "turns over" twice annually. Water at the lower level generally remains at 30 degrees, but in the spring when the warm winds blow, the water circulates from the lake bed up to the surface. Then in the fall, the autumn winds cause the water to "turn over" again.

West Okoboji has a maximum depth of 134 feet, and an average depth of 40 feet. Its shoreline is 19.6 miles long.

ACTIVITIES - Camp in one of GULL POINT's 112-unit campsites, with 62 containing electrical hookups. A lodge is available for overnight stops.

Record-sized fish have been caught from this lake, and bass tournaments are held on West Okoboji. East Okoboji is known for its walleye, pike, bullhead and catfish caught in the spring and early summer.

Summer sailboat races are sponsored weekly by the Okoboji Yacht Club, and are held on Wednesdays, Saturdays and Sundays. A sailing regatta is held in August, and sailing lessons are available. For information, call 712-337-0121.

Scuba divers frequent the lake with its various drop-offs and geological formations. Divers can rent equipment at the lake.

Hike the 1.3-mile nature trail, go boating, and have a picnic in the enclosed shelter.

ISTHMUS ACCESS, located between Big Spirit Lake and East Okoboji, has a boat ramp, dock, lake shore fishing, and swimming.

EMERSON BAY has 117 campsites, 60 with electrical hookups, and a trailer dump station. Go boating where boat rentals and a ramp are available, fishing for bass and swimming in the lake.

While in the area, attend an Okoboji Summer Theater performance. The theater is located on U.S. 71 between Arnolds Park and Spirit Lake, and its season runs mid-June–mid-August. For information, call 712-332-7773.

Ride the Queen II that conducts five daily cruises beginning at noon. The cruises are available from Memorial Day through Labor Day. The boat leaves from the dock on West Lake Okoboji, the Amusement Park, or from Arnold's Park. Call 712-332-5159 for additional information.

INFORMATION
Gull Point State Park
R. R. 2
Milford, Iowa 51351
712-337-3211

ISTHMUS ACCESS STATE RECREATION AREA
11
See under GULL POINT STATE PARK

LACEY-KEOSAUQUA STATE PARK
12

LOCATION - The park is in the southeast corner of the state south of Keosauqua on Iowa 1 along the Des Moines River.

FEATURES - The park is one of Iowa's largest state parks, and has some large sandstone outcroppings towering above Ely's Ford. Here, the Mormons crossed the river during the 1840s on their way west. A prehistoric Indian village site is close to the park.

ACTIVITIES - Go camping in its modern campground with 45 campsites providing electricity and 115 without. The campground has a dump station. You can also stay in one of the cabins, or in the lodge.

Hike the trails, fish for bass in either the Des Moines River, or fish and swim in the lake. Boat rentals are available.

If you're in the area in October, attend the Forest Crafts Festival featuring chain saw carvers, and watch the operating sawmill.

INFORMATION
Lacey-Keosauqua State Park 319-293-3502
P.O. Box 398
Keosauqua, Iowa 52656-0398

LAKE AHQUABI STATE PARK
13

LOCATION - To reach the park, 5.5 miles southwest of Indianola, from the intersection of Iowa 69 and 349, go west for a mile on Iowa 349 to Rock Road, and then continue north for one more mile.

ACTIVITIES - The park has 85 campsites with electrical hookups, and 76 campsites without. The campground is open April 15–November 1. You can also rent a room in the lodge or stay in one of the cabins.

Visitors can enjoy fishing for bass, swimming with supervision, and boating from the ramp in the lake. Hikers also have several trails to explore.

In Indianola, tour the National Balloon Museum with artifacts and memorabilia from over 200 years of ballooning history. Get a close-up look at some of the equipment used in both hot air and gas ballooning. Admission is free.

If you're here the first part of August, be sure to attend the U.S. National Hot Air Balloon Championships. Watch the mass ascension of over 200 balloons both in the morning and in the evening. Enjoy a carnival, car show, craft show, parade, pancake breakfast and Civil War battle re-enactments. For information, call 515-961-8415.

During the summer, the Des Moines Metro Opera is headquartered in Indianola. Attend an opera presented at the Blank Performing Arts Theater on the Simpson College Campus. For information, call 515-961-6221.

INFORMATION
Lake Ahquabi 515-961-7101
1650 118th Avenue
Indianola, Iowa 50125

LAKE ANITA STATE PARK
14

LOCATION - The park is eight miles southwest of Adair on Iowa 83 and then another half mile on Iowa 148. It's also five miles south of Anita off I-80.

ACTIVITIES - Triathletes can participate in the Whaletown Triathlon that begins with a one-kilometer swim in Lake Anita, followed by a 25-mile bike ride, and finished by a 10-kilometer run.

Camp in the campground with 144 sites, 69 with electrical hookups. Swim and fish for bass in the lake. Boating docks, ramps and rentals are available. Boaters on the lake must operate at a no-wake speed. Speed boating and water skiing are prohibited.

Incoming pilots can land at Harlan Municipal's Rushenberg Field located three miles southwest of town. Rental cars are available.

INFORMATION
Lake Anita State Park
R. R. 4, Box 145
Harlan, Iowa 51537
712-762-3564

LAKE KEOMAH STATE PARK
15

LOCATION - The park is five miles east of Oskaloosa. From the intersection of Iowa 92 and 371, continue south one mile on Iowa 371.

ACTIVITIES - Enjoy camping April 15–November 1 on one of their 88 grass sites, 40 with electrical hookups. You can also rent one of their cabins or stay in the lodge. The park has a concession stand.

Go boating from the ramp on Lake Keomah, fishing for panfish, swimming, hiking and horseback riding.

During the summer, Oskaloosa's city bank presents concerts in the city square.

INFORMATION
Lake Keomah State Park
c/o Iowa Department of Economic Development
200 East Grand Avenue
Des Moines, Iowa 50309
515-673-6975

LAKE MACBRIDE STATE PARK
16

LOCATION - From Solon, drive four miles west on Iowa 382 to reach the north campground, or west from town for four miles on 5th Street, County Road F-28, to reach the south campground.

ACTIVITIES - Camp in the modern campground located in the northern end of the park where 40 of the units have electrical hookups and 20 are without. If you're towing a trailer 26 feet or longer, the turn-around at the end of the campground is a real squeeze.

The south campground has 60 non-modern campsites, and is closer to the lake and to the boat ramps.

Fishermen enjoy fishing in Lake Macbride where they catch walleye, catfish, crappie, muskies and bluegill.

The area has several good hiking trails, one winding around the lake. During the summer, swim from the supervised beach.

Boaters can launch from six boat ramps, and rent boats near the swimming beach. Only boats with up to ten horsepower are allowed on the lake.

Coralville Lake is adjacent to Lake Macbride. To reach the entrance to this lake, go five miles north of Coralville off I-80. Here, you can find additional campsites and water recreation activities. Hike the trails, or take a guided tour with one of the park rangers. Attend campfire programs in the campgrounds each weekend during the summer.

Tour the visitor center located at the east end of the dam to see a working model of the Coralville Dam. For camping, fishing or lake level information, call 319-354-4466.

The Amana Colonies are located west of the upper end of this lake. Visitors thoroughly enjoy looking over their many crafts, and dining in their special restaurants. Take a self-guided tour of the various shops by picking up a map at the Amana Colonies Convention and Visitors Bureau in town. For information, call 319-622-3828.

West Branch, ten miles east of Iowa City, is the birthplace and boyhood home of Herbert Hoover, our 31st President. Tour the original Hoover home, the Friends Meeting House, and an old schoolhouse constructed in 1853. For information, call 319-643-2541.

INFORMATION
Lake MacBride State Park
R.R. 4, Box 426
Solon, Iowa 52333
319-644-2200

LAKE MANAWA STATE PARK
17

LOCATION - The park is 2.5 miles south of I-80, Exit 3, at Council Bluffs, and 2.5 miles west of I-29, Exit 47.

FEATURES - The lake was formed when part of the river channel was cut off by the Missouri River as it meandered over the land. It left behind an "oxbow" lake.

ACTIVITIES - Swim from the supervised beach. Hike along the shoreline, follow the paved nature trail, and picnic at one of the open shelters. The campground has 73 campsites with 37 providing electrical hookups, and a dump station. It's open April 15 to November 1.

Go boating on the lake that can accommodate any size motor. Ramps are located on the north, south and west sides of the lake. Enjoy fishing for crappie, bluegill, bass and catfish.

INFORMATION
Lake Manawa State Park
South Shore Drive
Council Bluffs, Iowa 51501
712-366-0220

LAKE OF THREE FIRES STATE PARK
18

LOCATION - From Bedford, go to the junction of Iowa 2 and Iowa 49, and continue northeast on Iowa 49 for three miles.

ACTIVITIES - Go camping in one of the 160 campsites, 30 with electrical hookups, and a trailer dump, or stay in one of the cabins. Go fishing, swimming or boating from the ramp in the lake.

Enjoy hiking and bicycling during summer, and snowmobiling in winter.

INFORMATION
Lake of Three Fires State Park
Route 4
Bedford, Iowa 50833
712-523-2700

LAKE RED ROCK/ELK ROCK STATE PARK
19

LOCATION - Elk Rock State Park is approximately 10 miles west of Pella and is accessible via Iowa G-28. It's located on both the north and south sides of Lake Red Rock, and is connected by a mile-long bridge. The south side of the lake is reached via Iowa 14.

ACTIVITIES - Elk Rock's north side is for day-use only, and has a launching ramp, picnicking areas and a self-guided nature hiking trail.

The south side has picnicking, a launching ramp and a campground with 18 campsites set aside for equestrian campers. Horseback riders have eight miles of bridal trails to explore.

Red Rock Lake is surrounded by several other recreation areas including North Overlook, Whitebreast and Howell Station Recreation Areas. Here you can go camping with some electrical hookups and a dump station, boat from their launching ramps, and attend talks at the Whitebreast amphitheater. During the summer, Army Corps park rangers give dam tours. Tour the visitor center at the west end of the dam.

Bikers and walkers will enjoy the paved path that parallels the river next to Ivan's Campground and North Overlook Park.

Visitors enjoy bird watching with approximately 300 species of birds spotted here. During the winter, watch for bald eagles below the dam.

Fishermen test their skill in capturing crappie, bass, walleye, pike and catfish.

Go floating on the Des Moines River, beginning from the Red Rock Reservoir tailwaters, and float 31 miles to Eddyville.

If you're in Pella the second weekend in May, you'll be in time for their annual Tulip Time Celebration. The Dutch community puts on a three-day parade that is presented during the afternoon, and then is lit for night viewing. Watch Dutch dancers perform, and stop by the various tulip beds scattered throughout the town. Be sure to see the tulips at the Scholte home, Sunken Gardens, and at Fairhaven. For information, contact the Chamber of Commerce at 515-628-4311.

Tour Historical Village to get the flavor of old Holland. Listen for the 147 bell carillon that chimes hourly. The figures appear daily at 11 a.m., 3:00, 5:00 and 9:00 p.m.

Each Labor Day, the Red Rock Lake Association sponsors Family Days featuring many free events for the family including fiddling and harmonica contests, turtle races, cross-country races and hot air balloon ascensions.

Incoming pilots can land at Pella Municipal located one mile west of town. Rental cars are available.

INFORMATION
Elk Rock State Park
Red Rock Reservoir
Otley, Iowa 50214
515-828-7522

LAKE WAPELLO STATE PARK
20

LOCATION - The park is 20 miles south of Ottumwa.

ACTIVITIES - Go swimming, boating, or fishing in the lake, and camping in the modern campground with 44 sites with electrical hookups and 44 without. You can also stay in the lodge or rent a cabin.

Chief Wapello Trail begins in Ottumwa, with one branch going southeast to Chief Wapello's grave in Agency, 12 miles away, and the other to Eldon, southeast of Agency, approximately 25 miles away.

In Ottumwa, attend the Midwest Country Musical Festival that occurs in May. The annual pro balloon races occur the second week in July.

INFORMATION
Lake Wapello State Park
R. R. 1
Drakesville, Iowa 52552
515-722-3371

LEDGES STATE PARK
21

LOCATION - The park is twenty miles southwest of Ames on Iowa 17.

ACTIVITIES - Go camping in the modern campground with 40 sites providing electrical hookups and 42 without. Go hiking and fishing in the stream.

Ride on Iowa's only operating antique carousel located 10 miles north of Ames on Iowa 69. It's open Memorial Day–Labor Day. For information, call 515-733-4214.

Attend weekly outdoor concerts held in Ames during June and July in Bandshell Park at 6th Street and Duff Avenue. For information, call 515-292-6228.

INFORMATION
Ledges State Park
R. R. 1, Box 84
Madrid, Iowa 50156
515-432-1852

MAQUOKETA CAVES STATE PARK
22

LOCATION - From the intersection of U.S. 61 and Iowa 428 near Maquoketa, drive northwest for seven miles on 428.

ACTIVITIES - Seven miles of trails lead to 13 caves scattered throughout the park. The main cave is lit with electrical lights, but you'll need to bring your own flashlight to tour some of the other caves such as "Ice Cave," "Hernando's Hideaway," or "Steel Gate Passage."

Hike around the top of the cliffs to overlooks of the lush valley below. Flower lovers will be treated to a carpet of hepaticas in the spring.

Camp in the campground with 29 sites. Stop by the concession stand for snacks, ice and information on the caves and trails. Visit the educational center to see a nature display.

The Hurstville Lime Kilns, listed on the National Register, and constructed in the 1870s, are north of Maquoketa, and are open for exploration. Because of the improvement in cement and the use of gypsum wallboard, the kilns were closed in 1920.

Incoming pilots can land at Maquoketa Municipal Airport located three miles west of Maquoketa. Rental cars are available.

INFORMATION
Maquoketa Caves State Park
R. R. 2
Maquoketa, Iowa 52060
319-652-5833

McINTOSH WOODS STATE PARK
23

LOCATION - The park is located on the northwest shore of Clear Lake between Clear Lake and Ventura.

ACTIVITIES - Go camping in one of the 50 campsites, 45 with electrical hookups. The park has a boating access point for Clear Lake. Enjoy hiking, swimming, and fishing for bluegill, crappie, bass and northerns.

INFORMATION
McIntosh Woods State Park
Ventura, Iowa 50482
515-829-3847

PALISADES-KEPLER STATE PARK
24

LOCATION - From the intersection of Iowa 1 and U.S. 30, drive 3.5 miles west of Mount Vernon on U.S. 30.

ACTIVITIES - The park has 70 campsites, 46 with electrical hookups, and a dump station. You can also rent cabins or a room in the lodge. Enjoy hiking, swimming, fishing for bass, and boating from the ramp on the Cedar River.

The Cedar Valley Nature Trail, extending 52 miles from Waterloo to Cedar Rapids, passes through here. For information on this trail, call 319-233-8431.

Incoming pilots can land at Waterloo Municipal Airport located four miles northwest of Waterloo. Rental cars are available.

INFORMATION
Palisades-Kepler State Park
700 Kepler Drive
Mt. Vernon, Iowa 50314
319-895-6039

PIKES PEAK STATE PARK
25

LOCATION - From McGregor, take Wisconsin 340 at the south end of town for approximately 1.5 miles to the park entrance. The park is located on the highest bluff on the Mississippi River overlooking the confluence of the Wisconsin and Mississippi rivers.

FEATURES - The park has some Indian effigy mounds built by the Native Americans of the Woodland Culture who lived here from A.D. 800 to 1200.

ACTIVITIES - The campground is nestled beneath trees on top of the 1,350-foot bluff above the confluence of the Wisconsin and Mississippi rivers, and has 120 campsites, 60 with electrical hookups. A park concession is a short distance from the campground. Go fishing for trout in the Mississippi River.

Hikers can explore 13 miles of trails through the woods. Pictured Rocks Trail goes to Bridal Veil Falls, and has sheer walls of limestone and sandstone banded with various colors. This colored sandstone was used by the great sand artist, Andrew Clemens, for his famous sand paintings. You can also hike along a section of the Ice Age Trail that passes through the park.

While in the area, go to Effigy Mounds National Monument, seven miles north of McGregor on Iowa 7G. This monument has 191 preserved prehistoric Indian burial mounds and effigies in the shapes of birds and animals estimated to be 2,500 years old. Join one of the naturalists for a guided tour from June–August. For information, call 319-873-3491.

McGregor is over 150 years old, and has several restored 19th-century storefronts along its main street. Huntting Mansion at 322 Kinney Avenue was built in 1890, and has nine fireplaces constructed of Italian mosaic tiles and marble. For information on the historic homes, contact the Chamber of Commerce at 319-873-2186.

Nearby Spook Cave, located seven miles west on U.S. 18, and then north two more miles, offers you an underground river cavern tour. Tours run May–November 1. Bring along a jacket since the cave temperature remains at a constant 47 degrees. Camp next to the cave by Beulah Falls. For information, call 319-873-2144.

INFORMATION
Pikes Peak State Park
McGregor, Iowa 52157
319-873-2341

PILOT KNOB STATE PARK
26

LOCATION - The park is four miles east of Forest City on Iowa 9.

FEATURES - The park is on top of Iowa's second highest point. A tower rising 1,450 feet offers the visitor a wonderful view. As the early pioneers traveled west, they used Pilot Knob as one of their landmarks.

ACTIVITIES - Go camping in one of 80 campsites, 48 with electrical hookups. The park is open April 15–November 1.

Go hiking or horseback riding along the multi-use trail, or boating and fishing for bass in Lake Pilot Knob.

Dead Man's Lake is actually a floating sphagnum bog, and is a botanist's dream with its unique pond lilies, native trees and shrubs. Many waterfowl breed and feed within its tall grasses.

Wintertime visitors come to go ice skating, sledding, tobogganing, cross-country skiing and ice fishing since they can warm up in the warming house.

INFORMATION
Pilot Knob State Park
Route 1, Box 205
Forest City, Iowa
515-582-4835

PINE LAKES STATE PARK
27

LOCATION - The park is one mile east of Eldora in central Iowa.

ACTIVITIES - Stay overnight in the lodge, or camp in the modern campground with 92 campsites providing electrical hookups and 36 sites without. The campground is open April 15 to November 1.

Go fishing for bass and catfish. Enjoy hiking, fishing, and boating with boat rentals available.

INFORMATION
Pine Lakes State Park
R. R. 3, Box 45
Eldora, Iowa
515-858-5832

RICE LAKE STATE PARK
28

LOCATION - The park is three miles south of Lake Mills in central Iowa.

ACTIVITIES - The park is for day-use only. Enjoy picnicking, hiking, swimming, lake fishing, boating from the nearby ramp, or golfing on an 18-hole course.

INFORMATION
Rice Lake State Park
Route 1, Box 205
Forest City, Iowa
515-582-4835

VOLGA RIVER STATE PARK
29

LOCATION - The park is four miles north of Fayette on Iowa 150 in northeast Iowa.

ACTIVITIES - The park is the state's largest recreation area, and offers camping in a non-modern campground with 42 campsites. Go fishing in both the stream and in the lake, and go boating from the ramp. Enjoy hiking the nature trails, bicycling and horseback riding along the bridle paths. Boat rentals are available.

Go snowmobiling here during the winter.

INFORMATION
Volga River State Park
R. R. 1, Box 72
Fayette, Iowa 52124
319-425-4161

WAPSIPINICON STATE PARK
30

LOCATION - The park is next to Anamosa in southern Iowa.

ACTIVITIES - The area has rugged bluffs and a hardwood timber forest for scenic hiking or bicycling. Go canoeing or boating on the river, or stay in one of the 15 campsites that have electricity, or in one of the 15 that come without. You can also rent a room in the lodge.

The Wapsipinicon River has great fishing for bass, catfish, bullhead, and carp because of its excellent habitat. The lower section of the river flows into the Mississippi River, and occasionally fishermen can land trophy-sized walleye, pike and catfish.

INFORMATION
Wapsipinicon State Park
R. R. 2
Anamosa, Iowa 52205
319-462-2761

WAUBONSIE STATE PARK
31

LOCATION - The park is seven miles southwest of Sidney in southern Iowa on Iowa 239.

FEATURES - From the park, you get a good view of the Loess Hills and the Missouri River flood plains.

ACTIVITIES - Attend a rodeo in early August, called "America's largest continuous rodeo." It features a parade, and seven performances over four days. For information, contact the Rodeo Ticket Office, P.O. Box 426, Sidney, Iowa 51652.

The state park has a modern campground with 22 sites with electrical hookups and 73 without, and a trailer dump station.

Go bicycling or hiking on the trails.

INFORMATION
Waubonsie State Park
R. R. 2, Box 66
Hamburg, Iowa 51640
712-382-2786

WILDCAT DEN STATE PARK
32

LOCATION - Wildcat Den is 12 miles northeast on Iowa 22 from Muscatine, and 18 miles from Davenport.

FEATURES - An historic grist mill constructed in 1848 is one of the best examples of mid-19th-century mills to be found in the U.S. Tour the restored schoolhouse built at the turn-of-the-century, located near the mill.

ACTIVITIES - The park has some interesting trails that lead to sites such as "Steamboat Rock," "Devil's Punch Bowl," "Fat Man's Squeeze," and "Horseshoe Bend."

Camp in one of their non-modern 28 campsites. If you need hookups, camp six miles away on Iowa 22 at the Fairport Campground. These sites are located on the Mississippi River and all 44 campsites have electrical hookups, and a dump station. Fairport also has two boat ramps.

If you're in Muscatine the third week in August, you can attend the Great River Days, a five-day celebration featuring outdoor concerts, parades, fireworks, and participate in either the five or ten-kilometer race.

INFORMATION
Wild Cat Den State Park
R. R. 3
Muscatine, Iowa 52761
319-263-4337

WILSON ISLAND STATE RECREATION AREA
33

LOCATION - The park is five miles west of Loveland in southwestern Iowa. The SRA is only 20 minutes from Omaha, Nebraska.

FEATURES - The Loess Hills, a long line of bluffs along the Missouri River flood plain, were formed by winds thousands of years ago. These bluffs resemble sand dunes, and are similar to formations found in northern China.

ACTIVITIES - The island's dense woods provide 65 campsites with electricity and 67 without, or you can stay in one of the cabins. Two boat ramps provide access in the Missouri River. Enjoy hiking, or fishing in the river.

Nearby you can visit the DeSoto National Wildlife Refuge where, at the peak of the waterfowl migration, approximately one million geese pass through. Up to 120 bald eagles have been spotted here.

Stop by the visitor center to learn about the steamboat "Bertrand" that was fully laden with supplies headed for the Montana gold mines when it sank in 1865. You'll see over 200,000 preserved artifacts from the ship, enabling you to get a look at life at the end of the Civil War.

Missouri Valley celebrates its heritage annually the last weekend in June. See Iowa's largest pizza, a carnival and tournaments. In the spring, attend the Apple Blossom Cruise.

The Classic Car Show and Parade are held on the third weekend in August, and the Iowa 1 Box Hunt festivities are featured in the fall. For more information on any of these events, contact the Chamber of Commerce at 712-642-2553.

Incoming pilots can land at Eppley Airfield located three miles northeast of Omaha, Nebraska. Rental cars are available.

INFORMATION
Wilson Island State Recreation Area
R. R. 2, Box 203
Missouri Valley, Iowa 51555
712-642-2069

There's nothing like a cool shower to beat the heat of a summer afternoon in one of 27 state parks in the Sunflower State.

CORPS OF ENGINEERS

KANSAS

Visitors to Kansas can't help but notice all the concrete grain elevators as you traverse the state. Kansas is one of the leading wheat-producing states. It also contains the geographic center of the continental forty-eight states, found two miles northwest of Lebanon. Kansas is also home to the Smoky Hillls, the Cimarron Breaks, and the Great Bend Prairie.

Kansas has 27 state parks. The park season generally extends from April 15 through October, or until the water pipes begin freezing; however, campsites with electrical hookups remain open year-round.

Cedar Bluff, El Dorado and Eisenhower are three of the largest parks. Tuttle Creek Lake has the longest shoreline, and Milford Lake is the largest man-made lake in the state.

For hunting pheasant and great sport fishing, go to the northwest region near Lovewell and Glen Elder. Crawford and Milford both have state fish hatcheries that are open for tours.

To get a feel for the state's history, go to Webster State Park located near Twin Mounds and Sugar Loaf Mound where Indians watched the early settlers traveling west. Fall River and Toronto are located in an area previously inhabited by prehistoric Indians, evidenced by the petroglyphs left behind in the area's caves. Meade is near the hideout of the notorious Dalton Gang.

Sand Hills is in the sand dune region of the Arkansas River Valley. Scott State Park is in an area of deep canyons. Hang gliders enjoy visiting Wilson because of its deep canyons and steep hills. Elk City is flanked by the beautiful Ozark Hills, and Kanopolis has mushroom rock sandstone formations.

CEDAR BLUFF STATE PARK
1

LOCATION - The park is 36 miles southwest of Hayes off Kansas 147, and 23 miles southeast of Wakeeney.

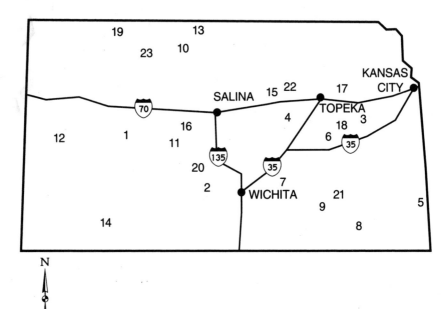

19   13

23   10

KANSAS
CITY

SALINA   15   22   17

70

TOPEKA

4

16   18   3

12   1   6

11   35

135   20   35

2   7

WICHITA   21

9

14   8

5

N

FEATURES - Cedar Bluff has two areas, one on the north and the other on the south shore of the Cedar Bluff Reservoir, overlooking the Smoky Hill River valley that winds through some old, fossil-rich chalk beds. Look for Castle Rock, a chalk spire rising 70 feet over the valley floor.

ACTIVITIES - Go camping in one of 10 sites with full hookups, 81 with electrical hookups, and two trailer dump stations. Enjoy picnicking, hiking the trails, boating from the ramp with 13 boating ramp lanes, fishing and swimming. Boat rentals are available.

Golfers can play golf on the nine-hole Big Creek golf course on South Highway 283, one mile south of I-70. For information and tee-off times, call 913-743-2617.

Visit the Trego County Historical Society and Museum located on the fairgrounds in Wakeeney. For information, call 913-743-2964.

If you're in town starting with the Saturday after Thanksgiving, you'll be in time to see "Christmas City of the High Plains." All along Main Street, several tons of Colorado greenery are used to form a huge tree, and over 3,000 bulbs are used for its illumination. For information, call 913-743-2077.

INFORMATION
Cedar Bluff State Park
Box 47
Ellis, Kansas 67637-0047
913-726-3212

CHENEY STATE PARK
2

LOCATION - It's 20 miles northwest of Wichita via U.S. 54 and Kansas 251, on Cheney Reservoir.

ACTIVITIES - Because of its prevailing winds, sailboaters throng to this area, and regattas are quite popular during the summer.

The upper part of the lake is reserved for fishing, and is a waterfowl refuge because of its location along the international flyway.

Concessions are provided by a full-service marina, and the Ninnescah Yacht Club provides facilities for sailing boats.

The park has three areas offering camping, two trailer dump stations, picnicking, boating from 20 boating ramps, boat rentals, bass fishing, swimming and hiking trails.

Cheney's East Shore State Park has 95 campsites with water and electrical hookups, 185 with electrical hookups only, and a trailer dump station. Limited groceries are available.

Cheney's West Shore State Park has 90 campsites with water and electrical hookups, and a trailer dump station.

While in town, tour the Souders Historical Farm Museum to see their large collection of farm machinery and artifacts from the town's early days. It's open by appointment only. Call 316-542-3573.

Flower lovers can visit the Wichita Garden at 701 N. Amidon in Wichita. It's open year-round. For information, call 316-264-0448.

The Lake Afton Public Observatory, 15 miles southwest of Wichita, at 250th Street West and 39th Street South (MacArthur Road), provides you with a look at such wonders as Saturn's rings, star clusters, and distant galaxies. It's open during the summer on Friday–Sunday evenings after sunset, and during the winter on Friday and Saturday evenings.

Museum goers can tour a couple of museums in Wichita. The Mid-America All-Indian Center and Museum at 650 N. Seneca has permanent collections of the Plains, Southwest, Northwest Coast and Eskimo Indians. For information, call 316-262-5221.

The Museum of Anthropology at Wichita State University, 17th and Hillside, McKinley Hall, Room 118, features exhibits on human cultures around the world. It's open weekdays 12–5. For information, call 316-689-3195.

For musical performances, contact the Music Theater of Wichita, 225 W. Douglas to see when their summer shows are presented. For information, call 316-265-3107.

Pilots can land at Wichita Mid-Continent Airport located five miles southwest of town where rental cars are available.

INFORMATION
Cheney State Park
R. R. 1, Box 167A
Cheney, Kansas 67025-9405
316-542-3664

CLINTON STATE PARK
3

LOCATION - The park is four miles west of Lawrence off U.S. 40.

FEATURES - The park is located on Clinton Reservoir and has 85 miles of shoreline.

ACTIVITIES - Fish for bass, crappie, catfish, pike and bluegill in small coves along the shoreline.

Concessions are provided at the full-service marina. The park also has 600 campsites, 240 with water and electrical hookups, and a trailer dump station. Enjoy a picnic, hiking the trails, boating from the ramp, and swimming from the beach where there is a bathhouse.

Art lovers can tour the Spencer Museum of Art located in Lawrence at 1301 Mississippi. The museum is one of the best university art museums in the U.S.

It's open Tuesday–Sunday from 8:30–5:00, and is free. For information, call 913-864-4710.

Incoming pilots can land at Lawrence Municipal Airport located three miles north of town. Rental cars are available.

INFORMATION
Clinton State Park
R. R. 1, Box 120E
Lawrence, Kansas 66044-9801
913-842-8562

COUNCIL GROVE STATE PARK
4

LOCATION - Council Grove State Park is on Council Grove Lake, located north of Council Grove .

ACTIVITIES - Camp in the campground with 62 campsites with electrical hookups. Go fishing for catfish and crappie, and swimming from the beach with a bathhouse. Enjoy boating from the ramp, and purchase supplies at the marina. The reservoir has large areas designated for public hunting.

INFORMATION
Council Grove Chamber of Commerce
117 West Main
Council Grove, Kansas 66846
316-767-5413

CRAWFORD STATE FISHING PIT LAKE STATE PARK
5

LOCATION - The park is four miles north of Pittsburg.

FEATURES - The park is in the heart of the coal strip-mining area, and is near the Ozarks.

ACTIVITIES - Camp here in the spring when the flowering trees and red-buds are in bloom, or in the fall when fall colors abound. The campground has 60 campsites with electrical hookups and a trailer dump station.

The lake is known primarily for its excellent fishing. Its fish hatchery, located below the dam, is open to the public.

Concessions are provided by the full-service marina and restaurant. Go boating from the two boating ramps.

An historical landmark to visit is Fort Scott National Historic Site where a Civil War Encampment is held in mid-May. The fort was established in 1842 as a base for the U.S. Army peacekeeping efforts on the Indian frontier, but was abandoned and sold in 1853. Later it was reactivated to be used as a Union supply depot during the Civil War. Many of the fort's 20 buildings have been restored and furnished. Tour the museum to learn more about the fort's history. On weekends and holidays during the summer, attend interpretive and living history programs. For information, call 316-223-0310.

Attend the Good Ol' Days celebration held in the city of Fort Scott in early June. For information, call 316-223-2334.

Pilots can land at Fort Scott Municipal located five miles southwest of the city. Rental cars are available.

INFORMATION
Crawford State Fishing Pit Lake State Park
Farlington, Kansas 66734-9999
316-362-3671

EISENHOWER STATE PARK
6

LOCATION - The park is 30 miles east of Emporia, three miles west of Melvern on Kansas 278, and eight miles southwest of Lyndon on Kansas 278. The state park is located on the north side of the reservoir that has 64 miles of shoreline.

ACTIVITIES - Melvern Lake has five additional parks besides the state park, and is ideal for camping with 200 campsites complete with electrical hookups. Go boating from one of the two boating ramps. Rental boats are available. Fish for catfish, crappie, walleye and bass. Attend interpretive programs in their amphitheater.

Go swimming from the beach where there is a bathhouse. A 12-mile equestrian trail follows the lake's southern shoreline between the Arrow Rock and Sundance areas. Two self-guided trails are located in the Outlet Area. Below the dam in the Outlet Area is a replica of the historic suspension bridge that was located south of the town of Melvern.

The Morton Farmstead is located approximately one mile west of West Turkey Point Park, and may be seen from your boat, or if you choose to explore it on foot, watch for venomous snakes that enjoy sunning themselves on the rocks during the summer.

The area has five trails to explore, including a 12-mile-long equestrian trail located along the south lake shore between Arrow Rock and Sun Dance Parks.

A marina's cafe is open during the summer from Wednesday–Sunday. A heated dock is open 24 hours daily.

The park's annual bluegrass weekend and arts and crafts fair is in mid-July.

INFORMATION
Eisenhower State Park
Melvern Reservoir
Route 2, Box 306
Osage City, Kansas 66523-9546
913-528-4102

EL DORADO STATE PARK
7

LOCATION - The park is on El Dorado Reservoir, five miles east of El Dorado on Kansas 177.

ACTIVITIES - El Dorado is one of the most heavily used state parks. Camp in the campground with 78 full hookups, 208 with electrical hookups only, and three trailer dump stations. Go boating from the ramp that features 16 boating lanes. Concessions and boat rentals are available at the full-service marina.

The end of July, attend the Prairie Port Festival in El Dorado. For information, call 316-321-1717 or 316-321-3150.

Go to the Rosalia High School, 13 miles east of El Dorado where you can get a look at life of the early settlers. Take a ride with the Flint Hills Overland Wagon Trips, Inc., which provides horseback transportation, covered wagon and coach rides plus meals and campfire musical entertainment. They're open the first and third weekends in June, September and October . For information, call 316-321-6300.

In El Dorado, tour the Kansas Oil Museum at 383 E. Central. See its re-created oil field featuring a 100-foot derrick, pumping units and a railroad tank car. It's open Tuesday–Saturday from 1–5. For information, call 316-321-9333.

INFORMATION
El Dorado State Park
Box 29A, R. R. 3
El Dorado, Kansas 67042-9803
316-321-7180

ELK CITY STATE PARK
8

LOCATION - The park is seven miles northwest of Independence off U.S. 75. It's located on the Elk City Reservoir, and has 50 miles of shoreline.

FEATURES - East of the park is Table Mound, where one of the last Osage Indian villages was located. Occasionally arrowheads and other artifacts are still found there.

ACTIVITIES - Camp in one of the 180 campsites with water and electrical hookups and two trailer dump stations.

Fish in the Elk City Lake for catfish, go boating from the ramp, and swimming from the beach. The park provides a complete trail system for the hiker and backpacker.

Thirteen miles southwest of Independence, visit the Little House on the Prairie, a reproduction of the cabin made famous by Laura Ingalls Wilder. The cabin is open May 15–September 1. Information: 316-331-6247 or 331-1890.

The Independence Museum at 8th and Myrtle has several interesting room displays. It's open Thursday–Saturday from 1:00–4:30 p.m. during the summer, and from 9:30–1:00 p.m. during the winter. For information, call 316-331-3515.

INFORMATION
Elk City State Park
P.O. Box 945
Independence, Kansas 67301-0945
316-331-6295

FALL RIVER STATE PARK
9

LOCATION - The park is northwest of Fall River adjacent to the Fall River Reservoir near Toronto, and 17 miles northwest of Yates Center on Kansas 105, off U.S. 54.

There are three state parks here: the Quarry Bay Area, Fredonia Bay Area, and the South Rock Area. Quarry Bay is four miles west of town on Kansas 96, and then north three more miles on the County Road.

Fredonia Bay is reached by driving south for 12 miles on Kansas 99 to Kansas 96, east nine miles to the park access road, and then north for another 2.4 miles.

South Shore State Park is off Kansas 95, and on the west side of Fall River Lake.

FEATURES - The park was once inhabited by prehistoric Indians, and is surrounded by oak and pine-covered hills.

ACTIVITIES - The park has 40 miles of shoreline, and is well known for its excellent pan fishing for catfish, bass and crappie. Bird watchers will find up to 400 species of birds in the area.

Concessions are located near both Toronto and the Fall River's bathhouses.

Fredonia Bay has 150 campsites, 45 with water and electrical hookups, and a trailer dump station. Quarry Bay has 50 campsites, and South Rock also has 50 campsites.

You can go boating from the ramp or swimming from the beach with a bathhouse.

A canoe trail is located on the Fall River beginning from the Kansas 99 Bridge and extending to the Climax boat ramp. The trail is 12 miles long, and requires six to eight hours to complete.

In Yates Center, arrange in advance with the Chamber of Commerce to take a guided walking tour of the Town Square that showcases numerous examples of restored Victorian architecture. The square has 41 buildings built between 1883 and 1928, and is the only courthouse square in Kansas listed on the National Register of Historic Places.

INFORMATION
Fall River State Park
c/o Toronto State Park
R. R. 1, Box 44
Toronto, Kansas 66777-9715
316-637-2213

GLEN ELDER STATE PARK
10

LOCATION - The park is twelve miles west of Beloit on U.S. 24. It's also ten miles west of Glen Elder.

FEATURES - The park was an early Indian historical site. Waconda Lake inundated Waconda Springs and mineral pool, site of the state's only health spa.

ACTIVITIES - Go camping with 350 campsites available with 140 offering electrical hookups . Enjoy a picnic, hike the trails, and go boating in Waconda Lake from one of the four boating ramps. The park has a full-service marina where you can rent boats. You can also go fishing for channel catfish, walleye, crappie, bass and flathead, enjoy swimming from the beach, and tour the visitor center.

Tour Honey Creek School, part of the Kansas State Living Library, located at the Roadside Park on U.S. 24. It's open May 1–October 1, Monday–Saturday from 1–4.

Beloit hosts a Chautauqua, featuring historic speeches and debates. Many are re-enacted from the past, while others cover present-day topics. It's held on a weekend in September, and offers folk and bluegrass music plus a display of arts and crafts.

In late July, Beloit hosts the Annual Quilt Show featuring hundreds of quilts placed on display, many made in the 1800s by the early pioneers.

INFORMATION
Glen Elder State Park
Box 298
Glen Elder, Kansas 67446-0298
913-545-3345

KANOPOLIS STATE PARK
MUSHROOM ROCK STATE PARK
11

LOCATION - Kanopolis State Park is 12 miles south of Kanopolis off Kansas 141, and 11 miles northeast of Marquette. The state park has two locations: one on the east shore and one on the south shore. The east shore is reached by driving west nine miles from Marquette on Kansas 4, and another three miles north. The south shore is 14 miles east of Ellsworth on Kansas 140, and then south ten more miles.

Mushroom Rock State Park is 10 miles east of Ellsworth, and is maintained as a satellite park by the Kanopolis State Park officials.

FEATURES - Mushroom State Park is the only state park that isn't on a reservoir. Mushroom Rock and the surrounding area was a major landmark during the 1800s. People who visited here included Wild Bill Hickcock, John C. Fremont during his 1848 expedition, and Kit Carson who insisted that the area was his "favorite little place."

ACTIVITIES - Camp in KANOPOLIS STATE PARK'S campground which has 15 campsites with full hookups, and 113 with electrical hookups. Enjoy a picnic, go boating from the ramp in the Smoky Hill River, rent a boat from the marina and go fishing for bass. You can also go for a swim from the beach where there's a bathhouse and food service.

The park includes the Buffalo Track Canyon Trail with its remnants of the once vast herds of buffalo, and caves used as homes by early settlers.

Hike the nature trail in Horsethief Canyon famous for its 150-foot Inscription Rock where three Indian cultures are represented in the petroglyphs.

The Salina Coyotes Motorcycle Club sponsors motorcycle meets here.

A 10.5-mile-long canoe trail is located along the Smoky Hill River, and requires four to five hours to cover.

MUSHROOM ROCK STATE PARK has hiking and picnicking available.

In the town of Kanopolis, the Fort Harker Guardhouse and Museum is located on the northwest corner of Ohio and Wyoming streets. The 1867 building is on the National Register of Historic Places, and is open Tuesday–Saturday 9–12, and 1–4, and Sundays from 1–5. Admission is free.

INFORMATION
Kanopolis State Park
R. R. 1, Box 26D
Marquette, Kansas 67464-9619
913-546-2565
Mushroom Rock State Park
c/o Kanopolis State Park

LAKE SCOTT STATE PARK
12

LOCATION - The park is twelve miles north of Scott City via U.S. 83 and Kansas 95.

FEATURES - The park is the site of El Cuartelejo, a ruined pueblo believed to have been home for Taos Indians fleeing north from the Spanish around 1664. Later Plains Apache Indians, Spanish explorers, and French traders camped here. The site was the northernmost Indian pueblo in the Americas, and the first white settlement in Kansas. A monument is located in the central picnic area.

Lake Scott is fed by springs flowing at 400 gallons per minute.

ACTIVITIES - Tour the old Steele home, go catfish fishing in Lake Scott where only fishing boats are allowed from the ramp. Camp in the campground with 205 campsites, 61 with electrical hookups, and a trailer dump station. Hike the trails.

The El Cuartelejo Ruins offers a special appeal to both amateur and professional archeologists.

INFORMATION
Lake Scott State Park
Route 1
Scott City, Kansas 67871-9721
316-872-2061

LOVEWELL STATE PARK
13

LOCATION - The park is fifteen miles northeast of Mankato off Kansas 14, and near Courtland.

ACTIVITIES - Camp in the campground with 63 pull-throughs, all 63 sites have electrical hookups. Go swimming from the beach with a bathhouse, boating from one of the four boating ramps, or rent a boat from the full-service marina. See the historical landmark, and go fishing for catfish.

INFORMATION
Lovewell State Park
Box 293
Courtland, Kansas 66939-0207
913-753-4305

MEADE STATE PARK
14

LOCATION - The park is thirteen miles southwest of Meade on Kansas 23.

FEATURES - The park was carved out of the Turkey Track Ranch in 1927, and is like an oasis in what is an otherwise treeless grassland. The world's largest volcanic ash mine is located near Meade, also home of the Dalton Gang Hideout and Museum.

ACTIVITIES - Go fishing for catfish in Meade State Lake, swimming from the beach where there is a bathhouse, and boating from the ramp or dock. Enjoy camping where there are 120 sites, 32 sites electrical hookups, some groceries, and a trailer dump station.

The Dalton Gang Hideout Museum and Park is four blocks south of U.S. 54 on Pearlette Street, and has furnishings from 1887. The home has been reconstructed to look as it did during the 19th century, and the secret passage tunnel that led to the barn where the gang kept their horses has been reconstructed. The W. S. Dingess antique gun collection is on display in the museum. For information, call 916-873-2731.

INFORMATION
Meade State Park
Box 1
Meade, Kansas 67864-0001
316-873-2572

MILFORD STATE PARK
15

LOCATION - The park is two miles northwest of Junction City on Kansas 57.

FEATURES - Milford Lake is Kansas's largest man-made lake.

ACTIVITIES - Camp in one of the 240 campsites with 62 pull-throughs, and 121 sites with full hookups. Go fishing for channel catfish, walleye, crappie, flathead and bass in the lake with 135 miles of shoreline. Go swimming from the beach with its own bathhouse, or boating from the ramp with 10 boating lanes.

Concession facilities are provided by the full-service marina. The Southwind Yacht Club offers facilities for sailing.

On the 4th of July, the Sundown Salute, one of the state's largest Independence Day celebrations, is staged in the park, and features the Coors Freedom Run.

East of the park is Fort Riley, the first territorial capital and still a major military reservation housing the First Infantry Division. Tour the Custer House built in 1854, and named for Colonel George Custer of the Battle of Little Bighorn. It's open year-round except on legal holidays. For information, call 913-239-2737.

The U.S. Cavalry Museum is on the corner of Custer and Henry in Fort Riley, and has artifacts from the cavalry when it played its role in the development of the west. For information, call 913-239-2737.

In July, you can attend "Music in the Park," in Heritage Park in Junction City. For performance times, call 913-238-8321.

Pilots can land at Junction City's Freeman Field located one mile northwest of town. Rental cars are available.

INFORMATION
Milford State Park
Route 3, Box 192
Junction City, Kansas 66441-8702
913-238-3014

MUSHROOM ROCK STATE PARK
16

See under KANOPOLIS STATE PARK

PERRY STATE PARK
17

LOCATION - It's sixteen miles northeast of Topeka off U.S. 24, and three miles west of Perry on U.S. 24 to Kansas 237 where you continue north for another 3.5 miles.

ACTIVITIES - The park features camping in one of the 150 campsites, 104 with electrical and water hookups, and a trailer dump station.

You can also go boating from ten boat ramp lanes, rent boats at the marina, go swimming from the beach with a bathhouse nearby, and hike the trails.

In Topeka, visit the Ward-Meade Home at 124 North Fillmore. It was built in 1870, and is listed on the National Register of Historic Places. Tour the botanical gardens with its 500 varieties of trees and shrubs, 9,000 annual flowers and 5,000 tulips.

Pilots can land at Topeka's Forbes Field located six miles south of the city, where rental cars are available.

INFORMATION
Perry State Park
Box 129
Perry, Kansas 660073-0129
913-289-3449

POMONA STATE PARK
18

LOCATION - The park is located two miles northeast of Vassar on Kansas 268. The park is on 110 Mile Creek and Dragoon Creek in the Marais des Cygnes River Valley. It's also 16 miles west of Ottawa on Kansas 368.

ACTIVITIES - Camp in the campground with 160 primitive sites, 109 with water and electricity, and 47 with full hookups, and four dump stations. The park is open year-round, but is in full operation April 15–October 15. Besides camping, you can stay in rent-a-camp sites.

Naturalist programs are offered from Memorial Day to Labor Day.

Go bass, catfish, and crappie fishing in Pomona Reservoir with 52 miles of shoreline. Enjoy swimming from the unsupervised beach with a bathhouse, and boating from one of the boat ramp lanes. Food service and boat rentals are available.

An amateur bluegrass festival is held in the park the third weekend in August. Near the park, you can participate in tennis, golf or attend the summer stock playhouse.

The Marais Des Cygnes River Canoe Trail has two sections. Its first section runs from Miami County State Lake to La Cygne and is 14 miles long, requiring four to six hours to cover. Its second section runs from La Cygne to Marais des Cygnes Waterfowl Management Area. This section is 18 miles long and requires five to seven hours.

The Marais des Cygnes Museum, five miles north of Pleasanton on U.S. 69, then three miles east on Kansas 52, is located on the site of a famous confrontation between pro-slavery and abolition forces in 1858. Five victims of the massacre were immortalized as martyrs in the cause of freedom. It's open Tuesday–Saturday from 10–5, and on Sunday from 1–5.

INFORMATION
Pomona State Park
Vassar, Kansas 66543-9999
913-828-4933

PRAIRIE DOG STATE PARK
19

LOCATION - Prairie Dog State Park is located on the north shore of the Keith Sebelius Reservoir, three miles west of Norton off U.S. 36.

ACTIVITIES - Camp in the 90-site campground, 30 with electrical and water hookups, and a trailer dump. The campground is open year-round, but water isn't turned on until April 15.

The reservoir has a shoreline of 32 miles, and limited concessions are available in the park. The lake is rated as one of the best fishing lakes in Kansas where you can go bass, crappie, and bluegill fishing.

Go boating from the two-lane boat ramp and swimming in the lake. Visit Hillman School, an adobe house originally constructed in the 1890s, and now restored and furnished with articles from the homesteading era.

Norton Wildlife Area is located on land adjacent to the lake, and both the reservoir and wildlife area are open to public hunting.

In mid-July, attend the Annual Carp Derby at Sebelius Reservoir. For information, call 913-877-2501.

In Norton, tour State Station 15 on Horace Greeley Avenue. Historians believe that Horace Greeley, Roy Bean and Billy the Kid's parents stopped over at the station. The present building is a replica, and is open 24 hours a day, year-round.

Norton is known as the Pheasant Capital of the World, and attracts hundreds of hunters during pheasant hunting season.

The Presidential Also Ran Gallery and Doll Collection are in Norton at 105 W. Main Street, and feature paintings and biographies of unsuccessful presidential candidates. It's open Monday–Friday from 9–3. For information, call 913-877-3341.

INFORMATION
Prairie Dog State Park
Box 431
Norton, Kansas 67654-0431
913-877-2953

SAND HILLS STATE PARK
20

LOCATION - Sand Hills State Park is three miles northeast of Hutchinson on Kansas 61. Access is either via E. 56th Street or E. 69th Street.

FEATURES - The park consists of acreage transferred both from the Hutchinson Reformatory and the Dillon Family.

ACTIVITIES - The park has three hiking trails and two self-guided interpretive trails. Prairie Trail, 1.8 miles long, is the longest trail, and may be connected to the Dune Trail to form a figure-eight pattern. Both trails are accessible from the parking lots located at E. 56th and E. 69th.

Horseback riding is only allowed by permit. Horses are restricted from the dunes and hiking trails, except the 1.5-mile Pond Trail.

In Hutchinson, tour the Kansas Cosmosphere and Space Center at 1100 No. Plum. The center has an OMNIMAX movie theater, and a complete set of the original spacecraft, the largest collection of space suits, and computerized "hands-on" exhibits. The complex is open daily, but is closed Mondays from Labor Day through Memorial Day. For information, call 316-662-2305.

If you enjoy watching softball, check on dates that over 1,000 tournament teams play at Fun Valley at 4000 W. 4th. It's open March–October whenever tournaments are being played. For information, call 316-669-9999.

Pilots can land at Hutchinson Municipal Airport located three miles east of town. Rental cars are available.

INFORMATION
Sand Hills State Park
3002 E. 30th
Hutchinson, Kansas 67502
316-663-5272

TORONTO STATE PARK
21

LOCATION - The park is 17 miles west of Yates Center off U.S. 54. Toronto Dam is four miles southwest of Toronto and 17 miles west of Buffalo.

FEATURES - The state park overlooks Toronto Reservoir with 51 miles of shoreline.

ACTIVITIES - Camp in the campground with 15 campsites with full hookups, and 47 others with water and electrical hookups. Swim from the beach with its bathhouse, go boating from one of six boating ramps, and hike the trails. The lake has some of the largest white bass in the world plus crappie, catfish, bluegill and walleye.

A prehistoric cave located 12 miles north of Toronto contains pictorial writings. The cave's mouth is 50 feet wide and extends back around 20 feet.

INFORMATION
Toronto State Park
R. R. 1, Box 44
Toronto, Kansas 66777-9715
316-637-2213

TUTTLE CREEK STATE PARK
22

LOCATION - Tuttle Creek State Park overlooks Tuttle Creek Reservoir, five miles north of Manhattan on U.S. 24 and has four developed areas.

ACTIVITIES - The campground has 12 campsites with full hookups, 128 with water and electricity, and a trailer dump station.

Go boating on the reservoir from one of 11 boat ramp lanes, rent boats at the marina, and hike the trails. Go fishing for bass, catfish, walleye and crappie in the Big Blue River, or swimming from the beach with its own beachhouse. Concessions are available in the River Pond Area.

Pilots can land at Manhattan Municipal Airport located four miles southwest of the city. Rental cars are available.

While in Manhattan, visit Pioneer Park, 2309 Claflin Road, site of three of the city's historical attractions: the Goodnow House/Museum, the Riley County Historical Museum featuring historical exhibits and changing displays, and the Hartford House, a re-creation of the prefabricated house brought on the Hartford Steamboat in 1855. The house has been restored to near original condition and refurbished with period replicas. For information, call 913-776-8829.

INFORMATION
Tuttle Creek State Park
804 Beckman Circle
Manhattan, Kansas 66502-4408
913-539-7941

WEBSTER STATE PARK
23

LOCATION - The park is eight miles west of Stockton on U.S. 24.

FEATURES - The park, located on Webster Reservoir, has 27 miles of shoreline, and is located near Twin Mounds and Sugar Loaf Mound, both used by Indian lookouts during the state's pioneer days. The mounds were also used as signaling stations when pioneers and railroads traversed the area.

ACTIVITIES - Camp in one of 60 campsites with electrical hookups. Go swimming from the beach with a bathhouse, boating from one of four boating ramp lanes, hiking the trails, and fishing for pike.

While in Phillipsburg, tour Fort Bissell located a half-mile west on U.S. 36. It's a replica of a fort built by the settlers in 1872 to protect themselves from Indian raids. Also here are two log cabins built in the 1870s, the 1879 Glade depot, a one-room schoolhouse, and a sod house replica where you can see a gun collection. They're open Monday–Saturday, April through October except on legal holidays. Admission is free.

In mid-May, attend the Phillipsburg Riverless Festival held at the Court House Square. For information, call 913-543-2321.

INFORMATION
Webster State Park
Box 293
Stockton, Kansas 67669-0293
913-425-6558

Bicycling is a popular family activity on Mackinac Island, where one must rely on horse-drawn carriages or one's own pedal power to get around.

MACKINAC STATE HISTORIC PARKS

MICHIGAN

Four Great Lakes touch the shores of Michigan: Lake Michigan, Lake Huron, Lake Erie, and Lake Superior. The state has two peninsulas. Lower Peninsula is bounded by Lake Michigan, Lake Huron, and the western end of Lake Erie. Upper Peninsula is bordered by Lake Michigan, Lake Huron and Lake Superior. The Straits of Mackinac lies between these two peninsulas, and is spanned by one of the world's longest suspension bridges. The state has over 11,000 inland lakes, and more miles of fresh-water shoreline than any other state.

Michigan has 81 state parks with over 14,000 campsites. Family rent-a-tents may be reserved at 14 of the state parks. Rentals run May 15–September 15.

For a unique camping experience, stay in one of the parks with a rent-a-tipi. Tipis are located in Bewabic, Holly, Indian Lake, Interlochen, Pontiac Lake and Wilson state parks. Southern Michigan has six equestrian campgrounds and 185 miles of bridle trails.

There are over 500 miles of Great Lakes and inland lake shorelines in the parks, along with 82 designated swimming beaches. Also bicyclists are treated to the 21-mile-long Hart Montague Trail, the 38-mile Kal-Haven Trail, and an even longer 220-mile Shore to Shore Riding and Hiking Trail that crosses the state from Empire on Lake Michigan to Tawas City on Lake Huron. In addition, the state has 10 marked Backroads Bikeway trails beginning and ending in Three Oaks in southwestern Michigan near the state line.

Michigan's Grand Traverse area's summers are generally warm and sunny, but with low humidity. Spring and fall temperatures are moderate, but can fluctuate significantly from day to day. Come prepared with a raincoat and warmer clothing.

Within 50 miles of Traverse City are five Blue Ribbon trout streams including the Boardmana River, Betsie River, Platte River, Little Manistee River and the Pere Marquette River. A special highlight of fall fishing is the salmon spawning run when anglers can reel in 20-30 pound catches. The area features chinook, coho and Atlantic salmon, whitefish, bass, northern pike and several types of trout.

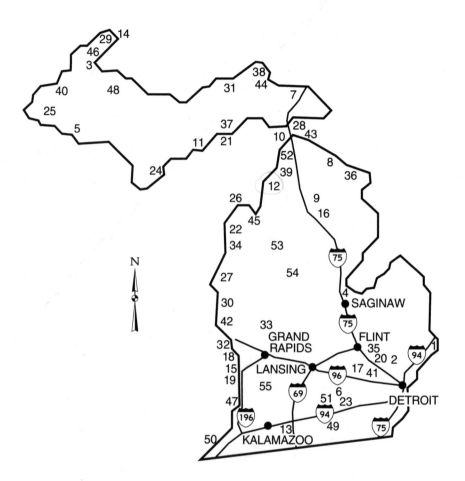

Michigan's Upper Peninsula has over 150 waterfalls. Some are tall like Laughing Whitefish, but some are broad and massive like Tahquamenon. It also features over 1,100 miles of Great Lakes shoreline and 4,300 inland lakes. Over 600 water access sites are available for small boats.

Scuba divers have many diving opportunities here, especially at the Alger Underwater Preserve located near Munising. Ten shipwrecks are protected for the divers. Other underwater preserves are at Whitefish Point, Keweenaw, Marquette, Sault Ste. Marie to Whitefish Point, and sections of Lake Michigan from Menominee to Manistique. The Straits of Mackinaw Underwater Preserve also has shipwrecks where ships have sunk while negotiating the straits' passage between Lakes Huron and Michigan. Even though over 600 ships have been lost in Lake Superior, only 150 have been located. Because of the lake's frigid temperatures, they are in well-preserved condition.

To find out the best fishing spots and seasonal activities on the Upper Peninsula, call 1-800-292-5404 in Michigan, and 1-800-248-5708 from other states.

Lake Superior, 350 miles long and 160 miles broad, is the world's largest body of fresh water.

A total of 104 lighthouses are located along Michigan's coastline. Some are open for touring, and some are located on private property for which special permission may be necessary.

ALGONAC STATE PARK
1

LOCATION - The park is two miles north of Algonac on Michigan 29 on the St. Clair River.

ACTIVITIES - Visitors can enjoy getting a close-up look at large freighters from all over the world as they pass by the park's half-mile frontage on the river.

Camp in the campground with 220 campsites with electrical hookups. Go salmon and walleye fishing in the St. Clair River and boating from the boat ramp. The park also has archery and trap ranges.

INFORMATION
Algonac State Park
8732 N. River Road
Algonac, Michigan 48001
313-765-5605

BALD MOUNTAIN STATE RECREATION AREA
2

LOCATION - The park is seven miles north of Pontiac off Michigan 24.

FEATURES - The park is dotted with eleven lakes and bisected with two trout streams.

ACTIVITIES - Rent one of two cabins. Go boating from the ramps at Chamberlain, Lower Trout and Graham Lakes, and fishing for trout, bass, bluegill and crappie in the streams. Many of the smaller lakes may be reached by way of trails. If you plan to fish in them, bring along a light-weight canoe or an inflatable boat.

Hikers can explore marked trails leading to some of the more remote areas including cedar swamps, duck ponds, bogs and scenic vistas. Trails range in length from 1.5 miles to a loop covering 3.6 miles in the north unit, and a loop of 4.8 miles in the south unit of the area.

Go horseback riding, bird watching, or swim from the large beach with bath-houses and a concession stand.

During the winter, you can cross-country ski along eight miles of trails.

INFORMATION
Bald Mountain State Recreation Area
1350 Greenshield Road
Route 1
Lake Orion, Michigan 48360
313-693-6767

BARAGA STATE PARK
3

LOCATION - The park is .25-mile south of Baraga on Keweebaw Bay.

ACTIVITIES - The campground has a rental tipi, 137 campsites with 109 offering electrical hookups. Go swimming from the beach, hike the nature trail, or go boating from the boat launching ramps. Go trout fishing in the stream, or fishing and searching for agates along Lake Superior.

Attend the Ojibwa Indian Powwow the fourth weekend of July in Baraga. The Baraga Lumberjack Days are held over the July 4th weekend.

The historic Hanka Homestead, settled in 1896, is being restored near Baraga. This farmstead is one of the last unaltered examples of pioneer handi-work and is of Finnish origin.

The area around Baraga has some beautiful waterfalls. Lower Silver Falls is six miles northeast of L'Anse off the Skanee Road. Canyon Falls, often referred to as the "Grand Canyon of Michigan," is eight miles south of L'Anse.

Sturgeon Falls and Gorge are 17 miles southwest of Baraga. From U.S. 41, take the Baraga Plains cutoff road, turn left at the four corners, right on the next road, and then follow the signs. From the parking area, you'll need to walk in 1.3 miles.

INFORMATION
Baraga State Park
Route 1, Box 566
Baraga, Michigan 49908
906-353-6658

BAY CITY STATE PARK
4

LOCATION - The park is five miles north of Bay City on Michigan 247. If going north on I-75, get off at Exit 164. Stay on this road, which becomes Michigan 13, until reaching the second light at Beaver Road. Go right on Beaver Road for two miles to reach the park.

If traveling south on I-75, get off at the Beaver Road Exit, Exit 168, and continue left on Beaver Road for approximately five miles.

FEATURES - Bay City State Park is located on Saginaw Bay which boasts one of the best sport walleye and perch fisheries in the state.

ACTIVITIES - The park has a long beach along Saginaw Bay where you can enjoy a picnic. Camp in family rent-a-tents or in one of 263 campsites with electrical hookups and a trailer dump station.

Go pan fishing for pike, perch, sunfish and bass, or go swimming in Saginaw Bay. Take a hike through the woods.

The park has a store and a nature center open every afternoon, except Monday, from noon until early evening.

An artist series is presented throughout the summer with concerts, speakers and dancing. Contact the park superintendent for dates and times.

The Tobico Marsh State Refuge Area is a short distance from the park, and features two 30-foot observation towers, a marsh boardwalk and five miles of hiking trails.

In Bay City, take a cruise aboard the Bay City Belle, a 49-passenger sternwheel riverboat docked in Wenonah Park. It cruises on the Saginaw River daily May–mid-October.

Stop by the Bay City Hall to see the 31-foot-long Chmielewska Tapestry hanging in the historic 1894 building.

INFORMATION
Bay City State Park
Bay City, Michigan 48706
517-684-3020

BEWABIC STATE PARK
5

LOCATION - The park is four miles west of Crystal Falls on U.S .2, and three miles southwest of Brighton off I-96, U.S .23 and Michigan 36.

ACTIVITIES - The park is on the northwest end of Fortune Lake, a chain of four lakes, where you can go swimming from the beach and canoeing and boating from the boat launch site. Canoe and boat rentals are available nearby.

Go fishing for bass, perch, bluegill and walleye. A hiking trail begins in the campground and takes you through the woods and down to the lake. Also hike across a wooded bridge to an island.

Rent a tent or a tipi for your family. The campground has 144 sites with electrical hookups and a trailer dump station.

Nearby attractions include Pentoga Park with an Indian burial ground, and the Iron County Museum located in Caspian, where you can learn more about the history of logging and mining industries.

You can also visit Chicaugon Falls with its two-mile scenic hike, Bond Falls, and Horse Race Rapids, six miles south of Crystal Falls on U.S. 2-141, known to the locals as the Little Grand Canyon. Watch the experts shoot Hemlock Rapids along the Paint River, upstream from the Bates-Amasa Bridge on Michigan 643.

INFORMATION
Bewabic State Park
1933 U.S. 2 West
Crystal Falls, Michigan 49920
906-875-3324

BRIGHTON STATE RECREATION AREA
6

LOCATION - The area is three miles west of Brighton off I-96, U.S. 23 and Michigan 36.

ACTIVITIES - Rent one of their two cabins. Go camping in one of the 222 sites, 150 with electrical hookups, or in one of the three rustic campgrounds. The park also has a 25-site equestrian campground.

Enjoy a picnic, or swim from one of the two beaches along Bishop Lake and Chilson Pond. The park has concessions and boat rentals available.

Rent horses from the riding stable. You can ride along 18 miles of bridle trails, or hike along seven miles of hiking trails. Kahchin Trail is two miles long, and Pwenosha is five miles long.

Many lakes are scattered throughout the park, providing good fishing. Go boating from ramps located at Appleton, Bishop, Lime and Long lakes.

INFORMATION
Brighton State Recreation Area
8360 Chilson Route 3
Howell, Michigan 48843
313-229-6566

BRIMLEY STATE PARK
7

LOCATION - The park is located one mile east of Brimley off Michigan 221, and 12 miles southwest of Sault Ste. Marie.

ACTIVITIES - Rent a tent for your family, or stay in one of 270 campsites with electrical hookups and a trailer dump. You can also stay in the lodge, and food is available from a store located at the edge of the park.

The park features a 2,400-foot sand beach and boat launching site. Whitefish Bay offers unlimited boating and trout fishing. Rock hounds can enjoy searching for agates by Lake Superior.

In the Sault Ste. Marie vicinity, you can visit the Tower of History, a 210-foot edifice, and the highest point of the Upper Peninsula. Take one of the two-hour Soo Locks Boat Tours. For information, call 906-632-6301.

Poke into the nooks and crannies of the S.S. Valley Camp, complete with a marine museum in cargo hold #3, and learn the history of the Great Lakes. Information: 906-632-3658.

Walk along the Locks Park Historic Walkway along the waterfront. Stop by the information center to get some background history on the locks. It's open mid-May–November 1.

The area boasts two historic lighthouses. Point Iroquois Lightstation, built in 1870, is located along the shore of Lake Superior in the Hiawatha National Forest. The Whitefish Point Lightstation located in Whitefish Point, was built in 1849, and was the first lighthouse on Lake Superior. The lighthouse is now the site of the Great Lakes Shipwreck Museum, and overlooks the shipwreck graveyard of the Great Lakes. For information, call 1-800-647-2858 in Michigan or 906-632-3301.

For a scenic, all-day trail excursion, take a train ride into Agawa Canyon. Especially beautiful during the fall, the train stops in the canyon for a couple of hours so you can stroll along the river to get a better view of the waterfalls. Bring along a picnic lunch. For reservations, call 705-946-7300.

INFORMATION
Brimley State Park
Route 1, Box 202
Brimley, Michigan 49715
906-248-3422

CHEBOYGAN STATE PARK
8

LOCATION - The park is four miles northeast of Cheboygan on U.S. 23 on Lake Huron.

ACTIVITIES - Stay in the lodge or rent one of their four cabins, each sleeps 8. The campground has 78 campsites with electrical hookups, a trailer dump, and a trailside cabin. Go bass fishing in Lake Huron, swimming, hiking, and boating from the ramp.

INFORMATION
Cheboygan State Park
4480 Beach Road
Cheboygan, Michigan 49721
616-627-2811

CLEAR LAKE STATE PARK
9

LOCATION - The park is eight miles north of Atlanta off Michigan 33. The park is geographically situated halfway between the north pole and the equator on the 45th parallel.

ACTIVITIES - Rent one of the tents for your family, or stay in one of the 200 campsites with electrical hookups and a trailer dump. A nature display structure is located between the park's two campgrounds. Food service is available in the park.

Go trout, bass, smelt and perch fishing in Clear Lake, swimming from the sandy beach, or boating and sailing from the paved boat ramp. As you boat or fish, watch for bald eagles diving for fish in the lake. The surrounding lakes and streams also provide for additional fishing opportunities.

Canoeists can find excellent canoeing on Thunder Bay River at Atlanta and on Au Sable River beginning in Mio or Grayling.

Hike the five-mile nature trail that begins between the two campgrounds. It hooks into other trails outside the park including the Jackson Lake Trail, extending your hiking opportunities up to 70 additional miles.

Cross-country ski along the Clear Lake Trail to Canada Creek Cross Country Ski Trail. It's four miles long and fairly level.

Drive the 48.5-mile-long scenic drive that goes past Clear Lake and the Mackinaw State Forest.

Nearby attractions include the Old Mill Creek Historic State Park, Fort Michilimackinac at Mackinaw City, Father Marquette National Memorial across the Mackinac Bridge, or Mackinac Island via ferry. For a look at some limestone sinkholes, go ten miles north of the park to Sinkholes Pathway.

INFORMATION
Clear Lake State Park
Route 1
Atlanta, Michigan 49709
517-785-4388

COLONIAL MICHILIMACKINAC STATE PARK
MACKINAC ISLAND STATE PARK
10

LOCATION - The island can be reached by ferry from either St. Ignace or Mackinaw City. The Arnold Mackinac Island Ferry departs from both St. Ignace and Mackinaw City and runs from early May to late October. For information, call 906-847-3351. You can also take a hydro-jet from Mackinaw City and St. Ignace. Information: 616-436-5044 or 906-643-7635.

FEATURES - Mackinac Bridge, completed in 1957, is the world's longest suspension structure and leads to Michigan's Upper Peninsula. "Mighty Mac," the gateway to the peninsula, is considered the eighth wonder of the world and is five miles long.

ACTIVITIES - Tour historic homes, churches, forts and natural attractions where Michigan's past has been preserved. The 19th century is kept alive in both the buildings and transportation. No cars or motorized vehicles are allowed on the island, so all traffic is by horse-drawn carriage, bicycle or on foot. To book a Mackinac Island carriage tour, call 906-847-3325. The tours operate mid-May–October. They stop at Surry Hill so you can wander through the horse and carriage museum. Exhibits here follow the evolution of the carriage business on the island from 1850.

Bicyclists will love cycling around the perimeter of the island, a ride of 8.2 miles, with no automobile traffic to deal with. It's also fun to ride the trails in the interior of the island. Some of the scenic sights to see include Skull Cave, Devil's Kitchen, Sugar Loaf and 146-foot-high Arch Rock. Fish for chinook salmon in the Straits of Mackinac.

Most visitors to the island sample some its fudge, the island's trademark. A dozen shops churn out thousands of pounds of the candy annually, and visitors who try some are nicknamed "fudgies."

Be sure to visit the Beaumont Memorial, Biddle House, Fort Mackinac, the Indian Dormitory and the Grand Hotel, constructed in 1887 as a retreat for the wealthy. At Fort Mackinac, experience the sounds of musket and cannon fire, and learn about the military history of the straits. The fort was built by the British in 1779 as a stronghold. The fort has been under three flags: British, French and American.

In mid-June, attend the Lilac Festival on the island. In late July, watch the Chicago to Mackinac Yacht Race. On Labor Day, participate in the Mackinac Bridge Walk beginning from St. Ignace.

Pilots can land on the island one mile northwest of the city. To get into town, either bring your own bicycle in the plane, or contact the Carriage Tour Company at 907-847-3323.

Tour the reconstructed Colonial Michilimackinac at Mackinaw City. Open mid-May–mid-October, the reconstructed sailing sloop, Welcome, carried supplies to Fort Mackinac. Costumed staff provide black powder weapons demonstrations and children's programs.

Visitors planning to tour Colonial Michilimackinac, Fort Mackinac and Mill Creek may purchase combination tickets to get a special rate.

The 40-foot Old Mackinac Point Lighthouse, built in 1892, now serves as the Mackinac Maritime Museum. Its light was visible for 16 miles and was in active service until 1957.

During the fall, when the colors are at their peak, attend the Annual Kite Festival in Mackinaw City at the Mackinaw City Airport. For information, call 616-436-5574.

On the last Saturday in June, "Down Memory Lane" becomes a two-mile-long exhibit of antique and custom-made cars. Come to see the many vintage cars, watch the Mackinac Bridge Rally on Thursday, and on Friday, watch the area tour of cars built in 1935 or before. For information, contact the St. Ignace Chamber of Commerce.

Mill Creek State Historic Park is located on U.S. 23, and is southeast of Mackinaw City. The park features a reconstructed 18th-century waterpowered mill, nature trails, an ongoing archeological dig, and an orientation program. It's open from mid-May through mid-October. For information, call 616-436-7301.

INFORMATION
Mackinac Island State Park
Colonial Michilimackinac State Park
Box 370-MB
Mackinac, Michigan 49757
906-847-3328 or 3761

FAYETTE STATE PARK
11

LOCATION - The park is on Big Bay de Noc, eight miles southwest of Garden off U.S. 2.

ACTIVITIES - The park is open daily from 9–7 from mid-May through mid-October. Walk through the ghost town of Fayette that has an old hotel, iron smelter, lime kiln and visitor center. The town was once a profitable iron smelting community from 1867 to 1891, but was abandoned when its blast furnaces closed.

Stay in one of 80 semi-modern campsites with electrical hookups, or go boat camping in Snail Shell Harbor.

Go hiking along approximately seven miles of trails winding through beech and maple hardwoods and through the historic town site. You can also enjoy a picnic, go pan fishing in Lake Michigan, or fishing for perch, bass and pike in Big Bay de Noc. Fishing is allowed in the harbor area.

Scuba divers come here to dive in Snail Shell Harbor. A swimming beach is located on Sand Bay, a short distance from the campground.

A boating launch site is located between the campground and picnic area and provides access to Big Bay de Noc. The protected waters of Snail Shell Harbor are deep enough for larger boats.

INFORMATION
Fayette State Park
13700 13.25 Lane
Garden, Michigan 49835
906-644-2603

FISHERMAN'S ISLAND STATE PARK
12

LOCATION - The park is three miles southwest of Charlevoix off U.S. 31 on Lake Michigan.

ACTIVITIES - The park has 90 rustic campsites, hiking trails, fishing and swimming from a sandy beach in Lake Michigan.

In Charlevoix, take a cruise on the "Star of Charlevoix" docked in Round Lake Harbor. The 114-foot cruiser sails Lake Charlevoix or Lake Michigan, weather permitting. For information, call 616-547-9032.

You can also take a 2.5-hour boat trip to Beaver Island from the city dock on Bridge Street from mid-April through December. You'll need reservations if you take your car. This is an especially beautiful cruise during fall.

Take the Beaver Island Mini-Bus Tour, an hour ride around "The Emerald Isle" where you see the Old Mormon Print Shop and the Marine Museum. You'll also see 30 stone cottages called mushroom homes.

In Charlevoix, attend the annual Apple Festival in mid-October. Northern lower Michigan is orchard country and grows 38 varieties of apples. Festivities include not only great eating, but hayrides, square dancing and a scarecrow competition. For information, call 616-547-2101.

INFORMATION
Fisherman's Island State Park
P.O. Box 45
Charlevoix, Michigan 49720
616-547-6641

FORT CUSTER STATE PARK
13

LOCATION - The park is seven miles southwest of Battle Creek on Michigan 96.

ACTIVITIES - The park has 219 campsites. Explore the hiking, biking or equestrian trails, or go swimming, fishing and boating on three lakes with boat launch sites.

Stay in one of their three frontier cabins located near Jackson Lake or in a riverside family walk-in cabin on the Kalamazoo River.

In Battle Creek, tour the Kingman Museum of Natural History on West Michigan Avenue at 20th Street. Located in the Leila Arboretum, the museum has exhibits from the Michigan Ice Age. Shows include "A Journey Through the Crust of the Earth," and "A Walk in the Footsteps of the Dinosaurs," plus planetarium shows. For information, call 616-965-5117.

INFORMATION
Fort Custer State Park
5163 Fort Custer Drive
Augusta, Michigan 49012
616-731-4200

FORT WILKINS STATE PARK
14

LOCATION - The park is two miles northeast of Copper Harbor on the shore of Lake Superior, on the northern tip of Keweenaw Peninsula.

FEATURES - The fort was built to keep order among the miners and to defend against Indian attacks that never happened. The fort was begun in 1844 only to be abandoned two years later. It was re-garrisoned in the late 1860s and operated until 1870. It's the last remaining original wooden fort east of the Mississippi River. The preserve has restored 16 buildings of the U.S. Army post, 12 of them original structures.

ACTIVITIES - The park is open year-round, but the fort is only open May 15–October 15. The fort complex features not only museum exhibits, period rooms, and an audiovisual presentation, but also has a living history program. Costumed interpreters are on duty from late June through late August. Summer evening programs begin at 7:30. A Civil War encampment is held annually in August.

Take a 20-minute, narrated boat ride to the restored Copper Harbor Lighthouse and Museum. Built in 1866, the lighthouse is the oldest operating, fully restored lighthouse on Lake Superior. Once ashore, you can tour the museum at your own pace, take a self-guided nature tour of Lighthouse Point, have a picnic lunch, and hunt for agates. The lighthouse opens in June. Lighthouse boat tours begin Memorial Day weekend and run through Labor Day. For information, call 906-289-4410 or 906-289-4688.

Overnight in the campground that has 165 campsites with electrical hookups, a trailer dump and some groceries, or stay in the lodge or cabins.

Go rainbow trout, bass and perch fishing, and boating from the ramp on Lake Fanny Hooe or in Copper Harbor. Hike or bike the park trails.

For a scenic drive, take the Brockway Mountain Drive on Michigan 26, four miles west of Copper Harbor. This drive is the highest above sea level drive between the Rockies and the Alleghenies, and is one of the most scenic drives in the Midwest. You get a panoramic view of Lake Superior, and have a great vantage point for observing eagle and hawk flyways.

In late May, you'll be in time for the Keweenaw Peninsula Game and Fish Tournament held in Houghton. Octoberfest is held in Copper Harbor early in September.

INFORMATION
Fort Wilkins State Park
U.S. 41 East
Copper Harbor, Michigan 49918
905-289-4215 or 517-373-3559

GRAND HAVEN STATE PARK
15

LOCATION - The park is one mile southwest of Grand Haven on U.S. 31 at the mouth of the Grand River.

ACTIVITIES - Grand Haven has a broad sandy swimming beach on Lake Michigan, and offers trout fishing in Lake Michigan, and perch fishing in Grand River. It has a store and a campground with 182 campsites with electrical hookups and a trailer dump. It's crowded during the weekends, attracting some of the largest crowds that visit any of Michigan's state parks.

The end of June, watch the "Sun-N-Fun" co-ed beach volleyball tournament. For details, call 1-800-292-2729.

In Grand Haven, take a ride aboard the Harbor Steamer, a stern-wheel paddle boat. It departs from Chinook Pier on U.S. 31, near downtown Grand Haven. It takes you on 1.5-hour tour of the waterfront via the Grand River and Spring Lake. It opens Memorial weekend, and offers special weekend trips during Tulip Time. For information, call 616-842-8950.

In town, you can also tour the Tri-Cities Historical Museum at Harbor Avenue at Washington off U.S. 31, or see the World's Largest Musical Fountain at Washington and Harbor Avenue on the Grand River, two miles west of U.S. 31. Here you'll find a unique display of synchronized water, lights and music featured in their nightly 20-minute performance. It opens Memorial Day and continues through August. For information, call 616-842-2550.

Annual events in the park include the Great Lakes Stunt Kite Competition in early May. The last week of July, the Coast Guard Festival is featured along with the Queen's Pageant, parade, ship tours and athletic events.

The Spring Lake Heritage Festival occurs in mid-June when you can take a tour of some of the area's historic homes. The second week in October, attend the Fall Color Fest, when you can get a look at the colors while riding the Harbor Trolley or the Harbor Steamer.

The Grand Haven South Pier Lighthouse is located in the park. Its light was first lit in 1839. The beacon is 52 feet high, and its light can be seen for 15 miles.

INFORMATION
Grand Haven State Park
1001 Harbor Avenue
Grand Haven, Michigan 49417
616-842-6020

HARTWICK PINES STATE PARK
16

LOCATION - The park is seven miles northeast of Grayling on Michigan 93, Exit 259 off I-75.

FEATURES - The Hartwick Pines Lumbering Museum is surrounded by one of Michigan's largest remaining stands of virgin white pine that managed to escape loggers active in the area. These pines are 155 feet tall.

ACTIVITIES - The park is the largest state park in the Lower Peninsula. Learn about the early lumbering activities by walking through the interpretive center and touring the logging camp's bunkhouse, blacksmith shop, saw filer's workshop and the steam operated sawmill exhibit. The exhibit buildings are open during April, May, September, and October from 8:00-4:30, and from June–Labor Day 8–7.

Several hiking trails criss-cross the park. The Au Sable River's three-mile-long trail winds through the forest, crossing the river. The Virgin Pines Trail leads you to the logging camp and beautiful Chapel in the Pines. For longer hikes, explore Weary Legs Trail, 7.5 miles long, five-mile Deer Run, or three-mile-long Aspen Trail.

One of the state's most famous trout streams, the Au Sable, passes through the park. You can fish for trout, perch and bass in Glory Lake. The Au Sable is also a great canoeing river, with no big rocks or rapids, and has a current flowing at 3-5 m.p.h.

The campground has 63 campsites, 42 with electrical hookups and a trailer dump. You can purchase supplies at the park store.

Annual events include "Old Time Days" in June, Mill Town Music Festival in July, and Black Iron Days in August. The steam-powered sawmill is operated during these festivals.

A beautiful time to visit here is in the fall when the maples turn deep red, blending in with the yellows and oranges of the other hardwoods.

The Michigan Riding and Hiking Trail passes through nearby Grayling, the halfway point along this 240-mile-long trail that stretches from Lake Michigan to Lake Huron.

Mushroom pickers come to the area in May, searching for the morel mushrooms. Good sites for the mushrooms are west of Four Mile Road around Frederic and Lovells.

INFORMATION
Hartwick Pines State Park
Route 3, Box 3840
Grayling, Michigan 49738
517-348-7068

HIGHLAND STATE RECREATION AREA
17

LOCATION - The area is two miles east of Highland off Michigan 59, and 17 miles west of Pontiac.

ACTIVITIES - Rent the cabin that sleeps six. Go camping in the campground with 35 campsites, but no electricity. Enjoy hiking and horseback riding from the equestrian campground.

Teeple Lake has a swimming beach and bathhouse. Boat launches are located at Alderman, Grass, Pickerell and Teeple lakes. You can also fish in the lakes.

This is a particularly beautiful park to visit during the fall when the hardwoods change.

INFORMATION
Highland State Recreation Area
5200 E. Highland Road
Milford, Michigan 48042
512-887-5135

HOFFMASTER STATE PARK
18

LOCATION - The park is in Norton Shores, three miles west of U.S. 31 on Pontaluna Road.

ACTIVITIES - Stay in the campground with 333 campsites with electrical hookups. Go swimming or salmon fishing in Lake Michigan. Hike among the sand dunes that border Lake Michigan. Ride horseback on the equestrian trails. Limited food service is available.

Tour the E. Genevieve Gillette Interpretive Center, open year-round, to learn the story of the sand dunes of Lake Michigan. Watch the slide show, and view the exhibits on the dunes. For information, call 616-798-3573.

This Lake Michigan seaport is home to the restored Queen Anne-style Hackley House located in Heritage Village. The homes are an outstanding example of Victorian architecture, and were built in 1889. Two hundred skilled workers and artists worked over two years to create the wood carvings, stained glass windows and ceramic tiles. Listen to descriptions of life during the late Victorian period in the Midwest. Beginning in mid-May, the complex is open Wednesday, Saturday and Sunday. For information, call 616-722-7578.

In June, Muskegon hosts the Lumbertown Music Festival. For information, call 616-722-3751.

INFORMATION
Hoffmaster State Park
6585 Lake Harbor Road
Muskegon, Michigan 49441
616-798-3711

HOLLAND STATE PARK
19

LOCATION - The park is seven miles northwest of Holland.

FEATURES - The Dutch settled here because it resembled their homeland, and the park is now steeped in Dutch traditions.

ACTIVITIES - Camp in one of 342 campsites with electrical hookups. One of the campgrounds is beside Lake Macatawa, and the other near Lake Michigan.

Go boating from the boat launch, perch fishing and swimming in Lake Michigan. Food service is available at the beach. Hike the sand dunes or the beach along the lake.

Come to Holland during Tulip Time in mid-May to enjoy their annual four-day festival complete with Dutch-style street scrubbing, and also view millions of tulips blooming all over town. During the festival, wooden shoe dancers perform, and three parades and nine musical/variety shows are staged. Shuttle buses operate from the Shuttle Bus station west of the U.S. 31 by-pass on 8th Street, or near the Civic Center. For information on the festivities, call 616-396-4221.

Tour the Dutch Village, one mile north of Michigan 21 on U.S. 31, to see its flowering gardens, carvings, and walk through the Dutch farmhouse and barn with its live animals. It also has canals, windmills, shops, folk dancing, movies and rides. For information, call 616-396-1475.

During tulip blossoming time, walk through the Veldheer Tulip Gardens located three miles northeast of town on U.S. 31 at Quincy. It has scenic windmills reminiscent of Holland. At other times during the summer, the tulips are replaced by other blooming plants.

Windmill Island is downtown at 7th and Lincoln, and features a miniature Dutch village and more tulip gardens. It also has an original, restored 200-year-old windmill built in the 1700s in Holland. It still operates and grinds graham flour that you can buy. Klompen dancing is presented in the summer, and guided tours are provided. It opens in May. For information, call 616-396-5433.

Have you ever watched the making of wooden shoes? If not, go to the Wooden Shoe Factory at 16th Street and U.S. 31. It's the largest wooden shoe factory in the U.S., and the wooden shoemakers use 100-year-old machines, modern machinery, plus old-fashioned hand carving to create the shoes. It's open year-round. For information, call 616-396-6513.

Saugatuck Dunes State Park is south of Holland near U.S. 31, and has several hiking trails winding through the dunes along Lake Michigan.

INFORMATION
Holland State Park
Ottawa Beach Road
Holland, Michigan 49424
616-399-9390

HOLLY STATE RECREATION AREA
20

LOCATION - The area is 12 miles northwest of Pontiac off I-75.

ACTIVITIES - Rent their cabin that sleeps six. Enjoy camping in one of the 160 campsites, or rent a tent or tipi overnight. The park has a store.

Go boating from the ramps located at Crotched, Crystal, Holdredge or Valley lakes. Their day-use area surrounds three other lakes—Heron, Valley and Wildwood—where you can go swimming, boating and fishing. These lakes have bass and bluegill. Heron Lake is stocked with walleye and tiger muskies.

Bridle trails wind around the Holdridge Lakes, the Valley and Wildwood lakes area, while several hiking trails traverse the McGinnis Lake area, and continue east beyond Young's Lake.

During the winter you can go cross-country skiing and snowmobiling along their trails, or ice fishing in the lakes.

In Holly, for some free wine tasting, stop by the St. Julian Wine Tasting Center located .25-mile west of I-75 exit 101 (Grange Hall Road). For information, call 313-634-4711.

The Seven Lakes Vineyard is located 1.5 miles north of Grange Hall Road, 1.5 miles west of Fish Lake Road, where you can do more wine tasting, have a picnic, and hike their wooded trails. For information, call 313-629-5686.

INFORMATION
Holly State Recreation Area
8100 Grange Hall Road
Holly, Michigan 48442
313-634-8811

INDIAN LAKE STATE PARK
21

LOCATION - The park is five miles west of Manistique off U.S. 2 and Michigan 149.

FEATURES - Indian Lake is the fourth largest inland lake in the Upper Peninsula, and is six miles long and three miles wide. At one time, Indians lived in log cabins near the outlet of the lake. The site is an area of unusual bridges and legendary springs.

ACTIVITIES - The campground has 302 campsites with electrical hookups and a trailer dump. The south shore has lake shore camping, while the west shore provides more secluded and sheltered campsites, but they're not on the lake. The park also has rent-a-tent and rent-a-tipi accommodations.

Go fishing for salmon, steelhead, pike, bass, bluegill, perch and walleye in Indian Lake. You can also go swimming, and boating from the ramp where boat rentals are available. Tour the visitor center, and hike the trails.

The park is near the Hiawatha National Forest and Lake Superior State Forest, so visitors also have access to these areas for hunting, fishing, canoeing, hiking, cross-country skiing and berry picking.

In Manistique, tour the 119-year-old Historic Iron Smelting Village located on the Garden Peninsula between Manistique and Escanaba, 17 miles south of U.S.

2 on Michigan 183. The village features restored buildings, exhibits, displays, a scale model of the town site, a visitor center, and a self-guided walking tour. For information, call 906-644-2603.

Siphon Bridge, built in 1919 in downtown Manistique, is featured in Ripley's "Believe it or Not," because of the road's location four feet below the river level. The bridge is supported by water that is forced under it.

In Escanaba, you can tour the Historic House of Ludington located at 223 Ludington on the shore of Bay de Noc. The hotel is a state historic site, and has been restored and redecorated. For information, call 906-786-4000.

Thompson State Fish Hatchery is only two miles from the park, and is open weekdays between 8:00–4:30.

INFORMATION
Indian Lake State Park
Route 2, Box 2500
Manistique, Michigan 49854
906-341-2355

INTERLOCHEN STATE PARK
22

LOCATION - The park is one mile south of Interlochen.

ACTIVITIES - You can either camp in one of 550 campsites, 479 with electrical hookups, or in a rent-a-tent or rent-a-tipi. Some groceries are available.

The park has one mile of beach on Green and Duck lakes. Go hiking, trout fishing and swimming. Enjoy boating from the ramp with boat rentals available.

Interlochen Center for the Arts, located off U.S. 31, 15 miles southwest of Traverse City on Michigan 137, features year-round cultural activities and entertainment with both professional and student productions. Summers feature daily concerts except on Mondays. For information, call 616-276-9221.

Before or after a concert, stroll through the unusual collection of musical instruments on permanent display at the north end of the Concourse. Included is the original Sousaphone made for John Philip Sousa in 1898, two saxophones made in Adolphe Sax's factory and signed by him, experimental instruments, and instruments from other cultures.

If you're in Traverse City in May, attend their Blossom Days Festival. If you're here in early July, attend one of Michigan's oldest events, the National Cherry Festival. This eight-day festival includes three major parades, jazz and band competitions, sporting events, nonstop live musical entertainment, and cherries prepared in a variety of ways.

Wine tasters can tour the Chateau Grand Traverse on Michigan 37, eight miles north of Traverse City. It's open April–December. For information, call 616-223-7335.

A replica of the 56-foot schooner, "Madeline," is moored at Clinch Park Marina. The original schooner sailed the waters of Lake Michigan during the mid-19th century, but its replica now houses a maritime history museum open May-August. Information: 616-941-8850.

For an unusual tour, go through the Music House located at the Junction of U.S. 31 and Michigan 72, 1.5 miles north of town. They have a display of automated musical instruments in live performance, historical phonographs and radios, a turn-of-the-century general store, theater, and a music shop. Tours are available May-October. For information, call 616-938-9300.

INFORMATION
Interlochen State Park
Interlochen M-137
Interlochen, Michigan 49643
616-276-9511

ISLAND LAKE STATE RECREATION AREA
23

LOCATION - The area is four miles southeast of Brighton off U.S. 23, south of I-96, Exit 151, Kensington Road.

ACTIVITIES - Rent one of two cabins, or stay in one of 45 campsites.

Fishing is available in Kent Lake, Spring Mill Pond, Island Lake and in the Huron River. Boat launching facilities are available on Kent Lake from Kensington Metro Park on the north side of I-96.

An outstanding feature of the park is the Huron River that meanders through the area. This section of the river was designated as "Country Scenic," and has canoe launching sites plus a campground set aside for canoe campers only. A boat/canoe livery is located at Kent Lake.

Enjoy swimming from one of the three swimming beaches located at Kent and Island lakes and at Spring Mill Pond. Food service is available.

A 14-mile loop hiking/skiing trail begins at park headquarters and winds through the entire length of the park. It's especially beautiful during the fall when the hardwoods change.

Nearby attractions include Gage House, a state-owned centennial farmhouse on Kensington Road, located between Grand River and Silver Lake roads near Brighton. It's open June 1–Labor Day on Saturdays and Sundays from 1–4.

INFORMATION
Island Lake State Recreation Area
12950 E. Grand River
Brighton, Michigan 48116
313-229-7067

J. W. WELLS STATE PARK
24

LOCATION - The park is one mile south of Cedar River on Michigan 35 and 25 miles north of Menominee.

ACTIVITIES - Rent one of six cabins, or camp in the campground with 178 campsites with electrical hookups. Go bass fishing, swimming and boating from the ramp in Green Bay.

Hike or go cross-country skiing on their seven miles of trails, and hunting on state land near the park.

INFORMATION
J. W. Wells State Park
Michigan 35
Cedar River, Michigan 49813
906-863-9747

LAKE GOGEBIC STATE PARK
25

LOCATION - The park is twelve miles northeast of Marenisco on Michigan 64.

FEATURES - Lake Gogebic is the largest lake in Michigan's Upper Peninsula and is surrounded by the Ottawa National Forest. The lake is less than a half hour drive from the state park.

Ten miles from Marenisco, on August 16, 1889, the last stage coach holdup in the U.S. took place on the Gogebic Stage Coach Road. The road is still used for a scenic drive.

ACTIVITIES - Camp in a family rent-a-tent. The campground has 165 campsites with electrical hookups, and a trailer dump. Go swimming from the sandy beach, boating from the ramp, and hiking the trails through the nearby dense hardwood forests.

Fish in Lake Gogebic for trout, walleye, perch, pike and whitefish. The area holds a spring smallmouth bass tournament in late May, a walleye tournament in mid-September, and a tagged fish contest throughout the season. Prize money worth thousands of dollars is awarded.

INFORMATION
Lake Gogebic State Park
M-64
Marenisco, Michigan 49947
906-842-3341

LEELANAU STATE PARK
26

LOCATION - The park is four miles north of Northport.

ACTIVITIES - Go camping in one of 50 campsites, pan fishing on Lake Michigan, swimming and hiking.

An historic 1852 lighthouse is on the tip of the Leelanau Peninsula in the state park. Its hours vary.

For a colorful fall tour, begin on Michigan 72 west of Traverse City, and continue on Michigan 72 to County Road 651. Head north on Michigan 651 merging with Michigan 616 to Cedar. Take a right on Michigan 645 just out of Cedar, and then another right on Michigan 643 heading east through Cedar Valley up along the west side of Lake Leelanau.

In the village of Lake Leelanau, go east on Michigan 204 to Suttons Bay. Follow Michigan 22 for a short distance before turning right onto Michigan 633. In Bingham, take Michigan 618 to M22 to drive along the shoreline and back to Traverse City. The approximate driving distance is 55 miles.

Sugar Loaf, located on the Leelanau Peninsula, has opened its cross-country ski trails to mountain bikers. The trails offer scenic views of Little Traverse Lake and Lake Michigan.

INFORMATION
Leelanau State Park
Route 1, Box 49
Northport, Michigan 49670
616-386-5422

LUDINGTON STATE PARK
27

LOCATION - The park is 8.5 miles north of Ludington.

FEATURES - Ludington is site of one of the largest charter fishing fleets on Lake Michigan. The Big Sable Point Lighthouse, located on the harbor was built in 1867, and is still in use today to guide sailors into port.

ACTIVITIES - The park has 398 campsites, hiking, boating from the ramp with boat rentals available, fishing, swimming, a visitor center, and food service.

In Ludington, tour the Rose Hawley Museum, 115 W. Loomis, to see exhibits of the personal effects and artifacts from the area's early settlers. It's closed Sundays year-round, and Saturdays in April. For information, call 616-843-2001.

Stop by White Pine Village. To reach it, follow U.S. 31 to three miles south of Ludington, then go west on Iris Road and continue to the end. Then drive north on South Lakeshore Drive for another .25-mile. Here you'll see Mason

County's first courthouse that has been restored on its original site. Other buildings from the 1800s include two museums, a chapel, blacksmith shop, and an early school. You can observe craft demonstrations daily. Closed Mondays, it's open Memorial Day weekend–Labor Day weekend. For information, call 616-843-4808.

On October 30, known as Devils' Night, celebrate "Halloween in the Village" at White Pine Village. Come trick or treating, bob for apples, and participate in the pumpkin carving and costume contests.

INFORMATION
Ludington State Park
Box 709
Ludington, Michigan 49431
616-843-8761

MACKINAC ISLAND STATE PARK
28

See under COLONIAL MICHILIMACKINAC STATE PARK

McLAIN STATE PARK
29

LOCATION - Located on Lake Superior 10 miles northwest of Hancock on Michigan 203, and seven miles west of Calumet, the park has frontage on both Lake Superior and Bear Lake.

ACTIVITIES - Camp in one of the 103 modern campsites with electrical hookups and a trailer dump station. The park also has 10 rustic campsites, a rent-a-tent for summer use, and a rustic cabin available year-round. Some groceries are available. Reservations are recommended for July and August.

Go hiking, trout fishing, search for agates on Lake Superior, swimming from the sand beach with a bathhouse beside Lake Superior, or boating from the ramp. Visitors can also go wind surfing, berry picking, rock hounding for agates along Lake Michigan, and attend an evening interpretive program.

One mile east of Hancock on Michigan 26, tour the Arcadian Copper Mine. For information, call 906-482-7502.

Quincy Mine Hoist No. 2, located one mile north of Hancock on U.S. 40, then .25-mile east on Quincy Hill, features the Nordberg Hoist, the largest steam-powered mine hoist ever manufactured. It is now a National Historic Site. Guides are available to tell you about the geology and mining era. It opens in mid-June. For information, call 906-482-3101.

INFORMATION
McLain State Park
Route 1, Box 82, Michigan 203
Hancock, Michigan 49930
906-482-0278

MEARS STATE PARK
30

LOCATION - The park is north of the village of Pentwater off U.S. 31.

ACTIVITIES - The park has .16-mile of sandy beach along Lake Michigan, and its campground has 179 campsites with electrical hookups. Hike the trails, go fishing in Lake Michigan for trout, salmon, coho, perch, pike and smelt from the Pentwater Pier located on the southern boundary of the park. You can also enjoy swimming with a bathhouse available, and purchase refreshments. A boat ramp is available in downtown Pentwater. No ramps are located in the park.

Events celebrated include the Memorial Day weekend fishing derby and parade, a Fourth of July fishing tournament, an art fair the second Saturday in July, and the Pentwater Homecoming Festival held the second full weekend in August. A 10-kilometer Sunset Run is held the last Saturday evening in August. For details, contact the Pentwater Chamber of Commerce at 616-869-4150.

In Mears, take a ride aboard the Silver Queen Riverboat's paddle wheeler and take a one-hour cruise on Lake of Sand Dunes. Rides begin June 1. For information, call 616-873-4741.

Take an eight-mile dune ride over the sand dunes to enjoy spectacular views of Silver Lake. Tours are offered from mid-May through mid-October. For information, call 616-873-2817.

Village band concerts are presented in Pentwater every Thursday in July and August.

INFORMATION
Mears State Park
Pentwater, Michigan 49449
616-869-2051

MUSKALLONGE LAKE STATE PARK
31

LOCATION - The park is on Lakes Superior and Muskallonge, 28 miles northwest of Newberry via Michigan 123, and 18 miles east of Grand Marais on H-58 and H-37.

FEATURES - The state park is the site of Deer Park, a lumbering town that was active during the late 1800s. At the time, a large dock extended into Lake Superior from which lumber was shipped. Muskallonge Lake was used as a mill pond for millions of white pine logs brought to the site by the narrow gauge railroad; however, by 1960, all the timber was gone and the mill closed. Today all you can see are some of the original dock pylons in Lake Superior.

ACTIVITIES - The park has 179 campsites with electricity. The fully modern facilities are open May 15–October 15. They have no winter camping.

You can also go hiking, boating from the ramp, and swimming from the sandy beach with a bathhouse. A 1.5-mile-long hiking trail connects with the North Country Pathway.

The park has two grocery stores nearby. Both stores and the nearby resort have rental boats.

Muskallonge Lake is known for its catches of northern pike, perch, smallmouth bass, rock bass and bullheads.

Rock hounds will enjoy searching for agates and other colorful stones along Lake Superior. Wild blueberries and raspberries are abundant in the area in July and August.

INFORMATION
Muskallonge Lake State Park
Box 245, Route 1
Newberry, Michigan 49868
906-658-3338

MUSKEGON STATE PARK
32

LOCATION - The park is four miles west of North Muskegon on Michigan 213.

ACTIVITIES - The park has three miles of sandy beach along the shores of Lake Michigan plus two more miles of frontage on Muskegon Lake. Muskegon Lake offers good fishing for bass, perch, pike, walleye and bluegill. Stop by the reconstructed Block House to get a great overlook of the lake and nearby sand dunes. The park has nine miles of hiking trails through the dunes and forest.

Camp in the campground with 357 campsites with electrical hookups. Refreshments are available in the park.

Visit the Blockhouse, a replica of an old fort on top of a high hill, to get a panorama view of the shoreline, dunes and Muskegon.

For a look at the reconstruction of an 1874 volunteer hose company fire barn, visit the C. H. Hackley Hose Company No. 2, located one block north of Business U.S. 31 in Muskegon. Here you'll see examples of both 19th- and 20th-century equipment, and a large photographic collection of Muskegon fires, and the fire fighters who put them out. It opens Memorial Day weekend, and is open Monday, Wednesday and Friday only. For information, call 616-722-1363.

INFORMATION
Muskegon State Park
3560 Memorial Drive
North Muskegon, Michigan 49445
616-744-3480

NEWAYGO STATE PARK
33

LOCATION - The park is two miles northeast of Newaygo from Michigan 37.

ACTIVITIES - The park has three miles of frontage on the Hardy Dam Point. Go camping in one of the 99 campsites, fishing in the river, swimming, and boating from the ramp.

Investigate the High Rollway Scenic Panorama, located on Michigan 82 east of Newaygo, to get a panoramic view from the edge of the steep slope where millions of feet of the state's virgin pine timber were plunged into the Muskegon River.

INFORMATION
Newaygo State Park
Box 309-A
Newaygo, Michigan 49337
616-856-4452

ORCHARD BEACH STATE PARK
34

LOCATION - The park is two miles north of Manistee on Michigan 110.

ACTIVITIES - Camp in one of the 176 campsites with electrical hookups, a trailer dump, and store. Go swimming and salmon fishing in Lake Michigan.

Hike either the .5-mile nature trail or two miles of hiking trails next to the campground. For additional hiking, the park is adjacent to the Manistee National Forest where additional trails are available.

Fishing in Lake Michigan and Manistee Lake is good year-round. Lake trout fishing peaks in June and July. During August and September, salmon make their spawning runs. Later, the steelhead make their fall run. Fishing tournaments are held during the summer, in this area often referred to as the "Fishing Capital of the Midwest."

Each Wednesday evening in Manistee, from Memorial Day until Labor Day, a concert is presented in the Victorian band shell on the river walk located on the north shore of the Manistee River off Memorial Drive. Concerts begin at 7 p.m.

A beautiful river walk begins at the Maple Street bridge and goes along the south side of the Manistee River.

In Manistee, tour the Manistee County Historical Museum at 425 River Street to see a century-old drugstore with all its original contents. It's closed Sunday and Monday, April–May, and closed Sundays beginning June 1.

The Old Waterworks Museum at the same location features an 1881 waterworks building that now houses marine, railroad and logging exhibits plus a lumber baron's carriage. It opens June 15, and is also closed Sundays.

The Ramsdell Theater located on Maple at First Street was built by lumber magnate T. J. Ramsdell, and is characteristic of a turn-of-the-century theater. It features professional productions and exhibits, and is open from May through October.

Tour Manistee to see the "Painted Ladies" houses. To qualify for this designation, the home must have three or more contrasting colors decorating the Victorian-style homes.

INFORMATION
Orchard Beach State Park
2064 Lakeshore Road
Manistee, Michigan 49660
616-723-7422

ORTONVILLE STATE RECREATION AREA
35

LOCATION - The area is four miles east of Ortonville off Michigan 15.

ACTIVITIES - Rent their cabin that sleeps 20. Enjoy camping in one of the 32 campsites, boating, fishing in one of the lakes, hiking, horseback riding, and swimming at Big Fish Lake with its own bathhouse. Boat launching facilities are provided at Algoe, Big Fish and Davison Lake.

INFORMATION
Ortonville State Recreation Area
6767 Hadley Road, Route 2
Ortonville, Michigan 48462
313-627-2838

P. H. HOEFT STATE PARK
36

LOCATION - The park is five miles northwest of Rogers City on U.S. 23.

ACTIVITIES - Rent one of the tents available June 1–September 15. Camp in the campground with 144 campsites with hookups, a trailer dump and limited groceries. Go boating from the ramp, salmon fishing in Lake Huron, and swimming from the beach. The park has a mile of frontage beside Lake Huron and features two buoyed beaches.

Hike the trails in the Huron Sand Dunes, or the 4.5 miles of trails running through the forest. This is a beautiful spot to visit during the fall because of the hardwood forest.

Ocqueoc Falls are located 12 miles west of U.S. 23 on Michigan 8. These are the largest falls in the Lower Peninsula, and their Indian name means "sacred." The falls have upper and lower falls 300 feet apart. Hike the seven-mile self-guided nature trail.

Rogers City is called "The Nautical City" because of its ample dock facilities providing anchorage for giant lake freighters. A nautical festival is held the first week in August.

If you're here over July 4th, watch the Double Handed Sailing Challenge in the Rogers City Yacht Harbor. For information on special events, contact the Chamber of Commerce at 517-734-4148.

The world's largest limestone quarry, from which 9.2 million tons of limestone were mined in 1989, is south of town.

Scuba divers dive in the waters off Rogers City where six known shipwrecks are located, most in 20 feet of water or less.

INFORMATION
P. H. Hoeft State Park
U.S. 23 North
Rogers City, Michigan 49779
517-734-2543

PALMS BOOK STATE PARK
37

LOCATION - The park is 12 miles north of Manistique on Michigan 149.

FEATURES - The spring is Michigan's largest, and is 45 feet deep and 200 feet across.

ACTIVITIES - Visit "Kitch-iti-ki-pi," the big spring, or what the Indians called the "Mirror of Heaven." Ride aboard a passenger-operated observation raft across the clear water, and watch the perfect reflection of sky, clouds and surrounding forests. Over 16,000 gallons of water bubble from the spring each minute, and the pool doesn't freeze during the winter or warm up during the summer, but remains at a constant 45 degrees. You can see large brown trout cruising about in the unusually clear water.

For day-use only, you can enjoy a picnic and purchase supplies from the concessions stand. For camping, go to nearby Indian Lake State Park.

In Manistee, you can see the Siphon Bridge and Water Tower featured in Ripley's "Believe it or Not." The road across the bridge is located four feet below the level of the river, and is supported by the water being forced under it.

INFORMATION
Palms Book State Park
c/o Indian Lake State Park
Route 2, Box 2500
Manistique, Michigan 49854
906-341-2355

PARADISE STATE PARK
38

LOCATION - The park is located on the Tahquamenon River 10 miles west of Paradise on Michigan 123.

ACTIVITIES - Camp in one of the 319 campsites, 259 with electrical hookups. Go pan fishing in the river and boating from the ramp where rentals are available.

Eight miles north of Paradise are the Whitefish Point Underwater Preserve and the Coast Guard station and lighthouse, now used as the Great Lakes Shipwreck Historical Museum. Here you can view exhibits of the "Invincible," the "Edmund Fitzgerald," and other vessels that were shipwrecked on Lake Superior.

INFORMATION
Paradise State Park
Paradise, Michigan 49768
906-492-3415

PETOSKEY STATE PARK
39

LOCATION - The park is four miles northeast of Petoskey near Little Traverse Bay. Take U.S. 31 to Michigan 119. Look for the park entrance on the west side of the road.

ACTIVITIES - The park has 190 campsites with electrical hookups, a trailer dump and some groceries.

Go swimming and salmon fishing in Lake Michigan. Also enjoy hiking along Portage or Old Baldy trails, and boating from the ramp.

In Petoskey, visit the American Spoon Foods Kitchens. It's on U.S. 131, 32 miles northwest of the I-75 Gaylord exit in the downtown gaslight district that has many shops for visitors who enjoy shopping.

The Kilwin's Candy Kitchen offers a tour through its kitchen, established in 1946. To reach it from the south, take I-75 north to Gaylord Exit 282. Turn left on Michigan 32 to U.S. 131. Turn right. It's closed Saturday and Sunday. For information, call 616-347-4831.

INFORMATION
Petoskey State Park
2475 Harbor-Petoskey Road
Petoskey, Michigan 49770
616-347-2311

PORCUPINE MOUNTAINS WILDERNESS STATE PARK
40

LOCATION - The park, Michigan's largest wilderness park, is 20 miles west of Ontonagon at the end of Michigan 107.

FEATURES - Porcupine Mountain Wilderness is dominated by the eroded remains of an ancient mountain range, and includes the Midwest's largest expanse of virgin timber plus the largest maple-hemlock climax forest in the U.S. The mountains were named by local Chippewa Indians who thought that the main range resembled a crouching porcupine when viewed from the distance.

The park includes the Porcupine Mountains, Lake of the Clouds, Mirror Lake and portions of both the Big Carp and Little Carp rivers.

ACTIVITIES - Hike along over 80 miles of hiking trails. Walk a short distance along one of the trails to reach the escarpment from which you can view Lake of the Clouds, lying hundreds of feet below you. Other trails lead to four secluded lakes, waterfalls and high peaks.

At the park's southwestern tip, the Presque Island River falls in four cascades as it flows towards Lake Superior. Take a very short hike through the woods to a boardwalk with platforms to view the Manido and Manabezho falls. Manido Falls drop 12 feet over a black slate ledge, while Manabezho Falls spills over a 30-foot ledge.

Trails in the park range in length from one to 16 miles. Trek to Mirror Lake, the highest lake in Michigan, located even higher than the escarpment above Lake in the Clouds. A 2.5-mile walk leads to this large, secluded lake.

Another great hike is out to the shoreline anywhere along Lake Superior's Trail, particularly at sunset. You'll often get a look at the northern lights in the spring, late summer or early fall.

Visitors also enjoy both alpine and cross-country skiing, fishing, swimming, and rock hounding. Climb the sand dunes and walk along the sandy beach. Climb the lookout tower at Summit Peak. Dining facilities are available.

The park has 13 cabins. Several of the cabins are located on lakes, and come equipped with rowboats for no extra charge. Call headquarters to make reservations for the cabins: 906-885-5275.

The visitors center at the east entrance is open mid-May to mid-October, and has a mini-museum, which offers a multi-media presentation in its theater.

Rainbow and brook trout swim in the Presque Isle and Big Carp rivers, and salmon congregate at their mouths.

The park has two modern campgrounds: Presque Isle and Union Bay. The Union Bay Campground has 95 campsites, a trailer dump station, and is located at the park's entrance. The park is open year-round, but the campsites are closed from December–April.

The Presque Isle Unit has 88 campsites without electricity. It's located at the mouth of Presque Isle River off the shores of Lake Superior, and 16 miles north of Wakefield on Michigan 519. Presque Isle offers boating, petting zoos, outdoor concerts and hiking. You can also go down a 160-foot water slide or swim in the largest outdoor pool in the Midwest.

For a colorful drive, particularly in the fall, begin in Boyne City, and take Front Street south of town along Lake Charlevoix to the historic Ironton Ferry. Ride the ferry across to Michigan 66 to U.S. 31. Follow U.S. 31 through the resort town of Charlevoix and on to Petoskey. You can see Beaver Island from here. This area is known for its mushroom hunting and pleasure boating.

Twelve miles east of Ontonagon, off Michigan 38, and west of Michigan 26 on Adventure Road, take a guided one hour, .25-mile tour of a copper mine. Miners of the 1850s discovered historic pits that had been dug by ancient miners as far back as 5,000 years ago. You can see these prehistoric workings, mine shafts, glacial markings on rock walls and remains of old mine buildings. The tour ends at the "ice cave" where cold air pours down from the side of the mountain. Tours are offered Memorial Day weekend through the fall color season.

INFORMATION
Porcupine Mountains Wilderness State Park
Star Route
Box 314
Ontonagon, Michigan 49953
906-885-5275

PROUD LAKE STATE RECREATION AREA
41

LOCATION - The park is four miles southeast of Milford and 12 miles southwest of Pontiac.

FEATURES - The park has three lakes: Proud, Commerce and Reed.

ACTIVITIES - Take a canoe ride down the Huron River. Camp in one of the 130 campsites with electrical hookups and a trailer dump. Go hiking, horseback riding, pan fishing and swimming from the beach with a bathhouse. Enjoy boating from the launch at Middle Straits, and in Proud and Reed lakes. Boat rentals are available in the park.

INFORMATION
Proud Lake State Recreation Area
3500 Wixom Road, Route 3
Milford, Michigan 48042
313-685-2433

SILVER LAKE STATE PARK
42

LOCATION - The park is seven miles west of Hart off U.S. 31, and five miles west of Mears on Silver Lake.

FEATURES - The park has frontage along Lake Michigan and Silver Lake.

ACTIVITIES - The park has 249 campsites with a trailer dump station, hiking along the sand dunes, boating from the ramp, fishing and swimming from the beach. The park also has its own store.

The 21-mile-long Hart-Montague Trail passes through the park, providing plenty of opportunity for bikers and hikers to explore the region.

Ten miles west of Hart and Shelby off U.S. 31, take an eight-mile ride over the desert-like dunes where you get spectacular views of Silver Lake. The area is closed Wednesday and Thursday, and open mid-May through the end of June. For information, call 616-873-2817.

INFORMATION
Silver Lake State Park
Route 1, Box 187
Mears, Michigan 49436
616-873-3083

STRAITS STATE PARK
43

LOCATION - The park is on the Straits of Mackinac at St. Ignace, and is off U.S. 1 west of the Mackinac Bridge.

ACTIVITIES - Camp in the campground with 318 campsites with a trailer dump. The campground overlooks Mackinac Bridge. Enjoy fishing, swimming, boating from the boat launch, and touring the interpretive center.

Tour Father Marquette National Memorial Museum in the park. It's an out-door memorial overlooking the Straits of Mackinac. The museum has memora-bilia of the French explorer and missionary, Father Jacques Marquette.

INFORMATION
Straits State Park
720 Church Street
St. Ignace, Michigan 49781
906-643-8620

TAHQUAMENON FALLS STATE PARK
44

LOCATION - The park is ten miles southwest of Paradise on Michigan 123. Paradise is located ten miles from the Upper Falls on the shore of Lake Superior's Whitefish Bay.

FEATURES - The Upper Tahquamenon Falls is the second largest waterfall east of the Mississippi River, and is sometimes called the "Little Niagara." The park includes both the Upper and Lower falls of the Tahquamenon River. Both falls are accessible via Michigan 123.

ACTIVITIES - The largest of a series of falls can be viewed from a lookout near the headquarters. However, there are three sets of falls located around the island, so you'll need to rent a rowboat to get out to the island. You can then follow trails around the island to get closer to the falls.

The shortest access to Tahquamenon Falls is via the Toonerville Trolley and Riverboat from Paradise. From the upper part of the river, an authentic nar-row gauge railroad and a riverboat built especially for sightseeing take you to the falls. The tours run from mid-June to early October. For information, call 906-876-2311.

You can also reach the falls by taking the Tom Sawyer Riverboat from Slater's Landing 10 miles north of Hulbert off Michigan 28. It's a 4.5-hour round trip and leaves only a short walk to reach the falls.

If you're here during the winter, you'll see huge rainbow-colored icicles on the walls of the Tahquamenon gorge. The coloring is natural because of the golden water.

The park's campground has 319 campsites, 259 with electrical hookups, and a trailer dump station.

The Great Lakes Shipwreck Museum is located at Whitefish Point on Lake Superior, 11 miles north of Paradise. For information, call 906-492-3436.

Tour Whitefish Point Lighthouse, the oldest working lighthouse on the lake, that began operating in 1849.

INFORMATION
Tahquamenon Falls State Park
Paradise M-123
Paradise, Michigan 49768
906-492-3415

TRAVERSE CITY STATE PARK
45

LOCATION - The park is two miles east of Traverse City on U.S. 31.

ACTIVITIES - The campground has 342 campsites with electrical hookups, and a trailer dump station. Go swimming from the beach with its own bathhouse. A store is close to the park.

Go fishing for bass, steelhead, walleye, trout, perch and muskies. From late August into mid-November, tributaries to Lake Michigan and Grand Traverse Bay host spawning king and coho salmon. Some salmon can be as large as 25 pounds. Kings run at their peak by the second week of September. Coho salmon enter the rivers later and hit their peak by early October.

The City Opera House, a restored 1891 landmark, features a variety of events throughout the year, including summer stock theater. It's located on Front Street. For information, call 616-941-8082

The Cherry County Playhouse offers professional theater and entertainment from late June through August. at the Park Place Hotel in Traverse City. For information, call 616-947-9560.

Take a cruise on the Tall Ship Malabar, a replica of the traditional two-masted schooner located in Traverse City. For information, call 616-941-2000.

Traverse City Symphony Orchestra performs from late fall to early spring. For tickets, call 616-947-7120.

Tour beautiful cherry orchards at 7407 U.S. 31 North. A complimentary cherry drink and dessert is served to all tour guests. It opens in May.

Take a tour of the Chateau Grand Traverse located on the Old Mission Peninsula, eight miles north of town. Here you'll find 45 acres of vineyards overlooking the Grand Traverse Bay area. The Old Mission Peninsula drive is · especially colorful in late May when the cherry trees are in bloom.`

Pilots can land at Cherry Capital Airport in Traverse City. Rental cars are available.

INFORMATION
Traverse City State Park
1132 U.S. 31 North
Traverse City, Michigan 49684
616-947-7193

TWIN LAKES STATE PARK
46

LOCATION - The park is on Lake Roland 23 miles southwest of Houghton on Michigan 26, and three miles north of Winona.

ACTIVITIES - Go camping in one of the 344 sites, all with electrical hookups. Enjoy boating from the ramp, salmon fishing and swimming in Lake Michigan.

In Houghton, tour the A. E. Seaman Mineralogical Museum located on the campus of Michigan Technological University's fifth floor. Here you'll find over 19,000 mineral and rock specimens from all over the world. It's only open weekends.

The Elm River Sugar Bush is located on the Keweenaw Peninsula. Go 20 miles south of Houghton-Hancock, then south on Misery Bay Road to Elm River Sugar Bush Road, and another 1.5 miles to the Sugarshack. Take a tour of the maple sugar processing facilities located here in the Elm River Valley. Observe the small herd of American buffalo. The facilities open May 15, but are closed on Sunday.

INFORMATION
Twin Lakes State Park
M-26 Twin Lakes Route
Tolvola, Michigan 49965
517-288-3321

VAN BUREN STATE PARK
47

LOCATION - Van Buren State Park is four miles south of South Haven.

ACTIVITIES - Van Buren has 220 campsites with electrical hookups, a trailer dump station, and some groceries. A beach and sand dunes are beside Lake Michigan, and are a five-minute drive from the campground.

Go swimming from the .75-mile-long sandy beach and boating in the lake.

Van Buren State Park administers the Kal-Haven Trail that stretches 34.1 miles, and passes through the park, making it a great way for bikers and hikers to explore the area. The trail follows an abandoned rail line between Kalamazoo and South Haven. Near South Haven is a large trestle that has been changed to a covered bridge.

To bike the trail on a rental bicycle, contact the Healy True Value Hardware and Lumber Company located at the intersection of Michigan 40 and the trail. For information, call 616-628-2584.

In South Haven, tour the Lake Michigan Maritime Museum located 1.5 miles west of I-196 at Exit 20. Turn right here, and turn right again at the second stoplight. The museum has exhibits of the people who built boats for sailing on the Great Lakes. See some historic Coast Guard vessels, a Lake Michigan commercial fishing tug, and tour the museum. It opens May 1, but is closed Mondays. For information, call 616-637-8078.

Ride aboard the Harbor Steamer at Chinook Pier near downtown Grand Haven. This riverboat takes you on a 1.5-hour narrated cruise. It departs at 1:00, 3:00, 5:30 and 7:30 every day of the week except on Wednesdays when the 1:00 cruise is replaced by an 11:30 cruise for lunch. For reservations, call 616-842-8950.

Annual events in the area include the National Blueberry Festival in July, a cross-country ski festival, Octoberfest, arts and crafts shows, fishing tournaments and farmers' markets.

INFORMATION
Van Buren State Park
23960 Ruggles Road
South Haven, Michigan 49090
616-637-2788

VAN RIPER STATE PARK
48

LOCATION - The park is three miles west of Champion on U.S. 41, and 17 miles west of Ishpeming on U.S. 41.

FEATURES - Van Riper contains .5-mile of frontage on the east of Lake Michigamme, and 1.5 miles of frontage along the Peshekee River.

ACTIVITIES - Camp in a family rent-a-tent. The park has 226 campsites, 150 with water and electrical hookups and a trailer dump station. Limited groceries and RV supplies are available.

Go pike, walleye, bass, perch and muskellunge fishing in Lake Michigamme, and swimming or boating from the ramp.

Hiking trails wander through hills on the north side of the highway, and give some great overlooks of Lake Michigamme. A few miles east of the park, iron ore was discovered in 1845, and you can still see evidence of the early mining operations along the trails. Some open pit mines are still operating.

In 1985, 59 moose were released in a site six miles north of the park, making this a good place to catch sight of one of these large animals.

INFORMATION
Van Riper State Park
P.O. Box 66
Champion, Michigan 49814
906-339-4461

W. J. HAYES STATE PARK
49

LOCATION - The park is nine miles west of Clinton on U.S. 12 and Michigan 124.

ACTIVITIES - The park has a half mile of sandy beach on Wamplers Lake, and contains all of Round Lake.

Enjoy fishing for largemouth and smallmouth bass, bluegill, perch and pike.

Go swimming from the beach where there is a store and bathhouse. Go boating from the boat launch. Rental boats are available.

The campground is wooded and has 210 sites, 160 with electrical hookups, and a trailer dumping station.

INFORMATION

W. J. Hayes State Park
1220 Wampler's Lake Road
Onsted, Michigan 49265
517-467-7401

WARREN DUNES STATE PARK
50

LOCATION - The park is 17 miles southwest of St. Joseph and is midway between New Buffalo and St. Joseph.

ACTIVITIES - Camp in one of their 197 campsites, all with electrical hookups. Go salmon fishing and swimming in Lake Michigan.

The park has over two miles of sand beaches along Lake Michigan. The spectacular sand dunes rise 240 feet above the lake, making it a favorite for hang gliders as well as hikers. A concession stand is located along the beach.

In the spring, bird watchers come to the dunes to watch the birds' migrations.

INFORMATION

Warren Dunes State Park
Red Arrow Highway
Sawyer, Michigan 49125
616-426-4013

WATERLOO STATE RECREATION AREA
51

LOCATION - The park is seven miles west of Chelsea off I-94.

ACTIVITIES - Rent one of nine cabins, or go camping in one of the two campgrounds: Portage or Sugarloaf. Portage has 194 campsites with electrical hookups, a trailer dump, and limited groceries. Sugarloaf has 186 campsites with electrical hookups and a trailer dump.

Tour the visitor center and go hiking or horseback riding. Also enjoy swimming, boating and bass fishing on Sugarloaf Lake.

In Chelsea, tour the Chelsea Milling Company, home of Jiffy Mixes. To reach it, take I-94 to Exit 159. Turn right. Go through the village of Chelsea and turn left at the first street past the railroad track. Watch the slide show, take a walking tour of the plant and warehouse, and enjoy some refreshments. It's closed weekends, and tours are by appointment only. Call 313-475-1361.

INFORMATION
Waterloo State Recreation Area
16345 McClure Rd, Route 1
Chelsea, Michigan 48118
313-475-8307

WILDERNESS STATE PARK
52

LOCATION - The park is eight miles west of Mackinaw City.

ACTIVITIES - The park has 210 campsites with electrical hookups and a trailer dump station. Rent one of their six cabins, or one of three rustic bunkhouses that sleep up to 24.

Go trout fishing, swimming or boating from the ramp in Lake Michigan.

In Mackinaw City, take a mini-cruise of the Straits of Mackinac featuring the Mackinac Bridge and surrounding islands.

Tour Fort Michilimackinac Maritime Park and Museum located off I-75, Exit 339. The entrance is under the south end of Mackinac Bridge. Here you'll find a reconstructed fur trade village dating to 1715 to 1781. The site has the longest continuous archeology ongoing dig in the U.S. Costumed interpretive staff are on duty. The maritime museum portrays the history of early boating on the Straits and the Great Lakes, and opens May 15.

The Revolutionary War Sloop, "Welcome," is docked at the Mackinaw City Marina, and is a reconstructed sloop owned by a British trader, and used by the British Navy in the 1700s. Explore the ship, crew's quarters, cargo hold and captain's cabin. Costumed guides from the British Navy tell the maritime history of the area. It opens June 15.

Tour Teysen's Woodland Indian Museum at 416 South Huron Avenue to see artifacts from Michigan's Indian culture dating back to 10,000 B.C. You'll also see artifacts from the fur trading and lumbering era.

INFORMATION
Wilderness State Park
Box 380
Carp Lake, Michigan 49718
616-436-5381

WILLIAM MITCHELL STATE PARK
53

LOCATION - The park is 2.5 miles west of Cadillac near Michigan 115.

ACTIVITIES - The park has frontage on both Lake Cadillac and Lake Mitchell, and has 270 campsites with electrical hookups and a trailer dump. Go hiking, and fishing for pike, perch, walleye, bass and bluegill in Lake Cadillac. Enjoy swimming from the beach with a bathhouse, and boating from the ramp where rentals are available.

The Heritage Fisheries and Wildlife Nature Study Area is adjacent to the park, where you can hike through the wetlands and observe the wide variety of plants and animals that live there. This wetland area serves as a filter for the city of Cadillac by capturing runoff and filtering out harmful pesticides before they reach the nearby lakes.

Near Cadillac, visit Johnny's Wild Game and Fish Park located west off Michigan 115 on the first road south of the Michigan 55 intersection. Here you'll see both wild and tame game in a natural setting. Enjoy petting the deer, goats, and other animals, and fishing in Johnny's stocked trout pond. For information, call 616-775-3700.

Attend the Viking Color Festival in Cadillac in early October where you're treated to a harvest dinner, pancake breakfast, art show, and parade. For information, call 616-775-9776.

INFORMATION
William Mitchell State Park
6093 East M-115
Cadillac, Michigan 49601
616-775-7911

WILSON STATE PARK
54

LOCATION - The park is located in the city of Harrison across from the Clare County Fairgrounds, and on the old sawmill site of the Wilson Brothers Lumber Company.

ACTIVITIES - Stay in one of the 160 campsites with electrical hookups, or in a rent-a-tent or tipi. Go canoeing, fishing for bass or swimming from a sandy beach in Budd Lake.

During the winter, you can go cross-country skiing or snowmobiling along their trails.

INFORMATION
Wilson State Park
910 North First Street
Harrison, Michigan 48625
517-539-3021

YANKEE SPRINGS STATE PARK
55

LOCATION - The park is 12 miles southwest of Hastings and eight miles east of Middleville.

FEATURES - The park has nine lakes connected by meandering springs and rugged wooded hills, and three miles of lake frontage on Gun Lake which has 93 miles of shoreline. This lake is the largest of some cluster lakes formed when the glaciers receded from the lower peninsula.

ACTIVITIES - Camp in the modern campground on the shore of Gun Lake with 220 campsites, 210 with electrical hookups, and a trailer dump, or in one of the rustic campsites at Deep Lake. Rent one of their 17 cabins, located by Long Lake, and are open year-round. Equestrians can stay in the horsemen's campground located on Duffy Road.

Early season fishing on Gun Lake offers excellent pan fishing for muskies, northern pike and bass. Picnic sites open in mid-April, but the walking trails never close. During the summer, enjoy swimming, water-skiing, sailing and boating. Boat launches are located at either end of the lake.

The park features 15 miles of hiking trails with five marked trails. Explore Devil's Soupbowl, a remnant of glacial "bulldozing," or hike The Pines Trail to get a panoramic view from Mt. Baldy observation point. For another good look-out of the area, go to Graves Hill southwest of Devil's Soupbowl.

Take a ride aboard the Pennasee Paddler, a 75-passenger, authentic stern-wheeler paddleboat that goes around Gun Lake. It leaves daily from Bay Pointe Restaurant and Yankee Springs State Park. For private party reservations, call 616-629-5655, for scheduled tours.

There are several golf courses nearby, and visitors can enjoy horseback riding as well. A chamber music festival presents Sunday evening concerts from July through August.

Winter also brings its own brand of fun activities to the area. Cross-country skiers and snowshoers can explore the trails that end at an alpine-style lodge. Many fishermen test their ice fishing abilities at landing bluegill and pike.

The annual Gun Lake Winter Festival, held the last weekend in January, has three days of racing, ice skating, snow sculptures and even polar bear dips in the frozen lake.

Located two miles north of the Yankee Springs entrance is historic Bowens Mills, a restored grist and cider mill. Built in 1864, it has ground flour and made cider for nearly 80 years. Now that it's been restored, its main floor museum is open Saturdays during 12–5 p.m. from Memorial Day through October. The mill's lower level houses a working water-powered machine shop and a blacksmith shop. Watch weaving, spinning, and the making of soap and baskets.

Also on this site is the 1860s Victorian Bowen House, a pioneer 1830s plant house, a covered bridge, and a beam barn housing a team of Belgium horses.

Festivals are held once a month during the summer featuring such activities as the Old Time Lace Makers' Convention, a Great Lakes Timber Show with log rolling, hatchet throwing and cross-cut sawing by championship showmen, and historical re-enactments. During the fall, various water-powered cider-making events are held. For information, call 616-795-7530.

The Charlton Park Village and Museum is at 2545 S. Charlton Road in Hastings. Here you'll see a 16-structure living historical village depicting life in a Midwestern rural village from 1850–1900. The village opens Memorial Day and is closed Monday–Wednesday. For information, call 616-945-3775.

Car buffs can tour the Gilmore Classic Car Club Museum located at Michigan 43 and Hickory Road north of Gull Lake. Here you'll find one of the most complete automotive collections in the U.S. with over 80 antique cars. You can also see a horse-drawn fire engine, narrow gauge steam locomotive, an English paddlewheel steamboat, and a replica of the Wright Brothers' "Kitty Hawk." For information, call 616-671-5089.

INFORMATION
Yankee Springs State Park
2104 Gun Lake Road
Route 3
Middleville, Michigan 49333
616-795-9081

The mighty Mississippi River begins its journey through America's heartland in the "Land of 10,000 Lakes." Minnesota has 64 state parks with over 780 miles of hiking trails.

MINNESOTA DEPARTMENT OF NATURAL RESOURCES

MINNESOTA

The Indians called this area "minisota," land of sky-tinted waters. The state boasts over 25,000 miles of rivers and streams, and almost 600 miles of state or national wild and scenic rivers. The state has 11,842 lakes measuring ten acres or larger, and 10,000 wetlands. Over 80% of the lakes are located in the northern two-thirds of the state.

Minnesota has 64 state parks with over 780 miles of hiking trails. Surfaced bike trails are provided in 12 of the parks, with St. Croix and Itasca offering rental bikes. Also, thirty-three of the parks offer swimming.

Because of all the water in the state, boating and fishing are very popular activities. Commercial boat tours are available at Itasca, Interstate and Lake Bemidji state parks. For some beautiful canoeing, go to the Minnesota Boundary Waters Canoe Area Wilderness in the northern part of the state. These lakes are open for paddling only, boats with motors are not permitted. For information, contact the Minnesota Travel Information Center at 1-800-657-3700.

Campers will find over 4,000 campsites throughout the parks, ranging from secluded canoe campsites to those set up for RVs. Reservations are accepted by calling 1-800-765-CAMP.

The Superior Hiking Trail provides an opportunity to explore the North Shore. From it you can walk in to places such as the Gooseberry River, the canyons of the Split Rock River, the Tettegouche Lakes, and the Cascade River gorge. When completed, the 250-mile-long trail will link Duluth to the Canadian Border. Until then, day hikers and backpackers can access the trail from several of the state parks. For information on the trail, contact The Superior Hiking Trail Association, P.O. Box 2175, Tofte, Minnesota 55615, 218-226-3539.

For a different kind of exploration, why not hike lodge-to-lodge along the Superior Trail? Several resorts, motels, and bed and breakfasts offer packages along a 30-mile-long stretch of the trail. For information and advance reservations, call 218-663-7804.

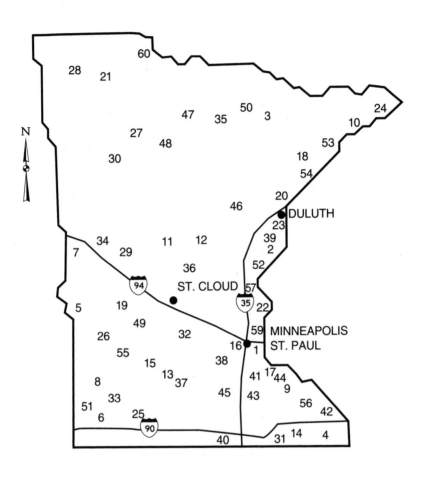

N

60
28 21
47 35 50 3
27 48 53 24
30 18 10
54
46 20
DULUTH
23
34 11 12 39
7 29 2
36 52
94 ST. CLOUD 57
5 19 35 22
49 59 MINNEAPOLIS
26 32 16 ST. PAUL
55 1
15 38
8 13 41 17 44
37 9
33 45 43
51 25 56 42
6 90 31 14 4
40

Join the Minnesota Hiking Club, a group organized to encourage walking designated trails in 62 state parks. The trails range in length from three to six miles, and hikers can earn patches for 25, 50, 75 and 100 miles hiked.

Because of the many lakes and wetlands, insect repellent will make your outings more enjoyable, since the mosquitoes are often quite thick. Hikers also need to be on the lookout for ticks, both wood ticks and deer ticks. The wood ticks are slightly larger, and usually disappear by mid-summer. Deer ticks remain active from April through October, and may carry Lyme disease. Be sure to check yourself and your hiking companions for these tiny ticks whenever you've been out hiking. Fortunately, the disease is treatable with antibiotics.

You can also join Club Fish, established to encourage visitors to fish the various lakes, rivers and streams in the parks for 30 species of fish.

Come to the North Shore during the fall to make your "colored leaf" tour. The area has two distinct color seasons: one in September when the inland maples turn, and the "second fall" in late September and October when the hardwoods along the shoreline change color.

The North Shore Hiking Trail winds through the forests between Duluth and Grand Marais, and has many accesses off Minnesota 61. Access is also available from the George H. Crosby-Manitou and Gooseberry Falls state parks.

AFTON STATE PARK
1

LOCATION - It's eleven miles north of Hastings. From St. Paul, drive eight miles east on I-94.

FEATURES - The park lies on the bluffs overlooking the St. Croix River and is cut by deep ravines dropping 300 feet down to the river.

ACTIVITIES - The park's campground, swimming beach and park's interior are only accessible by trail. You get some beautiful overlooks of the St. Croix River from 18 miles of trails also skied by cross-country skiers during the winter. Equestrians have access to five miles of trails, and bicyclists can cycle along four miles of trails.

The park doesn't have an established campground, but features 24 backpacking campsites and one canoe campsite. Go swimming and fishing in the river.

INFORMATION
Afton State Park
6959 Peller Avenue South
Hastings, Minnesota 55033
612-436-5391

BANNING STATE PARK
2

LOCATION - The park is four miles north of Sandstone on the Kettle River. The park's entrance is off I-35 and Minnesota 23.

FEATURES - The park is named for the ghost town that once occupied the site. Its land is next to a ten-mile-long stretch of the Kettle River, designated as a state wild and scenic river. Water sources within the park include the Kettle River, Wolf Creek, Log Creek, six streams, and three springs.

The Banning Rapids has five segments: Blueberry Slide, Mother's Delight, Dragon's Tooth, Little Banning, and Hell's Gate.

ACTIVITIES - Tour the historic ruins of the Banning Sandstone Quarry. Experienced canoers and kayakers enjoy going down the Hell's Gate Rapids on the Kettle River.

Visit Wolf Creek Falls, Log Creek Arches, Bat Cave and Robinson's Ice Cave.

Attend interpretive programs presented at the visitor center, open seasonally.

Hike along 17 miles of trails, or horseback ride along four miles. The Willard Munger Trail, a 36-mile-long surfaced trail, is nearby, where visitors can go bicycling, horseback riding and snowmobiling.

Go pike fishing or boating from three small boat landings on the Kettle River. No motors are permitted. Watch for the weathered concrete ruins from the former Banning town site and sandstone quarries.

The campground has 34 sites with 11 offering electrical hookups. Canoeists have four sites.

Go cross-country skiing along 11 miles of trails, or snowmobiling along five miles.

INFORMATION
Banning State Park
Box 643
Sandstone, Minnesota 55072
612-245-2668

BEAR HEAD LAKE STATE PARK
3

LOCATION - The park is on the edge of the Boundary Waters Canoe Area, 16 miles east of Tower. It's also 19 miles west of Ely off Minnesota 169.

FEATURES - Bear Head Lake features ten clear-water lakes. Four are stocked with walleye and trout. Eagle's Nest and Bear Head lakes have boat accesses. Rugged trails and portages provide access to the other lakes. The park also has six remote lake campsites, and two boat-in sites on Bear Head Lake.

ACTIVITIES - Hike along 17 miles of hiking trails, some following the old routes used by the narrow gauge railroad built to remove white and red pine.

Go fishing in Bear Head Lake or in the stream, and boating with both boats and canoes available for rent. The park has speed limit restrictions, and water-skiing is prohibited. Go swimming in one of the lakes, guarded during the summer months.

The campground has 73 modern campsites, five backpacking sites, and six remote canoe sites.

During the winter, cross-country ski along six miles of trails.

In Moorhead, visit the Heritage Hjemkomst Interpretive Center to see the replica of a Viking ship. In mid-July, attend the Strawberry Festival.

INFORMATION
Bear Head Lake State Park
9301 Bear Head State Park Road
Ely, Minnesota 55731
218-365-4253

BEAVER CREEK VALLEY STATE PARK
4

LOCATION - The park is five miles west of Caledonia off Minnesota 76 on Minnesota County Road 1.

FEATURES - The park is located in the "driftless area" of the state that was left untouched by the most recent glacial advances; however, as the glaciers melted, high volumes of melt water rushed through here, carving deep valleys and canyon walls rising as high as 250 feet above Beaver Creek.

Fresh water springs are commonly found beside the valley walls near the park, with one on East Beaver Creek near the campground.

ACTIVITIES - A great time to visit the park is in the spring when the wild-flowers are in bloom. Tour the visitor center that is open seasonally.

Hike along eight miles of trails. One of the trails goes along Beaver Creek through the wooded valley, while others lead up wooded slopes to blufftop views.

The campground has 42 campsites with 16 offering year-round electrical hookups and a trailer dump station. You can also backpack to six sites.

Go fishing in Beaver Creek, one of the best trout river streams in southeastern Minnesota.

During the winter, go cross-country skiing along four miles of trails. A warming house is open then.

Visit nearby historic Schrech's Mill, a two-story grist mill located in the northern part of the park. It's privately owned, but is open for tours. The mill is the only water-powered mill known to have its original, operational millstones.

INFORMATION
Beaver Creek Valley State Park
Route 2, Box 57
Caledonia, Minnesota 55921
507-724-2107

BIG STONE LAKE STATE PARK
5

LOCATION - The park is 17 miles northwest of Ortonville on Minnesota 7.

FEATURES - The area around Big Stone Lake has many granite quarries with some of the county's oldest rock formations. The top three inches of rock contain the fossil remains of sharks' teeth.

Giant bison bones have been found here along with evidence of "Brown's Valley Mans" presence. Traces of the early Vikings have also been found including runic writings on stones, mooring stones and metal spears.

Big Stone Lake, located on the Minnesota/South Dakota border, has 70 miles of shoreline, making it the state's tenth largest lake.

ACTIVITIES - Hike 1.5 miles of trails. Go swimming and boating in the lake. During the winter, snowmobilers can explore 3.5 miles of trails.

The campground has 52 sites with 10 offering electrical hookups. Tour the visitor center to learn more about the area's history. Enjoy excellent walleye fishing in the lake, a source of the Minnesota River.

During the fall, take a drive along the lake shore traveling through the apple orchards north of Ortonville.

Visit the Big Stone National Wildlife Refuge located two miles southeast of Ortonville. It offers hiking, and cross-country skiing and snowshoeing during the winter. Breeding colonies of western grebes, known for their courtship dances, are found in the refuge. To find out the best times for observing them, call 612-839-3284.

Arriving pilots can land in Ortonville on the 3,500-foot lighted hard-surface runway. Rental cars are available.

INFORMATION
Big Stone Lake State Park
Route 1, Box 153
Ortonville, Minnesota 56278
612-839-3663

BLUE MOUNDS STATE PARK
6

LOCATION - The park is five miles north of Luverne on U.S. 75, and 16 miles south of Pipestone.

FEATURES - The park is one of the largest prairie parks in Minnesota. Use caution around the bison in the park since they are wild animals and are quite unpredictable.

Most of the prairie is located on top of a massive outcrop of rock called Sioux Quartzite that terminates in a spectacular cliff 1.5 miles long, and at some places, is 90 feet high. As the early settlers passed this large outcrop, it had a bluish cast, causing them to call it The Blue Mound. If you get closer to the rock, you'll see glacial striations, scratches that have been gouged into the rock as loose rocks were dragged across the bedrock by the glacier.

At the south end of the park is a 1,250-foot-long line of rocks going east-west. No one knows who built it or why, but on the first day of spring, and again in the fall, sunrise and sunset line up along this stone alignment.

ACTIVITIES - Stop by the visitor center to learn about the history and geology of the park. Attend interpretive programs.

Walk along the Sioux Quartzite cliff. Hike along 13 miles of trails. During the summer, you'll see Big Bluestem grasses which can reach seven feet.

Go swimming, bass fishing, canoeing and boating in Lower Mound Lake. No motor boats or water-skiing is permitted.

The campground has 73 campsites with 40 offering electrical hookups year-round. During the winter, snowmobilers explore seven miles of trails.

In nearby Luverne, you can attend the Annual Tri-State Band Festival held the last Saturday in September. It features a parade and field competition for high schools from the surrounding states. Competition begins at 10:00 a.m. on Main Street.

The first weekend in June, attend Luverne's Buffalo Days, featuring a parade, auto show, horseshoe pitching contests, and a buffalo chip throwing contest.

Hard core triathletes can compete in a four-day event that combines bicycle riding, running and canoeing the entire length of Minnesota. For information, call 507-283-4061.

East of the park is Jeffers Petroglyphs, a state historic site that preserves a mural of ancient rock art.

Incoming pilots can land at Luverne Municipal Airport located two miles south of town. Rental cars are available.

INFORMATION

Blue Mounds State Park
Route 1
Luverne, Minnesota 56156

507-283-4892
507-283-4548 (visitor center)

BUFFALO RIVER STATE PARK
7

LOCATION - The park is thirteen miles east of Moorhead off U.S. 10.

FEATURES - The park is next to the Nature Conservancy's Bluestem Prairie Scientific and Natural Area. The park and preserve provide one of the most complete prairie landscapes in Minnesota.

ACTIVITIES - The park offers 12 miles of hiking trails including a hike along a glacial beach ridge. If you hike the nature trail, bring along some binoculars to watch for swallows nesting in the cliff. Each spring, watch prairie chickens dance their primitive ritual dancing.

Visitors can watch seasonal programs, and go pike fishing and swimming in the Buffalo River. Camp in one of the 44 campsites, eight with electrical hookups, and a trailer dump station.

During the winter, come to cross-country ski along eight miles of trails.

INFORMATION
Buffalo River State Park
Route 2, Box 256
Glyndon, Minnesota 56547
218-498-2124

CAMDEN STATE PARK
8

LOCATION - It's ten miles southwest of Marshall on Minnesota 23. It's also seven miles northwest of Montevideo on U.S. 59 and Minnesota 7, then four miles west on Minnesota 13.

FEATURES - Camden is located on top of the Altamont moraine, the second highest and easternmost moraine in the county.

ACTIVITIES - Fish in the Redwood River for stocked German brown trout, or for bass and bluegill in Brawner Lake. Go hiking on 15 miles of trails. Bicyclists can cycle along four miles of bike trails.

The visitor center is open seasonally, and offers interpretive programs and nature hikes from Memorial Day to Labor Day.

Enjoy swimming from the beach in the spring-fed pool guarded daily from Memorial Day weekend to Labor Day.

The lower campground has 37 campsites, nine with electrical hookups. The upper campground has 56 sites, 20 with electrical hookups. Equestrians have their own primitive campground plus 10 miles of trails to explore.

The third Sunday in August, attend the annual wildlife art exhibit where artists from the surrounding tri-state area display their works.

Cross-country ski along 3.5 miles of trails, or go snowmobiling along 10 miles of trails. A warming house is open during the winter.

Russell, four miles south of Camden, sponsors "Dairy Days" the second weekend in June. Lynd, four miles north of Camden, features "Prairie Days" the last Saturday in June.

INFORMATION
Camden State Park
Route 1, Box 9
Lynd, Minnesota 56157
507-865-4530

CARLEY STATE PARK
9

LOCATION - The park is four miles south of Plainview on Minnesota 4, and 10 miles northwest of Whitewater State Park.

ACTIVITIES - Come in the spring to see the woods full of Virginia bluebells. Hike five miles of forest trails along the North Branch of the Whitewater River. Attend interpretive programs that are offered seasonally.

Fish in the north branch of the Whitewater River designated a brown trout stream.

Stay in the campground with 20 campsites.

During the winter, go cross-country skiing along six miles of trails, or sledding down the hill near the picnic area.

INFORMATION
Carley State Park
Route 1, Box 256
Altura, Minnesota 55910
507-534-3400 or 507-932-3007

CASCADE RIVER STATE PARK
10

LOCATION - The park is ten miles southwest of Grand Marais off U.S. 61, or you can follow U.S. 61 northeast out of Tofte for 18 miles.

FEATURES - The park borders Lake Superior for six miles, and features the Cascade River, numerous small streams, spectacular waterfalls, and the Sawtooth Mountain range. The park was named for the stair-step cascades along the Cascade River. A footbridge provides a great look at them.

ACTIVITIES - The park has 18 miles of hiking trails. Hike up the forested hills to get scenic overlooks of Lake Superior. Walk along the shore of Lake

Superior, or follow the Cascade River. The Superior Hiking Trail passes through the park. Hike to the summit of Lookout Mountain for a great overlook of the surrounding lake, mountains and valley.

Go fishing for lake trout in Lake Superior, or at the mouth of the Cascade River. During the spring, steelhead run up the river, and salmon run in the fall. Rainbow and brook trout are found in the upper portions of the river.

The campground has 40 campsites, five backpacking sites, and a trailer dump station.

During the winter, cross-country ski or snowmobile along 17 miles of groomed trails that are linked with the North Shore Mountains Ski Trail System extending from Duluth to Grand Marais. A warming house is available.

INFORMATION
Cascade River State Park
HCR 3 Box 450
Lutsen, Minnesota 55612
218-387-1543

CHARLES A. LINDBERGH STATE PARK
11

LOCATION - The park is .5-mile southwest of Little Falls on Minnesota 27 and then one mile south on Lindbergh Drive.

FEATURES - Across the street from the park, on the banks of the Mississippi River, is the boyhood home of Charles A. Lindbergh, Jr., renowned for his trans-Atlantic solo flight in 1927. The house was built by his father in 1906.

ACTIVITIES - Hike six miles of scenic trails. Tour the Lindbergh home, the Weyerhauser Memorial Museum and prairie gardens, and stop by the visitor center to learn about three generations of the famous family. It's open daily May 1–Labor Day, and weekends after Labor Day. For information, call 612-632-3154.

Go pike, walleye, bass and muskie fishing or enjoy canoeing and boating from the ramp in the Mississippi River or on Pike Creek.

The campground has 38 campsites with 15 offering electrical hookups. Canoeists have a couple of campsites available.

Cross-country ski along 5.5 miles of trails with a warming house. The area around Little Falls has many miles of groomed snowmobile trails.

Play golf in Little Falls on the 18-hole course. In September, attend an arts and crafts fair, or the antique auto show and swap meet. For information, call 612-632-9441 or 632-3154.

To see memorabilia from military history in the state, tour the Minnesota Military Museum located at Camp Ripley. It's the nation's largest year-round

National Guard camp, seven miles north of Little Falls. For information, call 612-632-6631, extension 374.

Incoming pilots can land at Little Falls-Morrison County Airport located two miles south of town. Taxi transportation is available.

INFORMATION

Charles A. Lindbergh State Park
P.O. Box 364
Little Falls, Minnesota 56345
612-632-9050

Lindbergh House
Route 3, Box 245
Little Falls, Minnesota 56345
612-632-3154

FATHER HENNEPIN STATE PARK
12

LOCATION - The park is at the western city limit of Isle off Minnesota 27 on the shore of Mille Lacs Lake, the second largest fresh water lake in the state.

FEATURES - The park commemorates Father Hennepin's capture by Indians in 1860.

ACTIVITIES - Boating access is located on the northeastern shore of the lake. Hike four miles of trails along the lake shore or through the woods.

Enjoy fishing for pike, walleye, bluegill and bass in Mille Lacs Lake. Go swimming from the sand beach with a lifeguard on duty. Camp in the campground with 103 campsites with 30 electrical hookups, open year-round.

Cross-country ski along 3.5 miles of trails or snowmobile on 1.5 miles.

INFORMATION

Father Hennepin State Park
Box 397
Isle, Minnesota 56342
612-676-8763

FLANDRAU STATE PARK
13

LOCATION - The park is south of New Ulm off Minnesota 15.

ACTIVITIES - Hikers have access to eight miles of trails with a variety of terrain to explore including wooded river bottoms, oxbow marshes and prairie land. Naturalists offer guided hikes.

During the summer, go swimming in the sandy-bottom swimming pool. Go bass fishing or boating on the Cottonwood River.

The campground has 90 campsites with 35 offering year-round electrical hookups.

Cross-country skiers enjoy eight miles of trails and a warming house.

If you're in town the third week in July, attend Heritagefest, a four-day event featuring German entertainers who present musical concerts and dancing. The weekend before Ash Wednesday, attend Fasching with its masquerade ball, bonfire and parade.

The town has a glockenspiel in Schonlau Park Plaza. Its bells announce the hour, and figurines appear at noon, 3:00 and 5:00 p.m.

Incoming pilots can land at New Ulm Municipal Airport, two miles west of New Ulm. Rental cars are available.

INFORMATION
Flandrau State Park
1300 Summit Ave.
New Ulm, Minnesota 56073
507-354-3519

FORESTVILLE STATE PARK AND MYSTERY CAVE
14

LOCATION - The entrance to the park is four miles south of Preston off U.S. 16 on Fillmore County Highway 5, and then two miles east on Fillmore County 12.

The park is also five miles south of Wykoff on Minnesota 5, then two miles east on Minnesota 12.

FEATURES - The woods and trout streams surround a Civil War era town site containing the historic Meighen Store Museum.

The area contains many springs, underground rivers, caves and sinkholes as a result of the weak acids in the rain water and decaying vegetation dissolving the underlying limestone. Both Canfield and Forestville creeks enter the Root River in the park after emerging from caves several miles upstream.

During the 1800s, the town of Forestville was developed in the park's area, but gradually declined in population following the changing of stagecoach routes, and the railroad bypassing the town. Only the store and a brick house built in 1867 remain. The sites of the other buildings have been marked, and are within walking distance.

ACTIVITIES - If you're here in the spring, you can hear the ruffled grouse and wild turkey. During the fall, the hardwood trees provide a spectacular color display.

Tour the historic pioneer town site and historic pioneer cemetery. Browse through the Meighen store where you'll see items left behind by its owner when he closed the store in 1910. The visitor center is open seasonally, and interpretive programs are presented.

Explore 16 miles of hiking trails, or go horseback riding along 14 miles of trails. Fish for trout in three spring-fed streams.

The campground has 73 campsites, with 23 offering electrical hookups, and a trailer dump station. Equestrians have their own campground that accommodates 80 units.

Go cross-country skiing along 6.5 miles of trails, or snowmobiling along nine miles of trails. A warming house is open.

Mystery Cave, ten miles from the park, has 12 miles of underground passages to explore. It's open Memorial Day–Labor Day weekend. For information, call 507-937-3251.

INFORMATION
Forestville State Park and Mystery Cave
Route 2, Box 128
Preston, Minnesota 55965
507-352-5111

FORT RIDGELY STATE PARK
15

LOCATION - The park is six miles south of Fairfax on Minnesota 4, and then west on Minnesota 29/30. It's also 10 miles north of Sleepy Eye on Minnesota 4.

FEATURES - The park was named for the military post that occupied the site in the 1850s and 1860s. It was built to provide protection for the newly settled lands of southern and central Minnesota, and played a prominent role in the Dakota conflict of 1862.

ACTIVITIES - Tour the historic fort where the commissary and many of the original foundations have been restored. Examine exhibits on life in a military post from 1853 to 1867.

The last weekend in June, the park hosts the Fort Ridgely Historical Festival featuring an 1840s Fur Trader's Rendezvous, live musical entertainment, and educational history programs.

Play golf on the nine-hole course. Rental clubs are available at the park office.

Tour the visitor center, open seasonally, and attend their interpretive programs.

Hike 11 miles of trails which wind through wooded ravines and across open prairie meadows, or ride horseback along seven miles of trails.

The campground has 22 modern campsites with eight providing electrical hookups, and also has 17 more rustic campsites. Backpackers have access to four sites. Equestrians also have their own campsite.

Cross-country skiers have four miles of trails, while snowmobilers have access to seven miles. A warming house is open.

In nearby Sleepy Eye, attend a band concert and then a street dance on July 3, a buffalo burger feed and fireworks on July 4th, Buttered Corn Day on the fourth Thursday in August, the Great Grassroots Gathering the fourth Sunday in September, and Michaelmas the end of September.

In New Ulm, go to see the Glockenspiel, a musical clock tower with animated figures depicting the history of the community. A Heritagefest is held the third weekend in July, and the Minnesota Festival of Music is held the last weekend of April. Bus tours to several major historic sites are available with step-on guides. For information, call 507-354-4217.

Redwood Falls' Ramsey Park is the state's largest municipal park, and is often called "The Little Yellowstone of Minnesota." It has 217 acres of hiking trails, camping, a zoo, and is adjacent to a challenging nine-hole golf course.

During the second weekend in June, the town hosts the nation's oldest and most successful inventors' fair, the Minnesota Inventors' Congress. For information, call 507-637-2828.

To learn more about the Dakota Indians, visit the Lower Sioux Agency's interpretive center. It's located on Redwood County 2, nine miles east of Redwood Falls and four miles southwest of Morton. Admission is free, and is open from 10–5 daily May 1–Labor Day, and from 1–5 the rest of the year. The second weekend in June, the community hosts a powwow. For information, call 507-697-6185.

INFORMATION
Fort Ridgely State Park
Route 1, Box 65
Fairfax, Minnesota 55332
507-426-7840

FORT SNELLING STATE PARK
16

LOCATION - The park is located at the junction of the Minnesota and Mississippi rivers in St. Paul. The park entrance is on Post Road off Minnesota 5 in the heart of the Minneapolis/St. Paul metro area.

ACTIVITIES - Hike out to Pike Island where the Mississippi and Minnesota rivers converge, and visit the Pike Island Interpretive Center, open year-round.

The park has 18 miles of trails, and five miles of bicycle trails. It also has a 12-kilometer volksmarch course where you can earn credit towards the state park volksmarch incentive award. The sponsored walk is held the end of April, and again in early October.

Hike up to Fort Snelling on the bluff overlooking the river valley. The fort is separate from the park, and is near the intersection of Minnesota 5 and Minnesota 55 via the Fort Snelling Exit.

The fort has been restored, and has 17 buildings that include the commandant's house, hospital, barracks, and sutler's store. Observe costumed guides as they perform a cannon and musket drill, blacksmithing and baking. For information, call 612-726-1171.

An annual American Indian Movement Powwow is held over the Labor Day weekend.

Go swimming from the beach, boating, canoeing and fishing in either the lake or in the river. Canoe and paddle boat rentals are available in the park. Drive-in access to the water is on Picnic Island and at Cedar Avenue. Canoe carry-in access is on Snelling Lake and behind the park's office.

The park also has a golf course and polo grounds.

During the winter, go cross-country skiing along 18 miles of trails with a warming house open.

Incoming pilots can land at St. Paul Downtown Holman Field located one mile south of town. Rental cars are available.

INFORMATION
Fort Snelling State Park
Highway 5 and Post Road
St. Paul, Minnesota 55111
612-725-2390

FRONTENAC STATE PARK
17

LOCATION - The park is ten miles southeast of Red Wing on U.S. 61, on the north end of Lake Pepin.

FEATURES - Bird watchers can see many birds who migrate through the park along the Mississippi Flyway. Bald eagles are often spotted year-round.

At one time, the park area was a fur-trading post, and has Indian burial grounds.

ACTIVITIES - Hike along the wooded slopes to get some wonderful views of Lake Pepin. The park features 16 miles of hiking trails. Frontenac is part of the worldwide volksmarch program, and you can receive credit and a medal for walking their 11-kilometer trail. Sponsored walks go on weekends and holidays from mid-May through mid-October.

Take a boat excursion, go swimming, fishing, and boating on the lake.

The campground has 58 campsites, with 19 offering electrical hookups and a trailer dump station. You can also hike into six walk-in campsites. Some groceries are available.

During the winter, cross-country ski along 6.1 miles of trails, or go snowmobiling along eight miles. A warming house is open.

In Lake City, attend Lake City Water Ski Days held the end of June. Johnny Appleseed Days are held the first part of October.

INFORMATION
Frontenac State Park
Route 2, Box 134
Lake City, Minnesota 55041
612-345-3401

GEORGE H. CROSBY MANITOU STATE PARK
18

LOCATION - The park is located on Minnesota's North Shore, eight miles northeast of Finland.

FEATURES - The Manitou River passes through a gorge en route to Lake Superior, and offers some rugged hiking and backpacking opportunities.

ACTIVITIES - Only backpacking campsites are available along the cascading Manitou River and beside Benson Lake. If you decide to backpack in to one of the 21 backpacking sites, but don't have your own equipment, rent some from one of the outfitters located in the Twin Cities.

The park has 23 miles of hiking trails. The trails range from an easy walk around Lake Benson to the more difficult Humpback Trail. The River Trail follows the Manitou River as it drops 600 feet.

As you hike or backpack, be on the lookout for moose. If you spot one, use caution since they can be dangerous. Black bears also inhabit the park, so be sure to keep a clean campsite.

Bring along your fishing gear and see if you can land a brook or rainbow trout. You can also go boating, but no motors or water-skiing is permitted.

During the winter, cross-country ski along 11 miles of trails, and all trails may be snowshoed.

The park doesn't have any campgrounds, but several are within 20 miles.

Incoming pilots can land at Sky Harbor Airport located six miles southeast of Duluth. Rental cars are available.

INFORMATION
George H. Crosby Manitou State Park
c/o Tettegouche State Park
474 Highway 61 E
Silver Bay, Minnesota 55614
218-226-3539

GLACIAL LAKES STATE PARK
19

LOCATION - Go two miles south of Starbuck on Minnesota 29 and then two more miles south on Minnesota 41.

FEATURES - The park preserves a remnant of the native prairie land, with bluestem grasses, prairie clover, goldenrod and other prairie flowers. Several spring-fed lakes are located here, formed by the last retreating glacier. The park is located at the base of the 220-mile-long Glacial Ridge.

Some of the higher conical-shaped hills, called kames, contain glacial till up to 400 feet thick—some of the deeper glacial deposits found in the state. Between the hills are many potholes, or kettles, depressions left behind when glacial ice blocks melted.

Across from the park office is an esker, a worm-like ridge formed by a river that flowed under the glacier.

Several lakes, ponds and marshes are in the park, with Mountain Lake being the largest.

ACTIVITIES - The gravel campground has 41 campsites, 14 with electrical hookups, an equestrian campground, and two backpacking sites.

Hikers can explore 14 miles of trails including a .6-mile-long self-guided trail. Some of the trails wind past the various glacial formations, prairie potholes, marshes, woodlands and creeks, and others provide panoramic views from the top of the glacial ridge.

Glacial Lakes has nine miles of horseback riding trails. Drive-in access areas and primitive camping areas are available for visitors who bring their own horses.

Enjoy fishing for bass, pike, bluegill, crappie and perch in Mountain Lake. Go swimming from the small beach.

Enjoy boating on the lake where rowboat and canoe rentals are available. Only electric motors may be used.

Interpretive programs are offered occasionally by the park naturalists.

During the winter, cross-country ski on six miles of trails, or snowmobile on 9.5 miles.

INFORMATION
Glacial Lakes State Park
Route 2, Box 126
Starbuck, Minnesota 56381
612-239-2860

GOOSEBERRY FALLS STATE PARK
20

LOCATION - Follow U.S. 61 northeast from Two Harbors for 12 miles. The park is located on the north shore of Lake Superior.

FEATURES - The Gooseberry River cascades through the park in a series of five spectacular waterfalls and scenic overlooks.

Many of the buildings and the massive stone retaining wall built along the wayside of Minnesota 61 are evidence of the work of the Civilian Conservation

Corps established by President Franklin D. Roosevelt in 1933. Because of their work, the park is on the National Register of Historic Places.

ACTIVITIES - Tour the visitor center open daily from mid-May to mid-October. Watch their slide show, "Moods of the North Shore."

Try your skill at trout fishing in either the river or in Lake Superior.

Hike 18 miles of trails. Five of the trails wind along the Gooseberry River, providing great views of Lake Superior, as well as providing access to the Superior Hiking Trail. Favorites of visitors include the Upper and Lower Falls on the Gooseberry River, the Fifth Falls of the Gooseberry River, the Superior Ridgeline Hiking Trail, the Gitchi Gummi Trail, and hiking along the cliffs above Lake Superior. The sponsored volksmarch is held in mid-June along their 10-kilometer trail.

The campground has 70 semi-modern campsites, and a trailer dump station.

During the winter, cross-country ski along 15 miles of trails, or snowmobile on nine miles of trails. Snowmobilers also have access to the North Shore State Trail that opens up hundreds of miles of groomed trails from Duluth to Grand Marais.

In Two Rivers, you can watch giant ore carriers being loaded and maneuvered in and out of port from Paul Van Hoven Park on the waterfront.

Split Rock Lighthouse State Park is 18 miles northeast of Two Harbors via U.S. 61. Hike the nature trails.

Tour the interpretive center, and watch a video telling the history of the lighthouse, open mid-May–mid-October. For information, call 218-226-4372. Camp in the cart-in campground on Lake Superior. Carts are provided.

Incoming pilots can land at Two Harbors Municipal Airport located three miles northwest of Two Harbors. Rental cars are available.

INFORMATION
Gooseberry Falls State Park
1300 East Highway 61
Two Harbors, Minnesota 55616
218-834-3855 or 834-3787

HAYES LAKE STATE PARK
21

LOCATION - Go south from Roseau for 15 miles on Minnesota 89 and then nine miles east on Minnesota 4. The park is located on the edge of Hayes Lake.

ACTIVITIES - Attend seasonal interpretive programs, hike along 12 miles of trails, and go horseback riding on three miles of trails. As you walk the trails, watch for some beautiful orchids, particularly the lady-slipper, the state flower. To identify these beautiful flowers, pick up their brochure on "Orchids and Gentians."

Birders can pick up their bird checklist to see how many you can spot out of the more than 200 that have been spotted in the park.

Go fishing in the river for northern pike, crappie, bluegill and bass.

Swim or boat on the lake, but boats are restricted to electric motors.

The campground has 35 semi-modern sites, an equestrian campground, and two backpacking sites.

During the winter, cross-country ski or snowmobile on six miles of trails.

The park is located on the west side of the Beltrami Island State Forest, the second largest of the state's 56 state forests. The Beltrami Island Snowmobile Trail has 86 miles of marked and groomed trails. This trail connects with the Baudette/Norris Snowmobile Trail that adds an additional 52.5 miles of groomed trails to explore. The Baudette/Norris Trail may be accessed three miles south of Baudette. Since the forest has 250 miles of forest roads and logging trails, hiking opportunities are numerous.

INFORMATION

Hayes Lake State Park
Star Route 4, Box 84
Roseau, Minnesota 56751
218-425-7504

Beltrami Island State Forest
c/o Minnesota Department of Natural
   Resources
Division of Forestry/Trail and
   Waterways Unit
Information Center, Box 40
500 Lafayette Road
St. Paul, Minnesota 55155-4040
612-296-9747

INTERSTATE STATE PARK
22

LOCATION - The park is one mile south of Taylors Falls on Minnesota 8.

FEATURES - The falls were flooded when a dam was constructed in 1902.

ACTIVITIES - Stop by the visitor center to learn about the geological formations left behind by the glaciers. Visit the steep gorge formed by the St. Croix River. Hike three miles of trails. Fish for bass, or canoe down the river. Boat rentals are available, and canoe shuttles may be arranged.

Take an excursion boat tour in a double-deck paddle wheeler down the St. Croix River. For information, call 612-465-6315.

Visit the Dalles of St. Croix on the Minnesota-Wisconsin border. The 200-foot–high lava cliffs have been eroded by the river and form unusual rock formations.

The campground has 37 campsites with 22 offering electrical hookups.

INFORMATION
Interstate State Park
Box 254
Taylors Falls, Minnesota 55084
612-465-2411

JAY COOKE STATE PARK
23

LOCATION - The park is three miles east of Carlton on Minnesota 210.

FEATURES - The St. Louis River runs through a gorge in the park, providing a scenic, and sometimes steep backdrop for your outdoor activities.

The park was named for Jay Cooke, one of America's first great financiers during the mid-nineteenth century. His banking firm was instrumental in financing the Union Army during the Civil War.

ACTIVITIES - Hike along the historic Grand Portage Trail of the St. Louis River, used over 300 years ago. Walk over the swinging bridge erected over the rocky river gorge. This is the fourth one to be constructed over the river, and its 126-foot-long span provides access to trails on the south side of the river.

For a look back at history, visit historic Thomson Pioneer Cemetery.

Tour the visitor center open all year. Seasonal interpretive programs are presented, and snacks are available in the park.

Go trout fishing, ride horseback along 10 miles of trails, or enjoy hiking or mountain biking along 50 miles of forested trails. Part of the paved Willard Munger State Trail, 14 miles long, runs through the park.

The campground has 80 campsites with 21 electrical hookups. Backpackers have access to four sites.

During the winter, cross-country ski along 32 miles of trails, or go snowmobiling along 7.5 miles of trails. The park has a warming house.

INFORMATION
Jay Cooke State Park
500 E. Highway 210
Carlton, Minnesota 55718
218-384-4610

JUDGE C. R. MAGNEY STATE PARK
24

LOCATION - The park is on the Brule River, and its entrance is off U.S. 61, 14 miles northeast of Grand Marais.

FEATURES - The park has some wonderful waterfalls, including the beautiful Devil's Kettle Waterfall on the Brule River. Above Devil's Kettle, a rock jutting into the river divides the water. From here the eastern portion drops 50 feet into a deep gorge and pool, while the western portion plunges into a huge pothole, and according to legend, disappears forever.

ACTIVITIES - Hikers get great vistas of Lake Superior along six miles of trails.

Go salmon fishing in the Brule River or its tributary, Gauthier Creek. The river is stocked annually with trout, and steelhead trout make their spawning run in the spring, while pink salmon run in the fall.

Bird watchers can find many nesting warblers from May–July. Early fall brings the migrating hawks along the shore of Lake Superior.

Visit Devil's Kettle of the Brule River, and view the Upper and Lower Falls.

The campground has 36 rustic, grassy campsites.

During the winter, enjoy cross-country skiing along five miles of trails.

Visit nearby Grand Portage National Monument to tour the fur trading fort and to see the famous Witch Tree. The monument is on the western shore of Lake Superior, and its park entrance is from U.S. 61, 36 miles north of Grand Marais. For a great overlook, hike 300 feet to the summit of Mount Rose.

Rendezvous Days with voyageur contests, and the Ojibwa Powwow is held the second weekend in August.

The Boundary Waters Canoe Area accesses are near the park, and Lake Superior offers deep-sea fishing opportunities.

Incoming pilots can land at Devil's Track Municipal Airport at Grand Marais. Rental cars are available.

INFORMATION
Judge C. R. Magney State Park
Box 500, East Star Route
Grand Marais, Minnesota 55604
218-387-2929 or 226-3539

KILEN WOODS STATE PARK
25

LOCATION - The park is eight miles northeast of Lakefield, five miles east of Minnesota 86 on Jackson County 24. It's also 12 miles northwest of Jackson, and lies along the Des Moines River.

ACTIVITIES - Climb the tower to get a good overview of the surrounding countryside. Tour the visitor center open on a seasonal basis, or attend one of the interpretive programs offered year-round.

The park has five miles of hiking trails, 1.5 miles of cross-country skiing trails, and 3.5 miles of snowmobile trails. Ski rentals are available and a warming house is open.

Go canoeing in the Des Moines River. Canoe rentals are available nearby, and canoeists have their own campsites.

Go fishing in the river for walleye, northern pike, catfish and bullhead.

The campground has 33 campsites with 11 providing electrical hookups. There are also four walk-in sites, and three canoe sites.

Favorite spots to visit include Dinosaur Ridge, Prairie Meadows and Lookout Tower.

INFORMATION
Kilen Woods State Park
Route 1, Box 122
Lakefield, Minnesota 56150
507-662-6258

LAC QUI PARLE STATE PARK
26

LOCATION - The park is five miles northwest of Watson. Access is off U.S. 59 via Chippewa County Road 13. The park is on the southeast end of Lac Qui Parle Lake. It's also 12 miles northwest of Montevideo.

FEATURES - The park is a maple-basswood forest located in a small river valley along Lac Qui Parle Lake and River and the Minnesota River. Lac Qui Parle is French for "lake that talks."

ACTIVITIES - Bird watchers come here in the spring and fall when thousands of geese stop by the lake, and bald eagles are spotted. Flights of whistling swans pass over the area in April, and again in November. Pelicans nest in the area on a one-acre island. The lake is closed to boating in the fall.

Hike, cycle and horseback ride along six miles of trails.

Enjoy swimming in the lake, fishing either in the lake or the river, or boating with boat and canoes available for rent. The lake is primarily used for flood-control, so the lake's levels fluctuate and boating may be hazardous. Be sure to check the water levels and general boating conditions before going out onto the lake.

The campground has 56 campsites with 22 offering electrical hookups, and a trailer dump station. Equestrians also have their own campground that can accommodate 100.

During the winter, go cross-country skiing along five miles of trails, and warm up in the warming house.

INFORMATION
Lac Qui Parle State Park
Route 5, Box 74A
Montevideo, Minnesota 56265
612-752-4736

A paddle wheeler excursion boat chugs along the St. Croix River near Interstate State Park.

MINNESOTA DEPARTMENT OF NATURAL RESOURCES

LAKE BEMIDJI STATE PARK
27

LOCATION - The park is five miles northeast of Bemidji off U.S. 71. The park is located on the northeast shore of Lake Bemidji, 1.7 miles off Minnesota 21 on Minnesota 20.

FEATURES - Bemidji comes from the Chippewa word for "lake with river flowing through."

ACTIVITIES - The park has 14 miles of hiking trails. Walk the Bog Walk along a boardwalk, 1.5 miles long, where you can see orchids, mosses and insect-eating plants. Rocky Point Trail, .8 miles long, offers a scenic view of Lake Bemidji. The 10-kilometer seasonal volksmarch is held in late September, and a volksbike of 25 kilometers goes then too.

Go swimming and fishing for walleye on Lake Bemidji. Tour the visitor center, and attend interpretive programs offered year-round.

The campground has 100 campsites, 43 with electrical hookups, and a dump station.

During the winter, cross-country ski or snowshoe along nine miles of trails, or snowmobile along three miles of trails. A warming house is provided, and snowshoe rentals are available.

Take an excursion boat ride. If you're here July 4th, attend the Paul Bunyan Water Carnival featuring a parade, water show and fireworks.

Stop by the Information Building on Paul Bunyan Drive in Bemidji to see its "Fireplace of States" with stones from all the states and some foreign countries.

Go to the lakefront to see statues of Paul Bunyan and "Babe," his blue ox.

Attend a summer theater performance at the Paul Bunyan Playhouse. The season begins in June, and runs through the middle of August. For information, call the Ruttgers Birchmont Lodge at 218-751-1630.

Incoming pilots can land at Bemidji-Beltrami County Airport located three miles northwest of Bemidji. Rental cars are available.

INFORMATION
Lake Bemidji State Park
3401 State Park Road NE
Bemidji, Minnesota 56601
218-755-3843

LAKE BRONSON STATE PARK
28

LOCATION - The park is two miles east of Lake Bronson off U.S. 59. Access is from Minnesota 28.

FEATURES - The landscape you see in the park is the result of the ancient glacial lake, Lake Agassiz, that was once located in the northwest corner of Minnesota and extended into North Dakota and Canada. Ancient McCauleyville beach, formed as the lake gradually retreated, passes through the park.

ACTIVITIES - The park is open year-round from 8:00 a.m. to 10:00 p.m.

Climb the historic tower to get a good overlook of the area. Keep an eye out for moose, deer, and an occasional black bear as you hike through the park. Check with the park naturalists for current information on wildlife sightings.

Attend seasonal interpretive programs. Hike along 14 miles of trails, and go bicycling along five miles of bike trails. The sponsored volksmarch runs daily from the end of May through the latter part of September.

During the winter, snowmobiles have access to 10 miles of trails, while cross-country skiers ski along six miles of trails. A warming house is open.

Go water-skiing or swimming from the beach in Lake Bronson, or in the South Branch of the Two Rivers. Boat and canoe rentals are available.

Try your luck at fishing for walleye, northern pike, catfish or panfish.

The campground has 194 campsites with 35 electrical sites that are open all year, and a trailer dump station. Snacks are available in the park.

In nearby Karlstad, attend their June festival. Hallock hosts "Back Home Days" the third weekend in June. In Kennedy, runners come in July to participate in the "Troll Stroll." The Kittson County Fair is held the second weekend in July.

When the fall colors arrive, artists display their works at the Kittson County Historical Museum in Lake Bronson.

INFORMATION
Lake Bronson State Park
Box 9
Lake Bronson, Minnesota 56734
218-754-2200

LAKE CARLOS STATE PARK
29

LOCATION - The park is ten miles north of Alexandria on Minnesota 29 and then two miles west on Minnesota 38.

FEATURES - The park is located in a glacial moraine with woodland ponds, wetlands and lakes nestled in the hills.

ACTIVITIES - Go hiking or skiing from the tamarack bog into the maple-basswood forest.

Enjoy fishing in Lake Carlos known for its abundance of walleye, northern pike, bass and crappie.

Tour the visitor center, and attend their seasonal interpretive programs. Hike along 12 miles of trails, or bike on three miles of trails. Equestrians have eight miles of trails and their own campsites.

Go swimming or boating on the lake. Rentals are available nearby. The park has drive-in water access to Lake Carlos, and carry-in water access on Hidden Lake.

The park has two campgrounds with 127 campsites with 68 providing electrical hookups. Lakeside Campground is on the lake while Upper Campground is .25-mile from the lake. The park also has two walk-in sites.

During the winter, cross-country ski along five miles of trails, or snowmobile along nine miles.

In Alexandria, go by the Chamber of Commerce Museum to see the Rune Stone with an inscription dated 1362 telling of exploration of the area by a party of Swedish and Norwegian Vikings. Although some believe the stone is a forgery, others feel it is genuine.

INFORMATION
Lake Carlos State Park
Route 2, Box 240
Carlos, Minnesota 56319
612-852-7200

LAKE ITASCA STATE PARK
30

LOCATION - The park is 21 miles north of Park Rapids on U.S. 71.

FEATURES - Itasca is Latin meaning "true head." The park has over 100 lakes, and features 12,000 acres of aspen, red and white pine, and birch, and is the state's oldest state park. Here, the Mississippi River begins its lengthy journey of 2,552 miles to the Gulf of Mexico.

The bison kill site dates back to around 8,000 years ago when early hunters passed through here following the now extinct bison occidentalis, bison that were much larger than current-day buffalo.

The Itasca Indian Mounds are 500 years old, and were partially excavated in 1890. The Itasca Indian Cemetery and Chambers Creek Village Site contain artifacts left behind by the Woodland people who once lived here.

ACTIVITIES - Spots to visit include Preacher's Grove, a stand of red pine trees over 250 years old. Hike in a short distance from the road to see Minnesota's largest red pine, and its largest white pine, over 350 years old. The trailhead is by Elk Lake off Wilderness Drive.

Photographers should visit Peace Pipe Vista to get a wonderful view of Lake Itasca. It's a favorite spot to watch sunsets from and listen to the loons in the evening.

To learn about the 1900s logging era in the park, stop by the Logging Sled, join a naturalist-led hike to the Sawmill, or follow the self-guided Landmark Trail located along Wilderness Drive.

Stay in historic Douglas Lodge, Forest Inn, Nicollet Court or in one of the housekeeping cabins. Reservations may be made by calling 1-800-765-CAMP. The park recently opened a hostel where you can overnight. For reservations, call 218-266-3415.

Drive along 10-mile-long Wilderness Drive, passing Wilderness Sanctuary, one of Minnesota's seven National Landmarks, located 21 miles north of Park Rapids on U.S. 71. The drive is one way, heading west from the Headwaters, and is narrow and curvy in places. Before leaving on your tour, stop by the Itasca Gift Shop and pick up either their auto tour guide or cassette tape tour.

The park headquarters is open year-round, and at the headquarters and Brower Inn you can rent bicycles, canoes, and boats. Boat rentals are also available at Squaw Lake and Elk Lake through Itasca Landing, and at Mary Lake through the Douglas Lodge. Public boat accesses are located on Itasca, Squaw, Mary and Elk lakes.

Fish in Lake Itasca for pike, bass and crappie. Take a 1.5-hour narrated tour on Lake Itasca. For information, call 218-732-5318 or the park headquarters at 218-266-3654. The boat tours leave from the Douglas Lodge pier twice a day in June, and three times a day the rest of the summer.

Explore 24 hiking trails covering approximately 33 miles, and climb the lookout tower. Bicyclists are treated to 17 miles of bike trails.

The campgrounds have 210 campsites, 100 with electrical hookups. You can also camp in 11 walk-in sites. The campgrounds are open May 1–October 15. You can dine in Brower Inn or in Douglas Lodge's restaurant, open late May–September.

During the winter, cross-country ski or snowmobile along 31 miles of trails. When you get cold, stop by the warming house.

INFORMATION
Itasca State Park
Lake Itasca, Minnesota 56460
218-266-3654 or 266-3656

LAKE LOUISE STATE PARK
31

LOCATION - The park is 29 miles southeast of Austin, or 1.5 miles north of Le Roy on Minnesota 14.

FEATURES - The park has two spring-fed streams that join to form the Iowa River. A grist mill was located here during the late 1800s. The mill pond was named after a member of the Hambrecht family who owned the land beside the pond.

ACTIVITIES - Stroll along the shoreline of Lake Louise, or along the Little Iowa and Upper Iowa rivers. Go swimming, fishing in the lake or stream, boating and canoeing. Motorboats are prohibited.

Tour the Hambrecht Historical Cottage and Museum that is open weekends and holidays from 1:00–4:30 during the summer. The visitor center operates on a seasonal basis.

Hike along 12 miles of trails, or go horseback riding along 10 miles of trails. Go cross-country skiing during the winter.

The campground has 22 campsites with 11 offering electrical hookups, and a trailer dump station. Equestrians have their own campground with six campsites.

Attend Old Wildwood Days celebrated on the first Sunday in June, when you can participate in an old-fashioned ice cream social, and musical and play performances. The Hambrecht Beef Feed is held in September.

INFORMATION
Lake Louise State Park
Route 1, Box 184
Le Roy, Minnesota 55951
507-324-5249

LAKE MARIA STATE PARK
32

LOCATION - The park is 35 miles west of the Twin Cities, south of I-94, and may be reached either from the south via County State Aid Highway 39 and Wright County 111, or from the north via County State Aid Highway 8 and Wright County 11. It's also seven miles west of Monticello on Minnesota 39, and north one more mile on Minnesota 111.

ACTIVITIES - Be sure to visit here during the fall when the hardwoods have changed. The park has 13 miles of trails to explore, and six miles of equestrian trails. The volksmarch trail is 10 kilometers and sponsored walks occur on Fridays, Saturdays, Sundays and holidays from mid-April through mid-October.

Tour the visitor center. Go fishing or boating on the lake with both canoes and boat rentals available. There is no campground, but backpackers have access to 15 sites. Go cross-country skiing along 12 miles of trails with a warming house.

Incoming pilots can land at Pilots Cove Airport located two miles northeast of Monticello. They have a bus and a courtesy car for transportation into town.

INFORMATION
Lake Maria State Park
Route 1, Box 128
Monticello, Minnesota 55362
612-878-2325

LAKE SHETEK STATE PARK
33

LOCATION - The park is north of Currie via County Road 38. It's also 14 miles northeast of Slayton, and 33 miles southeast of Marshall.

FEATURES - The park is nestled in a shady oak forest on the shores of Lake Shetek, Minnesota's largest southwestern lake. Shetek is Sioux for pelican.

ACTIVITIES - Explore 7.9 miles of hiking trails. Rent a boat or a canoe and go boating. The park has its own canoe trail and launch site. Go fishing year-round in the lake for walleye, northern, bullhead and crappie.

Hike the interpretive trail out to Loon Island. The island is a bird sanctuary where you can observe the nesting of several birds, including several species of duck. Eagles visit Lake Shetek in the spring and again in the fall.

The visitor center is open seasonally, and offers interpretive programs.

Tour the 1858 Andreas Koch cabin, relocated in the park. The Wornson cabin is also over 100 years old, and may be toured. It's located in Slayton next to the museum that is dedicated to "Deke" Slayton, one of the first seven Mercury astronauts.

The campground has 98 campsites with 68 offering electrical hookups. There are also 10 additional walk-in campsites. Food service is available.

During the winter, go cross-country skiing along 2.8 miles of trail, or snow-mobiling along five miles of trail.

Go to Jeffers to see the largest petroglyph group found in the state. Jeffers also features a street dance the last weekend in June, and Corn on the Cob Days in early August.

Railroad buffs can visit the End-O-Line Railroad Park and Museum in Currie. It's open daily from Memorial Day to Labor Day. For information, call 507-763-3113.

INFORMATION
Lake Shetek State Park
Route 1, Box 164
Currie, Minnesota 56123
507-763-3256

MAPLEWOOD STATE PARK
34

LOCATION - The park is seven miles southeast of Pelican Rapids off Minnesota 108.

FEATURES - Three major prehistoric sites are located within the park. In one site, archeologists have found evidence of human habitation from approximately 6,000 years ago. Other artifacts indicate that other sites here were occupied from 1,200 to 900 years ago.

Watch for the tall ironwood trees, the largest found in the state. Because of these and other hardwoods, this is a beautiful spot to visit when the leaves change in the fall.

ACTIVITIES - The park has over 20 lakes with eight of the major lakes offering great fishing opportunities. South Lida Lake is the largest and one of the deepest. Beers Lake is known for its sunfish, crappie and bluegill fishing.

Explore 25 miles of hiking trails and 20 miles of equestrian trails. For a good overlook of the surrounding countryside, go to the top of Hallaway Hill, once used as a ski hill.

Go swimming from the beach or boating in Lake Lida. Both boats and canoe rentals are available. Boating ramps are provided both on South Lake Lida, and another on Beers Lake. Both lakes have good fishing for walleye, northern pike and panfish.

The campground has 61 campsites in three campgrounds located around Grass Lake, and 36 additional sites at the Shore Campground. It also has three backpacking sites, two canoe sites and an equestrian campground. You can rent Hilltop Home or the Wilson Lake cabin. Reservations: 1-800-765-CAMP.

During the winter, cross-country ski along 13 miles of trails, or snowmobile along 15 miles of trails. These trails are groomed on a weekly basis.

In Pelican Rapids, festivals held in July include an ugly truck competition where you'll see a display of rusted-out old trucks and pick-ups competing for a prize. Later that month you can attend their turkey festival, featuring a turkey "race."

INFORMATION
Maplewood State Park
Route 3, Box 422
Pelican Rapids, Minnesota 56572
218-863-8383

MC CARTHY BEACH STATE PARK
35

LOCATION - Take U.S. 169 north for five miles out of Hibbing to St. Louis County Road 5. Follow this road for 16 miles. It's another 1.7 miles west on Minnesota 915 to reach the park entrance.

FEATURES - A large glacier stopped where McCarthy Beach is located today, leaving behind glacially carved lakes and rolling hills called moraines.

ACTIVITIES - The park has many lakes including the Sturgeon Lake Chain with its four lakes. Side Lake, Pickerel Lake, Beatrice Lake and Mark Lake, Trestle Lake, and other smaller lakes provide great water sports recreation.

Go fishing, swimming, boating and sailing. Boats and canoes may be rented. Sturgeon Lake has a sandy swimming beach, changing house and boat access. Seven of the lakes offer fishing for trout, walleye, northern pike, bass, and panfish. Attend seasonal interpretive programs.

The park has 18 miles of hiking, bicycling and equestrian trails. The trails are used year-round. The park is also the midpoint of the Taconite State Trail.

The campground has 92 sites, three walk-in sites, and a trailer dump station. Forty-five of the campsites are semi-modern, and 14 rustic campsites are located on Side Lake, with 32 more rustic campsites located on Beatrice Lake.

During the winter, cross-country ski along five miles of trails, or snowmobile along 12 miles of trail. A warming house is open.

INFORMATION
McCarthy Beach State Park   218-254-2411
7622 McCarthy Beach Road
Side Lake, Minnesota 55781

MILLE LACS KATHIO STATE PARK
36

LOCATION - The park is eight miles northwest of Onamia on U.S. 169, then left for .8-mile on Minnesota 26.

FEATURES - The Dakota Sioux met at Kathio for centuries, until a battle in 1750 led to their defeat by the Chippewa, and they were driven off. The Dakota called the lake "Mde wahan," spirit lake or wonder lake.

ACTIVITIES - The park has a wonderful trail system of 35 miles. Equestrians have 27 miles of trails to explore. The sponsored volksmarch follows two 10-kilometer trails the end of October.

Be sure to climb to the top of the 100-foot observation tower to get a great look at the surrounding area. Tour the visitor center to learn about 5,000 years of life in this National Historic Landmark. Attend an interpretive program.

The campground has 70 campsites. Canoeists have access to four canoeing sites. Equestrians have their own campsites plus a corral for the horses.

Go bass fishing, swimming or boating on the Rum River.

During the winter, cross-country ski or snowmobile along their 19.6 miles of trails, and warm up in the warming house. You can rent skis and snowshoes.

Tour the Mille Lacs Indian Museum on U.S. 169 on the southwest shore of the lake near Onamia. For information, call 612-532-3632.

INFORMATION
Mille Lacs Kathio State Park
HC-67 Box 85
Onamia, Minnesota 56359
612-532-3523

MINNEOPA STATE PARK
37

LOCATION - The park is six miles west of Mankato on Minnesota 68 and U.S. 169.

FEATURES - The word Minneopa is a Dakota Indian word meaning "water falling twice." The park's highlight is the twin waterfalls dropping 45 feet and located in a deep gorge.

The park's Seppman Mill is a wind-driven gristmill constructed in 1864. It was one of the first stone grist mills in Minnesota, and with a favorable wind, could grind 150 bushels of wheat into flour daily.

ACTIVITIES - Hike five miles of wooded trails along the Minnesota River. The sponsored 10-kilometer volksmarch is in mid-June, and begins at the Minneopa Falls picnic area.

Bird watchers should watch for the loggerhead shrike, a unique bird since they are the only truly predatory songbird. Pick up a brochure at the visitor center to assist you in identifying one.

The visitor center is open seasonally. Go canoeing and fish for bass either in the river or stream. The campground has 62 gravel campsites. During the winter, cross-country ski along four miles of trails.

In nearby Mankato, attend the annual powwow held the third weekend in September when Native Americans from all over the U.S. and Canada participate. A People's Fair, a two-day musical festival, is held in mid-May, and features professional entertainment and crafts. For information, call 507-625-3031.

Bicyclists, hikers, cross-country skiers and snowmobiles have access to the 39-mile-long Sakatah State Trail that begins north of Mankato.

Incoming pilots can land at Mankato Municipal Airport located five miles northeast of town. Taxi service is available.

INFORMATION
Minneopa State Park
Route 9, Box 143
Mankato, Minnesota 56001
507-625-4388

MINNESOTA VALLEY STATE PARK
38

LOCATION - The park is west of Jordan off U.S. 169.

ACTIVITIES - Hike the trails along the river. The park has 46 miles of trails to explore, four for bicycling, and 31 miles of equestrian trails.

Go fishing, boating, and canoeing in the river.

The campground has 25 campsites, plus additional campsites for backpackers, canoeists and equestrians.

During the winter, go cross-country skiing along 12 miles of trails, or snowmobiling along 34 miles of trails. A warming house is open during the winter.

INFORMATION
Minnesota Valley State Park
19825 Park Blvd.
Jordan, Minnesota 55352
612-492-6400

MOOSE LAKE STATE PARK
39

LOCATION - The park is one mile southeast of Moose Lake off I-35. The park entrance is off County Highway 137.

FEATURES - Moose Lake, often called the "Agate Capital of the World," is surrounded by smaller lakes. When the last glacier melted, it left behind glacial outwash deposits that melted creating Moosehead and Echo lakes. Lake Moosehead's south shore was also Glacial Lake Nemadji's shoreline.

ACTIVITIES - Go swimming from the beach. Fish in either in Moose Lake or in Echo Lake. Both lakes are stocked with pike, walleye and bass.

Enjoy boating on Echo Lake with a drive-in boat entrance. Both boats and canoes may be rented in the park.

The campground has 18 rustic campsites.

Go cross-country skiing or snowmobiling along seven miles of trails that go beside Echo Lake, along Portage River, and to Moosehead Lake. During the summer, hike beside Echo Lake, or around one of the short loops encircling Wildlife Pond.

Moose Lake hosts a "Midsommar's Dag Festival" the third weekend in June, and features a 4th of July celebration.

INFORMATION
Moose Lake State Park
Route 2 1000 County 137
Moose Lake, Minnesota 55767
218-485-4059 or 218-384-4610

MYRE-BIG ISLAND STATE PARK
40

LOCATION - The park is three miles southeast of Albert Lea on Minnesota 38. Exit 11 off I-35 is the most convenient park access.

ACTIVITIES - Stop by the waterfowl blind during the spring migration, and again in the fall when thousands of white pelicans gather in the park. The island is considered to be one of the best birding sites in southern Minnesota.

The park has 16 miles of hiking trails including the 5.2-mile-long Bur Oak Esker Trail and the 1.1-mile-long Big Island Trail. The sponsored volksmarch 10-kilometer trail goes from late May through the first part of September.

Tour the visitor center and attend interpretive programs presented year-round.

Go boating or canoeing in Albert Lea Lake where canoe rentals are available.

Camp in one of two campgrounds with 100 campsites, 32 offering electrical hookups and a trailer dump station. Backpackers have access to four campsites. Campsites on the Big Island are shaded while White Fox Campground is in the open.

During the winter, cross-country ski along eight miles of trails, or snowmobile along seven miles of trails. A warming house is available.

The first weekend in October, attend the annual Big Island Rendezvous and Festival. Watch the voyagers bring their birch bark canoes ashore, enjoy listening to the banjos, fiddlers and cloggers, and try some buffalo burgers, fry bread and funnel cakes. For information contact the Big Island Rendezvous and Festival, Inc., P.O. Box 686, Albert Lea, Minnesota 56007.

From June through August, you can attend the Minnesota Festival Theater's performances in Albert Lea. For information, contact the Visitors' Bureau at 507-373-3938.

Incoming pilots can land at Albert Lea Municipal Airport located three miles north of town. Rental cars are available.

INFORMATION
Myre-Big Island State Park
Route 3, Box 33
Albert Lea, Minnesota 56007
507-373-5084

NERSTRAND BIG WOODS STATE PARK
41

LOCATION - Follow Minnesota 246 west of Nerstrand for two miles to County Road 40.

ACTIVITIES - Visitors come here during the spring to enjoy the spring flowers. As its name suggests, the large hardwood trees here are beautiful in the fall.

The park has 13 miles of trails to explore. Enjoy the boardwalk trail, or hike to Hidden Falls. The 10-kilometer sponsored volksmarch is held in late September.

The campground has 52 campsites, with 28 offering electrical hookups year-round, and a trailer dump station. You also have access to 13 walk-in campsites.

During the winter, cross-country ski along eight miles of trails, or snowmobile along five miles of trails.

INFORMATION
Nerstrand Big Woods State Park
9700 170th Street E.
Nerstrand, Minnesota 55053
507-334-8848

O.L. KIPP STATE PARK
42

LOCATION - The park is three miles north of La Crescent off I-90 at County Road 12. Follow Winona County 3, Apple Blossom Drive, to reach the park entrance.

It's also 20 miles southeast of Winona at the junction of U.S. 61 and I-90.

FEATURES - The park is part of Apple Blossom Drive, one of two scenic drives in Minnesota. The other scenic drive is along the North Shore above Duluth.

ACTIVITIES - The park is located on a high bluff overlooking the Mississippi River Valley, and lies within the Richard J. Dorer Memorial Hardwood Forest. The park has 6.5 miles of trails plus 2.5 miles of self-guided trails through the hardwood forest. Use caution on trails leading to overlooks or along the steep slopes. The 10-kilometer sponsored volksmarch is held in mid-May and again in early October.

Camp in the campground with 31 campsites and a trailer dump station.

Enjoy picking blackberries when they're in season. Because of the hardwoods, this is a wonderful place to visit during the fall.

During the winter, cross-country ski along 9.2 miles of trails. Snowmobiling and horseback riding are not permitted in the park.

Incoming pilots can land at Winona Municipal Max Conrad Field located three miles northwest of town. Rental cars are available.

INFORMATION
O.L. Kipp State Park
Route 4
Winona, Minnesota 55987
507-643-6849

RICE LAKE STATE PARK
43

LOCATION - The park is seven miles east of Owatonna on Steele County 19, and south of Minneapolis/St. Paul.

FEATURES - The area was originally located in an oak savanna called the Minnesota Southern Oak Barrens. Today only remnants of the original groves remain. The early Indians established campsites here while gathering food, especially wild rice, giving the lake its name.

ACTIVITIES - Bird watchers come here during the spring and fall to watch large numbers of migrating birds who visit the lake.

The visitor center is open seasonally.

Hike along three miles of trails through the woods, meadows and alongside Rice Lake. During the winter, cross-country ski along four miles of trails, or snowmobile along 2.5 miles.

Go fishing, swimming, boating and canoeing in the lake. Canoes may be rented in the park.

The campground has three campgrounds with 42 campsites, and a trailer dump station. Sixteen have electrical hookups. Canoeists have access to five canoe campsites.

If you go into Owatonna, you can visit the Village of Yesteryear located at the fairgrounds in the southeast corner of town. The village features the historic Dunnell House built in 1868, a railroad station constructed in the 1880s, a general store, and a country schoolhouse built in 1856. The village is open daily May 1–September from 1–5. For information, call 507-451-1420.

Incoming pilots can land at Owatonna Municipal Airport located three miles northwest of town. Rental cars are available.

INFORMATION
Rice Lake State Park
Route 3, Box 45
Owatonna, Minnesota 55060
507-451-7406

RICHARD J. DORER MEMORIAL HARDWOOD STATE FOREST
44

LOCATION - The forest is approximately five miles west of Wabasha off Minnesota 60 on Minnesota 81. You can also reach it by taking Minnesota 81 from Kellogg.

FEATURES - Much of the forest is on steep slopes that overlook the Zumbro River.

ACTIVITIES - You can camp in the campground with 19 campsites that provides access to the nearby Zumbro River.

Three marked trails begin from the campground. They range in length from the .75-mile Easy Wheeling Nature Trail to the five-mile multi-use trail that traverses the bluffs and valleys along the Zumbro River. A horse unloading site is located near the southwest corner of the forest.

Canoeists and boaters can enjoy the Zumbro River that flows below the Rochester Power Dam through a deep valley. However, the valley becomes wider below Theilman. The South Fork is the largest and most commonly used section of the river. For river level information from May 1–October 31, call 612-296-6699.

The river has good fishing for catfish, bass and bullhead.

INFORMATION
Richard J. Dorer Memorial Hardwood State Forest
c/o Forester
Box 69
Lake City, Minnesota 55041
612-345-3216

SAKATAH LAKE STATE PARK
45

LOCATION - The park is fourteen miles west of Faribault, or off Minnesota 60, one mile east of the intersection of Minnesota 13 and 60 at Waterville. It's also located in Mankato northwest of Minnesota 22 and U.S. 14 on Lime Valley Road, or in Morristown on Minnesota 60.

FEATURES - The park has two lakes, Upper Sakatah and Lower Sakatah, and features a mixed hardwood forest. The park got its name from the Dakota Indian tribe, and translates as "Singing Hills."

ACTIVITIES - Sakatah Singing Hills State Trail traverses the park. This multiple-use trail is utilized by bicyclists, hikers, snowmobilers and cross-country skiers. The first segment begins at the Lime Valley Road near Mankato and ends at the west city limits of Waterville. Its second segment begins at the eastern edge of Waterville, and ends west of Interstate 35 near Faribault. Bicycles can use the city streets of Waterville to connect the two segments.

The sponsored volksbike, over 25 kilometers one way, goes in early August.

The campground has 63 campsites with 14 offering electrical hookups year-round, and a trailer dump station. Attend interpretive programs at the interpretive center.

The Cannon River passes the park and is considered to be a good canoeing river with only a few rapids. You can also swim, boat and fish for bass, pike, walleye and catfish. For water level information, call 612-296-6699 or 507-285-7176.

INFORMATION
Sakatah Lake State Park
Route 2, Box 19
Waterville, Minnesota 56096
507-362-4438

SAVANNA PORTAGE STATE PARK
46

LOCATION - The park is 16 miles northeast of McGregor. Take U.S. 65 to Aitkin County Highway 14. Follow Highway 14 east for 10 miles to the park.

FEATURES - The park has two fishing lakes. The Savanna Portage once served as a vital link between the St. Louis River watershed and the Mississippi River for canoeists who came from Lake Superior to the Upper Mississippi.

ACTIVITIES - Hike the historic Savanna Portage Trail. Be sure to check on trail conditions with the park naturalists.

You can also hike the Continental Divide Trail where the water flows either into the Mississippi River or into Lake Superior. In all, the park has 22 miles of hiking trails to explore. Mountain bikers have access to 10 miles of biking trails.

The park offers excellent swimming and fishing. Loon Lake has trout. Lake Shumway has northerns, bass, walleye and panfish, and Savanna Lake has crappie and northerns.

Boat access is provided to Loon and Shumway lakes where only electric trolling motors are permitted. Both boats and canoes may be rented.

The campground has 60 campsites with 16 offering electrical hookups. Backpackers select from six backpacking sites. A trailer dump station is provided.

During the winter, cross-country ski along 17 miles of trails, or snowmobile along 60 miles of trails.

Stop by the park office to examine the exhibits and displays on the voyageurs and explorers.

Incoming pilots can land at Isedor Iverson Airport located one mile north of McGregor. Rental cars are available.

INFORMATION
Savanna Portage State Park
HCR 3 Box 591
McGregor, Minnesota 55760
218-426-3271

SCENIC STATE PARK
47

LOCATION - The park is seven miles east of Bigfork on County Road 7.

FEATURES - The park has been called one of the most scenic state parks in Minnesota, and has seven lakes: Coon, Sandwick, Tell, Spring, Cedar, Pine, and Lake of the Isles. The latter was established to protect the George Washington and Chippewa Forests' pine growth surrounding Coon and Sandwick lakes.

ACTIVITIES - Tour the visitor center that is open seasonally, and attend an interpretive program.

Explore 15 miles of hiking trails through the stands of some old white and red pine. One good .7-mile hike goes out to Chase Point where you can get a good look at Coon and Sandwick lakes. Go swimming, boating or fishing for walleye, northern and panfish in Coon and Sandwick lakes. Both boats and canoes may be rented in the park.

The campground has 117 campsites with 20 offering electrical hookups year-round. Backpackers can select among seven backpacking sites, and canoers have access to five campsites. You can also rent their lake shore guest house available year-round.

During the winter, cross-country ski along 10 miles of trails or snowmobile along 12 miles of trails.

INFORMATION
Scenic State Park
HCR 2, Box 17
Bigfork, Minnesota 56628
218-743-3362

SCHOOLCRAFT STATE PARK
48

LOCATION - The park is located along the banks of the Mississippi River, eight miles south of Deer River.

FEATURES - The park was named for Henry Rowe Schoolcraft, discoverer of the headwaters of the Mississippi River.

ACTIVITIES - Hike a couple of miles through the giant pine tree forest. Go canoeing, boating or pike fishing in the Mississippi or in the Vermilion River. Boat rentals and a boat launch are available.

The campground has 37 sites, and canoeists have access to 12 sites along the Mississippi.

Cross-country skiers can explore 10 miles of trails, and snowmobilers have access to 12 miles. A warming house is open.

INFORMATION
Schoolcraft State Park
HCR 4 Box 181
Deer River, Minnesota 56636
218-566-2383

SIBLEY STATE PARK
49

LOCATION - The park is seven miles west of New London on U.S. 71 or 15 miles north of Willmar.

ACTIVITIES - Attend one of the year-round naturalist programs. Climb 190 feet to the summit of Mt. Tom.

Since the park has five lakes, you can enjoy many water sports. Go swimming from the beach, fishing for northern, walleye and panfish, and boating or canoeing with both boats and canoes available for rent. From Lake Andrew you can follow a designated canoe route to the park's western lakes, Henschien and Swan.

Hikers can explore 23 miles of trails including eight miles of equestrian trails. Bicyclists have a five-mile trail that winds down from the interpretive center's parkinglot to Lake Andrew and continues along the lake shore. Bikes may be rented in the park.

The campground has 138 campsites, with 52 offering electrical hookups and a trailer dump station. Equestrians have their own campground with a capacity for 50 campers. Groceries may be purchased in the park.

During the winter, go cross country-skiing along 10 miles of trails, snowmobiling along six miles of trails, and warm up in their warming house. Snowshoes are available for rent.

In New London in mid-July, you can attend Water Days featuring a parade, water vehicle races, a show presented by the Little Crow Ski Club, and a water fight between the fire departments from neighboring communities.

In late August, you can attend the annual New London to New Brighton Antique Car Run featuring pre-1908 vehicles. The festivities last for four days.

Incoming pilots can land at Willmar Municipal-John L. Rice Airfield located one mile west of Willmar. Rental cars are available.

INFORMATION
Sibley State Park
800 Sibley Park Road NE
New London, Minnesota 56273
612-354-2055

SOUDAN UNDERGROUND MINE STATE PARK
50

LOCATION - The mine and park are located two miles east of Tower off Minnesota 169, and near the shore of Lake Vermillion at the edge of the Boundary Waters Canoe Area. It's also 22 miles southwest of Ely on Minnesota 169.

FEATURES - The mine is the region's oldest and deepest iron ore mine, dating back to 1883. It's the only underground iron ore mine in the world still open. However, it was closed to mining in 1963.

ACTIVITIES - Take a 1.5-hour tour, prefaced with a ten-minute movie, and followed by a ride down to 2,341 feet below the earth's surface. From there, you take a .75-mile electric train ride and climb a 32-step spiral staircase to see the last and deepest area mined. Tours leave from 9:30–4:00 from Memorial Day into the fall. Bring along a jacket since the mine temperature remains at 52 degrees year-round. Admission is charged.

Following your tour, enjoy a picnic, tour the visitor center, Dry House, and the Engine House to watch the hoisting apparatus for the elevator. Stop by the drill shop and mine rescue station.

The park has five miles of trails, some along the shore of Lake Vermillion. Hike the .2-mile interpretive trail to get an overlook of the open pit mines where the ore was originally mined. The Taconite Trail passes nearby.

The seasonal 10-kilometer volksmarch is held in mid-July, and 2.4 miles of the walk are done underground. Bring along a good flashlight.

Camp in the nearby McKinley Campground or at Hoodoo Point overlooking Lake Vermillion.

Lake Vermillion has 1,200 miles of shoreline and 40 miles of protected bays and inlets, attracting many fishermen and boaters.

INFORMATION
Soudan Underground Mine State Park
Soudan, Minnesota 55782
218-753-2245

SPLIT ROCK CREEK STATE PARK
51

LOCATION - The park is twenty miles north of Two Harbors on U.S. 61. It's also one mile south of Ihlen on Minnesota 23.

FEATURES - At one time, the park area was a treeless prairie, but after the dam was constructed, elm and ash shade trees were planted. Look along the west side of the road leading to the campground to see a remnant of this prairie.

After a November storm in 1905 wrecked six ships within 12 miles of the Split Rock River, the lighthouse was erected in 1910.

ACTIVITIES - The park offers 12 miles of well-marked hiking trails where you can go hiking two miles to the top of Day Hill, or to Corundum Point. You can also follow their eight-mile loop that winds past Lake Superior's shoreline, the Split Rock River, some waterfalls, the Split Rock Lighthouse and the Split Rock River Valley. The sponsored 10-kilometer volksmarch is held in mid-June, and begins from the Lakeview Trail Center. For a good day hike, go along the Split Rock River Gorge. For an even longer hike, take advantage of the park's access to the Superior Hiking Trail.

This is the only park with 20 "cart-in" campsites where you park your car in the parking lot and cart your gear into your site in a two-wheeled garden cart.

The visitor center is open seasonally.

Enjoy swimming from the beach, boating, canoeing and fishing for sunfish, walleye and perch in Split Rock Lake. Rental boats and canoes are available. Speed limit restrictions are in effect, and no water-skiing is permitted. Hike down to the dam area to see the picturesque stone bridge built by the WPA in 1937.

Split Rock Lake is the only reasonably sized body of water in Pipestone County, so it is a natural haven for waterfowl and migrating birds, particularly in the spring or fall.

During the winter, you can cross-country ski along the four-kilometer lakeshore trail between the Split Rock River and the lighthouse. The park has a heated trail center.

Tour the historic site grounds open during the summer, and tour the lighthouse, fog-signal building and the restored keeper's dwelling. Watch their 22-minute film, "Split Rock Light: Tribute to the Age of Steel." A fee is charged.

Pipestone National Monument is seven miles southwest of the park. Here you can see the famous pipestone quarries from which the red stone used by the

Indians in making their ceremonial pipes was quarried. Tour the visitor center to learn more about the history of these pipes.

Hike the Circle Trail past the quarries, Winnewissa Falls, Lake Hiawatha and Leaping Rock formations. For information, call 507-825-5464.

From mid-July through the first part of August, be sure to see their annual presentation of "The Song of Hiawatha" Pageant in Pipestone. For information, call 507-825-4126 or 825-3316.

INFORMATION

Split Rock Creek State Park
Box 2010A Highway 61 E
Two Harbors, Minnesota 55616
218-226-3065

Split Rock Lighthouse
218-226-4372

ST. CROIX STATE PARK
52

LOCATION - The park is fifteen miles east of Hinckley on Minnesota 48, and then five miles south on Minnesota 22.

FEATURES - The St. Croix River adjoining the park is a national wild and scenic river. The park's western boundary runs beside seven miles of the Kettle River, a state wild and scenic river.

ACTIVITIES - St. Croix is Minnesota's largest state park, and has three campgrounds with 217 sites: Riverview, Paint Rock Springs and Old Logging Trails. Electrical hookups for 42 vehicles are provided in Riverview. Equestrians and backpackers have their own campsites. Limited groceries may be purchased within the park. A modern Guest House can accommodate 15 people and is located at Norway Point.

Tour the interpretive center, and go canoeing on either the St. Croix or Kettle River. Six canoe landings and eight primitive campsites are located in the park, and canoe rentals are available. Shuttle service is available. For information, call 612-384-7806 or 384-6943.

Take a bike ride along the paved bike paths. Bike rentals are available.

Go swimming in Lake Clayton, and test your skill at pike fishing in the St. Croix River. You can also fish for trout on Hay Creek and Crooked Creek.

Hikers have access to 127 miles of trails, 6.5 miles of hard-surfaced bike trails, and 75 miles of equestrian trails. The Munger State Trail crosses through the park with 21 miles found within the park. For a good view of the St. Croix River, hike the River Bluff Trail adjacent to the campground. Drop down the steps for a short walk beside the river.

Tour the visitor center located in the campground from Memorial Day through Labor Day. You can rent bicycles here to cycle their paved 5.3-mile bike path.

During the winter, cross-country ski along 21 miles of trails, or snowmobile along 80 miles of trails. A warming house is open. Many miles of interconnecting snowmobile trails connect the park with state forests. You can winter camp, with 12 campsites providing electrical hookups.

For cross-country skiers who prefer skating, 6.4 miles of skating tracks are available.

In nearby Hinckley, attend summer concerts at the Mission Creek Theme Creek. For information, call 612-989-5151 or 218-727-2121.

For a longer hike, bicycle ride, or for snowmobiling, follow the Hinckley Fire Trail. It's 32 miles long, and follows the railroad grade used as an escape route during the great Hinckley Fire of 1894. The trail begins in Hinckley and ends at Moose Lake.

In nearby Pine City, attend free outdoor summer concerts presented on Friday evenings at 7:00 p.m. in June and July. The city also sponsors Art in the Park the third Saturday in July, Moonlight Madness the fourth weekend in July, the Pine County Fair with a parade the first weekend in August, and the Northwest Company Fur Post Rendezvous in mid-September. A flea market is held every Wednesday morning at the Pine County Fairgrounds. For information, call the Pine City Area Chamber of Commerce at 612-629-3861.

In Cloverdale, attend their annual pig roast complete with live music in mid-August. For information, call 612-384-6705.

In Sandstone, attend the Community Musical Theater the first two weekends in August. Bingo players can play every Thursday at the American Legion Hall on Main Street.

Pilots can fly in for breakfast from 8–12 at the Sandstone Municipal Airport the second Sunday in September. The airport is located two miles southwest of Sandstone and has rental cars available.

INFORMATION
St. Croix State Park
Route 3, Box 450
Hinckley, Minnesota 55037
612-384-6591

TEMPERANCE RIVER STATE PARK
53

LOCATION - The park is one mile north of Schroeder on U.S. 61, and 23 miles southwest of Grand Marais. It's midway between Duluth and the Canadian border, and three miles from Tofte, and has over a mile of shoreline along Lake Superior.

ACTIVITIES - Be sure to see the gorge with its many waterfalls carved by the Temperance River.

The park has eight miles of hiking trails. The main trail follows the winding river gorge of the Temperance River on its way to Lake Superior where you'll pass waterfalls, cauldrons and potholes. Both the North Shore Trail and the Superior Hiking Trail may be accessed from the park. You can also hike to Carlton or Britton peaks.

Go canoeing and fishing for trout in the lake, river or stream. The Sawbill Trail is one of the main entry points into the Boundary Waters Canoe Area, and is located close to the park. Area outfitters can rent you canoes and equipment.

The campground has 50 campsites in two campgrounds. Equestrians have 20 campsites and 5.5 miles of trails.

If you arrive here during the fall, take the Fall Color Tour sponsored by the U.S. Forest Service. Try your luck at shore casting at the river mouths and along the park's shoreline for the migrating salmon in the fall.

During the winter, cross-country ski along 12 miles of trails, or snowmobile along five miles.

INFORMATION
Temperance River State Park
Box 33
Schroeder, Minnesota 55613
218-663-7476

TETTEGOUCHE STATE PARK
54

LOCATION - The park is 4.5 miles east of Silver Bay on U.S. 61.

ACTIVITIES - The Baptism River has three waterfalls, including the state's highest waterfall.

The forested park has four lakes and 16 miles of trails. Stop at the overlooks of the Baptism River and Lake Superior. Hike out to wind-swept Shovel Point. Shovel Point is a spectacular example of some lava flows that occurred 1.1 billion years ago.

Other hikes include one to the old Tettegouche camp on Mic Mac Lake, or you can visit all the lakes in the park including Nicado, Tettegouche and Nipisiquit. The Superior Hiking Trail traverses the park past Conservancy Pines, and climbs Mt. Trudee in three miles for a great overlook of Tettegouche and Mic Mac lakes, the Palisade River Valley and Lake Superior's coastline.

The sponsored 10-kilometer volksmarch is held in mid-June.

During the winter, you can cross-country ski 12 miles of trails into several lakes. The 34-site semi-modern campground is open during the winter.

Stop by the visitor center to learn more about the area and the North Shore. Fish for trout and salmon in both the Baptism River and Lake Superior. Pike and walleye fishing are also available in four inland lakes, accessible by foot trail only.

During the winter, cross-country ski along 12 miles of trails or snowmobiling along seven miles of trails. Snowmobiles can also follow trails to Finland, Silver Bay, or go along the North Shore Trail.

INFORMATION
Tettegouche State Park
474 Highway 61 E
Silver Bay, Minnesota 55614
218-226-3539

UPPER SIOUX AGENCY STATE PARK
55

LOCATION - The park is eight miles southeast of Granite Falls on Minnesota 67. The park is located at the confluence of the Yellow Medicine River and the Minnesota River.

ACTIVITIES - Originally the area was the site for the Upper Sioux Agency, and still has several historic buildings. Tour the visitor center to learn more about the history of the park.

Go fishing in the river. Hikers and equestrians can explore 18 miles of trails, or camp in the campground with 45 campsites. During the winter, snowmobilers can travel along 16 miles of trails.

INFORMATION
Upper Sioux Agency State Park
Route 2, Box 92
Granite Falls, Minnesota 56241
612-564-4777

WHITEWATER STATE PARK
56

LOCATION - The park is in southeastern Minnesota, three miles south of Elba on Minnesota 74.

ACTIVITIES - Enjoy swimming or excellent trout fishing in the Middle Branch of the Whitewater River or in Trout Run Creek.

Hike along 10 miles of trails. The trails wander along the river on the valley floor, and climb 200 feet to the bluff tops. Be on the lookout for rattlesnakes.

The visitor center is open year-round, and has interpretive programs.

The campground has 106 campsites, and a trailer dump station.

During the winter, go cross-country skiing along five miles of trails with a warming house open. Snowmobiling is not permitted.

INFORMATION
Whitewater State Park
Route 1, Box 256
Altura, Minnesota 55910
507-932-3007

WILD RIVER STATE PARK
57

LOCATION - From North Branch, drive 12 miles east from I-35 on Minnesota 95, then three miles northeast on Minnesota 12. It's immediately north of the Wild Mountain Ski Area on Minnesota 16.

FEATURES - The St. Croix River flows through the park.

ACTIVITIES - The all-season trail system of 35 miles brings many hikers into the park. Equestrians have 20 miles of trails to explore.

Tour the visitor center to learn more about the area's history. Attend interpretive programs offered year-round. The center overlooks the St. Croix Valley, and features a unique weather station along with exhibits and slide programs.

Try your skill at fishing for catfish, northerns, walleyes, sauger and bass in the river.

Go boating or canoeing with canoe rentals available. Water users need to use caution because high water levels may result in swift currents after a heavy rainfall.

The campground has 96 campsites with 17 providing year-round electrical hookups. The park also has one walk-in site, six backpacking sites, and 12 canoe sites. Equestrians have their own campsites plus a corral for horses.

Cross-country skiers can explore 35 miles of trails with a warming house open during the winter.

INFORMATION
Wild River State Park
39755 Park Trail
Center City, Minnesota 55012
612-583-2125

WILLARD MUNGER STATE TRAIL
58

LOCATION - Parts of the trail are still being developed, and when completed, will go from St. Paul to Duluth.

FEATURES - The eastern section of the trail covers over 80 miles, connecting St. Croix State Park with the Nemadji and Chengwatana state parks. The western section of the trail has over 50 miles of abandoned railroad grade linking Banning, Moose Lake and Jay Cooke state parks. This section has an asphalt trail ideal for bicyclists.

The northern section goes from Carlton to West Duluth, and has wonderful views of the St. Louis River plus overlooks of Duluth, while the south portion goes from Barnum to Hinckley.

INFORMATION

Minnesota Department of Natural Resources,
Trails and Waterways Unit
Information Center
Box 40
500 Lafayette Road
St. Paul, Minnesota 55146
612 296-6699

Department of Natural Resources
Route 2, 701 South Kenwood
Moose Lake, Minnesota 55767
218-485-8647

WILLIAM O'BRIEN STATE PARK
59

LOCATION - The park is two miles north of Marine-on-St. Croix on Minnesota 95 on the St. Croix National Scenic Riverway.

FEATURES - You'll see sandstone outcroppings formed millions of years ago by inland seas lying along the St. Croix River. Later, glaciers passed through the area, scouring out the sandstone. As the ice melted, the large volume of water cut through the sandstone, creating the St. Croix River, and left behind a wide, boulder-strewn valley.

ACTIVITIES - The park is open year-round. Tour the interpretive center and attend year-round naturalist's programs. Hike or cross-country ski along 9.5 miles of trails, or bike two miles of bike trails. The 12-kilometer sponsored volksmarch is held in early October.

Go fishing in the St. Croix River for northern pike, walleye, bass and brown trout. Swimmers can swim from a guarded beach at Lake Alice, but swimming isn't permitted in the river because of the swift current.

You can go boating or canoeing on the river, considered to be one of the best in the U.S., and canoe rentals are available. A shuttle service for cars and/or passengers is provided during the summer months. The park has speed limit restrictions for boats, and no water-skiing is permitted.

There are two campgrounds with 125 campsites, 62 with electrical hookups plus a trailer dump station. Canoeists have a campsite of their own. Reservations for the canoeist campground are required. You can also camp in one of their backpacking sites.

During the winter, go cross-country skiing along 9.5 miles of trails, and warm up in the warming house.

INFORMATION
William O'Brien State Park
16821 O'Brien Trail North
Marine-on-St. Croix, Minnesota 55047
612-433-2421

ZIPPEL BAY STATE PARK
60

LOCATION - The park is on the shore of Lake of the Woods, and is located at the northern tip of the lake that is 80 miles long and 55 miles wide at its widest point. The lake is ten miles north of Williams and is mostly in the province of Ontario, Canada. Access to the park is from Lake of the Woods Road 8.

ACTIVITIES - Hikers can explore two miles of white sandy beach and six miles of trails. Because of the ocean-like waves in the lake, a recently constructed stone jetty provides safe access to the lake. For a good view of the bay, hike to the top of the granite-like outcrop next to the boat harbor.

During June and July, watch for four species of lady slippers and other orchids while hiking along the trails. You can also find blueberries, wild strawberries, pin cherries, cranberries, chokeberries and edible mushrooms.

Lake of the Woods is known for its outstanding walleye sauger and fishing. If you fish in the bay, you can find northern pike and walleye. You can arrange to go lake fishing aboard a fishing launch available from the boat harbor.

A public boat harbor, launching ramps and docks are located on Zippel Bay, providing access to Lake of the Woods. Also, go boating on Lake of the Woods from one of the protected boat harbors in the bay where boat rentals are available.

The campground has 60 campsites located in the forest, and a trailer dump station.

Hikers and equestrians share six miles of trails. During the winter, you can cross-country ski along two miles of trails, or go snowmobiling along six miles of trails.

INFORMATION
Zippel Bay State Park
Williams, Minnesota 56686
218-783-6252

*Hikers pause along the second loop on the Rocky Top Trail in
Lake of the Ozarks State Park.*

TOM NAGEL

MISSOURI

If you come to visit the Missouri Ozarks, you'll encounter not only rugged scenic beauty, but also a special folk culture. Missouri's eastern boundary is bordered by the mighty Mississippi, while the Missouri River forms its northern boundary. Besides these two large rivers is the Ozark National Scenic Riverway located along the Current and Jacks Fork rivers. Also, when the state needed to develop a means for flood control, several lakes and reservoirs were constructed, resulting in the increased availability of many water-based activities.

The state parks have been set aside to preserve Missouri's most outstanding natural and cultural features. Over 340 miles of trails may be found in the parks, ranging from primitive backpacking trails to paved bicycle trails. The Ozark Trail that will eventually stretch for 500 miles through the Ozarks, may be accessed from several of the state parks.

All the state parks containing historic sites are listed on the National Register of Historic Places, and four of the parks are national historic landmarks. These include Arrow Rock, Scott Joplin House, and Watkins Woolen Mill State Historic Site, and the Graham Cave State Park.

Tours at the state historic sites are available year-round, and are offered from 10–4 weekdays and Saturdays, and at varying times on Sundays and holidays. Some tours require a nominal admission fee.

Ten of the state parks have dining lodges including the 19th-century tavern at Arrow Rock State Historic Site. Eleven have lodging facilities ranging from stone cabins at the Sam Baker State Park to a modern motel overlooking the lake at Big Lake State Park.

Lodging facilities at three trout fishing parks, Bennett Spring, Montauk, and Roaring River, open the last day of February and remain open until October 31. Cabins and modern motel units in most of the parks open April 15 and close October 31. They are available in Big Lake State Park until December.

Most of the state parks' campsites are available on a first-come, first-served basis; however, ten will accept reservations: Watkins Mill, Meramec, Johnson's Shut-Ins, Bennett Spring, Lake of the Ozarks, Mark Twain, Sam A. Baker, Hawn, Roaring River, and Harry S. Truman State Park.

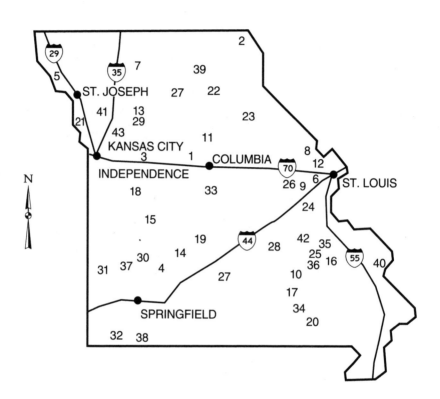

The campgrounds are open from April 1–October 31, except at Montauk, Roaring River and Bennett Spring state parks where the season begins on February 25.

Traditional story tellers present programs at some of the state parks from June–September. Check with the park naturalists for the schedule.

When hiking in the woods, be on the lookout for ticks, particularly during the spring and summer. They can cause four diseases that are usually hard to detect, since they mimic other diseases. To avoid a problem, stay on the established trails, wear light-colored clothing so ticks may be easily spotted, wear long pants tucked into your boots, and check periodically for their presence. Several brands of insect repellent have been found to be effective.

Civil War buffs can visit several parks to get a first-hand look at where several historic battles occurred. Over 400 battles, engagements and skirmishes occurred within the state, including the decisive Battle of Westport in 1864, considered to be the largest battle west of the Mississippi River. Only Virginia and Tennessee were more heavily fought over during the war.

Some of the parks to visit include the Battle of Athens State Park, Higginsville, Fort Davidson State Historic Site, Battle of Lexington State Historic Site, Wilson's Creek National Battlefield in Springfield, and the Jefferson Barracks Historical Park in St. Louis.

ARROW ROCK STATE HISTORIC SITE
1

LOCATION - The park is in Arrow Rock, 13 miles north of I-70 on Missouri 41.

ACTIVITIES - Stop by the Arrow Rock Tavern where authentic Missouri food is specialized. Here you can take a guided tour of the artist George Bingham's house, Dr. Matthew Hall's house, a gun shop, and the loom house. Tours are offered Monday–Saturday at 10:30 and 1:30, and on Sundays at 1:30 from Memorial Day through Labor Day, and by appointment the rest of the year. For information, call 816-837-3392.

Attend a performance at the Arrow Rock Lyceum, a noted summer theater.

The Sappington Cemetery State Historic Site is located in the park, and is the resting place for several prominent Arrow Rock citizens including Missouri's Confederate governor, Claiborne Jackson.

The campground has 43 sites with 13 providing electrical hookups, and a trailer dump.

INFORMATION
Arrow Rock State Historic Site
Arrow Rock, Missouri 65320
816-837-3330

BATTLE OF ATHENS STATE HISTORIC SITE
2

LOCATION - The site is located eight miles north of Revere off Missouri 81.

FEATURES - The Civil War battle of Athens, fought on August 5, 1861, was significant because it kept Missouri from following the southern states, and kept northeast Missouri under Union control.

The battle site contains most of the land on which the former town of Athens was situated. In 1860, it was one of the largest towns in the region, but today only a few structures and people remain.

The Thome-Benning House, owned by Joseph Benning during the Civil War, still stands. Below this house along the banks of the Des Moines River are the remains of the Thome Mill, constructed in 1844. At one time, it was one of the largest and most prosperous mills in the county.

ACTIVITIES - Every third year a re-enactment of the original battle is held in early August. The last re-enactment was held in 1990. A celebration of the battle is held annually.

Visitors can hike the trails, fish in the lake, take historic tours of the battle-ground, and camp in the 29-site campground with some electrical hookups. Over a mile of the park is located along the Des Moines River.

In nearby Kahoka, visit the Clark County Courthouse, built in 1871, and one of the few original courthouses still being used today. A mahogany staircase leads to the courtroom. The judge's bench and spectator's seats are original. Its jail is in the basement, and is much the same as when it was constructed. The courthouse is listed on the National Register of Historic Places.

INFORMATION
Battle of Athens State Historic Site
R. R. 1 Box 26
Revere, Missouri 63465
816-877-387

BATTLE OF LEXINGTON STATE HISTORIC SITE
3

LOCATION - The historic site is in Lexington on 13th Street.

FEATURES - Here, in 1861, the Missouri State Guard troops defeated the Union troops, and captured the Missouri River port of Lexington. The Anderson

House was used by both sides as a field hospital during the battle, and has been restored and furnished. Civil War relics and scars from the battle are still visible on the house.

ACTIVITIES - Learn about the history of the Battle of the Hemp Bales, one of three major battles fought in the state. Take a 30-minute tour of the Anderson-Davis House. An admission fee is charged. Walk the mile-long interpretive, self-guided trail through the battlefield.

The campground has 15 sites, and you can go boating, canoeing and sailing on the Missouri River.

In Lexington, you can see many homes built before the Civil War. One of the oldest courthouses still in use in Missouri today is located on Main Street. Look for the embedded cannon ball that hit the 1849 building in one of the front columns.

To stay in an historic place, check with the historic Graystone Park, a 10-room home built in 1833. For information or reservations, call 816-259-3476.

The Confederate Memorial State Historic Site is located 13 miles south of Lexington near Higginsville. It has the remains of the Confederate Home of Missouri, the Confederate Memorial Park and chapel, and a cemetery where over 600 Confederate veterans were buried.

Incoming pilots can land at Lexington Municipal located three miles north-west of town. Rental cars are available.

INFORMATION
Battle of Lexington State Historic Site
Lexington, Missouri 64067
816-259-2112

BENNETT SPRING STATE PARK
4

LOCATION - The park is 12 miles west of Lebanon on Missouri 64.

FEATURES - Bennett Spring has an average of 100 million gallons of water flowing daily. The water continues for 1.5 miles before it empties into the Niangua River.

The spring was an ideal location for the early grist and flour mills. Peter Bennett was known for his generous donations of hundreds of bushels of grain and flour to needy families during the Civil War. Unfortunately, fire destroyed the last mill in 1944.

ACTIVITIES - The park is known for its trout fishing. The trout are fed and cared for at the fish hatchery in the park and then released. Fishing season for the trout is March 1–October 31. During the winter, you can fish on a catch-and-release basis. Take a tour of the trout hatchery at designated times. Call for information: 417-532-4418.

Tour the nature center open daily, and Wednesday through Sunday from September through May. A full-time naturalist is on duty.

Swimming isn't permitted in the spring, but during the summer, you can swim in a modern pool.

Go floating on the Niangua River. Canoe rental and shuttle service are available both at the park and locally.

The campground has both basic and improved campsites. If you decide not to cook, eat at the rustic lodge that is open daily during the trout season. For information, call 417-532-4547. Cabins are available for rent during the fishing season. Advance reservations are required. Call 417-532-4307.

Hillbilly Days, a four-day summer festival, is held in the Bennett Spring-Lebanon area. Here you can watch square dancing, black powder shoots, canoe races, a ladies' nail driving contest, and listen to some fiddling. For information, call 417-588-3256.

Incoming pilots can land at Floyd W. Jones Lebanon Airport, three miles south of Lebanon. Rental cars are available.

INFORMATION
Bennett Spring State Park
Lebanon, Missouri 65536
417-532-4338

BIG LAKE STATE PARK
5

LOCATION - The park is eleven miles southwest of Mound City on Missouri 111.

FEATURES - Big Lake is actually an oxbow lake, or what remains from a channel in the Missouri River before its original course was rechanneled. It's the state's largest natural lake, and the park is located along its eastern shoreline.

The lake is shallow, and is a major stopping spot for migrating birds each spring and fall.

ACTIVITIES - Camp in the campground with 80 campsites, 60 with electrical hookups.

Go boating and water-skiing on Big Lake. Two boat docks and a launching ramp are located in the park. Fish for stocked catfish, carp, crappie, bass and bluegill.

Enjoy a refreshing swim in the modern swimming pool located near the 22-unit motel and dining lodge. The motel and dining room are open from April 1–December 15. You can also stay in one of eight housekeeping cabins located along the lake shore.

To see large numbers of migrating birds, visit Squaw Creek National Wildlife Refuge, eight miles from the park. In September, you'll see large groups of pelicans and blue herons arriving. In late fall and early winter, bald eagles migrate through here. In all, 301 species of birds have been spotted in the refuge.

INFORMATION
Big Lake State Park
Bigelow, Missouri 64425
816-442-3770

CASTLEWOOD STATE PARK
6

LOCATION - The park is six miles east of Ballwin on Kiefer Creek Road off Missouri 100.

FEATURES - During the early 1900s, the park was used as a resort when up to 10,000 weekend visitors gathered to go canoeing, dancing and sunning on Lincoln Beach located along the south bank of the Meramec River.

The Meramec River Recreation Area contains Castlewood State Park, and the area stretches 108 river miles from Meramec State Park to where the river joins the Mississippi River south of St. Louis.

ACTIVITIES - A boating access ramp to the Meramec River is on the east edge of the park and north of the river. Fish for bluegill and catfish.

Hikers, all-terrain bicyclists, and equestrians have access to over 14 miles of trails. Three-mile Grotpeter Trail takes you through the park's wooded uplands, with a trailhead near the first picnic shelter. River Scene Trail is three miles long, and climbs to the bluffs along the Meramec River. For a longer hike, follow Chubb Trail located on the south side of the river. Access is from Lone Elk or from the West Tyson county park.

INFORMATION
Castlewood State Park
Ballwin, Missouri 63021
314-527-6481

CROWDER STATE PARK
7

LOCATION - The park is four miles west of Trenton on Missouri 146.

FEATURES - The park honors Major General Enoch H. Crowder, who founded the nation's Selective Service System, the military draft.

ACTIVITIES - The park has 42 campsites, with 32 offering electrical hookups.

Crowder Lake is stocked with bass, bluegill, channel catfish and crappie. You can go boating, but no gas-powered motors are permitted. Go swimming from the sand beach and nearby beachhouse, and play tennis.

The park has two trails, one short one that connects the campground with the tennis court, and a longer one that takes hikers and equestrians down to the Thompson River.

In nearby Trenton, you can tour the Grundy County Museum, open from 2–5 on Saturday and Sunday, and on holidays from May–October.

Incoming pilots can land at Trenton Municipal Airport, located one mile east of town. Rental cars are available.

INFORMATION
Crowder State Park
Route 5
Trenton, Missouri 64683
816-359-6473

CUIVRE RIVER STATE PARK
8

LOCATION - The park is in east-central Missouri near Troy off Missouri 47.

FEATURES - The Cuivre River area was occupied by prehistoric man as early as 10,000 or 12,000 years ago, and archaeologists have found burial mounds and ceremonial complexes. The park covers over 6,000 acres of rugged, wooded hills surrounding Big Sugar Creek.

ACTIVITIES - The Northwoods Wild Area and Big Sugar Creek Wild Area offer primitive back-country recreation. Over 31 miles of hiking and equestrian trails are available, including the Lone Spring Trail that winds through the Northwoods Wild Area. The trail center has photographic displays and maps of the main park trails.

The campground has 110 sites, 32 with full hookups. Equestrians have their own campground.

You can go fishing for bass, catfish, sunfish and bluegill in Lake Lincoln, boating with trolling motors, or swimming from the beach. A park naturalist is on duty year-round.

INFORMATION
Cuivre River State Park
Route 1, Box 25
Troy, Missouri 63379
314-528-7247

DR. EDMUND A. BABLER MEMORIAL STATE PARK
9

LOCATION - The park is located around 20 miles west of St. Louis on Missouri 109 between U.S. 40 and Missouri 100.

ACTIVITIES - Because of the old oaks and maples, this would be a very colorful place to visit in the fall when the leaves change. Be sure to visit Cochran Woods where some of the trees are believed to be over 100 years old. The woods can either be reached by trail or by parking at the Cochran picnic shelter and following the hollow towards the east.

The interpretive center is open year-round, and is staffed by a full-time naturalist. It's located on Guy Park Drive near the pool. Go swimming in the modern pool, open daily from Memorial Day through Labor Day.

The park has over 13 miles of trails winding through the woods for you to hike or ride horseback. A riding stable is open June–August, but is closed Fridays. For information, call 314-458-3088. Ride your bicycle along the wide bike lanes, or play tennis on the tennis court. In mid-April, attend a workshop on spring wildflowers. Contact the park naturalist for details.

The campground has 84 campsites, 24 with electrical hookups, and a trailer dump station. The park also has over 250 picnic sites scattered throughout the grounds.

St. Louis has many interesting sights to see including the Gateway Arch, with its capsule transporter system that carries passengers to the observation room, where windows provide excellent views to the east and west. It's open daily, and during the busy times of the year, you can call ahead to check on ticket availability: 314-425-4465.

During the summer, be sure to visit the Missouri Botanical Garden, located at 4344 Shaw Avenue. It has shady paths to walk, formal gardens, greenhouses, and is a National Historic Landmark. Admission is charged. For information, call 314-577-5100.

INFORMATION
Dr. Edmund A. Babler Memorial State Park
Route 1, Box 468
Chesterfield, Missouri 63017
314-458-3813 (office)
314-273-6925 (pool)
314-458-3088 (stables)

ELEPHANT ROCKS STATE PARK
10

LOCATION - The park is located northwest of Graniteville on Missouri 21.

FEATURES - Billion-year-old giant granite rocks are lined up end-to-end resembling a train of circus elephants. Dumbo, a pink granite formation, stands 27 feet tall, is 35 feet long, 17 feet wide, and weighs 680 tons.

The state's oldest recorded granite quarry is located outside the park, and furnished stone for the Eads Bridge piers and cobblestones for St. Louis streets.

ACTIVITIES - No camping is permitted here, but 30 picnic sites are scattered throughout the park. Hike the one-mile Elephant Rocks Braille Trail, a National Recreation Trail.

The highest point in Missouri, 1,772-foot Taum Sauk Mountain, is 15 miles south of Elephant Rocks. A paved road leads to the top providing an excellent panorama of the surrounding countryside.

INFORMATION
Elephant Rocks State Park
Belleview, Missouri 63023
314-697-5395

FINGER LAKES STATE PARK
11

LOCATION - The park is in central Missouri, 10 miles north of Columbia on U.S. 63.

FEATURES - Before becoming designated as a state park, the land was heavily mined by the Peabody Coal Company that removed over 1.2 million tons of coal. Following the end of their mining operations, the company replanted and reseeded much of the acreage, leaving behind a dozen small lakes that have been connected by a series of dams and canals.

ACTIVITIES - The series of dams and canals extend over 1.5 miles along the eastern border of the park, making it a good place to go boating, canoeing and kayaking.

Over 70 miles of off-road motorcycle trails pass through the park. A new moto-cross course has been designed by professional riders, and is located in the western part of the park. The course and staging area became the site of a dozen moto-cross and motorcycle racing events during the summer and fall months; however, the off-road trails are only for motorcycles and not for four-wheel vehicles.

The campground has 35 campsites, available year-round.

Swimmers have a sandy beach and changing house located on one of the eastern finger lakes.

Incoming pilots can land at Columbia Regional, located 10 miles southeast of town. Rental cars are available.

INFORMATION
Finger Lakes State Park
Route 7
1505 E. Peabody Road
Columbia, Missouri 65202
314-443-5315

FIRST MISSOURI STATE CAPITOL STATE HISTORIC SITE
12

LOCATION - The site is in St. Charles at 200-216 South Main.

FEATURES - The capitol was used by the state's first legislators who met here to reorganize Missouri's territorial government into a state system. The legislators met here from 1821 through 1826 when the new capitol building in Jefferson City became ready for occupancy.

ACTIVITIES - Tour eleven rooms in the capitol complex that have been restored to their original state, with nine containing furnishings from the 1821–26 period. Tour the Peck brothers' residence and general store restored to how they looked during the mid-1800s. Also tour the restored Shepard residence located under the governor's office. A nominal entry fee is charged. For information, call 314-946-9282.

In St. Charles, attend the Lewis and Clark re-enactments presented the third weekend in May, featuring a court-martial, black powder shoot and parade.

In late August, attend the Fete des Petites Cotes that features 19th-century entertainment. Oktoberfest is held the third weekend in October.

Take a walking tour of St. Charles' historic Main Street. Booklets are available at the visitor center at 230 So. Main.

INFORMATION
First Missouri State Capitol State Historic Site
200-216 South Main
St. Charles, Missouri 63301
314-723-3256

GENERAL JOHN J. PERSHING BOYHOOD HOME STATE HISTORIC SITE
13

See under PERSHING STATE PARK

HA HA TONKA STATE PARK
14

LOCATION - The park is on the Niangua Arm of the Lake of the Ozarks, five miles southwest of Camdenton.

FEATURES - The park is an example of topography called karst, and features caves, sinks, underground streams, large springs and natural bridges.

Ha Ha Tonka Spring is one of the 15 largest springs in Missouri, and approximately 48 million gallons of water flow from the spring daily.

Visitors can arrive in the park by boat as well as by car. Two courtesy docks are available.

ACTIVITIES - You'll see the ruins of a castle, begun in 1906, and completed in 1922. Unfortunately, sparks from its fireplace caused fire to gut the castle, leaving behind the stone walls you see today. Near these ruins, you can see a stone stable, an 80-foot water tower, and the trenches for nine greenhouses. A post office operated here from 1928 to 1937.

As you hike, you'll see many interesting geological features including the Natural Bridge that is 70 feet wide, spans 60 feet and rises 100 feet. The bridge is actually the remains of the roof of a cave that collapsed. Watch for sinkholes that are further evidence of the old cavern's presence.

The Colosseum, located at the southern end of the Natural Bridge, was also formed when a large cavern collapsed, and it is believed to be the site of early Indian tribal meetings.

Trails lace the park, passing the various geological features. Get a trail map from the park office. The park is for day-use only and has no camping facilities. Before entering any of the caves, be sure to obtain a permit from the park superintendent.

Nearby is Bridal Cave, two miles northwest on Missouri 5, and then 1.5 miles west on Lake Road. Take a tour of the cave, stop by the observation deck overlooking the lake, tour the visitor center, go boating on the lake, and hike the nature trail. For information, call 314-346-2676.

In May, come for the Dogwood Festival celebrated in Camdenton, and enjoy a colorful walk through these flowering shrubs.

Incoming pilots can land at Camdenton Memorial located three miles southeast of town. A courtesy car is available.

INFORMATION
Ha Ha Tonka State Park
Route 1, Box 658
Camdenton, Missouri 65020
314-346-2986

HARRY S. TRUMAN STATE PARK
15

LOCATION - The park is seven miles west of Warsaw in the northern part of the Ozark Mountains, off Missouri 7 on Benton County UU. The Harry S. Truman Dam is built across the Osage River, and the park is located on a triangular-shaped peninsula two miles northwest of the dam.

FEATURES - The upper Osage River valley contains evidence that during the last glacial period, animals including mastodon, tapir, musk ox, ground sloth and giant beaver roamed the area. Later the Osage River Valley was used as part of the Santa Fe Trail. Now these valleys plus the river's tributaries are inundated by the Harry S. Truman Reservoir, the largest flood control lake in Missouri.

ACTIVITIES - The western section of the park has a campground with 201 campsites scattered through the forest and near the lake. It has 151 basic and primitive sites, and 50 with electrical hookups.

A two-lane boat ramp is located near the campground, and a sandy swimming beach for campers is nearby.

Two-mile Bluff Ridge Trail is located on the western side of the park.

The eastern section of the park is a day-use area; it has swimming, picnicking, boating with a fully equipped marina, and a four-lane boat ramp.

The Lakeside Trail is located below the shelter house, and takes you on a short hike through a wooded area near the lake shoreline.

Millions of fish have been stocked in the lake, making the fishing excellent.

Stop by the visitor center and exhibit area located in the dam's powerhouse to see the control area, and watch their presentation on the Ozarks and on the dam's operations. Hike the self-guided nature trail. For information, call 816-438-2211.

An annual 10-kilometer Dam Run is held in the park in early June. This same weekend, attend the Warsaw Jubilee Days with with a parade, carnival, fiddlers' contest, tractor pull, and country and western entertainment.

On the Fourth of July, come to the Harry S. Truman Dam to watch the fireworks display either from the surrounding hillsides or from aboard a boat.

Each year on the last weekend of October, Warsaw celebrates its heritage, and you can watch demonstrations of spinning and weaving. You can see displays of Civil War relics and steam engines, and enjoy square dancing or clogging. For information, call the Chamber of Commerce at 816-438-5922.

If you're in Warsaw at Christmas, watch the lighting of the Swinging Bridge, one of 15 swinging bridges built over the Osage River between 1895 and 1937. This is the only one that still stands.

Visit the John Hooper House, built in 1884 and placed on the National Register of Historic Places because of its unique roof construction. The house has been reconstructed near the Truman Visitor Center.

To see some old steamboat mooring rings dating back to before the Civil War, go to the rocky ledge bordering the Osage River in Lay Park. The coming of the narrow gauge railroad in the 1870s dealt a deadly blow to the steamboat trade.

Hike part of the Butterfield Overland Trail located in Warsaw.

INFORMATION

Harry S. Truman State Park
HCR 66, Box 14
Warsaw, Missouri 65355
816-438-7711
816-438-2423 (marina)

HAWN STATE PARK
16

LOCATION - The park is fourteen miles southwest of Saint Genevieve on Missouri 32.

FEATURES - The park is located in an historic area. Saint Genevieve is the oldest incorporated community in the state, founded between 1723–35, and became an important port for shipping along the Mississippi River.

The park has Lamotte sandstone bedrock that has been carved into an unusual landscape with rounded sandstone knobs and vertical cliffs.

ACTIVITIES - If you arrive here in the spring, you can see colorful azaleas and dogwood in full bloom.

Go backpacking, hiking, or bird watching in the Whispering Pine Wild Area. The Whispering Pine Trail consists of two loops and passes beside Pickle Creek and the River Aux Vases. Three primitive campsites are available along the trail. For a shorter hike, follow the mile-long Pickle Creek Trail past the sandstone bluffs and shut-ins.

The campground has 50 campsites, 17 with electrical hookups.

Naturalists offer guided nature walks and evening summer programs.

Pickle Creek is a state natural area, and the tea-colored stream has 21 fish species including the rainbow darter, striped shiner and silverjaw minnow.

Take a self-guided tour of Saint Genevieve to see some historic homes. Information is available at the information center on South Third Street next to the historical museum. For information, call 314-883-5750.

Felix Valle State Historic Site, constructed in 1818, is on the corner of Second and Merchant in Saint Genevieve's historical district.

Attend the Jour de Fete in mid-August when the 18th-century homes are on display, watch folk dances, parades and attend the grand ball. On New Year's Eve, members of the community perform the traditional songs and dances of the French settlers, a 250-year-old custom.

INFORMATION
Hawn State Park
Route 3, Box 124
Saint Genevieve, Missouri 63670
314-883-3603

Felix Valle State Historic Site
Merchant and Second Streets
Saint Genevieve, Missouri 63670
314-883-7102

JOHNSON'S SHUT-INS STATE PARK
17

LOCATION - The park is eight miles north of Lesterville on Missouri N, in the scenic St. Francois Mountains.

ACTIVITIES - Take a short walk from the parking lot to see these spectacular shut-ins, chutes, and nearly vertical gorge. Watch for the rare eastern collared lizard, also called a mountain boomer, which stands in an upright position and then runs on its hind legs if disturbed.

The Shut-Ins Trail does a 2.5-mile loop that takes you past some shut-ins, and then passes through the East Fork Wild Area.

The Taum Sauk section of the Ozark Trail is in the park. It takes hikers to Proffit Mountain, Mina Sauk Falls, the highest waterfall in the state, and up 1,772-foot Taum Sauk Mountain, the state's highest point.

The Ozark Trail, 1,000 miles long, passes through Arkansas and Missouri and goes north and west from the park into the Bell Mountain Wilderness Area in Mark Twain National Forest. Spring and fall are prime hiking times. In April and May, the redbud and dogwood trees are in bloom, while in October, the forests take on their fall splendor. June through September, hiking tends to be hot, humid and thick with insects. For information on the Missouri section of the trail, contact the Ozark Trail Coordinator at 314-751-2479 or 1-800-334-6946.

Backpack camping is allowed along the Taum Sauk part of the trail unless otherwise posted.

The park campground has 52 campsites, half with electrical hookups. Camping is available year-round, but water is turned off from November 1–April 1.

Go swimming in the smooth shut-ins, or fishing in the East Fork Black River for bass, bluegill and goggle eye.

INFORMATION
Johnson's Shut-Ins State Park
Middlebrook, Missouri 63056
314-546-2450

KNOB NOSTER STATE PARK
18

LOCATION - The park is two miles south of Knob Noster off U.S. 50 on Missouri 132 in Johnson County.

FEATURES - The park was named for two hills northeast of Knob Noster. The Indians called these hills "knobs." According to legend, the mounds were constructed as monuments to slain warriors after an Indian war. Later settlers added "noster," Latin for "our."

Most of the park is covered by thick second-growth forests of oak, hickory and other deciduous trees.

ACTIVITIES - Stop by the visitor center where a park naturalist is available year-round to present interpretive programs. The amphitheater, the Lil' Forest Theater, is near the campground.

The Pin Oak Slough Natural Area along Clearfork Creek has been designated as a Missouri Natural Area.

Camp in one of 33 basic and 40 improved campsites available year-round.

Clearfork Lake, plus smaller lakes, have fishing for catfish, bass, crappie and bluegill. Small boats without motors are permitted on Clear Fork.

Hikers will find seven hiking trails ranging in length from Clear Fork Savanna Trail, a .5-mile loop in an upland savanna, to the McAdoo Equestrian Trail, a seven mile multi-use trail by hikers, bikers and equestrians. The Boy Scouts maintain a compass trail through the park for which maps are available at the park office.

INFORMATION
Knob Noster State Park
Knob Noster, Missouri 65336
816-563-2463

LAKE OF THE OZARKS STATE PARK
19

LOCATION - The park is off Missouri 42 from U.S. 54 near Kaiser, Missouri.

FEATURES - Lake of the Ozarks is Missouri's largest state park, and the lake has over 80 miles of lake frontage located within the park.

ACTIVITIES - Visit Coakley Hollow Fen near Ozark Caverns, a Missouri Natural Area, complete with a boardwalk and self-guided trail.

The Patterson Hollow Wild Area is south of Missouri 42 and west of Missouri 134. If you come during the spring, you can see dogwood in bloom. The fall features beautiful colors in the hardwood forest of oak and hickory.

Hikers will find 10 trails covering 23 miles to explore, ranging in length from .5-mile to six miles. Backpacking is available on six-mile Woodland Trail.

Equestrians can ride on eight-mile Trail of Four Winds and Squaw's Revenge, and all-terrain bicyclists can cycle on the Trail of Four Winds.

Tour the Ozark Caverns located off County Road A, 8.5 miles from U.S. 54. One of the unusual sights is Angel's Shower, featuring a continuous shower of water that appears to come from the solid cave roof.

INFORMATION

Lake of the Ozarks State Park
P. O. Box 170
Kaiser, Missouri 65047
314-348-2694

Ozark Caverns
Route 1, Box 390
Linn Creek, Missouri 65052
314-346-2500

LAKE WAPPAPELLO STATE PARK
20

LOCATION - The park is 12 miles north of Poplar Bluff on U.S. 67, and nine miles east on Missouri 172.

FEATURES - According to legend, Wappapello was named for a friendly Shawnee chief who hunted in the forest during pioneer days. The park has a large oak-hickory forest. Watch for mistletoe that grows in the black gum and sycamores trees along the edge of the lake, a sight rarely seen in Missouri.

The area along Asher Creek is a winter waterfowl refuge. You can see wintering eagles, blue herons and great horned owls.

ACTIVITIES - Go fishing for bass, crappie, bluegill and catfish. Largemouth bass have been caught that weigh as much as nine pounds.

You can also go water-skiing, swimming from the 150-foot sand beach, and boating from the paved boat ramp. A fully equipped marina is in the park. It rents fishing boats, pontoons, motors, fishing tackle and sells food. For information, call 314-297-3247.

The Lake Wappapello Trail is 15 miles long, and is designed for hiking, backpacking and all-terrain bicycling. The Allison Cemetery Trail is 3.5 miles long and goes past Allison Cemetery. Two-mile Asher Creek Trail includes a section beside the waterfowl refuge area of the lake. The .5-mile Lake View Trail provides an easy hike to get good views of the lake.

Go camping in one of its 80 campsites, some basic and some with electrical hookups. Eight cabins are available for rent from April 1–October 31. Reservations are required. Call 314-297-3247.

INFORMATION

Lake Wappapello State Park
Route 2, Box 102
Williamsville, Missouri 63967
314-297-3232

LEWIS AND CLARK STATE PARK
21

LOCATION - The park is twenty miles southwest of St. Joseph on Missouri 138 along the shoreline of Sugar Lake.

FEATURES - The park is dedicated to explorers Lewis and Clark who visited here on their well-known journey west.

ACTIVITIES - The park is one of Missouri's smallest state parks, but has a 364-acre lake, Sugar Lake, a popular site for boating, canoeing, water-skiing and swimming. Because of its shallowness, fishing is good for bass, bluegill, catfish and carp. A fish hatchery is located in the park, and stocks many of the northern streams and lakes.

The campground has 70 campsites with some providing electrical hookups. Many picnic areas are scattered along the lake's shoreline.

In St. Joseph, visit the St. Joseph Museum at 11th and Charles, and the Pony Express Museum located at 914 Penn Street.

INFORMATION
Lewis and Clark State Park
Route 2, Box 226
Rushville, Missouri 64484
816-579-5564

LONG BRANCH STATE PARK
22

LOCATION - The park is located on the banks of Long Branch Lake, three miles west of Macon. From the intersection of U.S. 63 and 36, go west on Missouri 36.

ACTIVITIES - The lake is known for its excellent bass, catfish and bluegill fishing. Fishing is available in 24 coves located along the water's edge. Swimmers can go swimming from a sandy beach along the shoreline. A marina has gas, tackle and fishing equipment.

The campground has 40 campsites, all with electrical hookups. Sites are located in the wooded area and along the lake. The water is turned off from October 31–April 1.

Stop by the visitor center located at the east end of the dam to see their displays on the lake's history and recreational opportunities.

INFORMATION
Long Branch State Park
Macon, Missouri 635
816-773-5329 (park office)
816-877-3871 (marina)

MARK TWAIN BIRTHPLACE AND MUSEUM STATE HISTORIC SITE
MARK TWAIN STATE PARK
23

LOCATION - The Mark Twain Birthplace State Historic Site is located in Hannibal at 208 Hill Street. Mark Twain State Park is six miles south of the intersection of U.S. 24 and Missouri 107.

FEATURES - Samuel Clemens adopted his pen name of Mark Twain, a phrase used by the leadsman when a boat had reached safe water of two fathoms. His birthplace is a small two-room dwelling that has been preserved inside a modern museum. It measures only 420 square feet, but managed to house eight other family members when Clemens was born.

ACTIVITIES - The birthplace is open year-round from 10–4 Monday through Saturday, and from 12–5 p.m. on Sunday. Look at the first edition of Mark Twain's works, a handwritten manuscript of The Adventures of Tom Sawyer, and see the furnishings from his Connecticut home. A nominal admission fee is charged.

When the Clarence Cannon Dam was built across the Salt River, Mark Twain Lake was created, and now visitors can go boating and fishing. A six-lane boat ramp provides easy access into the lake stocked with bluegill, crappie, catfish, bass, carp and perch.

Go to "Buzzard's Roost" for a scenic overlook of the lake. Along this bluff, you can find some hillside strawberries, an unusual form of wild strawberry found only in the Salt River valley.

The campground has 56 sites, 35 with electrical hookups.

The only remaining Burr-arch style covered bridge in the state is over the South Fork of the Salt River near Paris, 25 miles west of the park. Completed in 1871, it is one of four remaining covered bridges in Missouri.

Hikers and backpackers have access to many miles of trails found throughout the Mark Twain Lake area. The lake has two full-service marinas located along its shoreline, plus many developed campgrounds, swimming beaches and good fishing.

Four miles south of Hannibal on U.S. 61, attend an outdoor production of "Reflections of Mark Twain." It's presented daily in the evening June–August, and the first three weekends in September. For information, call 314-221-2945.

Take a boat ride aboard the Mark Twain excursion boat docked at the foot of Center Street. The cruises go from May–October. For information and schedules, call 314-221-3222.

To see the cave where Tom Sawyer and Becky Thatcher were lost, tour the Mark Twain Cave located two miles southeast of Hannibal on Missouri 79. For information, call 816-252-1892.

If you're in town over July 4th, watch the National Fence Painting contest held during National Tom Sawyer Days. The first weekend in November, attend the Autumn Historic Folklife Festival.

INFORMATION
Mark Twain Birthplace State
  Historic Site
Stoutsville, Missouri 65283
314-565-3449

Mark Twain State Park
214-586-3440

MERAMEC STATE PARK
24

LOCATION - The park is four miles east of Sullivan on Missouri 185.

FEATURES - The park includes a gorge along the Meramec River.

ACTIVITIES - Hike into the Meramec Upland Forest Natural Area, featuring an old-growth, oak-hickory forest.

The park's campground borders the spring-fed Meramec River. It has 170 basic campsites and 80 improved campsites, or you can overnight in one of 18 cabins. The park has a dining lodge, a general store, canoe rentals and a visitor center. Take a float trip down the Meramec River.

Several springs and over 30 caves are found in this park, and a naturalist leads tours through Fisher Cave. An admission fee is charged.

INFORMATION
Meramec State Park
Route 4, Box 4
Sullivan, Missouri 63080
314-468-6519 (cabin and canoe reservations)
314-468-6072 (park)

MISSOURI MINES STATE HISTORIC SITE
25

See under ST. JOE STATE PARK

MISSOURI RIVER STATE TRAIL
26

LOCATION - Currently the trail runs from the U.S. 40-61 bridge at the eastern boundary of the Weldon Spring Wildlife Area to Marthasville, covering a distance of 26.6 miles.

FEATURES - Eventually the trail will cover 200 miles, extending between Machens in northern St. Charles County to Sedalia in Pettis County.

ACTIVITIES - Daniel Boone lived between Defiance and Marthasville, and his grave site is on the Boone Monument Road one mile east of Marthasville.

Incoming pilots can land at Jefferson City Memorial located two miles northeast of town. Rental cars are available.

INFORMATION
Missouri River State Trail   1-800-334-6946
c/o Missouri Department of Natural Resources
P. O. Box 176
Jefferson City, Missouri 65102

MONTAUK STATE PARK
27

LOCATION - The park is in the southwestern Missouri Ozarks, six miles southeast of Licking on Dent County VV off Missouri 137.

FEATURES - The park was named by a group of pioneers after their former home, Montauk, on Long Island. It's an Indian word and is believed to mean "hilly" or "fort country."

ACTIVITIES - The Current River and nearby Jack's Fork River have been designated National Scenic Riverways. Since the park is on the headwaters of the Current River, it's a favorite for trout fishermen. March 1–October 31 is the official trout season, and a fishing license is required. The Rose Holland Trout Derby is held annually on the first weekend in October, with smaller trout derbies held during the trout season. Tour the trout hatcheries.

During the winter, a fish-for-fun season runs from the second Friday in November to the second Sunday in February on weekends only.

This river is one of the best canoeing rivers in the Midwest, and the northernmost canoe access, Inman Hollow, is located just below the park's southeast border.

The park has several springs that once fed some grist mills, one which still stands in the park. This mill, built in 1896, is currently being restored, and is not yet open to the public.

Over 200 tent and trailer campsites are available, with 52 of the sites offering electrical hookups year-round. You can also stay in one of 25 housekeeping cabins or the motel which is open during the fishing season. Advance reservations are required. Reservations for both the motel and cabins may be secured by calling 314-548-2434 or 1-800-334-6946.

The park borders the Mark Twain National Forest, located east of the park. Hike along their nature trails to see the native wildflowers around the springs and along the Current River.

INFORMATION
Montauk State Park
R. R. 5, Box 278
Salem, Missouri 65560
314-548-2201 or 1-800-334-6946

ONONDAGA CAVE STATE PARK
28

LOCATION - The park is seven miles southeast of the I-44 Leasburg exit on Highway H. It's 65 miles southwest of St. Louis on I-44.

FEATURES - Missouri is called the cave state, leading every other state in the number of known caves with over 5,000 of them. The Onodaga Cave is one of the most beautiful with its abundance of stalactites, stalagmites, rimstone dams, flowstones, draperies, soda straws and cave coral. Since a stream meanders through the cave, many of the formations continue to grow. The cave contains six or seven sites with the bones of extinct animals.

ACTIVITIES - Take a guided walk through the electrically lit passages of the historic cave, listed as a National Natural Landmark. You'll see the spectacular Lily Pad Room and the large Queen's Canopy flowstone. The canopy is estimated to be worth one million dollars in polished onyx.

Onondaga Cave is open for daily tours March through October, and is closed November through February.

Vilander Bluff is located less than 10 miles from the park's main section, and contains some of the highest bluffs along the Meramec River.

Campers will find 72 campsites, 17 with electrical hookups. A cave is located in the visitor center.

Hikers can hike along three miles of hiking trails. The Blue Heron Trail is .5-mile long, and the Deer Run Trail makes a 2.75-mile loop.

The crystal clear waters of the Meramec River flow through the park, and you can go swimming, fishing and canoeing. Canoes may be rented at the gift shop. Reservations for canoes are highly advisable on summer weekends.

Take a nature float trip on Thursdays at 9:00 a.m. past the park's Vilander Bluff unit to the Blue Springs Access. The float trips are only offered June–August, and reservations are required the day before.

Naturalists present regularly scheduled programs during the summer.

INFORMATION
Onodoga Cave State Park
Route 1, Box 72
Leasburg, Missouri 65535
314-245-6417

PERSHING STATE PARK
GENERAL JOHN J. PERSHING BOYHOOD HOME STATE HISTORIC SITE
29

LOCATION - The Pershing Boyhood Home State Historic Site is located in Laclede, one mile north of U.S. 36 on Missouri 5.

The state park is two miles southwest of Laclede, off U.S. 36 on Missouri 130.

FEATURES - General John J. Pershing was the highest ranking military officer in U.S. history, and served as General of the Armies after World War I.

ACTIVITIES - Tour his boyhood home which includes displays related to both local history and to Pershing's life and career. Tour Prairie Mound, the one-room school where he once taught.

Go bass fishing in one of the two small lakes, hike the trails, and go swimming. The campground has 38 campsites, 21 basic, and 17 with full hookups.

Locust Creek Covered Bridge State Historic Site is located three miles west of Laclede on U.S. 36, and one mile northeast. It's one of only four remaining covered bridges left in the state, and is the longest of the four. The Howe-truss bridge was built in 1868, and features arched entrances with ramps sloping away from both ends.

INFORMATION
General John J. Pershing Boyhood   Pershing State Park
  Home State Historic Site   Laclede, Missouri 64651
Laclede, Missouri 64651   816-963-2299
816-963-2525

POMME DE TERRE STATE PARK
30

LOCATION - The park is five miles south of Hermitage via Missouri 64 along the banks of the Pomme de Terre Reservoir.

FEATURES - You can see remnants of a presettlement savanna landscape, complete with 200-year-old oak trees.

ACTIVITIES - The park is geared for water activities and has hundreds of coves where you can fish for muskie. Rent boats at the marina with a general store.

There are two public beaches and two campgrounds. The basic campground has 134 basic campsites, and the improved campground has 130 sites, and a dump station.

Go swimming from the beach, or attend one of the programs offered by their seasonal naturalists.

INFORMATION
Pomme de Terre State Park
Pittsburg, Missouri 65724
417-852-4291 or 417-745-6909

PRAIRIE STATE PARK
31

LOCATION - The park is twenty-five miles north of Joplin off Missouri 43 on Missouri P.

FEATURES - Two hundred years ago, prairie land covered 400,000 square miles in North America, and this park contains the state's largest example. Bison roam freely in parts of the park, so look around before leaving your car.

ACTIVITIES - Go hiking on one of the three hiking trails. Coyote Trail is three miles long. Drover's Trail is 2.5 miles long, and goes from the center of the park to the East Drywood Creek drainage. Gayfeather Trail is 1.5 miles long and passes through the Regal Prairie Natural Area.

A naturalist conducts year-round interpretive programs.

INFORMATION
Prairie State Park
Liberal, Missouri 64762
417-843-6711

ROARING RIVER STATE PARK
32

LOCATION - The park is located seven miles south of Cassville on Missouri 112.

FEATURES - The river spring, gushing over 200 million gallons of water, once provided the power needed for early milling endeavors. During the Civil War, the steep terrain and canyon-like gorges provided great hideouts for Civil War bushwhackers.

ACTIVITIES - Stay overnight in one of the rustic cabins or in the modern motel. Reservations for either may be made by calling 417-847-2330 or 1-800-334-6946. The campground has 200 campsites, both basic and with hookups.

Go fishing for trout during the fishing season that runs from March 1–October 31. The river is stocked daily, and you need a license.

Get a meal in the park's dining lodge featuring Ozark specialties; it's open during trout season. Go swimming in the modern pool open daily from 12–6 from Memorial Day through Labor Day.

Stop by the nature center, staffed year-round. Its naturalists conduct hikes and trout hatchery tours on a regular basis.

Hikers have access to 10 miles of trails. The 1.5-mile Devil's Kitchen Trail takes you to a rock shelter known as Devil's Kitchen. The 3.5-mile Fire Tower Trail provides access into the heart of the Roaring River Hills Wild Area.

Equestrians have access to a stable in the park.

INFORMATION
Roaring River State Park
Route 2, Box 256-H
Cassville, Missouri 65625
417-847-2330

ROCK BRIDGE MEMORIAL STATE PARK
33

LOCATION - The park is seven miles south of Columbia and I-70 on Missouri 163.

FEATURES - The park is for day-use only, and has many natural geological formations including Devil's Icebox Cave, a natural rock bridge, and many sinkholes that are part of a large limestone cave system dating back thousands of years.

ACTIVITIES - Take a short walk from the parking lot off Missouri 163 to see Rock Bridge. It's a remnant of an ancient cave roof that remained standing after the surrounding cave collapsed.

Devil's Icebox is a double sinkhole created when the roof of a cave collapsed, and now serves as the surface access to the underground cave system. Visitors can see this cave entrance from an observation platform. Only experienced spelunkers with permission from the park superintendent are allowed to enter and explore the six-mile cave interior.

Visit the Gans Creek Wild Area to see the wildflowers in the spring, and the oak and hickory foliage in the fall. Access to the area is either from the north via Bearfield Road, or from the east off Missouri 163 from the gate to the old Cunningham farm.

The park has four trails with 4.5 miles of hiking possibilities in the western section of the park. Rock Bridge Trail, .5-mile long, is where you can see some of the park's geological history. To see some sinkholes, hike the Sinkhole Trail, 1.5 miles. During winter, go cross-country skiing on these trails.

The University of Missouri Orienteering Club has developed an orienteering course with checkpoints scattered throughout the park.

General camping facilities aren't available in the park, but 33 picnic sites offer places to stop for a meal.

Incoming pilots can land at Columbia Regional Airport located 10 miles southeast of town. Rental cars are available at the airport.

INFORMATION
Rock Bridge Memorial State Park
Columbia, Missouri 65201
314-449-7402

SAM A. BAKER STATE PARK
34

LOCATION - The park is located 20 miles west of St. Louis on Missouri 109, off St. Louis County CC, and six miles north of Patterson via Missouri 34 and 143.

FEATURES - The park is located in the St. Francois Mountains, some of the oldest mountains in North America, and features rounded hills or domes of igneous rock. One of the largest domes, Mudlick Mountain, is located here.

ACTIVITIES - Take a hike, or go for a trail ride through the forest. Go for a swim in the modern swimming pool. Go bass fishing in the stream, or rent a boat and go boating.

A 15-mile National Recreation Trail provides access to the Mudlick Mountain's wild and natural area. Stop by the visitor center to learn more about these ancient mountains.

Camp in the campground with 211 campsites, 67 with electrical hookups, or stay in the lodge or in one of the cabins. Food service is available.

INFORMATION
Sam A. Baker State Park
RFD 1, Box 114
Patterson, Missouri 63956
314-856-4411

ST. FRANCOIS STATE PARK
35

LOCATION - The park is four miles north of Bonne Terre on U.S. 67.

FEATURES - The park is thick with deciduous trees including oak, hickory, maple, ash and black gum.

ACTIVITIES - Visit the Coonville Creek Wild Area, designated as part of the Missouri Natural Areas System. The area is especially colorful in the fall when the leaves change.

Hike Mooner's Hollow Trail, a 2.7-mile loop, named for the past activity of moonshiners. The Pike Run Trail is 11 miles long and has two loops to explore. Swimming Deer Trail is 2.7 miles, and begins at the east end of the campground.

Old Logger's Trail uses old logging roads and is a 10-mile equestrian and hiking trail passing through the eastern section of the park. This trail also provides access to the Coonville Creek Wild Area.

The park has 82 basic campsites, with 28 providing electrical hookups.

The Big River, which forms the southern boundary of the park, is ideal for novice canoeists. You can put in at St. Francois and float to Washington State Park, covering 24 miles.

Fishermen can try their luck at snagging bass, catfish and sunfish.

A park naturalist is available in the summer for nature walks, interpretive programs, and slide shows.

INFORMATION
St. Francois State Park   314-358-2173
Box 268
Bonne Terre, Missouri 63628

ST. JOE STATE PARK
MISSOURI MINES STATE HISTORIC SITE

36

LOCATION - The park is three miles southeast of Flat River off Missouri County B via Missouri 32.

FEATURES - St. Joe is the state's second largest state park, and is located in the heart of the "Lead Belt" in southeastern Missouri.

ACTIVITIES - The sandflats have been set aside for off-road vehicles including motorcycles, dune buggies and four-wheel drive vehicles. Free all-terrain vehicle safety classes are offered Memorial Day–Labor Day.

Off-road vehicle riders have a campground located near the riding area with 35 basic sites, and 15 campsites with electrical hookups.

Equestrians have a 23-mile-long trail winding through wooded portions of the park, and an equestrian campground with 10 campsites.

Bicyclists and hikers have 11 miles of paved trails to explore, including Hickory Ridge Trail, a three-mile loop, and Harris Branch Trail, an 11-mile paved bicycle trail. These trails are used for cross-country skiing during the winter.

The mining operations left behind four lakes located adjacent to the tailings' area, and here visitors can swim, go fishing and boating. Excellent beaches are located at Monsanto and Pim lakes. All four of the park lakes have boat ramps, and are stocked with bass, bluegill and catfish.

While in the area, tour the Missouri Mines State Historic Site, located one mile south of Main Street on Federal Mill Drive in Flat River. The powerhouse of Federal Mill No. 3 has been converted into a museum of mining, history and technology. One of the three galleries contains a fluorescent mineral room with minerals that are viewed under short- and long-wave ultraviolet light.

INFORMATION

St. Joe State Park
Elvins, Missouri 63601
314-358-2173

Missouri Mines State Historic Site
P. O. Box 492
Flat River, Missouri 63601
314-431-6226

STOCKTON STATE PARK
37

LOCATION - The park is on Stockton Lake at the western edge of the Missouri Ozarks, and 10 miles south of Stockton on Missouri 215. It's on a peninsula that juts out between the Big and Little Sac arms of Stockton Lake.

FEATURES - Archaeologists have found burial mounds, village sites and campsites left behind by prehistoric man who occupied the Sac River valley approximately 10,000 years ago.

ACTIVITIES - Visitors can go camping in one of 45 basic campsites with 38 offering electrical hookups. You can also overnight in the motel, and eat at the Stockton State Park Inn.

Stockton Lake has 298 miles of shoreline, and 12 parks surround it. It's known for its excellent fishing, and is stocked with bass, crappie, walleye, catfish, pike and bluegill.

It's also good for sailing and boating because of its dependable southwest breeze. A marina has groceries, and rents fishing boats. The park has two launching ramps and a marina.

Scuba divers enjoy diving in the clear water. Swimmers have a beach.

INFORMATION

Stockton State Park
Dadeville, Missouri 63635
417-276-4259

TABLE ROCK STATE PARK
38

LOCATION - The park is eight miles west of Branson on Missouri 165 on Table Rock Lake.

FEATURES - The lake has 800 miles of shoreline, and is within a few minutes' drive of Lake Taneycomo.

ACTIVITIES - Go boating, canoeing or sailing on Table Rock Lake. The clear water makes the park ideal for water activities and scuba diving. The marina has a general store with boating and fishing supplies plus scuba diving equipment.

You can also go hiking, or camp in the campground with 86 basic campsites, and 73 sites with full hookups.

Tour the dam and powerhouse. For their schedule, call 417-334-4104.

Take a ride on "The Ducks" two miles west of Branson on Missouri 76. This 70-minute narrated tour of the lake and nearby Wilderness Safari Animal Park is conducted in restored military amphibious vehicles. The season runs from mid-April through October, and weekends in November. For information, call 417-334-5350.

If you enjoy looking through caves, take the hour-long tour through Marvel Cave located under Silver Dollar City. It has 32 miles of explored passageways. Admission to the cave is included in the price of a Silver Dollar City passport. For information, call 417-338-8210.

Visit Table Rock Dam and Visitor Center located four miles west on Missouri 76, and five miles south on U.S. 165. The powerhouse is four miles from the center. Tour the dam and watch their audio-visual presentation. For information, call 417-334-4104.

INFORMATION
Table Rock State Park
Branson, Missouri 65616
417-334-3069
417-334-4704 (marina)

THOUSAND HILLS STATE PARK
39

LOCATION - The park is four miles west of Kirksville off Missouri 6 on Missouri 157.

FEATURES - When the glaciers passed over the area, they flattened the land that was then cut through by many rivers and streams. This erosion created what appeared to be "thousands of hills."

Rock carvings in the park left behind by the very early Indian inhabitants date back as far as the Middle Mississippi culture whose people lived here between A.D. 1000 and 1600.

ACTIVITIES - Stay in one of the 73 campsites, 27 with electrical hookups. A modern lodge with a dining room is located on Forest Lake, or you can stay in one of the five modern cabins overlooking the lake's shoreline. The cabins are open from March 1–December 21. The dining lodge is open daily from April 1–October 31, and on weekends from November 1–December 21.

Park programs offered during the summer include evening programs Wednesday–Saturday, nature hikes Friday and Saturday, pontoon boat rides around the lake Tuesday–Sunday, and a petroglyph open house 2–4 Saturday and Sunday. These ancient rock carvings have been listed on the National Register of Historic Places.

Forest Lake has 17 miles of shoreline, and is popular for sailing, canoeing, and motor boating with boats having a maximum of 90 horsepower. A fully equipped marina is located on the lake. For information, call 816-665-3712.

The Thousand Hills Trail is five miles long, and passes through one of the few remaining bigtooth aspen stands in the state. Its western portion follows Forest Lake's shoreline.

Incoming pilots can land at Kirksville Regional Airport located six miles south of town. Rental cars are available.

INFORMATION
Thousand Hills State Park
Route 3
Kirksville, Missouri 63501
816-665-6995 (park office)
816-665-7119 or 816-665-2811 (cabin reservations)

TRAIL OF TEARS STATE PARK
40

LOCATION - The park is ten miles north of Cape Girardeau on Missouri 177, and 10 miles east of Fruitland off I-55.

FEATURES - In 1830, President Andrew Jackson authorized the removal of the Cherokees who were living in North Carolina, Georgia and Tennessee. Many left voluntarily, but 13,000 who refused to go, were forced to march 1,200 miles to reservations in the west. At least a quarter of the Indians died en route, leading to the name "Trail of Tears."

Trail of Tears State Park is Missouri's only state park located directly on the Mississippi River.

ACTIVITIES - Visit Indian Creek Wild Area with its magnificent hardwood forests. The 10-mile Peewah Trail, named for the Indian word meaning "come follow in this direction," provides access into the wild area. The trail is used by hikers, backpackers, and equestrians.

A one mile hiking trail takes you to Shepard's Point for an overlook of the river. If you're here during the winter, watch for bald eagles nesting in the large trees on the bluffs and along the river cliffs.

The Vancill Hollow Natural Area's forest is similar to those found in the Appalachians, and has a large growth of American beech, tulip poplar and cucumber magnolia trees.

Camp in one of the 35 basic campsites located in the woods. Twelve campsites have electrical hookups and eight have both electrical and sewer hookups. Two backpacking sites are located along the northern loop of the Peewah Trail.

Go fishing in the Mississippi for catfish, perch, and carp. You can also fish in Lake Boutin stocked with bass, bluegill and catfish. The lake also is good for boating, canoeing and swimming from its beach with a change house.

INFORMATION
Trail of Tears State Park
Route 4
Jackson, Missouri 63755
314-334-1711

WALLACE STATE PARK
41

LOCATION - The park is six miles south of Cameron off I-35.

FEATURES - The Trice-Dedman Memorial Woods, owned by the Nature Conservancy, is one of the best examples of a presettlement forest found in northwest Missouri.

ACTIVITIES - Camp in the campground with 68 campsites, 23 offering electrical hookups, and a trailer dumping station.

Go boating, swimming, or fishing for bass and catfish in Lake Allaman. You can either fish from the shore or from boats with electric motors. No gas-powered motors are permitted.

Picnic in one of the numerous picnic shelters, or go hiking. The three trails, Rocky Ford, Skunk Hollow and Deer Run, range in length from .75-mile to two miles.

INFORMATION
Wallace State Park
Cameron, Missouri 64429
816-632-3745

WASHINGTON STATE PARK
42

LOCATION - The park is 14 miles northeast of Potosi on Missouri 21.

FEATURES - The Big River, a tributary of the Meramec River, forms the northern boundary of this park. The site was once used as ceremonial grounds for the Middle Mississippi people who left behind rock carvings called petroglyphs.

ACTIVITIES - Enjoy a home-cooked meal in the dining lodge overlooking the Big River, open from April 15–October 31. Camping supplies and groceries are sold at the general store located in the lodge.

Go swimming in the modern swimming pool or in Big River. The pool is open daily from 12–6:00 Memorial Day–Labor Day.

You can rent a canoe for float trips ranging from a half-day to two days. The floating trips may be arranged to cover anywhere from three to 22 miles. Transportation is provided to a "put-in" point. Tubing is another favorite activity, and innertubes may be rented from the concessionaire at the dining lodge.

See the Indian rock carvings located near the southern boundary of the park.

Stay overnight in one of the park's cabins that may be rented April 15–October 31. For reservations, call 314-586-6696 Memorial Day–Labor Day, or 314-438-4106 (after 5:00 p.m.) the remaining months. You can also camp in the campground with 73 basic campsites of which 18 offer electrical hookups.

The Washington Hardwoods Forest, located along the bluffs near Big River, feature 100-foot trees including Kentucky coffee, sugar maple and slippery elm.

Stop by the interpretive center located near the park entrance to learn more about the park, and to attend evening slide shows and nature walks during the summer.

The park has three marked hiking trails ranging from the 1,000 steps trail which winds through the forest, to the Rockywood Trail, a hiking/backpacking trail that traverses 10 miles of the rugged Ozark terrain.

INFORMATION
Washington State Park
Route 2, Box 450
De Soto, Missouri 63020
314-586-2995 or 1-800-334-6946

WATKINS MILL STATE PARK
WATKINS WOOLEN MILL STATE HISTORIC SITE
43

LOCATION - Watkins Mill State Park is six miles north of Excelsior Springs, off Missouri 92 on Missouri RA. Watkins Woolen Mill State Historic Site is 6.5 miles north of Excelsior Springs on U.S. 69, and then 1.5 miles west on Missouri MM.

FEATURES - The historic site was once part of the Bethany Plantation, a 3,660-acre livestock farm owned by Waltus Watkins. The factory is the only

19th-century American woolen mill with its original machinery still intact, and is registered as a National Historic Landmark.

ACTIVITIES - Tour the woolen mill, restored owner's house, and various outbuildings. A small fee is charged for the tour. The campground has 36 campsites.

Watkins Mill State Park has a small lake for fishing, swimming from the beach, and boating or canoeing. You can also camp in the campground with 60 campsites, some with full hookups, ride on an asphalt bicycle trail, or go hiking. A naturalist is on duty seasonally.

INFORMATION

Watkins Mill State Park
Lawson, Missouri 64062
816-296-3387

Watkins Woolen Mill State Historic Site
Lawson, Missouri 64062
816-296-3357

Scout's Rest Ranch, in Buffalo Bill State Historical Park near North Platte,
was the home of famed showman and Wild West hero William F. Cody.
BUFFALO BILL RANCH STATE HISTORICAL PARK

NEBRASKA

When you drive across Nebraska on I-80, you become aware of the many lakes that were formed during the construction of the highway. These lakes, along with "Big Mac," Lake McConaughy, provide visitors with numerous opportunities to enjoy water-based activities along with scenic camping. Nebraska has 69 state recreation areas, seven state parks and ten historical parks for you to explore.

Those who enjoy history should visit Arbor Lodge, Rock Creek Station, Fort Atkinson, Fort Kearny, Fort Hartsuff, Buffalo Bill Ranch, Arthur Bowring Ranch, Champion Mill and Ash Hollow.

For a glimpse into life on frontier military posts during the late 1800s, visit Forts Atkinson, Kearny and Hartsuff. Arbor Lodge is the former home of J. Sterling Morton, founder of Arbor Day. Buffalo Bill Ranch was the home of pioneer scout and showman, Buffalo Bill Cody. Ash Hollow and Rock Creek Station give some of the history of the Overland and Oregon Trails.

Overnight lodging is available at five of the state parks, and at two recreation areas. Fort Robinson, Chadron, Niobrara, Ponca, and Platte River state parks have lodging facilities. Some cabins at Platte River State Park are open year-round. Two Rivers State Recreation Area and Victoria Springs both have cabins.

ARBOR LODGE STATE HISTORIC PARK
1

LOCATION - The park is northwest of Nebraska City.

ACTIVITIES - The park is home of Arbor Day founder J. Sterling Morton. Arbor Day, celebrated the last weekend in April, originated in Nebraska City.

Visitors coming here in October can watch the early day crafts such as spinning and quilting. You'll also hear hoof beats echoing along the brick streets as antique carriages carry visitors on tours of the grounds.

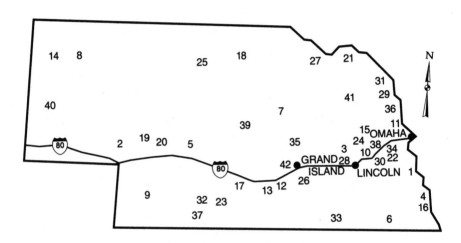

14 8
25
18
27 21
N
31
41 29
40
36
7
11
39
15 OMAHA
80
2 19 20 5
35
24 38 34
3
10 30 22
42 ● GRAND 28
ISLAND LINCOLN 1
80
17 13 12 26
9
32 23
4
37
33 6
16

The 52-room lodge has been redecorated circa 1905, and is open for tours from mid-May through Labor Day from 10–5, and from 1–5 September and October.

Hike the Arbor Tree Trail surrounding the park with over 250 varieties of trees and shrubs.

Stroll through the 1901 carriage house to see historic coaches, horse-drawn carriages, and other historic vehicles, and enjoy a cup of fresh apple cider. Wander through the rose garden, and follow the self-guided Trees Trail.

Living history demonstrations are presented on Sundays during October.

Since the park is open for day-use only, camping is available at the Riverview Marina State Park east of town. This campground has 30 campsites, fishing and boating on the Missouri River.

You can drive through the park daily all year round or drive through the valley in the fall to see the area's orchards.

Incoming pilots can land at Grundman Airport in Nebraska City, one mile southwest of town. Rental cars are available.

INFORMATION
Arbor Lodge State Historical Park
R. R. 2, Box 15
Nebraska City, Nebraska 68410
402-873-7222

ASH HOLLOW CAVE STATE HISTORICAL PARK
2

LOCATION - Ash Hollow Cave is three miles south of Lewellen, and a .5-mile east of U.S. 26.

FEATURES - Bones of prehistoric mammals were found at Ash Hollow Cave along with evidence that early man was here around 8,000 years ago. The area is also the site of the historic Blue Water Battlefield.

ACTIVITIES - Tour the visitor center on the bluff, overlooking the canyon mouth. Hike down to the fresh-water spring. Camping facilities are available. You can also visit a pioneer cemetery, an old-time schoolhouse, and an ancient Indian cave.

In Windlass Hill, 2.75 miles south of the visitor center, you can see deep ruts carved by the wagon trains traveling along the Overland Trail. Ash Hollow was a welcome sight to the westward-bound emigrants, and one traveler wrote, "Steep does not begin to describe the final descent into the Hollow. We had to rough lock the wheels for the first time and several times I felt sure that the wagon would tip over on the tongue yoke of cattle." Today a nature trail leads to the top of Windlass Hill, so you can experience the steep pitch they descended.

INFORMATION
Ash Hollow Cave State Historical Park
Box A
Lewellen, Nebraska 69147
308-778-5651

BRANCHED OAK STATE RECREATION AREA
3

LOCATION - The area is 3.5 miles north of Malcolm and four miles west of Raymond.

ACTIVITIES - This park is the most heavily utilized area in the state and is the site of the largest Salt Valley reservoir, with 1,800 miles of shoreline.

Camp in one of the 195 campsites where 114 offer electrical hookups, and a nearby concession stand.

Each spring, enjoy fishing for walleye, crappie and catfish along the dam. In late spring, fish for bass, bluegill and crappie. During the summer, fish in the submerged weed beds for walleye and bass. In the fall, move to the shallow water and areas with submerged trees to fish for bass, bluegill and crappie. Winter fishermen go after crappie in the deep water along the dam. Branched Oak Inn and Branched Oak Marina provide snacks, fishing tackle and gasoline.

Go boating from the ramp where boat rentals are available, water-skiing, swimming, and sailing on Branched Oak Lake. Tour the arboretum with over 100 species of trees and shrubs.

INFORMATION
Branched Oak State Recreation Area
R. R. 1, Box 61
Raymond, Nebraska 68428
402-783-3400

BROWNVILLE STATE RECREATION AREA
4

LOCATION - The area is a half-mile southeast of Brownville.

ACTIVITIES - Go fishing or boating on the Missouri River. The small campground has 15 sites.

Take a two-hour cruise aboard the "Spirit of Brownville." The cruises depart Tuesday through Sunday beginning in mid-June and running through Labor Day. For information, call 402-825-644.

One of the main attractions in town is the Meriwether Lewis Steamboat dredge, named for the explorer who explored the Missouri River in 1804. Now the Museum of Missouri River History is located on the dry-docked dredge, and has displays of early river life.

During the summer, you can attend Nebraska's oldest summer repertory theater. Performances are given on Friday evenings. Saturday and Sunday have both matinee and evening performances, and additional performances are given on Thursdays in August. For information, call 402-825-4121.

INFORMATION
Brownville State Recreation Area
Brownville, Nebraska 68321
402-883-2575

BUFFALO BILL STATE HISTORICAL PARK
5

LOCATION - The park is 3.5 miles northwest of North Platte via Nebraska 30, Rodeo Road. Turn west on Buffalo Bill Avenue and follow the signs.

ACTIVITIES - Tour his 18-room mansion, called Scout's Rest Ranch, which he had built in 1886 at the height of his entertainment career. Here you can see an exhibit on dime novels and comic books featuring Buffalo Bill plus artifacts of Sioux Indian chief Sitting Bull, who toured briefly with his show.

The barn, built in 1887, and once a rehearsal site for his Wild West troupe, has his personal saddle, pictures and posters from his shows, plus a collection of horse-drawn farm implements. Watch some rare footage of Cody's Wild West show shot by Thomas Edison.

Attend a rodeo presented nightly during the summer across the street from the ranch.

Buggy rides are available from 12:00 to 4:00, Wednesday through Sunday during the summer. Visitors can enjoy old-fashioned buffalo stew at cookouts on Wednesdays, Thursdays and Fridays from July 4–August 10.

The park is closed holidays.

While you're in town, visit the Railroad Museum at Cody Park, one-half mile north of Rodeo Road on Nebraska 83. See Challenger 3977, a large steam locomotive, and Centennial 6922, one of the largest diesel-electric locomotives ever built. The park is open during the summer from Memorial Day through Labor Day.

Don't miss the Western Heritage Museum in North Platte, adjacent to the park. Tour the western prairie village and museum with its many artifacts from the early settlers.

Incoming pilots can land at Lee Bird Field, three miles east of North Platte. You can also land at Clinch Airpark located five miles south of town. Both have rental cars.

INFORMATION
Superintendent, Buffalo Bill State Historical Park
Rt. 1, Box 229
North Platte, Nebraska 69101
308-535-8035

BURCHARD LAKE STATE PARK
6

LOCATION - The lake is three miles east of Burchard and south of Nebraska 4.

ACTIVITIES - This is a good place for bird-watchers. White pelicans arrive here in the spring along with prairie chickens who arrive on the hills at the western end of the lake. There, each April and May, they perform their dawn drumming dance, a mating ritual that may be observed from a blind.

You can go fishing, camping, have a picnic or go hiking year-round.

INFORMATION
Burchard Lake State Park
c/o State Wildlife Management Area, District 5, Southeast Office
Tecumseh, Nebraska 68450
402-335-2534

CALAMUS RESERVOIR STATE RECREATION AREA
7

LOCATION - The Calamus Reservoir is six miles north of Burwell.

FEATURES - Its name came from a plant common to the river valley called "food of the muskrat," by the native Americans. Its Latin name, *Acorus calamus*, is known today as sweet flag, and the herb was used to relieve stomach disorders.

ACTIVITIES - The reservoir is the third largest in the state with 31 miles of shoreline. Go swimming from the swimming beach, or enjoy fishing for bass, walleye, trout, pike, carp, catfish and crappie.

Camp in one of the two campgrounds. Homestead Knolls on the lake's north shore has 83 hard-surface campsites with hookups, and Nunda Shoal has 39 hard-surface pads, and two boat launches.

Additional boat ramps are at Valleyview Flat and at Hannamon Bayou. Both these sites have primitive camping available.

INFORMATION
Calamus Reservoir State Recreation Area
HC 79, Box 20L
Burwell, Nebraska 68823
308-346-5666

CHADRON STATE PARK
8

LOCATION - Chadron State Park is nine miles south of Chadron on 385.

FEATURES - Chadron is Nebraska's oldest park, and was established in 1921.

ACTIVITIES - Visitors can enjoy picnicking, boating with boat rentals available, trout fishing in the park lagoon and creek, or in the other Pine Ridge streams. Also go swimming in the lake or in a heated pool, go horseback riding, and tour the visitor center.

Go camping along Chadron Creek in one of the 170 sites, four with electrical hookups. You can also choose to stay in the lodge, in one of 22 two-bedroom rental cabins, or in one of six housekeeping units in the Multi-Use Facility, available from the Memorial Day weekend through Labor Day weekend. For information and reservations, call 308-432-2036.

The Forest Service maintains 33 miles of marked hiking trails through Pine Ridge. The Pine Ridge Trail begins five miles south of Chadron east of U.S. 385 at the Spotted Tail trailhead. After winding through the hills, creek bottoms and two canyons, it enters the state park.

Limited concessions are available in the park, and for memorable eating, enjoy a cookout where trapper's stew made with buffalo meet is served on Saturday nights.

Attend the Chadron Fur Trade Days over the first full weekend after the 4th of July. A Buckskinner's Camp is set up on Bordeaux Creek where you can see how these camps originally appeared with their furs, handicrafts and beadwork on sale. You can also watch rifle shoots, and tomahawk and knife throwing. Anyone staying in this campground must wear old-time dress and live in teepees or shelters made from materials such as canvas tents held up by wooden poles.

Watch the parade, a 10-kilometer or two-mile fun run. Enjoy cowboys showing off their skills, and watch the World Championship Buffalo Chip Toss.

An Elderhostel Program is available at Chadron State College. For information on the program, contact the Conference Office at Chadron State College at 308-432-6374.

Incoming pilots can land at Chadron Municipal Airport located four miles west of town. Rental cars are available.

INFORMATION
Chadron State Park
HC 75, Box 33
Chadron, Nebraska 69337
308-432-2036

ENDERS RESERVOIR STATE RECREATION AREA
9

LOCATION - Enders Reservoir is one mile south of Enders, and five miles east and 4.5 miles south of Imperial.

FEATURES - The dam rises 134 feet, and forms a lake with 26 miles of shoreline.

ACTIVITIES - Enjoy excellent white bass, crappie and walleye fishing, swimming and boating. Also picnic or camp in the campground with 60 sites. The main campground parallels the east shore and has a boat ramp and a trailer dump station. Another boat ramp is at Center Dam. Concessions are available in the nearby town of Enders.

The Enders Wildlife Refuge is on the western end of the lake where large flocks of mallards and geese winter on the water.

Golf at the Enders Lake Resort Golf Course overlooking the reservoir.

INFORMATION
Enders Reservoir State Recreation Area
c/o Southwest Reservoirs
602 Missouri Avenue
McCook, Nebraska 69001
308-394-5118

EUGENE T. MAHONEY STATE PARK
10

LOCATION - The state park is near Ashland, off I-80 at Exit 426.

ACTIVITIES - This is Nebraska's newest state park, and is the state's first year-round state park. It can accommodate 1,000 overnight visitors. You can dine in the restaurant, and stay in the large lodge with 40 guest rooms, in one of 34 cabins, or in one of the two campgrounds with 150 asphalt camping pads with electrical hookups and a trailer dump station. Tent camping is available southeast of the Little Creek campground.

While there, you can play golf on the 18-hole miniature golf course, fish in the lake on the east side of the park, go horseback riding, play tennis, dine in the restaurant, swim in the pool, and boat on the lake. Owen Marina is located next to the campground, and has snacks and boat rentals.

To get a good look of the area, climb the 70-foot observation tower.

Soon, you'll be able to attend plays in the playhouse.

INFORMATION
Mahoney State Park
Rt. 1, Box 305
Ashland, Nebraska 68003
402-944-2523

FORT ATKINSON STATE HISTORICAL PARK
11

LOCATION - The park is off Nebraska 75 in Fort Calhoun, and 10 miles north of Omaha.

FEATURES - The fort commemorates the first and largest military post to be built west of the Missouri River. It was established in 1820 on the site selected by the Lewis and Clark Expedition, and for the next seven years had a garrison of over 1,000 men stationed here. By 1827, however, the fort was abandoned, and much of the fort was either destroyed by fire or removed.

ACTIVITIES - Walk through the park grounds, open year-round. Tour the Harold W. Anderson Visitor Center during the summer to learn the story of this outpost through its artifacts, scale model of the fort, and a re-creation of a treaty signing done with mannequins that speak.

Explore the partially reconstructed stockade-barracks. Hike the bluffs overlooking the channel where the Missouri River flowed 150 years ago.

While in the area, stop by the DeSoto National Wildlife Refuge, east of Blair, where you can get a good look at thousands of migratory ducks and geese in the spring and fall from a glass-enclosed observation deck.

Walk through the Bertrand Museum located in the refuge to see thousands of artifacts retrieved from the steamboat "Bertrand" when it sank in the Missouri River in 1865. During the mid-19th century, steam boating along the Missouri River hit its peak, but the river proved to be very hazardous with its constantly changing course, sandbars and floating snags. This steamboat wasn't the only one to suffer this fate. Between 1842 and 1865, 58 steamboats were wrecked in the hazardous channels of the river.

You can go hiking in the refuge, tour the lake by boat, or take a self-guided car tour. For information, call 712-642-2772.

Incoming pilots can land at Eppley Airfield three miles northeast of Omaha where rental cars are available.

INFORMATION
Fort Atkinson State Historical Park
Box 240
Fort Calhoun, Nebraska 68023
402-468-5611

FORT KEARNY STATE HISTORICAL PARK
12

LOCATION - The historical park is 8.5 miles southeast of Kearney on Nebraska 50A. It is three miles south of I-80, and is accessible either via Exit

272 (Kearney), or Exit 279 (Minden). The recreation area is 1.75 miles north of Fort Kearny State Historical Park.

FEATURES - Fort Kearny was the first fort built to protect travelers traveling the dangerous Oregon Trail. Around 1849, 30,000 people passed through the fort during an 18-month period. The fort then became a headquarters for the military and civil government, a stage and pony express station, and an outfitting station for various Indian campaigns. In 1871, it provided protection for the crews building the Union Pacific Railroad, after which it was abandoned.

ACTIVITIES - The recreation area is open year-round, and its modern facilities operate from early April through the end of October. The historical park is open daily from Memorial Day weekend through Labor Day, and from 12–5 on weekends in May and September.

Watch the slide show at the visitor center, and tour their museum to get a flavor of the Kearney area during the 1800s.

Not much is left of the original fort, but you can tour the rebuilt blacksmith shop and stockade located behind the visitor center.

Living history demonstrations and cannon firings occur from Memorial Day through the first part of September. The annual Fort Kearney Stampede is held on the Saturday nearest July 4. It offers living history demonstrations, blacksmithing, covered wagon rides, and firings of muskets and cannons, including the park's 24-pound howitzer. The cannons are also fired on major summer holidays.

The nearby recreation area provides camping under century-old cottonwoods with 134 sites, 80 with electrical hookups. The campground is open from Memorial Day through Labor Day. Primitive camping is available year-round.

Go fishing in the Platte River or in one of the eight lakes for bass, bullhead, bluegill, catfish and crappie. Boats are limited to non-powered craft or ones with electric motors. Go swimming in eight sandpit lakes with change houses.

The Fort Kearney Hike-and-Bike Trail begins here, and goes for 1.8 miles to the Bassway Strip State Wildlife Management Area. The trail crosses both channels of the Platte River over some scenic wooden bridges. Another trail follows the old 1864 river channel. Pick up a copy of the booklet, "The Fort Kearney Hike-Bike Trail" at the visitor center.

Each spring, the world's largest concentration of sandhill cranes meet to feed near the park in the central Platte River Valley.

History buffs will enjoy stopping by the Fort Kearney Museum located at 311 So. Central Avenue, to see thousands of artifacts collected from all over the world. Included is one of the state's largest Indian collections, a natural history exhibit, and a gun collection with over 100 rifles and shotguns. While there, take the Midwest's only glass bottom boat ride from Memorial Day weekend-Labor Day weekend. For information, call 308-234-5200.

To tour an unusual museum, visit the Pioneer Village in Minden, 12 miles south of I-80 at Exit 279. Walk through thousands of items that have been arranged to show you how many of the things we use today were developed. Just a few things you can do here are to take a ride on the steam-powered carousel, see 20 historic flying machines, trace the development of lights, and see the largest collection of antique farm machinery collected in the U.S. Information: 1-800-445-4447 or 308-832-1181.

Incoming pilots can land at Kearney Municipal Airport four miles north of town. Rental cars are available.

INFORMATION

Fort Kearney State Historical Park Riverview Marina
Route 4 402-873-7222
Kearney, Nebraska 68847
308-234-9513

FORT KEARNY STATE RECREATION AREA
13

See under FORT KEARNY STATE HISTORICAL PARK

FORT ROBINSON STATE PARK
14

LOCATION - Drive three miles west of Crawford to the intersection of U.S. 385 and Nebraska 20, and continue west for 28 miles on Nebraska 20.

FEATURES - Thousands of military personnel were stationed at the fort over the years starting with the Indian Wars of the 1870s and continuing through 1941.

ACTIVITIES - The park is open from mid-April through the middle of November. Camp in the campground with 150 sites, all with electrical hookups. You can also rent a cabin, or stay in a room in the lodge. You can also overnight in one of the original calvary officers' quarters or enlisted men's barracks. All accommodations are available from Memorial Day weekend through Labor Day weekend.

Hike along nine miles of trails through the Wood Reserve west of the park. Trooper Trail is four miles long, and passes Soldier's Creek. Boots and Saddle Trail is six miles long, and if combined with Trooper Trail, provides an eight-mile loop.

Bicyclists can rent bikes. Tennis courts and a covered pool are available.

Enjoy a buffalo stew cookout on Tuesday, Wednesday, Friday, and Saturday. Western entertainment and nightly performances are presented at the Post

Playhouse from the end of May through mid-August. For information, call 308-665-1976, or write Post Playhouse, Box 271, Crawford, NE 69339.

Ride aboard the tour train, or take a jeep ride to the top of the surrounding Red Cloud Buttes. Stroll through the Trailside Museum to see one of the largest elephants ever unearthed plus other prehistoric artifacts.

For a unique experience, ride through the park on a stagecoach drawn by mules and driven by a mule-skinner.

Watch for the buffalo herd that roams near the fort and along the Smiley Canyon Road west of the fort.

Stop by the information center for details about the various park programs, rent rowboats, and obtain activity reservations and tickets.

Tour the Fort Robinson Museum, the Trailside Museum, and some of the restored exhibit buildings.

A free rodeo is offered at 8:00 p.m. on Sunday and Thursday evenings.

Professional western artists who travel around the country exhibit their work in the 4th of July Professional Western Art Show.

The park is two miles west of Carter Johnson Reservoir where you can go trout fishing, swimming or boating with boat rentals available.

The Peabody Hale Fiddle Contest and Pioneer Days Festival are held in Crawford the end of July. For information, call 308-665-1243 or 665-2587.

While in Crawford, drive northwest of town to see Toadstool Park, named for its unusual land formations formed by the erosion of the clay rocks. Enjoy a picnic in the moon-like landscape of the Badlands.

East of town is the Museum of Fur Trade, the only museum of its kind.

The Crawford State Fish Hatchery in Crawford's City Park produces brown and rainbow trout that are used to stock Nebraska's lakes and streams. It's open to the public Monday through Friday.

Play golf on the Legend Buttes Golf Course's nine-hole course located along White River between Crawford and the park.

INFORMATION
Fort Robinson State Park
P. O. Box 392
Crawford, Nebraska 69339
308-665-2660

FREMONT LAKES STATE RECREATION AREA
15

LOCATION - The state recreation area is three miles west of Fremont on U.S. 30.

ACTIVITIES - Enjoy camping in one of the 100 campsites with 44 offering electrical hookups and a trailer dump.

The area has 20 sandpit lakes where you can rent paddle boats, canoes, flat-bottom boats and bicycles. Go fishing, boating and swimming.

Go for a train ride on the steam-powered excursion train that runs between Fremont and Hooper, 15 miles northwest. The dinner train offers you the chance to dine while crossing the Mormon Trail, once an historic Indian road, and followed by Major Stephen Long on his military expedition. Reservations are required. Call 402-727-0615 or 1-800-942-7245.

Incoming pilots can land at Fremont Municipal Airport two miles northwest of town where rental cars are available.

INFORMATION
Fremont Lakes State Recreation Area
Route 1
Ames, Nebraska 68621
402-721-8482

INDIAN CAVE STATE PARK
16

LOCATION - The park is northeast of Shubert on Nebraska 67. The eastern edge of the park is bordered by the Missouri River.

FEATURES - Indian Cave was named for the large sandstone cave next to the Missouri River in the southeast corner of the park. Ancient Indian petroglyphs were found on its inside walls. They are the only ones of their kind known in Nebraska.

St. Deroin was built on the site of a small trading fort set aside for people who were left behind by the traders and trappers who married Indian women, and then moved on, abandoning their homes and families.

ACTIVITIES - The park is open year-round.

Observe a variety of old-time crafts from 9–5 daily in the restored village of St. Deroin that dates back to the late 1800s. You'll see soap-making, candle-dipping and broom-making. On Saturday nights, attend the buffalo stew cook-out at 6:00 p.m. The Pioneer Long Rifles demonstrate muzzle loading of their rifles on the first weekend of each month, and on holidays through October. Tour the authentic trapper's cabin reconstructed using methods originally employed in the 1850s, and walk through the St. Deroin General Store, ice-house and schoolhouse.

The campground has 134 hard-surface sites with electrical hookups. Backpackers have access to many primitive campsites, and to 10 Adirondack shelters located along its 20-mile-long trail system. Indian Cave State Park is the only major state park not offering cabin accommodations.

Visitors can catch pan fish in the Missouri River, go horseback riding, and attend living demonstrations as part of the park's American Heritage Program. Also stroll through the historic Halfbreed and St. Deroin cemeteries, enjoy a picnic, or go hiking along 20 miles of trails.

INFORMATION
Indian Cave State Park
R. R. 1, Box 30
Shubert, Nebraska 68437
402-883-2575

JOHNSON LAKE STATE RECREATION AREA
17

LOCATION - The area is ten miles southwest of Lexington on U.S. 283.

FEATURES - The lake lies between two reservoirs: Callagher Canyon Reservoir and Elwood Reservoir.

ACTIVITIES - Enjoy water-related activities such as boating, water-skiing and swimming from the unsupervised beach. Go camping in the main area on the southeast end of the lake with 130 campsites, 81 providing electrical hookups, or across the lake in the South Side Inlet Area that has 29 campsites with electrical hookups. The campground is open year-round.

Fish for walleye, white bass, catfish, crappie and perch.

Only basic canoeing skills are necessary to navigate the Plum Creek segment of the Tri County canal system, making it ideal for family excursions.

Public boat ramps and shops are located around the lake, and two are in the park. Several concessions are also located on or close to the lake.

History buffs can tour the Dawson County Museum in Lexington located on the east side of town. Go north on Nebraska 283, right on 6th Street, and then left on Taft Street. Among its attractions is the McCabe Airplane with its curiously bowed wings, a Union Pacific Depot, locomotive and caboose, one-room school, and log home.

Incoming pilots can land at Lexington Municipal Airport two miles northwest of town. Rental cars are available.

INFORMATION
Johnson Lake State Recreation Area
Route 2, Box 42
Elwood, Nebraska 68937
308-785-2685

KELLER STATE RECREATION AREA
18

LOCATION - The area is five miles east and nine miles north of Ainsworth, and north of U.S. 20 on U.S. 183.

ACTIVITIES - The park is located on Bone Creek, and offers 27 camper pads with electrical hookups, and a trailer dump station. Go hiking on the trails through the grasslands and canyons, and fishing in Bone Creek plus five other ponds. Pond #5 is regularly stocked with trout. The other ponds have bass, bluegill and channel catfish.

Access to pond #1 is via a county road off U.S. 183 north of the park. Visitors are asked not to wade Bone Creek to reach these ponds.

Incoming pilots can land at Ainsworth Municipal Airport located six miles northwest of town. Rental cars are available.

INFORMATION
Keller State Recreation Area
Ainsworth, Nebraska 69210
No phone. Contact the District Office in Bassett: 402-944-2523

LAKE McCONAUGHY STATE RECREATION AREA
19

LOCATION - Lake McConaughy is nine miles north of Ogallala on Nebraska 16 and 61 or 10 miles east of Lewellen on Nebraska 92.

FEATURES - Lake McConaughy, Nebraska's largest lake, boasts 100 miles of white sand, and is 22 miles long. Kingsley Dam is one of the largest of its kind in the world, and stretches almost three miles across the North Platte River. Tours are available.

ACTIVITIES - For camping, you have a wide selection of sites to choose from. Campsites include 600 gravel sites at Arthur Bay, 116 paved sites at Cedar Vue, 100 sites at Eagle Canyon, 200 sites at Lemoyne Bay, 600 at Martin Bay, 400 at Otter Creek, 400 at Sandy Beach, 150 at Spring Park, 30 dirt sites at Omaha Beach, and 582 at Lake Ogallala State Recreation Area located just below Lake McConaughy. Lake Ogallala is apart from "Big Mac," and is open year-round for camping. It has two boating ramps available.

This large, scenic lake offers you many water sports including boating from the various ramps, swimming from sandy beaches, and fishing for bass, trout, channel catfish and walleye. The fish here often grow to trophy size.

You can also water-ski, scuba dive, sail, and during the winter, enjoy ice boating.

The lake has 13 boating ramps, and is the site of one of the nation's largest open class inland sailing regattas. Annual events include the Ogallala Round-Up Rodeo and Fair in early August. The Governor's Cup Sailboat Regatta on Labor Day, and Ogallala Indian Summer Rendezvous are held downtown in mid-September.

In mid-September, attend the Big Mac Rod and Custom Run when street rods and fixed-up older cars participate in a two-day event. Attend the car show and parade in town on Saturday, and then go to Martin Bay for a picnic and games. On Sunday, a poker run is featured. For information, call 308-284-4654.

While staying here, tour nearby Ash Hollow Cave State Historical Park located near the upper end of the lake on U.S. 26 to see the wagon ruts carved by the wagon trains traveling along the Oregon Trail. The visitor center and the ancient Indian cave are open from May–September. You can also take a drive through the scenic Sandhills.

Incoming pilots can land at Searle Field two miles west of Ogallala where rental cars are available.

INFORMATION

Lake McConaughy State Rec. Area
Lake Ogallala State Recreation Area
Route 2, Box 62Z-2
Ogallala, Nebraska 69153
308-284-3542

Ogallala/Keith County Chamber of
Commerce
P. O. Box 628
Ogallala, Nebraska 69153
1-800-658-4390 or 308-284-4066

LAKE OGALLALA STATE RECREATION AREA
20
See under LAKE MC CONAUGHY STATE RECREATION AREA

LEWIS AND CLARK LAKE STATE RECREATION AREA
21

LOCATION - The lake is ten miles north of Crofton off U.S. 81 on the Missouri River.

FEATURES - Gavins Point Dam was constructed to hold back the water of the Missouri River.

ACTIVITIES - Stop by the visitor center near the dam, approximately 10 miles north of Crofton. It's open daily throughout the summer, and weekdays during the winter months.

Take an escorted tour of the power plant conducted on a daily basis during the summer, and by appointment the remainder of the year.

Downstream from the dam you'll find Gavins Point National Fish Hatchery and Aquarium that produces both warm and cold water fish to stock in the state's lakes. Fish for walleye, sauger, catfish, pike, bass and crappie. Fishing is available year-round in the open tail waters of the dam.

Lewis and Clark Lake has 200 campsites with 100 electrical hookups. You can enjoy fishing, boating and water-skiing.

Golfers can tee-off and play the Lakeview Golf course's nine holes adjacent to the visitor center.

Attend the Lewis and Clark Tri-State Dairy Expo in early August. Not only will you see a dairy show, but you can watch the Northeast Nebraska Cow Chip Flip, cow calling contest, bossie bingo and cow milking contests. For information, call 402-388-4798.

The 55-mile stretch of the Missouri River between this lake and Ponca is designated as a National Recreational and Scenic River.

INFORMATION
Lewis and Clark Lake State Recreation Area   402-373-2440
P. O. Box 171
Bloomfield, Nebraska 68718

LOUISVILLE STATE RECREATION AREA
22
See under PLATTE RIVER STATE PARK

MEDICINE CREEK RESERVOIR STATE RECREATION AREA
23

LOCATION - The area is two miles west and seven miles north of Cambridge on Nebraska 47.

FEATURES - Medicine Creek's dam is 165 feet high, and the lake behind it has 29 miles of shoreline.

ACTIVITIES - The small islands in the lake provide fishermen with king-sized crappie and other panfish. Walleye fishing is very good in June, while white bass are caught during the summer.

Shady Bay Campground on Trail No. 4 on the lake's east side has 77 hard-surfaced camping pads, with 34 electrical hookups. Shady Bay also has boating ramps, a swimming beach, and trailer dump station.

Additional campsites are located on Trail No. 1. Other boat ramps are on Trail No. 3, and still more campsites are scattered around the lake wherever there are trail road accesses.

Medicine Creek Lodge, located on the south side of the dam on Trail No. 1, has a restaurant, grocery store, boat rentals, cabins, and fishing.
INFORMATION
Medicine Creek Reservoir State Recreation Area
c/o Southwest Reservoirs
602 Missouri Ave.
McCook, Nebraska 69001
308-697-4667

MEMPHIS LAKE STATE RECREATION AREA
24

LOCATION - Drive seven miles northwest of Ashland on Nebraska 63 to reach Memphis, and continue another .25-mile to reach the recreation area.
FEATURES - Memphis Lake was originally created for harvesting ice. An ice plant was constructed in 1897, and at one time, was believed to be the largest ice plant in the world. Unfortunately, the ice house burned down in 1921, but you can still see some of the old concrete footings. To see pictures of the ice plant, visit Ye Old Snack Shop.
ACTIVITIES - Memphis Lake offers fishing for carp, bullhead, bluegill, crappie and catfish.
Only electric motors and no gas-powered boats are allowed on the lake. Rentals are available.
The campground has 122 sites and a trailer dump station.
INFORMATION
Memphis Lake State Recreation Area
Ashland, Nebraska 68003
402-464-0641

MERRITT RESERVOIR STATE RECREATION AREA
25

LOCATION - The reservoir is in a narrow valley of the Snake River, 26 miles southeast of Valentine.
FEATURES - The reservoir is located in the heart of the Nebraska Sandhills, and its depth prevents it from being drawn down by irrigation during the summer. Access is available from ramps in the Powder Horn, Main, Beed's Landing and Snake River areas.
ACTIVITIES - Merritt Reservoir offers you the opportunity to swim, water-ski, sail or fish. Try your luck at landing walleye, bass, perch, muskie, catfish and crappie. Many state record-sized fish have been caught here.

The shoreline of 73 miles provides for camping and picnicking facilities along with lighted ramp areas. Enjoy hunting on the prairie, or walk along miles of white sandy beaches.

If you prefer not to camp, stay at the Merritt Resort located on the reservoir, and is open year-round. For information, call 402-376-3437.

Snake River Falls, the state's largest waterfall, is near Merritt Dam. Watch for the sign near the dam.

Incoming pilots can land at Miller Field one mile south of Valentine. Rental cars are available.

INFORMATION
Merritt Reservoir State Recreation Area
Valentine, Nebraska 69201
No phone is available in the state recreation area.
Merritt Dam Trading Post
402-376-3437

MORMON ISLAND STATE RECREATION AREA
26

LOCATION - The area is in Grand Island.

FEATURES - The park was named for the winter stopover of Mormons heading west for Salt Lake City, and is part of Nebraska's "Chain of Lakes."

ACTIVITIES - Enjoy swimming where a change house is provided, boating in non-powered boats, fishing for largemouth bass, walleye, channel catfish and bluegill, or camping in one of its 34 campsites with complete facilities. The park is open year-round.

Each spring, thousands of sandhill cranes stop along the Platte River to rest and pursue their courtship rituals. They begin arriving in mid-February, and by the first part of April, begin flying north to their breeding grounds.

While in the area, tour the Stuhr Museum of the Prairie Pioneers located at the intersection of U.S. 34 and U.S. 182, and four miles north of I-80. The museum has a permanent display of a railroad town, and includes 60 original buildings and an operating steam train. The Rotunda houses Indian memorabilia. The main buildings and the Gus Forner Memorial Rotunda are open year-round, while the outdoor attractions open Memorial Day weekend, and close Labor Day weekend.

Henry Fonda narrates an historical account of the pioneer era. The cottage in which this Oscar-winning actor was born is one of 60 restored structures in Railroad Town, an elaborate re-creation of a prairie community, where you can board the last working turn-of-the-century steam engine.

Incoming pilots can land at Central Nebraska Regional located .5 mile northeast of town. Rental cars are available.

INFORMATION
Mormon Island State Recreation Area
Route 2, Box 190A
Grand Island, Nebraska 68832
308-381-5649 (park)

NIOBRARA STATE PARK
27

LOCATION - The park is 1.5 miles west of Niobrara on Nebraska 12 at the junction of the Niobrara and Missouri rivers.

FEATURES - Niobrara means "running water" in Ponca Indian language. Historically, the river was used as a highway into the wilderness.

ACTIVITIES - Because of recent flooding, the old park, located in the bottom lands, has been replaced by a new park on the bluffs overlooking the Missouri River.

Stay in one of their two-bedroom cabins affording you a great view of the Missouri River valley, available from mid-April through mid-November. The campground has 75 sites with 36 electrical hookups and a trailer dump station.

Play golf on the old Niobrara town site's nine-hole course.

You can also go swimming, boating, hiking and horseback riding. A new system of trails has been constructed through the park's hills giving the hiker a great view of the Niobrara and Missouri River valleys.

Park fishermen and boaters have access to the Missouri River. You can fish in the Missouri River for walleye, bass and catfish, and in the Niobrara River for walleye, sauger and catfish. The park offers guided fishing and boating excursions. Each September, Niobrara holds an annual Pancake Day.

Tour the J. Alan Cramer historical interpretive center to learn more about the early inhabitants including the early Indians, the Lewis and Clark expedition, and later Mormons who wintered nearby.

INFORMATION
Niobrara State Park
P. O. Box 226
Niobrara, Nebraska 68760
402-857-3373

PAWNEE LAKE STATE RECREATION AREA
28

LOCATION - The area is seven miles northwest of Lincoln off U.S. 6, and three miles west of Emerald on West Adams Street.

ACTIVITIES - During the spring when the fish are spawning, fish for walleye and crappie from the dam. Largemouth bass and bluegill fishing is good along the shallow shoreline on the west, north and east sides of the lake. Catfish are found by the dam and in the shallow water on the lake's west side. Winter fishermen can find crappie in front of the dam, and bluegill from coves on the lake's east side. The concession stand on the east side of the lake has food, fishing gear and gasoline. The campground has 275 campsites with 68 electrical hookups and a trailer dump.

Launch your boat from four ramps, or stop by the New Pawnee Lake Marina for boat rentals and fishing supplies. For information, call 402-796-2330.

You can also enjoy hiking and swimming in the park.

Incoming pilots can land at Lincoln Municipal located four miles northwest of town where rental cars are available.

INFORMATION
Pawnee Lake State Recreation Area
R. R. 4, Box 41B
Lincoln, Nebraska 68524
402-796-2362

PELICAN POINT STATE RECREATION AREA
SUMMIT LAKE STATE RECREATION AREA
29

LOCATION - Pelican Point is in northeastern Nebraska, four miles east, four miles north and one mile east of Tekamah on the Missouri River. Summit Lake is one mile south and three miles west of Tekamah.

ACTIVITIES - PELICAN POINT has 28 gravel camper pads, but its real attraction is its access to the Missouri River where you can either go boating from the ramp or go fishing along its banks.

SUMMIT LAKE has picnic shelters, 24 camping pads, and good fishing in a lake stocked with catfish, bass, bluegill, walleye and northern pike.

Incoming pilots can land at Tekamah Municipal located two miles southeast of town where rental cars are available.

INFORMATION

Pelican Point State Recreation Area
Tekamah, Nebraska 68061
402-468-5611

Summit Lake State Recreation Area
Tekamah, Nebraska 68601
402-468-5895

PLATTE RIVER STATE PARK
LOUISVILLE STATE RECREATION AREA
SCHRAMM PARK STATE RECREATION AREA
30

LOCATION - Platte River State Park is reached by driving south 14 miles on Nebraska 50 from the intersection of I-80 and Nebraska 50. The park is 17 miles southwest of Omaha. It's also three miles west of Louisville, and is right in the middle of the state's two largest cities: Lincoln and Omaha.

The park complex includes the Louisville Lakes State Recreation Area and the Schramm Park State Recreation Area, six miles south of Gretna off I-80.

Louisville State Recreation Area is .5-mile northwest of Louisville off Nebraska 50, on the south bank of the Platte River.

ACTIVITIES - PLATTE RIVER STATE PARK is open year-round, but the food facilities and visitor services only operate from Memorial weekend to Labor Day, and on a limited basis in May, September and October.

You can go picnicking, boating, fishing for channel catfish, carp, perch, bass, crappie and northern pike. Go horseback riding, rent a room in the lodge, in one of the camper cabins, or in a more modern cabin. Lodging is available from May 1–October 31.

You can also rent a teepee year-round in the Oto, Pawnee, or Lewis and Clark teepee villages. Because of the rugged terrain, no camping is available in the park.

The park has 10 miles of hiking trails, plus additional trails in Stone Creek.

SCHRAMM STATE RECREATION AREA is the site of the state's first fish hatchery. Three miles of Schramm Park's nature trails have been designated as part of the National Recreation Trail system.

Rent a paddle-boat and cruise around Jenny Newman Lake, or climb to the top of the 85-foot Lincoln Journal Tower to get a panoramic view of the former Indian, trader and settler routes. You can see over 20 miles on a clear day.

Attend a campfire program in the amphitheater, or try out your archery skills on the archery range. Supervised shooting is available several hours each weekday.

Decker Creek Lodge offers daily craft activities, and recreational equipment may be rented at Owen Landing.

Want to try some buffalo meat specialities? Visit the Scott Lodge Restaurant. A buffalo stew hoe-down and campfire sing-along are offered Friday, Saturday and Sunday evenings. Reservations are advised. Call 402-234-2217.

Visit the Ak-Sar-Ben Aquarium and the World Herald Theater located 15 minutes from Platte River State Park. The aquarium is the only one of its kind in the Midwest, and is closed Tuesdays. The World Herald Theater presents a regular schedule of movies shown at 11:00 daily.

Gretna Fish Hatchery Museum, located on the site of the state's first fish hatchery, tells the story of the evolution of fish beginning in prehistoric times, and gives you information about the early days of fish management.

LOUISVILLE STATE RECREATION AREA is located about 10 minutes from the Platte River State Park, and has five sandpit lakes surrounded with cottonwood trees. Enjoy a picnic, go swimming, or fishing for catfish, bluegill, crappie, walleye, carp and bullheads. Game and Parks has an active stocking program of bass, catfish, bluegill, crappie and walleye in Lakes 1, 1A, 2 and 2A. Children can fish for stocked carp in Lake 3.

The A.C. Nelson Campground is located in the Louisville State Recreation Area, on the south bank of the Platte River. The campground has 145 all-weather camping pads with electrical hookups, 84 sites with no electricity, and 75 primitive, non-designated sites. The modern facilities are open from late May through October 31, but primitive camping is available year-round.

Go boating on any of the lakes, and enjoy canoe access, a concession stand, and a campground on the Platte River.

Swimming is available from a designated beach area on Lake No. 2. The beach is open from Memorial Day through Labor Day, and change houses are available. There are no lifeguards, however.

Incoming pilots can either land at Eppley Field, three miles northeast of Omaha where rental cars are available, or at Lincoln Municipal four miles northwest of town where there are also rental cars.

INFORMATION

Platte River State Park	Louisville State Recreation Area
Route 1, Box 161A	Box 279
Louisville, Nebraska 68037	Louisville, Nebraska 68037
402-234-2217	402-234-6855

Schramm Park State Recreation Area
21502 West Highway 31
Gretna, Nebraska 68028
402-332-3901

PONCA STATE PARK
31

LOCATION - This park is two miles north of Ponca, above the Missouri River in northeastern Nebraska.

FEATURES - Both the town and park were named for the Indian tribe that once roamed the area.

ACTIVITIES - Camp in the campground with 100 hard-surfaced campsites with electrical hookups, and another 200 non-designated primitive campsites.

The campground is open from mid-May through October 31. You can also stay in housekeeping cabins from mid-April through mid-November.

Go fishing in the Missouri River for channel catfish, boating from the ramp, and swimming in the modern swimming pool. Enjoy horseback riding through the bluffs on three miles of established trails.

Both hikers and winter cross-country skiers can explore 17 miles of hiking trails that wind through the park.

For a "three-state lookout," go to the world's largest pipeline suspension bridge.

Annual events in town include the Days of '56 Rodeo in late June, and the Nifty 50s Day and Car Show in early August.

INFORMATION
Ponca State Park
P. O. Box 688
Ponca, Nebraska 68770
402-755-2284

RED WILLOW STATE RECREATION AREA
32

LOCATION - The area is eleven miles north of McCook.

ACTIVITIES - This reservoir has a bushy shoreline 35 miles long, with many submerged trees and underwater structures, making it a haven for bass. You can also fish for crappie, pike and walleye.

Willow View Campground has 50 hard-surfaced campsites overlooking the lake, 45 with electrical hookups. Two boat ramps and a designated swimming beach are at Kiwanis Point. Concessions, restaurant, camping, and fishing supplies, and boat rentals are located on the Spring Creek access road.

Incoming pilots can land at McCook Municipal Airport located two miles east of town where rental cars are available.

INFORMATION
Red Willow State Recreation Area
c/o Southwest Reservoirs
602 Missouri Ave.
McCook, Nebraska 69001
308-345-5899

ROCK CREEK STATION STATE HISTORIC PARK
33

LOCATION - The park is seven miles east of Fairbury off Nebraska 8.

FEATURES - Visitors can still see the deep ruts carved by the covered wagons traveling along the Oregon Trail. When the station was originally built, it was used as a primitive store where supplies could be bought or traded by these early pioneers.

Shortly thereafter, it was used as a stage station for travelers with the Overland Stage Company, and as a swing station for riders on the Pony Express who rapidly changed mounts here; however, the site is better known as being the spot where James Butler Hickock began his bloody career as a gunslinger.

ACTIVITIES - Camp in the campground in adjoining Rock Creek State Recreation Area with 25 sites with electrical hookups and a trailer dump station, and go hiking along the trails.

Take an ox-drawn covered wagon ride from the East Ranch, and watch blacksmithing demonstrations on weekends from Memorial Day through Labor Day. A reconstructed ranch house gives the visitor a glimpse into living conditions during the time early travelers passed through here.

During the summer, watch the slide show at the Burlington Northern Visitor Center, and see artifacts of the era to learn the story of Rock Creek.

INFORMATION
Rock Creek Station State Historic Park
RFD #4 Box 36
Fairbury, Nebraska 68352
402-729-5777

SCHRAMM PARK STATE RECREATION AREA
34
See under PLATTE RIVER STATE PARK

SHERMAN RESERVOIR STATE RECREATION AREA
35

LOCATION - The area is six miles east of Loup City off Nebraska 92.

ACTIVITIES - This reservoir has 65 miles of shoreline, and is a favorite for fishermen and power boaters. During the spring, walleye fishing is good along the dam, while summer brings catches of white bass and catfish all over the lake.

One of the most popular fishing accesses is Fisherman's Bridge at the northern end of the reservoir, where pedestrian fishermen have access to the supply canal below the reservoir's inlet. Be on the lookout for any rain moving into the area, for the road becomes difficult when wet.

INFORMATION
Sherman Reservoir State Rec. Area
Route 2, Box 117
Loup City, Nebraska 68853
308-745-1270

Tradewind's Marina
308-745-1187

SUMMIT LAKE STATE RECREATION AREA
36

See under PELICAN POINT STATE RECREATION AREA

SWANSON RESERVOIR STATE RECREATION AREA
37

LOCATION - The area is three miles west of Trenton on U.S. 34.

ACTIVITIES - Swanson Reservoir is the largest of the four reservoirs found in the southwest on the Republican River. The water is very clear, and fishing for trophy-sized northern pike, large walleye, and black bass is one of its best-known attractions.

Camp in Spring Canyon with its 50 hard-surfaced campsites, 45 with electrical hookups. Here you'll also find two boating ramps. Nearby are a marina and a trailer court with electrical hookups. Where U.S. 34 crosses the northern tip of Mackin Bay, you'll find 17 additional campsites with electrical hookups.

The Massacre Canyon Historical Marker on east-bound U.S. 34 marks the site of the last great battle between the Sioux and Pawnee.

INFORMATION
Swanson Reservoir State Recreation Area
c/o Southwest Reservoirs
602 Missouri Avenue
McCook, Nebraska 69001
308-276-2671

TWO RIVERS STATE RECREATION AREA
38

LOCATION - The area is fifteen miles east of Wahoo on Nebraska 92, or one mile southwest of Venice at the confluence of the Platte and Elkhorn rivers.

ACTIVITIES - Stay in the lodge or in one of the cabins. For a unique experience, stay in one of their cabooses that sleep six. The campground has 96 sites, 93 with electrical hookups. Food concessions are available in the park.

Go trout fishing in the Platte River. Lake No. 5 is the only trout fishing site in southeastern Nebraska, and is restocked each year. There are five additional lakes where you can fish for bass, crappie, bullhead and catfish.

You can also go hiking, swimming from the sandy swimming beach at Lake No. 2, boating on Lake No. 3 where boat rentals are available, or rent a bicycle to tour the park. Canoeing access to the Platte River is west of the Riverside Campground.

INFORMATION
Two Rivers State Recreation Area
Route 1, Box 203
Waterloo, Nebraska 69069
402-359-5165

VICTORIA SPRINGS STATE RECREATION AREA
39

LOCATION - The area is seven miles east of Anselmo, or seven miles north of Merna. It's also six miles east of Virginia Springs on Spur 21A.

FEATURES - Victoria Springs is the third oldest area in the state park system, and is described as being an oasis within the Sand Hills. It was named for the mineral springs located there.

Charles R. Matthews, a Custer County judge, homesteaded here, and the log cabins he built are still on the site. One was used as his home, and the other was the first post office in Custer County.

ACTIVITIES - The park is open from mid-April through the middle of November. Two housekeeping cabins generally open May 15 and close September 15. For reservations, call 308-749-2235. You can also camp in the campground with 160 grassy campsites, 15 with electrical hookups.

Go trout, crappie, catfish, carp, perch and bass fishing in Victoria Creek, and non-power boating on the small lake. Paddle boats and rowboats may be rented.

INFORMATION
Victoria Springs State Recreation Area
P. O. Box 254
Anselmo, Nebraska 68813
308-749-2235

WILDCAT HILLS STATE RECREATION AREA
40

LOCATION - From the junction of Nebraska 71 and 92, it's ten miles west of Gering on Nebraska 71.

FEATURES - The area overlooks the North Platte River Valley, and Scotts Bluff National Monument can be seen off to the northwest.

ACTIVITIES - Hike along three miles of marked trails through the canyons and rocky bluffs. The main trail begins below the large shelter-house. You'll be hiking at elevations up to 5,000 feet, and footbridges and a rain shelter are located along the way.

Watch for their herds of buffalo and elk in the game reserve south of the state recreation area. Visitors aren't permitted within the fenced reserve. The best observation times are in the early morning or evening.

You can also enjoy a picnic in one of the three stone shelters, or camp here; however, the campsites aren't designated sites, and are more suitable for tents. Trailers can overnight in the parking lot.

INFORMATION
Wildcat Hills State Recreation
P. O. Box 65
Gering, Nebraska 69341
308-436-2838

WINDMILL STATE RECREATION AREA
41

LOCATION - Take the Gibbon Exit from I-80. The area is located between Kearney and Grand Island.

FEATURES - Windmill State Recreation Area was created as part of the state's "Chain of Lakes," located along I-80. The area was named from its locale, Windmill Crossing, where the Pawnee Indians forded the Platte River during their annual buffalo hunts.

It has some restored antique windmills collected from around the Midwest. The largest windmill is a railroad windmill rising over 60 feet. Watch for two old windmills, a Waupan first utilized in 1902, and a Dempster Model nine, constructed around 1910.

ACTIVITIES - See their exhibit of antique wind machines. Camp in their campground with 69 sites, all with electrical hookups, and a trailer dump station. It's open from April 1 to October 31.

Go swimming in the unguarded lake. You can also go fishing or boating in a non-powered boat.

Incoming pilots can land at Central Nebraska Regional Airport in Grand Island. It's .5 mile northeast of town, and rental cars are available.

INFORMATION
Windmill State Recreation Area
Box 427
Gibbon, Nebraska 68840
308-468-5700

*North Dakota's Badlands boast some of the most rugged,
character-building country in the United States. Cross Ranch State Park,
named after Theodore Roosevelt's old Maltese Cross brand is near here.*

NORTH DAKOTA

North Dakota, one of the country's leading wheat producers, has several lakes that provide visitors with many water-based activities. Lake Sakakawea, a large man-made reservoir that goes 200 miles up the Missouri River, and Devils Lake, the state's largest natural body of water, are two sites visited by many who come to vacation here. As President Theodore Roosevelt once said, "I would never have been president if it had not been for my experiences in North Dakota."

Canoeists can get up-to-the-minute information on canoeing conditions on several rivers throughout the state during the canoeing season by calling the hotline at 1-800-472-2100 (in state), or 1-800-437-2077 (out of state). Canoeists particularly enjoy canoeing the Sheyenne River that traverses eastern North Dakota, the Missouri River, and the Little Missouri.

The state parks are connected with over 250 miles of snowmobile and cross-country ski trails. The Loppets, a cross-country ski race series, is held every January and February in the Missouri River Natural Area, and in Turtle River, Fort Ransom, Lake Metigoshe and Icelandic State Parks.

You can't downhill ski in the state parks, but downhill skiing is available near Lake Metigoshe, Devils Lake and Fort Ransom. For information on skiing conditions, call Frostline at 1-800-472-2100 (in state), or 1-800-437-2077 (out of state).

Ice fishing is available at Icelandic, Metigoshe, Beaver Lake, Lake Sakakawea, and Devils Lake state parks.

You can camp not only during the summer, but also during the fall and winter in all the state parks. From the first of October through early spring, primitive camping facilities are available at all major state parks. Three parks offer lodging during the winter: Cross Ranch, Lake Metigoshe and Turtle River.

The northern end of the North Country National Scenic Trail follows the shoreline of Lake Sakakawea, and continues along the Garrison Diversion Project Canals. Upon reaching the Sheyenne River, the route turns north to go to Fort Totten State Historic Site and Sully's Hill National Game Preserve. Then it turns south to go to Fort Ransom and Sheyenne National Grassland, a

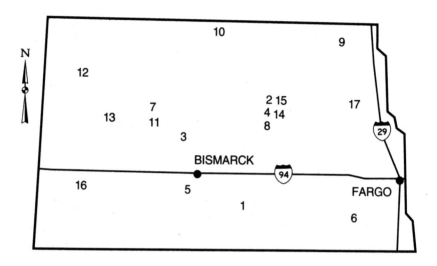

71,000-acre remnant of tall grass prairie. It continues east where it traverses the shores of the Great Lakes, and winds up in the Adirondack Mountains.

Rent-a-camps are available in the following state parks: Fort Abraham Lincoln, Lake Metigoshe, Lake Sakakawea, Turtle River, Fort Stevenson, Icelandic, Lewis and Clark, Fort Ransom and at Cross Ranch.

The state parks have over 1,100 campsites, with 200 campsites available for reserved camping from Memorial Day through Labor Day.

For further information, contact Parks and Tourism, 604 E. Blvd., Bismark, South Dakota 58505, 1-800-437-2077.

BEAVER LAKE STATE PARK
1

LOCATION - The park is on the west shore of Beaver Lake and is three miles northeast of Burnstad. It's also 17 miles southeast of Napoleon.

ACTIVITIES - Go strolling along the trails that passi over gentle prairie hills, go swimming from the beach, or fish for northern pike and walleye. Fishermen also enjoy ice fishing during the winter months.

Camp in the campground with a dump station.

Golfers can play on a nine-hole course in Wishek, or play tennis on one of their courts.

INFORMATION
Beaver Lake State Park
Route 1, Box 216
Wishek, North Dakota 58495
701-452-2752

BLACK TIGER BAY STATE RECREATION AREA
2

See under DEVILS LAKE STATE PARK

CROSS RANCH STATE PARK
3

LOCATION - The park is nine miles southwest of Washburn on North Dakota Alternate 200. It's on the west bank of the Missouri River, halfway between Center and Washburn. It's also five miles south of Hensler.

FEATURES - The park has 560 acres, and is adjacent to the Missouri River. It adjoins the 6,000-acre Cross Ranch Nature Preserve that contains the largest remaining tract of flood plain woodland along the Missouri River.

The Mandan Indians lived here from the 15th through the early 19th century; however, they were unable to withstand a series of smallpox epidemics, and were gradually removed to individually owned reservation plots.

The area was then turned into a ranch in the 1800s, and when its last owners, the Levis, purchased the land, they named it the Cross Ranch after acquiring Roosevelt's old brand, the Maltese Cross.

ACTIVITIES - The park offers primitive camping in 30 campsites, showers, a dump station, rent-a-camp facilities, and rental of the log cabin.

You can also have a picnic, go boating and backpacking. Explore 16 miles of hiking trails that connect the park to the preserve land where you can see a large buffalo herd and some archaeological remnants thousands of years old. The preserve has over 100 archaeological sites including examples of the Mandan-Hidatsa culture plus Archaic period artifacts dating back to 6000 B.C.

Tour the visitor center and check out the schedule of naturalist programs offered from Memorial Day through Labor Day, and in 1991, sponsored both Native American and Bluegrass Festival weekends.

During the winter, go cross-country skiing along marked, groomed trails.

Knife River Indian Villages National Historic Site is 24 miles west of Washburn on North Dakota Alternate 200. Here you can see the remnants of Hidatsa Indian villages. Archeological sites suggest possible habitation of the area 8,000 years ago. Tour the visitor center, hike the various trails ranging in length from .9 miles to three miles, with one of the trails passing a buffalo preserve. Take a guided walk through the village remnants. The area also has some cross-country skiing loops to explore.

On some summer weekends, the old Indian ways are recreated as they were when the Mandan, Hidatsa and Arikara Indians inhabited the site.

The Smith Grove Wildlife Management Area, located three miles south of Cross Ranch State Park, contains a grove of the state's largest cottonwood trees, some approximately 200 years old. You can hike a .25-mile-long trail, or enjoy a picnic.

Fort Mandan is four miles west of Washburn, and has a replica of the fort constructed by the Lewis and Clark expedition in the fall of 1804. You can tour the fort, go camping, tour the visitor center, and enjoy a picnic.

Incoming pilots can land at Washburn Municipal Airport located four miles north of town. A courtesy car is available.

INFORMATION
Cross Ranch Centennial State Park
HC 2, Box 152
Hensler, North Dakota 58530
701-794-3731

DEVILS LAKE STATE PARK
GRAHAM'S ISLAND STATE PARK
SHELVER'S GROVE STATE RECREATION AREA
BLACK TIGER BAY STATE RECREATION AREA
THE NARROWS STATE RECREATION AREA
4

LOCATION - Devils Lake is in the northeast part of the state off U.S. 2.

FEATURES - The Fremont Expedition called the area "Enchanted Waters" when they traversed the area in the 1830s. Devils Lake is the largest natural lake in North Dakota with almost 300 miles of shoreline, and 55,000 surface acres of water. Today it's called the "Perch Capital," and was written up in *Field and Stream's* "Top 25 Fishing Spots in the U.S."

ACTIVITIES - Fish for walleye, pike, perch and white bass.

The heavily wooded hills are covered with oak, ash, elm and aspen that attracts deer, wild turkey and small game to the area. Stop by the lookout tower at Sully's Hill National Game Preserve. It's located on the Fort Totten Sioux Indian Reservation off the shore of the main lake, and south of Devils Lake. Here you get a panoramic view of the lake. In May you can hear wild turkeys gobbling in the morning, and in late September, you'll be in time to hear bugling of bull elk at sunset.

Enjoy a picnic, the four-mile auto tour, and a self-guided nature hike.

Sailboat races are held on the lake almost every summer weekend. Fishermen can try their skill in one of the fishing tournaments. Visitors can also go water-skiing and swimming.

The state's fish and game department runs a hatchery program here at the Minnewaukan Flats to obtain millions of eggs used to stock other lakes throughout the state.

During the fall, the lake becomes a temporary stopover for thousands of migrating geese and ducks heading south out of Canada.

The lake's shore is dotted with resorts, boat rentals, and bait shops and daily pontoon tours of the lake are available.

The park includes four recreation areas located on the lake. GRAHAM'S ISLAND STATE PARK, 14 miles southwest of Devils Lake, is the largest recreation area in the park, and has camping facilities for 75 trailers and 30 tent sites, boating from the ramp, fishing, and hiking a self-guided nature trail. It features views of the lake from the bluffs.

SHELVER'S GROVE STATE RECREATION AREA is two miles southeast of Devils Lake, and has picnicking, swimming, and a campground with 20 tent sites and 28 trailer sites with electrical hookups. Camping reservations are accepted. Call 701-662-7106.

In late August, attend Old Settlers Day weekend in the park when the lifestyle of the pioneers is celebrated. Watch demonstrations on their everyday chores, including butter churning, spinning, and washing clothes on a washboard. You can also see many crafts displayed, and watch Dutch clog dancing.

BLACK TIGER BAY STATE RECREATION AREA is 18 miles southwest of Devils Lake, and has a two-lane boat ramp for boating and fishing.

THE NARROWS STATE RECREATION AREA is four miles south of Devils Lake, and provides boat access to East Devils Lake with its three-lane boat ramp. Devils Lake is also known throughout the Midwest for its ice fishing. Winter access is at Graham's Island, Black Tiger Bay and The Narrows. Snowmobilers enjoy the nearby lake region where they have a groomed, marked trail.

Nearby Fort Totten, 13 miles south of Devils Lake, is the best preserved military post from the early frontier days, and its outdoor museum includes the Pioneer Daughter's Museum and the Fort Totten Little Theater. Plays are offered from early July through early August. For information, call 701-662-8459. Tour the interpretive center open mid-May through mid-September, and attend a show in the theater.

Attend Fort Totten Days the end of July, and observe the annual Russell Littleghost Memorial All Indian Fastpitch Softball Tournament, a rodeo, a moccasin tournament, parade contest and a half-court three-on-three basketball tournament.

Dancers compete in several categories including team dancing, traditional, fancy, grass and jingle dancing. Runners can compete in either a 5-kilometer, a 10-kilometer, or a one-mile walk.

Camp Grafton is located along the shore of Devils Lake adjacent to North Dakota 20 and 57, and south of Devils Lake. Its history dates back to the 1800s, and was originally designated as the Fort Totten Military Wood Reservation. The barracks complex can accommodate 800 people, and has dining facilities, a boat launch area and a theater.

Incoming pilots can land at Devils Lake Municipal located two miles west of town. Rental cars are available.

INFORMATION
Devils Lake State Park
Route 1, Box 165
Devils Lake, North Dakota 58001
701-766-4015

FORT ABRAHAM LINCOLN STATE PARK

5

LOCATION - The park is five miles south of Mandan on the Lewis and Clark Trail, North Dakota 1806, and at the confluence of the Heart and Missouri rivers.

FEATURES - The fort was established in 1873, and was originally manned by Colonel George A. Custer and his 7th Cavalry. Custer and his troops rode from here on May 17, 1876, to campaign against the Plains Indians, resulting in the deaths of 265 soldiers, scouts and civilians at the Battle of the Little Bighorn. The fort was abandoned in 1891, and part of the buildings have been reconstructed.

Ruins of the On-A-Slant Indian Village, occupied by the Mandan Indians from around 1650–1764, also are found within the park boundaries. The village had 68 earth lodges, and several have been reconstructed.

Lewis and Clark camped near the abandoned Indian village in 1804, and an interpretive marker is located at a park overlook.

ACTIVITIES - Tour the park museum to view various artifacts, and watch an audio-visual program. The visitor center has concessions and a trading post.

Tour part of the On-A-Slant Indian Village that includes four log and sod earth lodges. Follow a self-guided trail around Cavalry Square where you can see three wooden blockhouses.

Enjoy fishing for walleye and northern pike in the Missouri and Heart rivers.

Special programs during the summer months include Fur Traders Rendezvous and an Indian Cultural Weekend in August. Military Days is held in June, and the Historical Walking Drama is held over three July weekends when a narrator accompanies you to describe life in the past. The last weekend in June, watch homesteaders' demonstrations of such activities as butter churning, candle making, blacksmithing and spinning.

Take a nine-mile ride aboard the Fort Lincoln Trolley that takes you along the Heart and Missouri rivers. The trolley leaves from the Third Street Station in Mandan. For information, call 701-663-9018 or 663-9571.

One night a month the Dakota Astronomical Society leads a "tour" of the night skies. For information, call the visitor center.

A Fur Traders' Rendezvous is held in mid-August when you can watch trade demonstrations, and listen to authentic tales of life in the wilderness.

Participate in the Great American Horse Race the first part of September. This race is reminiscent of the Pony Express, and is run in heats for a prize-winning purse. For information on how to participate, prize money, and race times, contact the park headquarters.

Take an historic ride aboard the Lewis and Clark Riverboat, a replica of the paddle wheelers that once passed here. The riverboat leaves the port of Bismarck and docks at the state park daily. For information, call 701-223-3315.

Camp in the 97-site campground. Some sites have electrical hookups.

Bicyclists can ride along North Dakota Highways 1804 and 1806. Both roads have been designated as part of the Lewis and Clark National Trail System. If you hike the entire North Country National Scenic Trail route of 443 miles in North Dakota, you'll follow the Missouri River to the state's western border.

Take a guided tour of the last home occupied by Colonel Custer. Tours are offered daily from May through September.

During the winter, you can go ice fishing, cross-country skiing along groomed trails, and snowmobiling along the Roughrider National Recreation Trail with its 17 miles of groomed trails.

INFORMATION
Fort Abraham Lincoln State Park
Box 139
Mandan, North Dakota 58554
701-663-9571

FORT RANSOM STATE PARK
6

LOCATION - The park is in southeastern North Dakota two miles north of Fort Ransom. It's also 30 miles south of Valley City, and 18 miles northwest of Lisbon.

FEATURES - The park was established in 1867 to maintain order when the Northern Pacific Railroad was being built. Following the military era, the area saw an influx of white settlers who grew durum wheat, now the state's major grain. As you drive through the area, you'll pass many old farmsteads.

Artifacts from prehistoric dwellers indicate people lived here as long ago as 6000 B.C.

ACTIVITIES - The park has two early farmsteads. The Bjone farm home, built in 1879, is now being used as the park's visitor center. The Sunne homestead, built in the 1880s, is the center of an annual celebration of Sodbusters Days the first weekend after the Independence Day weekend. During these festivities, you'll see demonstrations of horse-drawn plowing, antique machinery displays, and farm-style cooking.

If you visit here during the fall, you'll be treated to some beautiful colors when the hardwoods change.

Camp in one of the 22 primitive campsites or in one of the five semi-modern campsites with electrical hookups. Walk-in tent and canoe campsites are located along the Sheyenne River.

Equestrians can ride along 3.5 miles of trails. No horse rentals are available. You can camp in the group equestrian campsite complete with a corral.

The Sheyenne River is one of the state's most popular canoeing rivers, and the park serves as the headquarters for a canoe trail, a canoe access campsite, and canoe rentals. Lake Ashtabula, one of the largest lakes in the eastern part of the state, skirts the park, and is a popular spot for both fishing and boating. Go shoreline fishing for walleye, pike, bass and bullhead.

Hike the 1.5-mile-long segment of the North Country National Scenic Trail that runs through the park. Hike a two-mile, self-guided nature trail.

During the winter, you can winter camp, go cross-country skiing along eight miles of groomed ski trails, or snowmobiling along the Sheyenne Trail that goes north 46 miles from the park to Valley City. A warming hut is open. For information on trail snow conditions, call 1-800-472-2100. Park snow conditions: 701-973-4331. General trail information: 701-845-9058. Cross-country skiers should check into the Loppet ski races held during the winter.

Downhill skiers can ski at the Fort Ransom Ski Area south of town. For information, call 701-973-2711.

Nearby attractions include the Fort Ransom State Historic Site, Writing Rock Historical Site, Viking Statue Monument, Swinging Bridge and Indian Village Sites.

INFORMATION
Fort Ransom State Park
Box 67
Fort Ransom, North Dakota 58033
701-973-4331

FORT STEVENSON STATE PARK
7

LOCATION - The park is three miles south of Garrison on the northern shore of Lake Sakakawea.

ACTIVITIES - Go fishing, water-skiing, and boating from the full-service marina with concessions, sailboats and houseboat rentals. Four additional recreation areas are located at Steinke Bay, Deepwater Bay, Douglas Bay and West Totten Trail. For information, call 701-462-8541.

Participate in the North Dakota Annual Governor's Cup Walleye Fishing Derby, or in the "bass only" fishing tournament held in early August.

Camp in the campground with both 100 modern campsites and 10 primitive campsites. Reservations are accepted.

Hikers and cross-country skiers have access to several trails in the park, and a seasonal naturalist is on duty.

Nearby attractions include the North Dakota Fishing Hall of Fame in Garrison, power plant tours, and the Broste Rock Museum.

Incoming pilots can land at Garrison Municipal Airport located one mile west of town. Courtesy car transportation is available.

INFORMATION
Fort Stevenson State Park
Route 1, Box 262
Garrison, North Dakota 58540
701-337-5576

GRAHAM'S ISLAND STATE PARK
8

See under DEVILS LAKE STATE PARK

ICELANDIC STATE PARK
9

LOCATION - The park is five miles west of Cavalier on North Dakota 5, and on the north shore of Lake Renwick.

FEATURES - The park was one of the major settlements for Icelandic pioneers. It's situated in the former glacial lake bed of Lake Agassiz.

ACTIVITIES - Tour the Gunlogson homestead believed to be one of the earliest in the state. The original house and barn were constructed in 1880, but were replaced later by the existing house and barn. Now the barn houses the visitor center with displays depicting six time periods.

The campground has 100 sites with both water and electrical hookups. Another 20-unit campground is available for trailers or tents, and you can also walk into several tent sites next to the lake. Reservations are accepted.

The park is open year-round, and visitors enjoy fishing for pike, walleye, crappie and perch. During the winter, go cross-country skiing on four miles of marked groomed trails, sledding, snowmobiling and ice skating.

Lake Renwick has a launching ramp for power boats, canoes and sailboats. You can also go swimming in the lake next to the picnic area with a concession stand.

Take advantage of one of the campfire programs, guided nature walks and historical tours on summer weekends. Wildwood Trail, a National Recreation Trail, winds through the Gunlogson Arboretum. An extensive trail system winds along the Tongue River.

Settlement Days are celebrated the end of June, and feature ethnic entertainment, foods, exhibitions, carriage rides, games and contests.

A kite festival is held the last Sunday in May when ribbons are awarded to the kids who compete in various categories such as best kite flying, longest tail and most colorful.

Nearby attractions include: the Chaboillay Trading Post site and Pioneer Daughters Museum, at Pembina; the Pembina County Museum, at Cavalier, Gingras Historic Park and Kittson Trading Post site, at Walhalla; Paton Isles of Memories, at LeRoy; and the Heritage Village, at Grafton.

Pembina's Gorge Trail provides 255 miles of trails for the snowmobiler, or you can go cross-country skiing along the Pembina Valley Nordic Trail's six miles of marked trails.

Incoming pilots can land at Cavalier Municipal Airport located one mile southwest of town. Courtesy car transportation is available.

INFORMATION
Icelandic State Park
HCR 3, Box 64A
Cavalier, North Dakota 58220
701-265-4561

LAKE METIGOSHE STATE PARK
10

LOCATION - The park is fourteen miles northeast of Bottineau.

ACTIVITIES - The campground has 198 campsites, 90 are modern sites and 108 are primitive. The park also has sleeping dormitories and rental cabins.

Enjoy fishing in the lake for walleye, muskie, pike, perch, bluegill, bass and trout. Boat launching facilities are located on the eastern shore of the lake. You can also swim in the lake from a terraced beach. The park has boat rentals, canoe trails, a grocery store, eating facilities, a golf course and a public fishing dock.

Forty-five miles of hiking trails lace the Turtle Mountains. Three of the most popular include Disappearing Lakes, Turtle's Back and the Old Oak National Recreation Trail. For longer hikes, contact the State Forest Service in Bottineau by calling 701-228-2278.

Triathletes can participate in a mini-triathlon held the end of June. Contact the park authorities for details.

Bird watchers can observe thousands of migratory waterfowl passing over and through the park during the spring and fall.

During the winter, you can go cross-country skiing along 12 miles of trails, including three groomed trails. Snowmobilers have access to over 70 miles of wooded trails, many groomed daily. These trails connect with over 125 miles of trails in the Turtle Mountains. Downhill skiers can ski at Winter Park near Bottineau. Information: 701-263-4556.

The park also hosts winter festivals. For details, contact the park naturalists. Cross-country skiers can participate in the Loppet ski races staged here.

The International Peace Garden, nestled in the center of the Turtle Mountains, near Dunseith on the Canada-North Dakota boundary, and northeast of the park, commemorates over 150 years of peace between the U.S. and Canada. Visitors can tour the formal gardens, arboretum, Peace Tower and Carillon Bell Tower. Two scenic drives take you on both sides of the international line to loop around the lakes.

The International Music Camp provides many concerts, plays and dance productions. More than 2,000 students and adults attend this camp where they not only receive instruction in music, but also participate in the various outdoor activities. For information on the camp, call 701-263-4211 from June–August. Otherwise, call 701-838-8427.

In Boissevain, Manitoba, come to the Canadian Turtle Derby that attracts large crowds to watch turtles race. Besides the big race, you can watch a demolition derby, parade, curling, a softball tournament and many other activities. The three-day event is held in mid-July. For information and dates, call 204-534-6472.

Incoming pilots can land at Bottineau Municipal Airport located one mile east of town. Rental cars are available.

INFORMATION

Lake Metigoshe State Park   701-263-4651
Route 1, Box 152
Bottineau, North Dakota 58318

LAKE SAKAKAWEA STATE PARK
11

LOCATION - The park is one mile north of Pick City, and three miles west of Riverdale on North Dakota 200.

FEATURES - Lake Sakakawea is 180 miles long, and is located along the Missouri River. It's sometimes referred to as the "Sixth Great Lake," with a shoreline longer than the coast of California.

ACTIVITIES - Camp in one of the 150 sites with electrical hookups, or in one of the 150 primitive sites. A walk-in tent site is next to the lake on the northeast corner of the park.

Captain Kit's Marina is located in the park where you can purchase gas, rent a fishing boat or pontoon, obtain your fishing license and purchase live bait. Anglers fish for giant walleye, salmon, bass and world-record sauger.

The North American Regatta is held on the lake at the end of July when hobie cats, catamarans, and sailboats compete. For registration and information, call 701-224-4887. A salmon fishing derby is featured here in August.

Tour the power plant on the lake daily during the summer, or by scheduling an appointment the rest of the year. Tours take you into the face of the dam where you can observe the power plant at work. The lobby has displays that can be viewed year-round. For information, call 701-654-7411.

The cold, deep lake water offers some very good scuba diving with underwater visibility ranging from 15 to 20 feet. Favorite dive spots include the face of Garrison Dam, Mallard Island, and the Riverdale Bluffs area.

INFORMATION

Lake Sakakawea State Park   Marina: 701-487-3600
Box 832
Riverdale, North Dakota 58565
701-487-3315

LEWIS AND CLARK STATE PARK
12

LOCATION - The park is 16 miles southeast of Williston on North Dakota 104 on one of the upper bays of Lake Sakakawea.

ACTIVITIES - Go boating from the modern boating facilities that include a marina, boat rentals and a boat ramp. Enjoy fishing for walleye, sauger and northern pike.

Hike along the self-guided nature trail. Camp in the modern campground with 58 campsites. Swim from the swimming beach, and attend a program in the amphitheater. During winter, go snowmobiling or cross-country skiing.

Nearby attractions include the Buffalo Trails Museum, and Fort Union Trading Post National Historic Site, 24 miles southwest of Williston on North Dakota 1804. The fort is a reconstructed fur trading post originally operated by John Jacob Astor's American Fur Company in the early and mid-1800s. Tour the visitor center and the Bourgeois House.

The Fort Buford State Historic Site is near Williston, and is the site of Sitting Bull's surrender.

INFORMATION
Lewis and Clark State Park
Route 1, Box 13A
Williston, North Dakota 58843
701-859-3071

LITTLE MISSOURI BAY STATE PARK
13

LOCATION - The park is 21 miles north of Killdeer.

FEATURES - The park is located in the North Dakota Badlands.

ACTIVITIES - The park offers primitive camping in 25 sites. Over 75 miles of trails criss-cross the badlands that are used by both hikers and horseback riders. Equestrians have a corral plus several artesian wells for watering horses. A horse concession is located adjacent to the park. Springtime is especially beautiful when the wild flowers bloom.

Little Missouri Bay is an extension of Lake Sakakawea, and offers good fishing. You need to ride horseback or hike to reach the water. You can also boat into the park, but the park itself has no boating facilities.

Nearby attractions include Theodore Roosevelt National Park's North Unit in Medora where you can see displays from Roosevelt's ranching days and attend an interpretive program. Cross-country skiing is also available there.

INFORMATION
Little Missouri Bay State Park   701-487-3315
c/o Lake Sakakawea State Park
Box 832
Riverdale, North Dakota 58565

NARROWS STATE RECREATION AREA
14

See under DEVILS LAKE STATE PARK

SHELVER'S GROVE STATE RECREATION AREA
15

See under DEVILS LAKE STATE PARK

SULLY CREEK STATE RECREATION AREA
16

LOCATION - The area is located in the heart of the Badlands, and minutes away from the town of Medora and Theodore Roosevelt National Park.

FEATURES - The park was named for General Alfred Sully, who, in 1864, was sent to North Dakota to retaliate for the 1862 "Minnesota Uprising" of the Sioux.

ACTIVITIES - Go horseback riding in the Badlands by providing your own horse. You can also hike or ride into nearby Little Missouri National Grasslands or into Theodore Roosevelt National Park South Unit.

The park has primitive camping in 24 sites, 12 drive-in sites, 10 tent sites, plus a horse corral. Water is available at the well house. Go fishing on the Little Missouri River for catfish, carp and bullhead.

Other nearby attractions include the Chateau DeMores State Historic Site, a mansion built by a French nobleman whose dream was to begin a cattle shipping empire here. It's open for daily summer tours.

Additional scenic sights to visit include the Little Missouri Scenic River, Burning Coal Vein, and Columnar Junipers Natural Area.

Attend one of the nightly professional musical productions given under the stars at the Burning Hills Amphitheater in Medora.

To get a feel for the area loved by President Roosevelt, stop by the visitor center at the Theodore Roosevelt National Park on the west side of Medora, and tour the park. In town, stop by the front desk of the historic Rough Rider Hotel.

INFORMATION
Sully Creek State Recreation Area
c/o Fort Abraham Lincoln State Park
Route 2, Box 139
Mandan, North Dakota 58501
701-663-9571

TURTLE RIVER STATE PARK
17

LOCATION - Turtle River State Park is 22 miles west of Grand Forks on North Dakota 2 in the eastern part of the state.

FEATURES - The Turtle River winds its way through the park. Watch for two old beach ridges left behind by receding glacial Lake Agassiz that covered the area approximately 10,000 years ago. A series of archeological sites are located within and near the park dating back to the Arvilla Mounds people who are believed to have lived here from A.D. 600 to 900.

ACTIVITIES - Visitors can enjoy fishing, swimming, horseback riding with a rental concession available outside the park, hiking, and camping. You can select from 80 modern campsites, 20 semi-modern sites, or rustic group cabins. Interpretive programs are presented each Friday and Saturday during the summer at the park amphitheater.

Over the Fourth of July, attend their free concert "Music in the Park" celebration. In late September, attend the Turtle River Arts and Crafts Show.

During the winter, come to enjoy snowmobiling, cross-country skiing along 12 miles of marked, groomed trails, sledding or skating on the ice rink. A heated chalet is open, and refreshments are sold. Attend the winter festival and Loppets' cross-country ski race.

In nearby Grand Forks, take a ride on the Dakota Queen Riverboat that offers tours from May through October. For information and reservations, call 701-775-5656.

In North Forks, tour the Center for Aerospace Science on the UNC campus, and learn about its state-of-the-art "Atmospherium." For information, call 701-777-4195.

Pilots can fly into Grand Forks Mark Andrews International Airport located 4.5 miles west of Grand Forks on North Dakota 2. Rental cars are available.

INFORMATION
Turtle River State Park
Arvilla, North Dakota 58214
701-594-4445

*The natural surroundings in Ohio's state parks range from
dense forests and misty meadows to towering geologic formations,
such as this impressive scene at Hocking Hills State Park, near Logan, Ohio.*

OHIO DEPARTMENT OF NATURAL RESOURCES PHOTO

OHIO

Ohio has an abundance of water resources including Lake Erie, many inland lakes, ponds and reservoirs, 7,000 miles of rivers and streams, plus 451 miles of the Ohio River shoreline. As a result, over 20% of the state's population participates in sport fishing each year. Lake Erie is often called the "Walleye Capital of the World." Others come to participate in sailing and powerboating.

The state boasts 72 state parks, ranking it third nationally in the number of state parks. Although Ohio ranks 35th in size, its state park system ranks as the sixth largest in the U.S. in land acreage and attracts over 61 million annual visitors.

You can overnight in six vacation lodges and almost 500 vacation cabins located within the state parks. The resort parks are located in Shawnee, Hueston Woods, Deer Creek, Salt Fork, Burr Oak and Punderson State Parks. Cabin rentals during June, July and August are available on a weekly basis only. Exceptions are the Lake Hope sleeping cabins and Buck Creek deluxe housekeeping cabins. Only the sleeping cabins at Lake Hope are available year-round.

The Buckeye Trail has a network of trails that encircle the state in a 1,200-mile loop. It has both on- and off-road segments, some designated for both equestrian and hiking traffic, and others just for hiking. In some areas, segments follow bike trails and tow paths. For information, call 614-385-6386.

Bicyclists should check into the Great Ohio Bicycle Adventure, a week-long, 50-mile-per-day bicycle tour through the state. For information, call 1-800-BUCKEYE.

A. W. MARION STATE PARK
1

LOCATION - The park is five miles east of Circleville off U.S. 22 and Ohio 188, and 30 miles south of Columbus.

FEATURES - The park is located in the roughest terrain in Pickaway County known as "The Devil's Backbone."

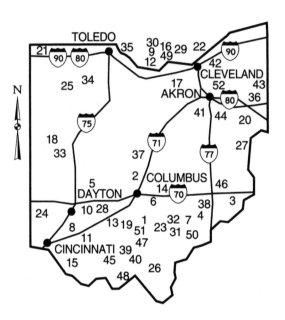

ACTIVITIES - Camp in the 60-site campground without hookups. Launch your electric-powered boat from the ramp. Rental boats are available at the concession stand on the northwest side of the lake. A boater's beach is at the south end of the lake.

Go fishing for panfish, bass, muskellunge and catfish. Catfish tournaments are held the third Saturday of each month, from May–September. Hike the Hargus Lake Trail following the five-mile lake shoreline.

During the winter, go sledding, ice fishing, ice skating and hiking.

The Circleville Canal, a five-mile portion of the Ohio and Erie Canal, is located one mile west of Circleville and south of U.S. 22. The waters are stocked with bass, bluegill and crappie.

Tarlton Cross Mound is south of the park, and one mile north of Tarlton off Ohio 159.

Incoming pilots can land at Clark's Dream Strip located four miles northwest of Circleville. Rental cars are available.

INFORMATION
A.W. Marion State Park
7317 Warner-Juffer Road
Circleville, Ohio 43113
614-474-3386

ALUM CREEK STATE PARK
2

LOCATION - Alum Creek Lake is north of Columbus between I-71 and U.S. 23, and seven miles southeast of Delaware off Ohio 36 and 37, one mile west of junction I-71.

FEATURES - The Adena Indians lived here from 800 to 200 B.C., and built seven mounds that were found around Alum Creek.

Campers will find a bronze plaque commemorating the site of Fort Cheshire, known to the colonists as the Blockhouse. It was built as protection against the Indians around 1812, but was never used for this purpose.

During the 1860s, the Alum Creek area was a main artery of Ohio's "underground railroad" used by slaves escaping to Canada. They walked in the waters of Alum Creek so their scent couldn't be picked up by pursuing dogs.

ACTIVITIES - The 3,000-foot-long beach located on the west side of the lake north of the dam on Lewis Center Road is the largest inland beach in the state. Visitors can purchase concessions at the main bathhouse. Lifeguards are on duty from Memorial Day to Labor Day.

The campground, open year-round, is located on the west side of the lake, south of Cheshire Road, and has 297 campsites with electrical hookups and a trailer dump. Five rent-a-camp sites are available May 1–October 31, and should be reserved in advance since they generally fill early in the season.

Boaters can use vessels of unlimited horsepower. Sailboats, canoes and row-boats are also permitted on the lake with five launching ramps. The lake's northern end has many hidden coves and quiet fishing spots accessible only to small boats. Powerboats usually use the south end of the lake where water-skiing is good. A marina is located on the west side of the lake at the end of Hollenback Road, and has a restaurant, launch ramp and rental boats. For information, call 614-548-6056.

Fishermen can try their luck at landing bass, bluegill, crappie, perch, catfish and walleye. The best fishing is at the northern end of the lake.

Hike along 8.5 miles of hiking trails. A six-mile multi-purpose trail is located at the New Galena launch ramp on the east side of the lake. You can also hike the nature trail in the Hollenback launch area, or the Park Office Trail on the west side of the lake.

Ride along 32 miles of bridle trails recommended for experienced riders. The majority of the trails are north of U.S. 36-37. No horse rentals are available. An equestrian camp is located on Howard Road on the north end of the lake.

During the winter, snowmobilers and cross-country skiers have access to seven miles of trails. Dog sled races are held annually.

Special events include the Fall Festival in October, and triathlons in June and July. Throughout the summer months, many bass tournaments and sailing regattas are held.

In Columbus, visit the Olentangy Indian Caverns, six miles north of the intersection of U.S. 23 and I-270, and another two miles west on Home Road. The caverns were once utilized as shelter by the Wyandot Indians, and its cave-house museum has artifacts and archeological displays. Tour the three-level cavern and the Indian Museum, or the Ohio Frontierland and the Indian country village. For information, call 614-548-7917.

Incoming pilots can land at Delaware Municipal Airport located three miles southwest of town. Rental cars are available.

INFORMATION
Alum Creek State Park
3615 South Old State Road
Delaware, Ohio 43015
614-548-4631

BARKCAMP STATE PARK
3

LOCATION - The park is one mile east of Belmont off Ohio 149.

FEATURES - The park got its name from Barkcamp Creek, site of an early logging operation where logs were stripped of their bark before being delivered to the mill.

ACTIVITIES - Stop by the Antique Barn to see their antique tool display and nature center. Nature programs are offered during the summer.

Stay in the campground with 176 sites and a dump station. The park also has five rent-a-camp sites.

Go hiking along four miles of trails, or horseback riding along six miles. Go boating from the ramp where rentals are available.

In August, attend the annual Civil War re-enactment in the park. In July, St. Clairsville presents "Jamboree in the Hills," and in August, they feature "Blue Grass in the Hills."

In nearby Wheeling, West Virginia, tour some Victorian homes, and take a cruise aboard the Valley Voyager's authentic stern-wheel riverboat docked at 1315 Water Street on the waterfront. For information, call 304-233-1010.

INFORMATION
Barkcamp State Park   614-484-4064
65330 Barkcamp Park Road
Belmont, Ohio 43718

BLUE ROCK STATE PARK
4

LOCATION - The park is fifteen miles southeast of Zanesville. The main entrance is on Cutler Lake Road, Ohio 45, six miles from Ohio 60.

ACTIVITIES - Camp in the campground located on the west shore of the lake with 101 campsites without hookups. Rent-a-camp facilities are also available. A walk-in, tents only area, is off Cutler Lake Road.

Go boating in rowboats, canoes or in boats powered by electric motors. A launch ramp is off Cutler Lake Road. Paddle boats may be rented at the beach concession building.

Fish for bass, catfish and bluegill. Hike three miles of trails in the park, or go hiking and horseback riding the trails located in nearby Blue Rock State Forest. Enjoy swimming from the beach on the north end of the lake.

To take a scenic drive, follow Ohio 60 from Zanesville along the Muskingum River to Marietta. In Zanesville, look for the famous "Y" bridge that spans both the Muskingum and Licking rivers.

Incoming pilots can land at Zanesville Municipal, located six miles east of town. Rental cars are available.

INFORMATION
Blue Rock State Park   614-674-4794
7924 Cutler Lake Road
Blue Rock, Ohio 43720

BUCK CREEK STATE PARK
5

LOCATION - The park is four miles east of Springfield on Ohio 4.

ACTIVITIES - Go boating from a four-lane launch ramp. The marina has a snack bar, and rental boats. Go scuba diving or swimming from a sand beach with a concession stand. Anglers can fish for walleye, bass and panfish.

Stay in the campground with 101 sites, 89 with electrical hookups and a dump station. The park also has 26 family housekeeping cabins.

Tour the restored Crabill House, listed on the National Register of Historic Places. Tour the visitor center operated by the U.S. Army Corps of Engineers, and take a tour of the dam.

Cedar Bog State Nature Preserve is located between Urbana and Springfield, and is open for tours on Saturday and Sunday from April–September.

Incoming pilots can land at Springfield-Beckley Municipal Airport located six miles south of town. Rental cars are available.

INFORMATION
Buck Creek State Park   513-322-5284
1901 Buck Creek Lane
Springfield, Ohio 45502

BUCKEYE LAKE STATE PARK
6

LOCATION - The park is nine miles south of Newark off Ohio 13.

ACTIVITIES - The park is for day-use only, and offers swimming, unlimited horsepower boating from several launch ramps, water-skiing, picnicking and fishing for bluegill, crappie, bass and catfish. Two boat rentals are located on Buckeye Lake's north side, and several other marinas and restaurants are located around the lake.

Bird watchers will enjoy watching the many species that come through here, particularly in the spring and fall. One of the state's largest great blue heron rookeries is adjacent to the park, and these birds can often be seen in the park.

During the winter, come to go ice fishing, ice skating, and snowmobiling. Motorcycle races are held every Sunday when ice conditions are favorable.

Cranberry Bog, a State Nature Preserve and a National Natural Landmark, is in the lake. It's a living relict of the Ice Age, dating back more than 13,000 years. The bog is a floating island made of sphagnum moss, and access to the island is by permit only from the Division of Natural Areas and Preserves.

Hebron Fish Hatchery is north of the lake on Canal Road, and is open to the public. From March to June watch the spawning of walleye and catfish.

Moundbuilders' State Memorial is one mile southwest of Newark on Ohio 79. You'll see a circular earthwork 1,200 feet in diameter with three smaller mounds in its center. The memorial is open from dawn to dusk from April through October. To learn more about the Moundbuilders, stop by the Ohio Indian Museum on the grounds. For information, call 614-344-1920.

Incoming pilots can land at Newark-Heath Airport located three miles southwest of town. Rental cars are available.

INFORMATION
Buckeye Lake State Park
Box 488
Millersport, Ohio 43046
614-467-2690

BURR OAK STATE PARK
7

LOCATION - The park is six miles northeast of Glouster off Ohio 13.

ACTIVITIES - Burr Oak is one of Ohio's seven resort parks, and Burr Oak Lodge has 60 guest rooms, a dining room, swimming beach, tennis courts, golf course, boat launch ramp, and an indoor-outdoor pool.

The campground has 123 sites without electrical hookups, and a trailer dump station. twenty-three additional sites are located on the other side of the lake at docks two and three. You can also stay in one of the three rent-a-camp sites or in one of the 30 deluxe housekeeping cabins.

Anglers can fish for bass, crappie, bluegill and catfish. A public beach is located on the west side of the lake and has a snack bar. You can also go scuba diving in the lake.

Boat rentals are available at docks one and four. Horseback riding and a nine-hole golf course are available nearby.

The park has 40 miles of hiking trails including a portion of the Buckeye Trail and the Burr Oak Backpack Trail's 29-mile loop.

During the winter come to go sledding, cross-country skiing and ice fishing.

INFORMATION

Burr Oak State Park
1901 Buck Creek Lane
Springfield, Ohio 45502
614-767-3570

Lodge and cabin reservations:
1-800-282-7275 (in Ohio)
or 614-767-2112

CAESAR CREEK LAKE STATE PARK
8

LOCATION - The park is five miles east of Waynesville and five miles west of I-71 on Ohio 73. The lake is 30 miles northeast of Cincinnati and 15 miles southeast of Dayton.

FEATURES - Caesar Lake is Ohio's deepest lake, with a water depth of 115 feet near the dam. It has many bays and inlets, and three islands.

ACTIVITIES - The lake permits unlimited horsepower boating from five launch ramps, and you can swim from your boat in the coves by Lukens Road and by Ward Road. Go water-skiing and swimming from the beach with a concession stand. Fish for bass and crappie, bluegill and walleye in Caesar Creek Lake.

The 287-site campground with electrical hookups is open year-round, and has rent-a-camps and a youth hostel. Equestrians have their own campground with 25 sites, but you have to bring your own horse.

Go hiking on one of the 15 trails covering 38 miles ranging in length from .4-mile to four miles. To see Flat Fork Gorge, follow the trail from the dam to Wellman Meadows Road on the east side of the lake.

Go horseback riding on 35 miles of trails, or backpacking on the 50-mile backpack trail. Nature programs are presented year-round.

To learn about the Hopewell Indians who built three miles of earthen walls making up Fort Ancient, visit the Army Corps of Engineers' Visitor Center located three miles southeast of Waynesville on Clarksville Road.

Visit the Pioneer Village in Waynesville where buildings dating from 1790 have been reconstructed. It's open year-round for self-guided tours, and has a living history demonstration area. Festivals are presented each month from May–September. For information, call 513-897-1120.

Nearby attractions include the Blue Jacket outdoor drama, and canoeing on the Little Miami Scenic River.

Incoming pilots can land at the James M. Cox Dayton International Airport located nine miles north of town. Rental cars are available. Moraine Air Park is located five miles southwest of town, and has rental cars.

INFORMATION

Caesar Creek Lake State Park   513-897-3055
8570 East State Route 73   513-382-2311
Waynesville, Ohio 45068

CATAWBA ISLAND STATE PARK
9

See under LAKE ERIE STATE PARKS

CLIFTON GORGE STATE NATURE PRESERVE
10

See under JOHN BRYAN STATE PARK

COWAN LAKE STATE PARK
11

LOCATION - The park is five miles south of Wilmington off U.S. 68.

ACTIVITIES - Go camping in the campground with 237 campsites with electrical hookups, or in one of the cabins. The campground and 27 deluxe cabins are available year-round. A boat launch ramp, boat docks and beach are available for camper use.

Go swimming in the lake with lifeguards on duty from Memorial Day to Labor Day. Fish for muskie, bass, crappie, bluegill and catfish. A record 50-pound shovelhead catfish has been caught in the lake.

Park naturalists are on duty from mid-June through August. Go hiking on one of the six trails. Lotus Cove, one of the most popular, leads to Lookout Pier where you can get an overlook of the lake, and walk along the boardwalk to see the American lotus (water lily) colony.

The marina is open seven days a week, and has a food concession and rental boats. You can go boating with low horsepower, sailing and canoeing. The lake is considered to be one of the best sailing lakes in the Midwest.

Rock hounds come here to hunt fossils, the remains or imprints of prehistoric plants and animals that have been preserved in the sediments for over 75 million years. Since the fossils are so abundant, collecting is permitted.

Incoming pilots can land at Clinton Field which is five miles northwest of Wilmington. Rental cars are available.

INFORMATION
Cowan Lake State Park
729 Beechwood Road
Wilmington, Ohio 45177
513-289-2105
Marina: 513-289-2656

CRANE CREEK STATE PARK
12

See under LAKE ERIE STATE PARKS

DEER CREEK STATE PARK
13

LOCATION - The park is seven miles south of Mount Sterling on Ohio 207.

FEATURES - Evidence has been found on Tick Ridge of an ancient Indian tribe who camped here around 2000 B.C.

ACTIVITIES - Visitors can stay overnight in Deer Creek State Park lodge's guest rooms, in one of the 25 deluxe housekeeping cabins, three rent-a-camps, or in the campground with 232 sites, all with electrical hookups. Equestrians have access to a small primitive campsite and 14 miles of trails.

Golfers can play on the 18-hole golf course. The lake allows unlimited horsepower boating from two ramps, fishing, water-skiing and swimming from the beach with a concession stand. The park has a fully equipped marina.

Hikers have access to three miles of trails. Nature programs are offered during the summer.

Drive into Chillicothe to watch "Tecumseh," an historical outdoor drama presented in the Sugarloaf Mountain Amphitheater, 6.5 miles northeast of Chillicothe on Delano Road. Performances run Monday–Saturday from mid-June until Labor Day. Come early to take a behind-the-scenes tour offered every hour from 2–5. Then enjoy dinner at the Tecumseh Restaurant Terrace before watching the play. For information, call 614-775-0700.

INFORMATION

Deer Creek State Park
20635 Waterloo Road
Mt. Sterling, Ohio 43143
614-869-3124

Golf course: 614-869-3088
Lodge/cabin reservations:
1-800-282-7275 or 614-439-2751
Marina: 614-869-4543

DILLON STATE PARK
14

LOCATION - The park is five miles northwest of Zanesville off Ohio 146.

ACTIVITIES - The campground has 195 sites with 183 offering electrical hookups, or stay in one of the 29 deluxe cabins.

You can hike along four trails including the Ruffed Grouse Nature Trail that is a branch of the longer six-mile hike on the Licking Bend Trail that skirts the lake shore.

Go swimming from a beach with concessions, boating from one of the four ramps with unlimited horsepower permitted, water-skiing, and fishing.

A unique feature of the park is its sportsmen's area that includes lighted trap and skeet fields, and a rifle and pistol range. Visitors can also play tennis, volleyball, handball and shuffleboard.

During the winter, come to sled and then warm up in the area provided.

Blackhand Gorge State Nature Preserve is located 10 miles northwest of the park on Licking County 273. Here you'll see a narrow gorge cut by the Licking River, and seven trails await your exploration. Bicyclists have access to the North Central Bike Trail that winds 4.2 miles along the western rim of the gorge. For information, call 614-265-6452.

In Zanesville, take a one-hour cruise aboard the Lorena Sternwheeler docked at Zanesville's Riverside Park. The cruises leave Wednesday–Monday at 2:00 and 4:00 p.m. from May through October. For information, call 614-454-6851.

The National Road-Zane Grey Museum is located in Norwich, ten miles east of Zanesville on U.S. 22/40, and east of I-70 at Exit 164. Here you can learn the history of the nation's first "highway," and see many of Zane Grey's memorabilia. He wrote almost 100 books, his most popular being his western novels. For information, call 614-872-3143.

In Roscoe Village, located in Coshocton, approximately a half-hour from the park, costumed tour guides take you through the reconstructed 18th-century Ohio village. The village hosts a variety of special events including Dulcimer Days and a Christmas candle lighting celebration. For information on tours and special events, call 614-622-9310.

The Flint Ridge State Memorial and Museum is northwest of the park near Brownsville, and three miles north of U.S. 40. The preserve has several nature trails to explore. Overlook the pits where the Indians quarried their flint. For information, call 614-787-2476.

Incoming pilots can land at Zanesville Municipal located six miles east of town. Rental cars are available.

INFORMATION

Dillon State Park   614-453-4377 (park office)
5265 Dillon Hills Drive   614-453-0442 (camp office)
P. O. Box 126   614-453-7964 (canoe rentals)
Nashport, Ohio 43830   614-453-4980 (marina)

EAST FORK STATE PARK
15

LOCATION - The park is four miles southeast of Amelia off Ohio 125.

ACTIVITIES - Camp in one of the state's largest campgrounds with 416 campsites, all with electrical hookups. A 17-site equestrian campground, and four rent-a-camps are also available.

Water sports enthusiasts can go boating from five ramps with no boating restrictions, water-skiing, and swimming from the beach with life guards and concessions. Hikers have a 12-mile-long trail to explore, and hikers and equestrians share the 37-mile East Fork Back Country Trail that includes an eight-mile section of the Buckeye Trail. Four overnight shelters are located along the trail. No rental horses are available.

A "Hoe-down in the Park" is held the second and fourth Saturday evenings from Memorial Day weekend through the end of September.

Check the naturalists' schedule for their guided fossil hunt, and search for evidence of the sea creatures that lived here millions of years ago.

Each year in mid-June, top rowers come from across the country to compete in the Cincinnati Regatta. For information on rowing opportunities, call 513-241-2628.

Visit President Ulysses S. Grant's birthplace in Point Pleasant. It's at U.S. 52 and Ohio 232, south of East Fork.

INFORMATION
East Fork State Park
Box 119
Bethel, Ohio 45106
513-734-4323

EAST HARBOR
16

See under LAKE ERIE STATE PARKS

FINDLEY STATE PARK
17

LOCATION - The park is three miles south of Wellington on Ohio 58.

ACTIVITIES - Visitors can go swimming, boating with rental boats available at the marina, and fishing for bass, bluegill and northern pike. Launching ramps are located at the campground or picnic area.

The campground has 280 campsites, a dump station, and three rent-a-camp sites. A naturalist is on duty during the summer.

Go hiking along ten miles of trails, including part of the Buckeye Trail.

Archibald Willard lived in nearby Wellington. He painted the famous "The Spirit of 76," and many of his originals are hung in the town library. Visit the Spirit of 76 Museum located at 202 No. Main Street to see a collection of his memorabilia. Wellington has over 113 homes and businesses listed on the National Register of Historic Places.

Incoming pilots can land at Cleveland Hopkins Airport located ten miles southwest of Cleveland. Rental cars are available.

INFORMATION
Findley State Park
25381 State Route 58 South
Wellington, Ohio 44090
216-647-4490

GRAND LAKE ST. MARYS STATE PARK
LAKE LORAMIE STATE PARK
18

LOCATION - Grand Lake St. Marys is two miles west of St. Marys on Ohio 703. Lake Loramie is south of the lake on Ohio 362 and 66.

FEATURES - The lake has 52 miles of shoreline, and is nine miles long. It's the largest artificial body of water in the world built without using any machinery, and served as a vital link between the Great Lakes and the Ohio River.

ACTIVITIES - In GRAND LAKE ST. MARY'S STATE PARK, go boating, water-skiing, wind sailing and hover crafting on the large, relatively shallow lake. It has four public swimming beaches, boat rentals, four launch ramps, and unlimited boating restrictions. Use caution if the weather turns bad since the water can become quite rough and dangerous.

Fish for bass, bluegill, crappie, perch and catfish. Participate in the annual 60-day Johnson Reel's Crappiethon tournament from the middle of April until the middle of June. For information, call 205-353-8447.

Camp in the campground with 206 sites, 50 with electrical hookups. Campers have access to their own beach and boat docks. A park naturalist is on duty during the summer.

The adjacent 40-mile stretch of the Miami-Erie Canal provides excellent horseback riding and hiking along the towpath. The trail begins at the St. Mary's Municipal Power Plant, and ends at 40-Acre Pond. Five miles of additional bicycling are available on the Coldwater-Celina bicycle trail between the two cities.

The 18-hole Northmoor Golf Course borders the lake, located on Ohio 703 between St. Marys and Celina. A fish hatchery is located on the extreme eastern edge of the lake on Ohio 364, and is open weekdays from 8–4. A 40-foot working lighthouse is located on the west bank of the lake, and has an observation deck. The city of St. Marys built a full-scale replica of a canal boat, and it's located in part of the old canal in Memorial Park in town. It can be visited any time.

Tour nearby Fort Recovery, a replica of a fort dating from the War of 1812. It's southeast of the park on Ohio 49, and is open 9:30–5:00 except Monday, from March to November.

LAKE LORAMIE STATE PARK has facilities for boating, fishing, picnicking, camping and swimming. The Miami and Erie Trail connects the Grand Lake St.

Marys and Lake Loramie state parks. Besides the 40-mile trail, you can ride on eight miles of bridle trails, or canoe along six miles of canoe trails. The trail begins at Delphos and ends at Lake Loramie State Park.

In nearby Wapakoneta, tour the Neil Armstrong Air and Space Museum located on the I-75 business loop at Exit 111. Exhibits chronicle the history of flight beginning with the Wright Brothers continuing through to the Space Shuttle program. An astrotheater gives you the experience of traveling through space on a moon mission. For information, call 419-738-8811.

INFORMATION

Grand Lake St. Marys State Park	Lake Loramie State Park
Box 208	11221 State Road 362
St. Marys, Ohio 45885	Minster, Ohio 45865-9311
419-394-3611	513-295-2011

GREAT SEAL STATE PARK
19

LOCATION - The park is three miles northeast of Chillicothe on Marietta Pike.

FEATURES - The park got its name from the state emblem, the Great Seal of Ohio, which depicts a sun over rolling hills and shocked wheat.

ACTIVITIES - Twenty miles of trails await the hiker and equestrian with terrain varying from steep to gently rolling hills. Climb Sugarloaf Mountain, a hike of 2.1 miles, but one that climbs around 500 feet in less than .25-mile.

The Shawnee Ridge Trail is 7.8 miles long, and includes Bald Hill, Sand Hill and parts of Rocky Knob. Mountain Eyes Trail is 6.4 miles long, and crosses several ridges, making the hike a strenuous one.

The park doesn't have a regular campground, but does accommodate equestrians with a 15-site Horsemen's Camp located off Marietta Road.

Sugar Loaf Mountain Amphitheater is located on the park's boundary, and offers a summer outdoor drama, "Tecumseh," depicting the life of Tecumseh and his struggle in preserving a home for his Shawnee Nation. Performances run from Monday–Saturday at 8:00 p.m. from mid-June through the first part of September. For information, phone 614-775-0700.

The surrounding region has many relics from the prehistoric Indians including the Mound City National Monument located on Ohio 104 five miles west of the park. Serpent Mound State Memorial is located south of Bainbridge off Ohio 41, and Seip Mound State Memorial is located west of Chillicothe on U.S. 50 near Bainbridge.

You can also tour Adena built in 1806, and located off Adena Road near Chillicothe. For information, call 614-772-1500.

Incoming pilots can land at Ross County's Shoemaker Field located seven miles northwest of town. Rental cars are available.

INFORMATION
Great Seal State Park
825 Rocky Road
Chillicothe, Ohio 45601
614-773-2726

GUILFORD LAKE STATE PARK
20

LOCATION - The park is 28 miles east of Canton, and seven miles west of Lisbon, off Ohio 172 and County 411. The park office is on the east side of the lake approximately .5-mile north of Ohio 172 on East Lake Road.

ACTIVITIES - Camp in the 42-site campground. Its entrance is off Ohio 411. A fishing dock is available for campers to use.

Go boating on the lake with motors up to ten horsepower allowed. Boat rentals are available from a marina on the south side of the lake. Launching ramps are located on the lake's north, east and south sides.

Enjoy fishing for bass, bluegill, crappie and pike from the north shore or from your boat. The swimming beach is on the northwest side of the lake, and lifeguards are on duty during the summer months.

Two public golf courses are located near the park, one with nine holes, and the other offering 18 holes.

In Canton, tour the Professional Hall of Fame. It's beside I-77, off Exit 24, Blake Avenue. For information, call 216-456-8207.

The McKinley National Memorial is next to Monument Park at 7th Street NW, where the 25th President and his family are entombed.

INFORMATION
Guilford Lake State Park
6835 East Lake Road
Lisbon, Ohio 44432
216-222-1712

HARRISON LAKE STATE PARK
21

LOCATION - The park is four miles south of Fayette off Ohio 66.

ACTIVITIES - Camp in the campground with 176 sites, 126 with electrical hookups. The park has three campgrounds, with the larger one on the lake's north side that includes three rent-a-tent sites.

Hikers can hike around the lake, and bicyclists can cycle 3.5 miles on paved roads in the park plus an additional 2.75 miles on nearby county roads.

Swimmers have a beach, while anglers can fish for bass, crappie, bluegill and pike. Boaters can take out rowboats, canoes, sailboats and boats with electric motors.

The nature center is on the north side of the lake, and features weekend hikes and Saturday night slide shows.

The Sauder Museum, Farm and Craft Village is east of the intersection of Ohio 66 and 2 near Archbold, and includes an 1860s home and barnyard, a museum with antique tools, and a restaurant located in the restored barn. The village is open seven days a week from mid-April through the end of October. For information, call 419-446-2541.

Goll Woods Nature Preserve, three miles northwest of Archbold, is one of the best remaining examples of the Black Swamp forest.

INFORMATION
Harrison Lake State Park
Route 1
Fayette, Ohio 43521
419-237-2593

HEADLANDS BEACH STATE PARK
22

LOCATION - The park is two miles north of Painesville at the end of Ohio 44 along Lake Erie.

ACTIVITIES - Go swimming in the lake, or walking its mile-long natural beach. Concessions are available.

The park has three miles of hiking trails. Adjoining these trails is a five-mile trail passing through Mentor Marsh Nature Preserve. The preserve has three trails that give you a close-up view of the preserve's many inhabitants. If you visit during the spring, you'll be treated to many wildflowers and migrating birds; however, around the end of May, the mosquitoes hatch, and visitors should be prepared with plenty of insect repellent, long-sleeved shirts, long pants, and a hat.

Fall visitors who arrive after the first frost will find most of the mosquitoes gone, and a riot of fall color in the marsh's wooded uplands.

INFORMATION
Headlands Beach State Park
9601 Headlands Road
Mentor, Ohio 44060
216-257-1330

HOCKING HILLS STATE PARK
LAKE LOGAN STATE PARK
23

LOCATION - Lake Logan is 48 miles southeast of Columbus, 18 miles southeast of Lancaster, and west of Logan off U.S. 33 between Ohio 180 and 664S. Hocking Hills State Park and Forest are reached via Ohio 664 and U.S. 33 out of Logan.

ACTIVITIES - LAKE LOGAN STATE PARK has ten miles of shoreline and has good fishing for bass, bluegill, crappie, pike and catfish. Swim from the beach, guarded Memorial Day–Labor Day, with a concession stand. Sailboats and powerboats, with a maximum of ten horsepower, are permitted. Rental boats are available. During the winter, come to ice skate, ice fish and sled.

A section of the Buckeye Trail passes through the northwest end of the park, or you can hike the one-mile-long Pine Vista trail to circle the hilltop.

Each July, the Ohio Department of Natural Resources sponsors the "Foothills Footstomp" near the spillway off State Route 664S. The free festival offers bluegrass music, and arts and crafts displays.

HOCKING HILLS STATE PARK's lake is only accessible via hiking trail, and is well stocked with catfish, trout and bass. The park has 170 campsites with 129 offering electrical hookups.

Equestrians have access to over 40 miles of bridle trails through Hocking State Forest. In addition, the Buckeye Trail plus other bridle trails connect the Hocking area with Tar Hollow State Park's bridle trail, making the area an equestrian's mecca. For information, call 614-592-6644.

If you come in the spring, pick up a waterfall and wildflower tour map at the park's information center and drive around to see many waterfalls.

Hocking Hill State Forest has a specially designated rock climbing and rappelling area. The area is located on Big Pine Road east of Conkle's Hollow. Conkle's Hollow is on Ohio 374, north of South Bloomingville, and its deep gorge—considered to be the state's deepest—ends at a small cave with cascading waterfalls. Hike Rim Trail that circles the gorge in a 2.5-mile-long hike.

Cedar Falls is two miles north of Ash Cave on Ohio 374, and is located at the head of a gorge. You can hike a three-mile-long trail from here to reach Old Man's Cave. You can stay at the lodge or in one of the cabins at Old Man's Cave. The park has a visitors' center, and naturalists provide year-round programs. The cave has the most spectacular view of the park's gorges and two waterfalls. Upper Falls can be seen from a scenic footbridge that spans it. Lower Falls requires a hike through the gorge.

Ash Cave is east of South Bloomingville on Ohio 56. The park's highest waterfall is here, dropping 90 feet. In the winter, a huge ice stalagmite forms.

Cantwell Cliffs is southwest of Rockbridge on Ohio 374, and is a 150-foot-high, horseshoe-shaped precipice sheltering a rock recess. A narrow passageway goes between two sandstone blocks, aptly called "Fat Woman's Squeeze." Trails climb to the top of the cliff to go along the rim to the gorge.

Take a ride aboard the Hocking Valley Scenic Railway. Go to Nelsonville where the 1916 locomotive offers trips on Saturdays and Sundays from Memorial Day through the end of October. You stop at Robbins Crossing where you engage in a living history interpretation of life in the valley during the mid-1850s. For information, call 513-335-0382 or 614-753-9531.

Drive over to Chillicothe to watch "Tecumseh," an outdoor drama. Performances run Monday–Saturday from mid-June through Labor Day. For information, call 614-775-0700.

Rockbridge State Nature Preserve, located off U.S. 33 near Rockbridge between Ohio 374 and 180, has the state's largest natural rock bridge. To reach the bridge, park in the preserve lot on Dalton Road, and hike or canoe in via the Hocking River. Interpretive programs are held at the preserve. For information, call 614-653-2541.

INFORMATION

Hocking Hills State Park	Lake Logan State Park
20160 State Route 664S	30043 Lake Logan Road
Logan, Ohio 43138	Logan, Ohio 43138
614-385-6841	614-385-3444
	614-385-6721 (boat rentals)

HUESTON WOODS STATE PARK
24

LOCATION - The park is five miles north of Oxford off Ohio 732.

FEATURES - The beech-maple forest is a National Natural Landmark.

ACTIVITIES - Camp in the campground with 507 sites, 255 with electrical hookups. You can also stay in the lodge's guest rooms, eat in the dining room, or stay in one of the 25 cabins.

The nature center is open year-round. Check the naturalists' schedule to see about a "canoe adventure" on Acton Lake. The park is known for its program specializing in rehabilitating birds of prey.

Hike along ten miles of trails, or horseback ride for six miles. The park has two swimming pools and a concession stand.

Golfers have access to an 18-hole course. Visitors can also go boating, sailing, and fishing for bass, crappie, bluegill, walleye and catfish on Acton Lake. Boat rentals are available at the marina.

Tour the Pioneer Museum furnished as a farmhouse of the mid-1800s. It's open Memorial Day to Labor Day on weekends from 12–4.

The Hueston Woods State Nature Preserve is located on the lake's west shore, and preserves a virgin stand of beech and sugar maple trees. Tours of the sugar house and sugar bush are offered in the spring during maple syrup weekends.

Fairhaven is known as one Ohio's best villages for antique finds. Its 12 shops are open weekends.

In nearby Oxford, tour the McGuffey House and Museum to see personal articles of William McGuffey, author of the McGuffey Readers.

Incoming pilots can land at Cincinnati-Blueash Airport located six miles northeast of town, or at one of the others near Dayton. Rental cars are available.

INFORMATION

Hueston Woods State Park
Route 1
College Corner, Ohio 45003
513-523-6347

Hueston Woods Lodge
513-523-6381
Lodge and cabin reservations:
1-800-282-7275 or 614-439-4406

INDEPENDENCE DAM STATE PARK
25

LOCATION - The park is four miles east of Defiance on Ohio 424 along the Maumee River. It's between the historic Miami and Erie Canal and the Maumee River.

ACTIVITIES - Camp in the campground with 40 campsites without electricity. The marina has a four-lane launch ramp, and is located on the north bank of the river west of the dam. Motors of unlimited horsepower are allowed. Water-skiers ski along four miles of the Maumee River.

The three-mile hiking trail goes between the old canal and river. It begins at the east end of the campground. The trail originally served as the towpath for the Miami and Erie Canal.

Enjoy fishing in the Maumee River for pike, bass, crappie and catfish. Bicyclists can cycle along the three-mile main access road.

In Defiance, stop by the site of General Anthony Wayne's Fort Defiance marked by plaques and stones in the city park. You can still see some old earthworks. Johnny Appleseed's nursery, circa 1811–26, is located here.

Auglaize Village, a re-created Ohio settlement, is open for tours on a seasonal basis. It's located two miles west of Defiance on U.S. 24. It's open Saturday and Sunday from 10–5 from Memorial Day through early October. For information, call 419-784-0107.

INFORMATION

Independence Dam State Park
Route 4, State Route 424, Box 27722
Defiance, Ohio 43512
419-784-3263

Good fishing abounds in the state parks of the Midwest,
but it does take patience, as this photo suggests!

DIVISION OF TOURISM

JACKSON LAKE STATE PARK
26

LOCATION - The park is two miles west of Oak Hill on Ohio 279.

FEATURES - Iron ore was mined here, some used to build the ironclad warship, the Monitor. The Jefferson Iron Furnace made its last cast in 1916.

ACTIVITIES - Go camping in the campground with 36 sites without hookups, and located near the swimming beach. Fish in Jackson Lake for bass, muskie, bluegill and pike. Go bird watching in the marshy areas near the northern end of the lake. Tour the reconstructed Jefferson Iron Furnace.

Three miles north of the park on Ohio 28 and northwest of Coalton is the Leo Petroglyph State Memorial. It has 40 figures cut into the sandstone by prehistoric Indians, and is open daylight hours.

The Buckeye Iron Furnace State Memorial is located 10 miles southeast of Jackson, and has reconstructed buildings typical of those used during the 19th century.

For family fun "down on the farm," go to the Bob Evans Farms on U.S. 25, .5-mile east of Rio Grande. You'll see a museum of antique farm implements, hiking trails, horseback riding, canoeing, and farm animal displays. Special events are sponsored throughout the year. The farm is open May–October from 10–5. For information, call 614-245-5305.

INFORMATION
Jackson Lake State Park
P. O. Box 174
Oak Hill, Ohio 45656
614-682-6197

JEFFERSON LAKE STATE PARK
27

LOCATION - The park is sixteen miles northwest of Steubenville off Ohio 43, and 2.5 miles northwest of Richmond. The park office and campground check-in station are at the north end of the park off County 54.

ACTIVITIES - Camp in the campground with 100 campsites without hookups. Non-motorized boats, and boats with electric motors with less than four horsepower are permitted on Jefferson Lake.

A public beach is located off the main access road. The lake is regularly stocked with bass, catfish, bluegill and sunfish.

Almost 15 miles of scenic, and often rugged trails go through the park.

In nearby Carrollton, visit the McCook House State Memorial located in the town square. The house, built in 1837, was home for the "Fighting McCooks," a family who contributed 13 men to the Union Army during the Civil War. The house is open June through September from 10–5. For information, call 216-627-3345.

The birthplace of General George Armstrong Custer is in New Rumley.

The Scio Pottery and Museum on Ohio 151 and 646 is one of the world's largest manufacturers of dinnerware. Tours are available.

Incoming pilots can land at Jefferson County Airpark located five miles west of Steubenville. Rental cars are available.

INFORMATION
Jefferson Lake State Park
Route 1
Richmond, Ohio 43944
614-765-4459

JOHN BRYAN STATE PARK
CLIFTON GORGE STATE NATURE PRESERVE

28

LOCATION - The park is two miles southeast of Yellow Springs on Ohio 370.

ACTIVITIES - Camp in the campground with 100 sites without electrical hookups. Go canoeing on the Little Miami River. The park has ten miles of hiking trails, and springtime is one of the best times to visit here. The Old Mill Bikeway and Buckeye Trail wind through the park.

During the winter, come to go cross-country skiing or sledding.

Visit the Clifton Gorge State Preserve to hike some gorge trails. The North Gorge Trail provides a view of the Amphitheater Falls and a glimpse of Steamboat Rock. The Narrows Trail takes you along the rim of the narrowest section of the gorge with four overlooks and two waterfalls. Use caution when following the trails along the gorge.

Aviation buffs can visit the Wright Brothers' Bicycle Shop at 22 S. Williams in Dayton. Listed on the National Register, here Wilbur and Orville Wright began the work that led to their first flight. The shop is open Wednesday–Saturday.

Visit the U.S. Air Force Museum, 4.75 miles northeast of Dayton at the Old Wright Field on Springfield Pike. You can see many exhibits starting with the flight at Kitty Hawk continuing through the Apollo-series space capsules. It's the oldest and largest military aviation museum in the world, with approximately 200 aircraft and missiles. Documentary films are shown in the museum theater on Saturday, Sunday and holidays. For information, call 513-255-3284.

Visit the historic Clifton Mill, established in 1802, and located at 75 Water Street in Clifton. It's the largest operating grist mill in the country, and has an 18-foot water wheel. You can also see 1,300 Santa Clauses, the country's largest collection. For information, call 513-767-5501.

In Xenia, attend a performance of "Blue Jacket," the story of a white man adopted by the Shawnee, who then became the War Chief for the Shawnee Nation 200 years ago. Backstage tours are offered at 4–5 except Mondays, and dinner is served before the show. For information, call 513-376-4318, or in Dayton: 513-427-0879.

INFORMATION
John Bryan State Park
Clifton Gorge State Nature Preserve
3790 State Route 370
Yellow Springs, Ohio 45387
513-767-1274

KELLEYS ISLAND
29

See under LAKE ERIE STATE PARKS

LAKE ERIE STATE PARKS
EAST HARBOR
CATAWBA ISLAND
SOUTH BASS ISLAND
KELLEYS ISLAND
CRANE CREEK
30

LOCATION - East Harbor is eight miles northeast of Port Clinton on the Marblehead Peninsula off Ohio 163. Catawba Peninsula State Park is in Catawba off Ohio 53. South Bass Island is three miles from the mainland. Kelleys Island is located in the western basin of Lake Erie about four miles north of Marblehead. Crane Creek State Park is west of Port Clinton off Ohio 2.

FEATURES - Perry's Victory and International Peace Memorial on Catawba Island is a tribute to Perry who defeated the British, captured the entire British fleet, and took control of Lake Erie and most of the old Northwest. His victory helped persuade the British to cease their hostilities, enabling the U.S. to claim the Northwest at peace talks in Ghent a year later. Put-in-Bay and the Lake Erie islands are considered part of the "Walleye Fishing Capital" of the world.

ACTIVITIES - EAST HARBOR STATE PARK has 570 campsites. The park has seven miles of hiking trails, and a launching ramp near the campground. Food service is available. Go swimming from the sandy beaches, and fishing for bass, bluegill, crappie and carp. Participate in their summer programs and winter recreational sports.

Bird watchers can hike Middle Harbor Trail that skirts the Middle Harbor Game Sanctuary, and includes a stop at a bird observation blind. Check the naturalists' schedule for their "swamp stomp."

CATAWBA ISLAND has a fishing pier, launch ramp and picnicking. Golfers have an 18-hole course at Catawba Willows. For tee-off times and information, call 614-734-2524.

Take the ferry to South Bass Island, three miles away, from Catawba Point, or from Port Clinton, 10 miles away. It operates from April through November. You'll travel more easily if you leave your car at Miller Ferry, and rent a bicycle, golf cart, or take the tour train on the island. The tour train leaves the downtown depot every half hour. For information, call 419-285-4855.

Perry's Monument is open daily from early May until late October, and closed the rest of the year. Its observation platform is 371 feet above the lake, and is reached by elevator. It has a campground, launch ramp, and cabins. The monument offers narrated summer tours.

Tour Crystal Cave and Perry's Cave, and fish for perch, walleye, bass and catfish. Walleye catches are larger in May and June, particularly off Buckeye Reef near the island.

SOUTH BASS ISLAND STATE PARK has 135 campsites without hookups, and a swimming beach. Visitors can also rent a cabent, a combination of a tent and a cabin, but rentals are by the week only. Incoming pilots can land on the island's airport, one mile southwest of town. Taxi and bus service are available.

KELLEYS ISLAND: Spring is a beautiful time to arrive, both because of the flowers, and because of the good fishing. Visitors can see some 25,000-year-old glacial grooves located in Glacial Grooves State Memorial on the northern shore.

Go camping in the 129-site campground, and bicycling around the island. Enjoy boating and swimming from the beach. Runners can participate in a five- or ten-kilometer race in June. Stop by Inscription Rock State Memorial to see some pre-historic Indian pictographs.

Access to Kelleys Island is via private boat, ferry from Marblehead, or by air from the mainland. Private aircraft can land on the island's airport located two miles north of town. Taxis are available.

CRANE CREEK adjoins the Magee Marsh Wildlife Area and the Ottawa National Wildlife Refuge, and has a boardwalk through the marsh. The

Sportsman's Migratory Bird Center has displays and lectures. You can also walk the beach, and fish for bluegill, crappie, perch and bass. Go swimming, have a picnic, or go boating. Tour the historic Marblehead Lighthouse, the oldest operating lighthouse on the Great Lakes, and open for tours on selected summer weekends.

In Marblehead, attend one of the programs offered at the Chautauqua including concerts, theater, ballet and speakers.

Incoming pilots can land at Carl R. Keller Field located three miles of Port Clinton. A courtesy car and taxis are available.

INFORMATION

Lake Erie Islands
4049 E. Moores Dock Road
Port Clinton, Ohio 43452
419-797-4530 (reservations)

Catawba Island State Park
4049 E. Moores Dock Road
Port Clinton, Ohio 43452
419-797-4530

Crane Creek State Park
13431 West State Route 2
Oak Harbor, Ohio 43449
419-898-2495

Kelley's Island State Park
Kelley's Island, Ohio 43438
419-746-2546

South Bass Island State Park
South Bass Island, Ohio 43456
419-285-2112

East Harbor State Park
1169 N. Buck Road
Lakeside-Marblehead, Ohio 43440
419-734-4424 (park)
419-734-5857 (camp office)

LAKE HOPE STATE PARK
31

LOCATION - The park is twelve miles northeast of McArthur on Ohio 278.

FEATURES - The Hope Furnace built here over 100 years ago processed iron ore extracted from the region's sandstone bedrock. Today, the lake covers the town, and all you can see are the skeletal remains of the furnace.

Rainwater percolating into the old mine shafts carries dissolved minerals, causing the lake's blue-green color.

ACTIVITIES - Two great times to visit are in spring when the wildflowers are blooming, and in fall when the trees take on their autumn foliage.

Camp in the campground with 223 sites without hookups. You can also stay in five rent-a-camps, in one of the 25 deluxe cabins, 23 sleeping cabins, or 21 standard cabins. Equestrians have 16 campsites.

Go swimming from the beach with its concession stand, and where canoes and rowboats can be rented. Hikers have 15 miles of trails to explore, 21 miles for backpacking, and equestrians have six miles of trails. Attend summer naturalists' programs, go boating from the ramp, and fishing in the lake. The park is surrounded by state forest lands adding more hiking, swimming, boating, fishing and camping opportunities. During the winter, come cross-country skiing, and stay overnight in one of the cabins.

In nearby Nelsonville, take a ride aboard the old-time passenger train over a restored 1840 canal lock, and through the small town of Haydenville listed on the National Register of Historic Places. For information, call 513-335-0382 (weekdays) and 614-753-9531 (weekends).

INFORMATION
Lake Hope State Park
P. O. Box 279
Zaleski, Ohio 45698-0279
614-596-5253
1-800-221-1122 (Horse and livery)

LAKE LOGAN STATE PARK
32
See under HOCKING HILLS STATE PARK

LAKE LORAMIE STATE PARK
33
See under GRAND LAKE ST. MARYS STATE PARK

MARY JANE THURSTON STATE PARK
34

LOCATION - The park is 20 miles southwest of Toledo off U.S. 24, 35 miles east of Defiance off Ohio 65, and 18 miles west of Bowling Green off Ohio 65. It's located on a 53-mile stretch of the Maumee River.

ACTIVITIES - Go boating on 20 miles of open water on the Maumee River. Two double boat launch ramps, boat docks and gas are available.

The Maumee has good fishing for pike, walleye, bass, catfish and crappie. Hike along the trail that follows the old canal from the river to the nearby village of Grand Rapids. During winter, go ice skating or ice fishing on the river.

Nearby is Independence Dam State Park on the west bank of the river, off Ohio 24. The park has camping, fishing and boating. Maumee State Forest is six miles north of the park on Ohio 295 near Whitehouse, and has 15 miles of hiking and equestrian trails. An area has been designated for all-purpose vehicles.

Fort Meigs is located near Perrysburg on U.S. 25 and Ohio 65.

Incoming pilots can land at Toledo Express Airport located 10 miles west of Toledo. Rental cars are available.

INFORMATION
Mary Jane Thurston State Park
Box 352
Grand Rapids, Ohio 43522
419-832-7662

MAUMEE BAY STATE PARK
35

LOCATION - Maumee Bay is located off Lake Erie, eight miles east of Toledo, and then three more miles north off Ohio 2.

ACTIVITIES - Go swimming, fishing in the bay, hiking along ten miles of trails, and riding along eight miles of trails. Overnight in one of the cabins, in the lodge, in the campground, or in a rent-a-camp facility.

Go boating in the lake where no motors are permitted, or canoeing in the canoeing lake. Play golf on the golf course. Obtain a permit to explore the Cedar Point National Wildlife Refuge.

Incoming pilots can land at Toledo Express Airport located ten miles west of Toledo. Rental cars are available.

INFORMATION
Maumee Bay State Park
6505 Cedar Point Road
Oregon, Ohio 43618
419-836-7758
419-836-1466 or 1-800-282-7275 (Lodge reservations)

MOSQUITO LAKE STATE PARK
36

LOCATION - The lake is ten miles north of Warren off Ohio 305.

ACTIVITIES - Mosquito Lake is one of Ohio's largest, and is attractive to boaters. Four launch ramps provide access to the lake, and much of the lake permits unlimited horsepower. However, the area north of the causeway is a no-wake zone. Boat rentals are available.

Anglers enjoy fishing for walleye, bass, pike and crappie. Swim from the 600-foot beach.

Camp in the campground with 234 campsites, some providing lake shore scenery. Hike from the campground to watch the active beaver colony.

The lake's marshes are a good place to visit during the spring and fall bird migrations. Tours may be arranged at the area office for the Mosquito Creek Wildlife area at the north end of the lake. The Grand River Wildlife Area west of the park on Ohio 88 has ponds and marshes, and is open to the public.

During the winter, come to snowmobile, sled, ice skate, ice fish, or go cross-country skiing.

INFORMATION
Mosquito Lake State Park
1439 State Route 305
Cortland, Ohio 44410
216-638-5700

MOUNT GILEAD STATE PARK
37

LOCATION - The entrance is located off Ohio 95, one mile east of Mount Gilead, and six miles west of I-71.

ACTIVITIES - Camp in the 60-unit campground or in the rent-a-camps.

Fishing in the Mount Gilead Lake is fair to good for bass, bluegill and other panfish.

The lake is divided into two tiers, where visitors can go canoeing, rowing, or boating with electric motors. Launching ramps are provided.

Three miles of trails pass through the park. Sam's Creek's self-guiding nature trail begins near the east end of the campground. Golfers can play on the golf course directly across from the park.

INFORMATION
Mt. Gilead State Park
Route 3
Mt. Gilead, Ohio 43338
419-946-1961

MUSKINGUM RIVER PARKWAY
38

LOCATION - The Muskingum River parallels Ohio 60 for most of the distance between Dresden and Marietta. Ten locks are located along its route. The park office is at Lock 10 in Zanesville, and is accessible by boat or on foot from the Canal Bridge off 6th Street.

FEATURES - The Muskingum River is the largest river lying entirely within Ohio. Boats are able to navigate the full length of the river, and continue onto the Ohio and Mississippi rivers, passing through the locks that are still manually operated.

ACTIVITIES - Go boating with unlimited horsepower. Public launch ramps are available at Locks 4, 5, 6, and 11. The river is navigable from Dresden to Marietta. The river channel from Dresden to Ellis is unmarked and difficult to follow. Pick up navigation charts at the parkway office. The Licking River, which joins the Muskingum River in Zanesville, is only navigable by canoe and row-boat. Boating on the parkway involves going through one of the locks.

One Class B campground is located at Lock 11, and there are 20 campsites off Ohio 60 and C.R. 49.

Go fishing in the river for muskellunge and catfish. Bass are found in several of the river tributaries.

In Marietta, where the Muskingum enters the Ohio River, you can ride aboard the W. P. Snyder, Jr., one of the last sternwheeler steamboats on inland waterways. Trips are provided from April 1–October 31.

Visit the National Road/Zane Grey Museum in Norwich, ten miles east of Zanesville, to learn about the development of our first "highway." Zane Grey wrote over 100 books, with westerns being his most famous. The museum has a collection of his manuscripts and first editions. For information, call 614-872-3143.

In Zanesville, you can also take a one-hour cruise aboard the Lorena Sternwheeler, Wednesday through Monday at 2:00 and 4:00 p.m. from May through October. For information, call 614-454-6851.

In Dresden, referred to as "Hometown, U.S.A.," you can shop in 19th-century shops, ride in Roaring Twenties railroad cars, and see the world's largest basket. It measures 48 feet in length, was made from maple trees, and is located on the corner of Fifth and Main.

Incoming pilots can land at Zanesville Municipal located six miles east of town. Rental cars are available.

INFORMATION
Muskingum River Parkway
P. O. Box 2806
Zanesville, Ohio 43701
614-452-3820

PAINT CREEK STATE PARK
39

LOCATION - The park is seventeen miles east of Hillsboro on U.S. 50.

FEATURES - Paint Creek is the longest creek in the U.S., and the lake has 25 miles of shoreline.

Rocky Fork Creek, located near the park, cut a 75-foot gorge through the rock, and pre-glacial tributary valleys were left 50 feet above the creekbed.

ACTIVITIES - Hike along one of the four trails ranging in length from .75-mile to 2.5 miles. Eight miles of trails lace the park, along with 25 miles of bridle trails. Pick up maps and begin riding from the staging area near the Pioneer Farm.

Enjoy fishing in the reservoir for bluegill, bass, catfish and crappie. The park has a beach and a marina with boat rentals. Three launch ramps provide access to the water, where boating limits are unlimited.

Camp in the campground with 199 sites, all with electrical hookups. Stay in one of the three rent-a-camp sites.

Stop by the Pioneer Farm located on the beach entrance road. The buildings were reassembled from original buildings, and represent a farm built here around 1810.

Fort Hill State Memorial, a prehistoric Indian hilltop earthworks, is located south of the park, and is open April–October.

Visit Seip Mound State Memorial, three miles east of Bainbridge, to see the 250-foot-long ceremonial mound built by the Hopewell Indians.

Seven Caves are four miles west of Bainbridge on U.S. 50, and then another mile south. Take the short hike up to the caves, located 50 feet above the creek. The area, complete with waterfalls, cliffs and canyons, is especially beautiful when the spring wildflowers are in bloom. Concessions are available. For information, call 513-365-1283.

Take a drive on one of the four Paint Valley Skyline drives that originate from Bainbridge. These are particularly spectacular during the fall, and range in length from 19 to 50 miles.

INFORMATION
Paint Creek State Park
14265 U.S. Route 50
Bainbridge, Ohio 45612
513-365-1401
513-981-7061: camp office
513-365-1485 or 513-981-2186: marinas

PIKE LAKE STATE PARK
40

LOCATION - The park is six miles southeast of Bainbridge.

FEATURES - Pike County's area has many earthworks constructed by Ohio's prehistoric people.

ACTIVITIES - The campground is located within the Pike State Forest and has 101 campsites with electrical hookups. You can also stay in one of the 12 deluxe cabins open year-round, or in one of the 13 standard cabins available from April 1–October 31.

Hikers have access to six miles of trails in the park, and the forest has additional trails established for equestrians, hikers and all-purpose vehicles.

Go swimming in the lake from the beach with concessions. Stop by the nature center and get a schedule of their summer programs and activities. Go boating on the lake where boat rentals are available.

In nearby Bainbridge, you can take a series of four scenic tours along the Paint Valley Skyline. One of these tours passes through the state park. Bainbridge is also site of the Annual Fall Festival of Leaves.

Three miles east of Bainbridge on U.S. 50 is Seip Mound State Memorial with an open exhibit pavilion detailing the history of the mound and the Hopewell Indians.

Fort Hill State Memorial is southwest of Bainbridge on Ohio 41, and is another example of the massive earthworks constructed by the Hopewell Indians. The memorial also has 16 miles of nature trails to explore, plus a museum containing Indian artifacts.

INFORMATION
Pike Lake State Park
1847 Pike Lake Road
Bainbridge, Ohio 45612
614-493-2212

PORTAGE LAKES STATE PARK
41

LOCATION - Portage Lakes State Park is in Akron on Ohio 93.

FEATURES - The park is located between two major lobes of the Wisconsin glacier, and has many glacial reminders. Portage Lakes was once used as a portage trail between the Cuyahoga and Tuscarawas rivers.

ACTIVITIES - The park has 13 lakes offering a variety of boating opportunities. Some have 400 horsepower limits, and others are quiet lakes for sailing or boats with electric power. Go swimming from Turkeyfoot Beach.

Anglers come here year-round to fish for bass, walleye, catfish and carp. Family camping is available in the 104-spot campground near Nimisila Reservoir, or camp in one of the 30 other walk-in campsites.

The Astronomy Club of Akron operates a small observatory in the park, and offers special seasonal programs.

In Akron, tour Stan Hywet Hall and Gardens, a Tudor showplace located at 714 N. Portage Path. Take a 50-minute guided tour. For information, call 216-836-5535.

Go to Quaker Square, 120 E. Mill St., where the restored Quaker Oats Company buildings have been turned into restaurants and boutiques, and where you can see artifacts from the railroad era.

To go hiking, bicycling, picnicking or canoeing, go to nearby Quail Hollow State Park and Cuyahoga Valley National Recreation Area.

Incoming pilots can land at Akron-Canton Regional Airport located four miles northwest of town. Rental cars are available.

INFORMATION
Portage Lakes State Park
5031 Manchester Road
Akron, Ohio 44319
216-644-2220

PUNDERSON STATE PARK
42

LOCATION - The park is two miles northeast of Newbury off Ohio 87.

ACTIVITIES - Hike along 14 miles of hiking trails. Attend summer nature programs. Check to see if the naturalists still offer an auto tour on Sundays to nearby Nelson-Kennedy Ledges State Park to hike to Gold Hunter's Cave, Dwarf's Pass, Devil's Den and the Ice Box.

Visitors have access to Punderson Lake plus two smaller lakes. Go swimming from the beach, canoeing and boating from the ramp, and fishing for bluegill, bass, trout and catfish. Boat rentals are available.

The campground has 201 sites, all with electrical hookups, and is located on the site of a former Indian village. You can also stay in the Manor House resort, and play golf on the championship 18-hole course, go scuba diving, or stay in one of the 26 cabins.

The park is open year-round, and since the park is in the heart of Ohio's "snow belt," during the winter you can go cross-country skiing, downhill skiing nearby, snowmobiling, tobogganing, and ice skating. Cross-country ski rentals are available. Annual winter events include the Punderson Cup cross-country ski races in February, and the Buckeye Classic Sled Dog Race each January.

The Cuyahoga River, from Burton to Route 303, offers 25 miles of easy canoeing water. To schedule canoeing trips, contact the Camp Hi Canoe Livery, Inc. in Hiram at 216-569-7621.

In Burton, tour the Century Village, a reconstruction of an 1800s village. Village tours are offered at 1:00 and 3:00 p.m. For information, call 216-834-4012. Bicyclists can travel along the Amish Bikeway down the winding county roads.

INFORMATION

Punderson State Park
Box 338, 11755 Kinsman Road
Newbury, Ohio 44065
216-564-2279

Punderson Manor House:
1-800-282-7275 or
216-564-9144
Cabin reservations: 614-439-4406

PYMATUNING STATE PARK
43

LOCATION - The park is six miles southeast of Andover off U.S. 85, on the western shore of Pymatuning Reservoir.

FEATURES - Pymatuning is taken from an Indian term meaning "the crooked-mouthed man's dwelling place."

The Pymatuning Spillway is famous as the place where "the ducks walk on the fish." Each year, so many visitors feed the ducks and carp that the ducks actually stand on top of the carp to catch their treat.

ACTIVITIES - The campground has 373 sites, with 352 providing electrical hookups. A 10-site primitive camping area is located north of the Ohio 85 causeway. You can also stay in deluxe housekeeping cabins available year-round, or in one of the 35 housekeeping cabins available from April 1–November 1.

Go hiking along three miles of trails, swim from the beach south of the causeway or near the cabin area. Snacks are available. Summer nature programs are presented. Check the schedule for the evening beaver dam stroll.

Boaters are allowed a maximum of ten horsepower, and have access to five launch ramps. Anglers will find good fishing for walleye, crappie, bass, bluegill and catfish.

Because the park is located in the "snow belt," winter sports including skating, snowmobiling, ice boating, ice fishing, cross-country skiing, and winter camping are popular.

The world's largest inland fish hatchery is near Linesville. The visitors' center is open 8–4 year-round. It also features a two-story aquarium.

INFORMATION

Pymatuning State Park
Route 1
Andover, Ohio 44003
216-293-6030
Cabins: 216-293-6329

QUAIL HOLLOW STATE PARK
44

LOCATION - The park is two miles north of Hartville on the Congress Lake Road.

ACTIVITIES - The park is open for day-use, and has over ten miles of trails enjoyed by hikers, joggers, and cross-country skiers. Bridle trails are also available for riders with their own horses.

A visitor center is located within the former Stewart family home, and is open weekends 1–4 p.m. During the summer, the meadow trails south and east of the center are recommended for hikers without insect repellent.

Fish in Congress Lake Outlet along the Beaver Lodge Hiking Trail.

The Quail Hollow Herbal Society offers guided tours of the herbal garden in the park the last Sunday of each month at 2 p.m. from May through September.

INFORMATION
Quail Hollow State Park
13340 Congress Lake Ave.
Hartville, Ohio 44632
216-877-6652

ROCKY FORK STATE PARK
45

LOCATION - The park is six miles southeast of Hillsboro off Ohio 124.

FEATURES - During the 1800s and early 1900s, six different mill sites were established along Rocky Fork's banks. Today only the foundations of these remain.

ACTIVITIES - The campground has 220 campsites, with 70 campsites having electrical hookups. The lake offers fishing for walleye, bass, and crappie, water-skiing, swimming and boating with unlimited horsepower. Two marinas have rentals and food. Swimmers have two beaches, and both are close to refreshments. A restaurant is located in the park.

Annual events include a fishing safari in May, a fishing tournament and the Rocky Fork Antique Tractor show in June, a campground hobo supper in August, and hydroplane races in September.

Two state historical sites are nearby. Fort Hill is south of Bainbridge off Ohio 41, and has a complex of Hopewell Indian mounds over 1,000 years old. Serpent Mound is a 1,000-foot snake effigy mound. For information, call 614-466-1500.

INFORMATION
Rocky Fork State Park
9800 N. Shore Drive
Hillsboro, Ohio 45133
513-393-4284

SALT FORK LAKE STATE PARK
46

LOCATION - The park is seven miles northeast of Cambridge on U.S. 22, at Exit 47 from I-77.

FEATURES - Salt Fork Lake is Ohio's largest state park, and is located in the foothills of the Appalachian Mountains.

ACTIVITIES - Go boating on the 3,000-acre lake with no horsepower limits. With 76 miles of sheltered shoreline, you have plenty of sandy beach to walk. Salt Fork has two marinas, rental boats, and excursion boat rides.

Swimmers can swim from Ohio's largest inland beach, and hikers have access to 14 miles of trails. Twenty miles of continuous bridle trails wind through the forest.

Play tennis, or golf on the 18-hole championship golf course. Anglers can fish in the well-stocked lake. Fishing is good in the many bay areas of the lake and on the artificial reef in the lake's north branch.

Stay overnight in the 148-room lodge, in one of the 54 two-bedroom cabins, or camp in the 212-unit campground.

Park naturalists conduct explorations of Hosak's Cave plus other programs.

In the winter, come to sled, snowmobile, ice fish and cross-country ski.

In nearby Cambridge, annual events include the Hopalong Cassidy Spring Festival in May, the Third Annual Gospel Sing in September, the Salt Fork Arts and Crafts Festival in August, and an Oktoberfest in Cambridge.

The Cambridge Performing Arts Center, located at 642 Wheeling Avenue, presents community theater productions September through May on varying weekends. For information, call 614-432-7958. The Living World Outdoor Drama's Passion Play is presented two miles west of Cambridge off Ohio 209 on College Hill Road, Thursday through Saturday, from late June through the end of August. For information, call 614-439-2761.

Visit Roscoe Village in Coshocton to tour an early 1800s Ohio village. In New Philadelphia, attend a performance of the "Trumpet in the Land" outdoor drama. Shows are presented Tuesday–Sunday from mid-June through late August. For information, call 216-339-1132.

The Schoenbrunn Village state memorial is near New Philadelphia, and has been rebuilt and furnished as the original village. For information, call 216-339-3636.

Incoming pilots can land at Cambridge Municipal located four miles south of town. Rental cars are available.

INFORMATION

Salt Fork State Park	Salt Fork State Park Lodge:
P. O. Box 672	614-439-2751 or 1-800-282-7275
Cambridge, Ohio 43725	Salt Fork marina: 614-439-5833
614-439-3521	

SCIOTO TRAIL STATE PARK
47

LOCATION - The park is ten miles south of Chillicothe off U.S. 23.

FEATURES - Scioto Trail State Park lies within the Scioto Trail State Forest, and its two areas are located around Caldwell and Stewart Lakes.

ACTIVITIES - Camp in the campground with 58 campsites, 20 with electrical hookups. Go hiking, bass fishing, and boating in Caldwell Lake. Climb the fire tower that is 60 feet high, and provides a look of the countryside.

In Chillicothe, attend "Tecumseh," an outdoor drama presented in the Sugarloaf Mountain Amphitheater from early June through the end of August from Monday–Saturday. Every hour from 2–5 Monday through Saturday, you can take a behind-the-scenes tour. For information and reservations, call 614-775-0700.

Tour the Adena State Memorial from Memorial Day weekend–Labor Day on Wednesday–Sunday. The 1807 restored mansion was the home of Thomas Worthington, governor and senator from Ohio. For information, call 772-1500.

The Mound City Group National Monument is three miles north of Chillicothe on Ohio 104, and is open year-round. You'll see 23 prehistoric Hopewell Indian burial mounds dating back to 200 B.C. Tour the visitor center and follow the self-guided trails. For information, call 614-774-1125.

Seven Caves, an Ohio Natural Landmark, are four miles west of Bainbridge on U.S. 50, and then one more mile south. The area has four nature trails traversing up and down the sides of cliffs into the canyons and gorges. Food service facilities are available. For information, call 513-365-1283.

The Feast of the Flowering Moon celebration is held Memorial Day weekend, and features Native Americans who have a powwow, Indian encampment, historical re-enactments, and live musical entertainment.

Incoming pilots can land at Ross County's Shoemaker Field located seven miles northwest of Chillicothe. Rental cars are available.

INFORMATION
Scioto Trail State Park
144 Lake Road
Chillicothe, Ohio 45601
614-663-2125

Scioto Trail State Forest
2731 Stoney Creek Road
Chillicothe, Ohio 45601
614-663-2523

SHAWNEE STATE PARK
48

LOCATION - The park is eight miles west of Portsmouth on Ohio 125.

FEATURES - Shawnee's hills have been called "Ohio's Little Smokies," and the state forest and park encompass part of the former hunting grounds of the Shawnee Indians. Shawnee means "those who have silver," and the tribe used the metal for trading.

ACTIVITIES - You can stay overnight in the resort lodge, in one of the 25 deluxe cabins, or in the campground with 107 sites, 104 with electrical hookups. The campground is close to the beach at Roosevelt Lake. Backpackers have access to additional campsites on the nearby Shawnee Backpack Trail.

Golfers have access to an 18-hole course near the main park area. Go boating or canoeing on the Ohio River with access from the park's marina. Rental canoes are available from the concession at Turkey Creek Lake.

Come hiking in the spring when the wildflowers are blooming, and go swimming, fishing, and visit the park's nature center. Year-long nature programs are presented.

Annual events include a trout derby, muzzle-loading rifle shoot, and a fall hike and camp out. During the winter, come to go ice skating, ice fishing, and cross-country skiing.

Nearby attractions include Tremper Mound, Serpent Mound, the Olde Wayside Inn, and an 1810 House. Details on these sites are available at the park office.

Incoming pilots can land at Greater Portsmouth Regional located 11 miles northeast of Portsmouth. Rental cars are available.

INFORMATION
Shawnee State Park
Star Route, Box 68
Portsmouth, Ohio 45662
614-858-6652

Lodge and cabin reservations:
1-800-282-7275 or
614-858-6621
Marina (May–October):
614-858-5061

SOUTH BASS ISLAND
49

See under LAKE ERIE STATE PARKS

STROUDS RUN STATE PARK
50

LOCATION - The park is eight miles northeast of Athens off U.S. 50A on Ohio 20.

ACTIVITIES - Camp in one of the 80 campsites without hookups. Swim from the sandy beach on the east side of the lake. Go scuba diving, or hiking on 13 miles of trails.

Boats may be launched at the north end of the lake off Ohio 20. Motors are limited to ten horsepower. Fish for trout, bass, crappie and catfish. Look for the dams constructed by beavers north of the lake.

INFORMATION

Strouds Run State Park   614-592-2302
11661 State Park Road
Athens, Ohio 45701

TAR HOLLOW STATE PARK
51

LOCATION - The park is ten miles south of Adelphi off Ohio 540.

FEATURES - The area was named for the pine tar taken from the pine trees, and used to make balm, animal liniments and lubricants for the pioneer wagons.

ACTIVITIES - Camp in the campgrounds north of the lake with 96 sites. A primitive campground with 16 sites is on the ridge off Park Road 10. Camp Dulen, a walk-in camp area, is in the state forest south of the fire tower off Park Road 9, Lipscomb Hollow Road.

Go swimming from the public beach located at the north end of Pine Lake. Go boating in canoes, rowboats and boats with electric motors less than four horsepower. Fishing is available for catfish, bass, bluegill and panfish.

Hikers can hike the two-mile Ross Hollow Trail, or on the 21-mile Logan Trail that begins at the Pine Lake dam parking lot. Part of the Buckeye Trail traverses the park.

Equestrians have access to nine miles of bridle trails, and a horsemen's camp is on Poe Run Road. No rental horses are available. During the winter, go sledding, hiking, cross-country skiing, and snow shoeing.

Nearby attractions include Adena, located in Chillicothe, an elegant Georgian mansion with formal gardens. It's open April 15–October 31, Tuesday through Sunday. For information, call 614-772-1500.

Mound City Group National Monument is on the east bank of the Scioto River, three miles north of Chillicothe. This prehistoric Indian complex has 23 burial mounds, and has a museum and visitor center.

INFORMATION
Tar Hollow State Park
16396 Tar Hollow Road
Laurelville, Ohio 43135
614-887-4818

WEST BRANCH STATE PARK
52

LOCATION - The park is located on the west branch of the Mahoning River five miles east of Ravenna off Iowa 5. It's also 19 miles east of Akron and 14 miles north of Alliance. Access is from Ohio 5 north of the lake, and from Ohio 52 south of the lake.

FEATURES - The river was named for the Delaware Indian word *Mahonink*, meaning "at the salt lick." Earlier, a salt works was located southeast of Warren along the river.

ACTIVITIES - The campground has 103 campsites without electricity. Five rent-a-camp sites are available.

The lake has over seven miles of shoreline where you can go boating. A marina is on the south shore where boat rentals and two launching ramps are located. Boats with unlimited horsepower motors are permitted.

Enjoy year-round fishing in the Michael J. Kirwan Lake for bass, walleye, catfish, bluegill and crappie.

The swimming beach is open from Memorial Day to Labor Day and has a refreshment stand and lifeguards on duty.

Over 17 miles of hiking trails lace the park, plus four miles of the state's Buckeye Trail. Equestrians have access to 20 miles of trails, but you need to bring your own horse. A horse camp is open by permit only.

For additional recreational activities, visit nearby Cuyahoga Valley National Recreation Area located along a 22-mile section of the Cuyahoga River between Cleveland and Akron.

During the winter, go sledding, ice skating, ice fishing, snowmobiling, and cross-country skiing. fourteen miles of snowmobiling trails are located on the south side of the lake.

Incoming pilots can land at Akron-Canton Regional Airport located four miles northwest of town. Rental cars are available.

INFORMATION
West Branch State Park
5708 Esworthy Road, Route #5
Ravenna, Ohio 44266-9659
216-296-3239

*The "needles" are bizarre but beautiful rock formations
and granite upthrusts. Needles Highway, part of Custer State Park,
curves and winds through 14 miles of the granite pinnacles.*

PHOTO COURTESY OF THE SOUTH DAKOTA DEPARTMENT OF TOURISM

SOUTH DAKOTA

Many visitors come to South Dakota and head for the Black Hills that rise 3,500 feet above the surrounding terrain. Legend holds that the hills are the site of the burial of "Babe," Paul Bunyan's blue ox. Others are attracted to the state's lakes including Lewis and Clark, Francis Case, Sharpe and Oahe where many water-based activities are available.

South Dakota has 13 state parks and 24 state recreation areas, all open year-round. Camp South Dakota's program was established to encourage visitors to "camp three, get the fourth night free." The offer is available year-round except on Memorial Day and Labor Day weekends, and from mid-June through the end of August.

The Black Hills have 18 peaks rising over 7,000 feet. The Black Hills' Centennial Trail is 111 miles long, and begins at Bear Butte State Park near Sturgis. The trail goes to Mount Rushmore, and continues through the Black Elk Wilderness, heading to Custer State Park. From there it goes to Wind Cave National Park. Although much of the trail was designed for hikers, parts of it are open to mountain bikers and horseback riders. Some segments are open to four-wheelers and ORVs since the Black Hills has over 6,000 miles of logging roads and fire trails.

Each summer the Black Hills hosts 15 volksmarches—organized, non-competitive hikes. For a schedule, contact Volksmarch, Custer State Park, HCR 83, Box 70, Custer, South Dakota 57730.

The Black Hills have many caves to explore. Seventy-two calcite crystal caves are found all over the world, and 68 of them are here. Two "must see" caves include Jewel Cave National Monument and Wind Cave National Park.

Canoers have access to two canoe trails, one on the James River between Mitchell and Olivet, and the other on the Big Sioux River from Sioux Falls to Newton Hills State Park. Campsites are located along each trail. For maps and information, contact Division of Parks and Recreation, Anderson Building, Pierre, South Dakota 57501, or call 605-773-3485. For general state park information, call 605-773-3391.

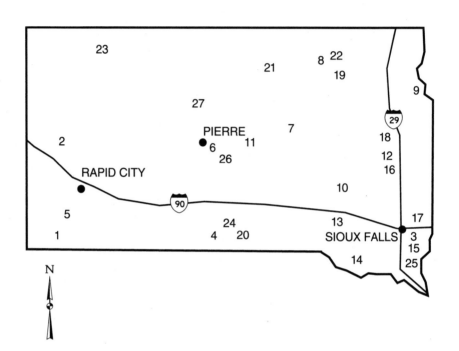

23

21　　8 22
　　　　19

9

27

PIERRE　　7
● 6　11
26

18

12
16

RAPID CITY
●

10

90

5

24　　　13
4　20

17

SIOUX FALLS　3
15

14

25

N

Some of the best fishing in the state is on South Dakota's Great Lakes: Lake Oahe, Lake Sharpe, Lake Francis Case, and Lake Lewis and Clark. Fish for mammoth paddlefish in the tail waters of the Big Bend or Gavins Point Dam.

Trails at Farm Island, Sica Hollow, Newton Hills, Bear Butte and Custer state parks are listed in the National Registry of Recreation Hiking Trails.

South Dakota is in two times zones: Central and Mountain. The Missouri River acts as the dividing line.

ANGOSTURA STATE PARK
1

LOCATION - The park is ten miles southeast of Hot Springs off U.S. 18. The park is located on the 5,000-acre Angostura Reservoir.

FEATURES - Angostura is Spanish for "narrow opening," which describes the narrow, steep-walled canyon of the reservoir.

The Smithsonian Institution has dated Indian artifacts from this area at over 10,000 years old. Unfortunately, the prehistoric village and campsites of these early Indians are covered by the waters of the reservoir.

ACTIVITIES - The campground is open May 1–October 31, and has 180 gravel sites, 50 with electrical hookups, and limited groceries. Lodging is also available in two resorts.

Go walleye, perch, catfish and bass fishing, swimming, and boating from the ramp or two marinas on the Angostura Reservoir where regattas are held during the summer. A canoe access for the Cheyenne River begins at the dam. Hike the hiking trail or walk along miles of sandy beaches.

In Hot Springs, go to the world's largest natural warm water indoor pool, Evan's Plunge. It's open year-round, and is on the north edge of town. For information, call 605-745-5165.

Take an historic walking tour of Hot Springs to see some turn-of-the-century buildings. Pick up maps at the Chamber of Commerce. Attend the Main Street Arts and Crafts Festival the last full weekend in June.

To visit a ghost town located at Cascade, drive nine miles southwest of Hot Springs on South Dakota 71.

Each summer, scientists come to Hot Springs to study the bones of the 26,000-year-old mammoths who died in a sinkhole near here. Guided tours are offered through Mammoth Site from April through October. The site is located 1.5 miles southwest of town on the U.S. 18 bypass. For information, call 605-745-6017 or 1-800-325-6991.

Wind Cave National Park is nine miles north of Hot Springs, and offers four daily guided tours. The cave is the world's eighth longest cave with over 34 miles of boxwork, frostwork and popcorn formations. For information, call

605-745-4600. You're also close to Mt. Rushmore National Monument and Custer State Park.

Incoming pilots can land at Hot Springs Municipal Airport, located five miles southeast of town. Rental cars are available.

INFORMATION
Angostura State Recreation Area
Star Route Box 131 A
Hot Springs, South Dakota 57747
605-745-6996

BEAR BUTTE STATE PARK
2

LOCATION - The park is six miles northeast of Sturgis off South Dakota 79.

FEATURES - The Sioux Indians called Bear Butte "Mato Paha," or "Bear Mountain."

The butte is a volcanic laccolith, an "un-erupted volcano," that rises 1,499 feet above the prairie. The Cheyenne Indians still come here to the "sacred mountain" for religious retreats, and artifacts over 10,000 years old have been found in the area.

Colonel George Custer led an expeditionary force of 1,000 men here, and verified the rumors of gold being found in the Black Hills. Soon three stage and freight routes converged near Bear Butte, followed by a history of holdups and Indian attacks now marked by historical markers.

Bear Butte is the beginning of the 111-mile Centennial Trail that traverses the Black Hills, Custer State Park, and terminates at Wind Cave National Park.

ACTIVITIES - Tour the visitor center open from early May through mid-September to learn the story of the mysterious mountain that still holds great religious significance for the Plains Indians. The park is open year-round. Interpretive programs are offered weekly from May 1 to mid-September. Interpreters conduct guided tours by appointment. The campground at Bear Butte Lake has 15 gravel sites without electrical hookups.

Visitors to Bear Butte Lake can go canoeing, swimming, boating and fishing. Hike to the summit of 4,426-foot Bear Butte, where you gain 1,000 feet in 1.5 miles. Either the Ceremonial Trail or Summit Trail leads to the top for a great view of the surrounding plains.

Old Fort Meade Museum is located one mile east of Sturgis on South Dakota 34. Here you can see an old military post constructed in 1878. The "Star-Spangled Banner" was played here as part of the military retreat ceremony 39 years before it became our national anthem. For information, call 605-347-3924.

Over 50,000 motorcyclists gather in Sturgis in early August for the Black Hills Motorcycle Classic. Attend the Annual Black Hills Balloon Rally on Mother's Day weekend. In August, come for the Steam and Gas Threshing Bee. September brings four-wheelers to the Black Hills for the Sturgis Jeep Jamboree.

Nearby attractions include Deadwood with its Broken Boot Gold Mine open for tours, Boot Hill (Mount Moriah Cemetery), and performances of "Trial of Jack McCall for the Murder of Wild Bill Hickock," given in Old Towne Hall from May 31 to the end of August. For information, call 605-578-3583.

Wonderland Cave is at Nemo, near Deadwood, and offers daily tours.

In nearby Lead, you can tour the Homestake Gold Mine, one of the largest producing gold mines in the Western Hemisphere. For tour information, call 605-584-3110.

Incoming pilots can land at Sturgis Municipal located six miles east of town. Rental cars are available.

INFORMATION
Bear Butte State Park
Box 688
Sturgis, South Dakota 57785
605-347-5240

BIG SIOUX STATE RECREATION AREA
3

LOCATION - The area is one mile west of Brandon.

FEATURES - The recreation area contains one of the best examples of the tallgrass prairie. The Big Sioux River is 390 miles long, and extends from northeastern South Dakota to the Missouri River, and winds over 1.5 miles through the park.

ACTIVITIES - Go fishing in the river, and take a hike along the Valley of the Giants Trail or follow the Big Sioux Loop. Tour the original log cabin built by Ole Bergerson in 1869.

Over half of the park is open to snowmobilers, cross-country skiers and snow-shoers. A warming house is open during the winter.

Only tent and canoe camping is permitted in the area. Canoe launching facilities are also available.

INFORMATION
Big Sioux State Recreation Area
c/o Palisades State Park
Garretson, South Dakota 57030
605-594-3824

BURKE LAKE STATE RECREATION AREA
4

LOCATION - The area is two miles east of Burke.

ACTIVITIES - Bird watchers come here to watch the many species of birds that nest here, or that pass through during their annual migrations.

The shaded campground located near the swimming beach, has 15 paved sites and 15 tent sites. It's open May 1–September 30.

Burke Lake offers swimming, boating from the ramp, sailing, canoeing and fishing for pike, bass, perch, bluegill and bullhead. The lake is surrounded by trees that protect its many coves, and has an average depth of eight feet. Hike the trail that goes around the lake.

For a scenic drive, particularly during fall, follow South Dakota 44 via Lucas.

INFORMATION
Burke Lake State Recreation Area
Box 84A
Herrick, South Dakota 57538
605-775-2968

CUSTER STATE PARK
5

LOCATION - The park is 15 miles east of Custer off U.S. 16A.

FEATURES - Custer State Park is the second largest state park in the U.S., and has one of the world's largest bison herds in the world. The Cathedral Spires rise 6,800 feet, and Mount Coolidge is 6,023 feet, making it the highest point in the central part of the park.

The Needles Highway leaves Legion Lake, and climbs to 6,400 feet, traversing through some needle-sharp, spectacular granite spires. The 14-mile highway was originally considered to be impossible to construct, but the use of tight hairpin curves and tunnels made it feasible. Cathedral Spires is registered as a National Landmark.

ACTIVITIES - Tour the Peter Norbeck Visitor Center and watch their movie on the park. The naturalists offer guided walks, summer theater and trail rides.

The park has four man-made lakes: Center, Legion, Stockade and Sylvan, where visitors can go trout fishing, swimming and boating. Stockade Lake is the only lake that permits all types of boating, and has rental boats.

A replica of the historic Gordon Stockade is near Stockade Lake where a living history program is presented June through August. The Badger Clark Memorial, the cabin of South Dakota's first poet laureate, Charles Badger Clark, is open daily from Memorial Day through Labor Day.

Attend a performance in the Black Hills Playhouse presented six nights a week from mid-June to late August. For information, call 605-255-4141.

Iron Mountain Road, U.S. 16A, passes between Mount Rushmore and Hermosa. Wildlife Loop Road is an 18-mile road that takes you through prime wildlife country. The best time to go is early morning or late afternoon. Watch for pan-handling burros searching for treats along the road. Originally, these burros were used to transport tourists to the top of Harney Peak, and are now wild.

Ten campgrounds have 323 sites, but none with electrical hookups. Dump stations are available in the Game Lodge campground. An equestrian camp is located in the French Creek area for riders bringing their own horses. Reservations are required.

Stay in the State Game Lodge, once used as the summer white house for Presidents Coolidge and Eisenhower. It has guest rooms, jeep rides to see the buffalo herds and wildlife, marked hiking trails, a lighted 4,100-foot sod airstrip, and a dining room. For reservations, call 605-255-4541.

You can also stay in the Blue Bell Lodge on French Creek (605-255-4531), the Legion Lake Resort (605-255-4521), or overnight at the Sylvan Lake Resort (605-574-2561). All lodges have cabins, restaurants, and general stores.

Harney Peak is the highest point between the Rockies and the Alps. To climb the 7,242-foot peak, begin from the Sylvan Lake Trailhead parking lot. It's three miles to the summit. You can also begin from the Little Devils Tower Trailhead, or from the Cathedral Spires Trailhead. The trail climbs 1,000 feet to a fire lookout. Look for some mountain goats roaming around at the summit. The Harney Peak trail system has a network of over 60 miles of marked trails that encircle the peak.

Custer has several other hiking trails including 22 miles of the Black Hills Centennial Trail. Sunday Gulch Trail, a National Trail, is below the Sylvan Lake Dam, and follows the stream for a 3.5-mile loop. Use caution when hiking around buffalo since they can be very dangerous.

Backpackers will enjoy camping in the French Creek Natural Area with its 12-mile-long trail passing through a gorge. Anglers can follow the three-mile Walk-In Fishing Area Trail, between the Center Lake Dam and the Grace Coolidge Campground.

For a great overlook of the Black Hills, visit the observation deck of the Mount Coolidge Lookout on top of the 6,023-foot peak. The turnoff is on South Dakota 87 where a 1.2-mile road winds to the top of the mountain.

Rock climbers come to The Needles to climb pinnacles rising 400-500 feet. If you've never climbed before, guides are available near Sylvan Lake. Contact the Sylvan Rocks Climbing School at 605-574-2425. Other popular climbing spots include Elkhorn Mountain, the surrounding peaks west of Horse Thief Lake, and the outlet rocks below Sylvan Lake.

During the winter, come snowmobiling along the Needles Highway.

Jewel Cave National Monument is 13 miles west of Custer via U.S. 16, and has over 76 miles of explored passageways, ranking it as the second longest in the U.S. and fourth longest in the world. It has several kinds of tours available. Tickets for either the scenic 1.5-hour tour, or the two-hour historic tour may be purchased at the visitor center. Historic tours are offered daily from mid-June through mid-August. Scenic tours run from May through September. Spelunkers can take a four-hour tour, and may reserve tickets up to two months in advance. For information, call 605-673-2288.

Mount Rushmore National Monument is three miles southwest of Keystone via U.S. 16A and South Dakota 244. Called the "Shrine of Democracy," you can see the heads of George Washington, Abraham Lincoln, Thomas Jefferson and Theodore Roosevelt carved into the side of the mountain. Come in the evening from mid-May through mid-September to watch a program that ends with the illumination of the faces from 9:30-10:30 p.m. For information, call 605-574-2523.

Wind Cave National Park is approximately 10 miles north of Hot Springs on U.S. 384. The cave is the world's eighth longest cave with over 34 miles of boxwork, frostwork and popcorn formations. It features 52 miles of known underground passages where you can take a guided tour, hike part of the Centennial Trail, and camp. For information, call 605-745-4600.

Badlands National Park is accessible via the Badlands Loop, South Dakota 240. Here you can drive through the Badlands on the 32-mile loop off I-90 via Exit 131 or 110, best done in the early morning or late evening. To see it up close, take a hike along 20 miles of trails in the hills preserving the world's greatest fossil beds dating back to the Oligocene Epoch, 30 million years ago. You can also take a ranger-guided tour offered from June through early September.

A challenging but scenic hike is the one-mile hike to the Notch where you climb a wooden ladder secured to the rocks. For a longer hike, hike the six-mile Castle Trail that traverses the Badlands. The terrain is quite rough, and hiking boots are advised. Be sure to carry plenty of water with you, and begin early in the day.

Take a helicopter ride over the park. The heliport is located at the east entrance to the park. For information, call 608-752-4001.

Tour one of the visitor centers, and attend an evening program Memorial Day through Labor Day followed by an hour-long night prowl. Watch for the large bison herd in the Sage Creek Wilderness Area. For park information, call 605-433-5361.

You can also visit the Crazy Horse Memorial, located five miles north of Custer off U.S. 16/385, to see the sculpture of Chief Crazy Horse. Crazy Horse was the Sioux warrior who lead the attack against General Custer at the Little Big Horn. When the statue is completed, it will be the largest statue in the world, rising 563 feet and 641 feet long. For information, call 605-673-4681.

Attend the Black Hills Passion Play in Spearfish. It's presented Sunday, Tuesday and Thursday. For reservations and information, call 605-642-2646.

On opposite nights to the play, go to the historic 1906 Matthew's Opera House for one of their performances. For information, call 605-642-1948.

In Spearfish Canyon, anglers can fish Spearfish Creek, a blue ribbon fishing stream. Hikers can enjoy hiking the canyons such as Iron Creek, Eleventh Hour Gulch, or go to a swimming hole on Squaw Creek called "The Devil's Bathtub." Bicyclists enjoy cycling in the canyon since U.S. 14A has wide shoulders, and follows an old railroad bed with a 3% grade.

INFORMATION
Custer State Park
HCR 83, Box 70
Custer, South Dakota 57730
605-255-4464 (summer); or 605-255-4515 Monday–Friday (rest of the year)
Campground reservations: 605-255-4000

FARM ISLAND STATE PARK
6

LOCATION - The park is three miles east of Pierre on South Dakota 34.

FEATURES - Fur traders named the site when they planted crops on the island to protect themselves from prairie thieves. Now a causeway connects the island to beaches, picnic sites, boating ramps and a campground on the mainland.

The island was the original state park until the Big Bend Dam was completed in 1965, when much of the island was flooded. Today the island is a nature area where you can go hiking along a National Recreation Trail.

ACTIVITIES - The recreation area is on the north side of Hipple Lake that is part of Lake Sharpe, and is a naturally protected bay for boating, swimming, water-skiing and fishing for bass and walleye. The park also provides access to the Missouri River where you can do additional boating and fishing.

The visitor center is near the site of Old Fort Sully. Park naturalists offer interpretive hikes on the island, and evening programs near the campground during the summer season.

The campground has 70 gravel sites, 41 with electrical hookups.

Tour nearby Oahe Dam, one of the largest rolled-earth dams in the world. The dam and reservoir are four miles northwest of Pierre on South Dakota 1804/1806. Tours are offered from Memorial Day–Labor Day. For information, call 605-224-5862.

Incoming pilots can land at Pierre Municipal Airport located three miles east of town. Rental cars are available.

INFORMATION
Farm Island State Park
R. R. 3, Box 111
Pierre, South Dakota 57501
605-224-5605

FISHER GROVE STATE PARK
7

LOCATION - The park is seven miles east of Redfield on U.S. 212, and is near the James River.

FEATURES - Fisher Grove was once a river crossing for the early pioneers.

ACTIVITIES - Camp in the campground with 28 campsites, 12 with electrical hookups, and 15 tent sites.

Go fishing, boating, and canoeing in the James River. During the spring and early summer, canoeists particularly enjoy following the 28-mile segment of the James River from Fisher Grove to the James River Lakeside Use Area near the Diversion Dam.

Walk through the 1884 country school house restored with artifacts of pioneer education in Spink County, and now used for the visitor center.

Hike the trails. One leads to Belchers Ford, a traditional rock river crossing used by the Indians to cross the James River. Concessions and food service are available in the park. Interpretive programs are presented, but not on a regular basis.

Golfers can play on the Redfield Country Club near the campground.

INFORMATION
Fisher Grove State Park
R. R. 1, Box 130
Frankfort, South Dakota 57440
605-472-1212

FORT SISSETON STATE HISTORIC PARK
8

LOCATION - The park is ten miles southwest of Lake City off South Dakota 25.

FEATURES - Fort Sisseton's name came from the nearby Sisseton Indian tribes, and was built in 1861 to protect settlers in the Dakota Territory, but instead the fort became the area's social center. Fifteen of the original 45 buildings have been preserved, and the fort is registered as a National Historic Landmark.

ACTIVITIES - Camp in the campground with 12 sites without hookups. Hike the interpretive trails. Stop by the visitor center and attend weekly interpretive programs offered from Memorial Day through Labor Day.

Tour the historic site. An annual historical festival is featured the first weekend in June. Cavalry troops practice precision drills, and buckskin-clad mountain men and women compete in shooting matches, tomahawk throws and rolling pin tosses. Watch Native Americans perform dances.

In Sisseton, attend the annual Antique Auto Festival held the first weekend in June. The Fort Sisseton Historical Festival is also held the first weekend in June, the Hills and Valley Trail Ride the second weekend in June, and the Sisseton-Wahpeton Sioux Tribe's powwow over the 4th of July.

INFORMATION
Fort Sisseton State Historic Site
P.O. Box 2993
Rapid City, South Dakota 57709
605-448-5701

HARTFORD BEACH STATE PARK
9

LOCATION - The park is on the western shore of Big Stone Lake, twelve miles north and two miles west of Milbank on South Dakota 15.

ACTIVITIES - Enjoy canoeing, swimming, boating from the ramp, fishing, skin diving and water-skiing in 38-mile-long Big Stone Lake. Hike the interpretive trails to some of the historical sites including early fur-trading posts, prehistoric Indian villages, and burial mounds.

Concessions and food service are available along with lodging and camping in the campground with 37 campsites, 25 with electrical hookups. Attend interpretive programs presented on the weekends from Memorial Day through Labor Day.

Visit nearby Big Stone Island Nature Area located southeast of the park. Big Stone Lake is part of the ancient Warren River channel that is listed in the registry of National Natural Landmarks. The island is accessible by boat during the summer, or by walking across the ice during the winter.

During the winter, come to cross-country ski, go ice fishing, snowmobiling, and downhill skiing on the bluffs.

INFORMATION
Hartford Beach State Park
R. R. 1, Box 50
Corona, South Dakota 57227
605-432-6374

LAKE HERMAN STATE PARK
10

LOCATION - The park is two miles south of Madison off South Dakota 34.

FEATURES - The park is on a peninsula that extends into Lake Herman. The area around the park was formed by melting glaciers, and was popular among the Mandan and Arikara Indians who came here en route to the nearby pipe-stone quarries. The log cabin, built for Herman Luce in 1871, still stands on its original site.

ACTIVITIES - Go canoeing, boating, fishing for walleye and other game fish, swimming from the beach, and horseback riding. Stay in the campground with 69 campsites, 43 with electrical hookups. Concessions are available, and interpretive programs are presented weekly in the campground during the summer, and by request in the off-season.

Hunters come to hunt for ducks, geese and pheasants in the fall, and hikers have access to five miles of trails.

From Memorial Day to Labor Day, come to Prairie Village and attend its summer repertory theater. An old fashioned threshing bee is held the last weekend in August during Jamboree Days.

INFORMATION
Lake Herman State Park   605-256-3613
R. R. 3, Box 79
Madison, South Dakota 57042

LAKE LOUISE STATE RECREATION AREA
11

LOCATION - The area is twelve miles northwest of Miller off U.S. 14.

ACTIVITIES - Camp in the campground along the wooded shoreline with 28 campsites, 15 with electrical hookups, and three tent sites. The lake has six miles of shoreline where you can go boating from the ramp, swimming from the beach, and fishing for bass, walleye, perch and catfish.

Hikers have access to trails both in the park and in the Game Production Area that surrounds Lake Louise.

During the winter, come to cross-country ski through the woods, or go snow-mobiling along the shoreline and by the lake's secluded bays.

INFORMATION
Lake Louise State Recreation Area   605-853-2533
R. R. 1
Miller, South Dakota 57362

LAKE POINSETT STATE PARK
12

LOCATION - The park is twelve miles north of Arlington off U.S. 81, and midway between Brookings and Watertown in the northeastern part of the state.

FEATURES - Lake Poinsett is the state's second largest natural lake, measuring 5.5 miles long and three miles wide, and features a mile-long sandy beach.

ACTIVITIES - Two modern campgrounds located on the south side of the lake have 97 sites, 60 with electrical hookups. Visitors can fish year-round, and enjoy swimming, walking the mile-long beach, boating, and water-skiing. Park naturalists conduct interpretive programs Memorial Day through Labor Day.

Flower lovers can visit McCrory Gardens located in Brookings at U.S. 14E, west of I-29. You'll see over 1,000 rose varieties, and many blooming annuals and perennials.

Incoming pilots can land at Brookings Municipal located southwest of town, or at Watertown Municipal located two miles northwest of town. Rental cars are available.

INFORMATION
Lake Poinsett State Park
c/o Oakwood Lakes State Park
R. R. 2, Box 10
Bruce, South Dakota 57220
605-983-5085

LAKE VERMILLION STATE RECREATION AREA
13

LOCATION - The area is five miles south of Montrose and 27 miles west of Sioux Falls.

FEATURES - The lake may have been named for the Sioux word "vermillion" meaning "red paint." Others believe it was named for the red dogwood found along the river banks.

ACTIVITIES - The recreation area is a State Game Bird Refuge, but trapping and deer hunting are permitted in season. No boating is allowed from October 1–December 31 except on its northernmost section.

Visitors come to go water-skiing, swimming, birding, canoeing, sailing and fishing for walleye, bass, pike, perch and crappie. Access to the lake is available from boat ramps located near the park entrance. Hikers can explore the bordering grasslands.

You can camp in a commercial campground adjacent to the park where gas, food and boat rentals are available.

If you come here the second Thursday in July, attend the annual Sport Day in Canistota featuring parades, sporting events, and ending with a giant fireworks display.

INFORMATION
Lake Vermillion State Recreation Area
Route 3, Box 79
Madison, South Dakota 57042
605-256-3613

LEWIS AND CLARK LAKE STATE RECREATION AREA
14

LOCATION - The area is five miles west of Yankton on South Dakota 52.

FEATURES - Lewis and Clark is the gateway to the Missouri River System. Twenty-five miles of the park border the Lewis and Clark lake. The lake was named for the leaders of the famous 1804–06 expedition, and was created by Gavins Point Dam. The lake is 45 feet deep, and stretches from Yankton 35 miles up the Missouri River.

ACTIVITIES - Go fishing for walleye and bass upriver, and for sauger, catfish and paddlefish below Gavins Point. Sailboating is a popular summertime activity. Visitors can enjoy boating, hiking miles of sandy beaches, and cycling on the bicycle trails.

The park has three units. Yankton Unit has a modern marina, restaurant, visitor center, and lodging in the Lewis and Clark Resort with 24 motel units or five modern cabins. Camp in the modern campground with 78 paved sites, 50 with electrical hookups.

The Midway Unit is next to the Yankton Unit, and has boat ramps, miles of sandy beaches, a modern campground with 103 paved sites (86 with electrical hookups), and rustic camping cabins.

Gavins Point's campground has 76 sites, with 34 offering electrical hookups. It also has hiking trails, sandy beaches, an equestrian campground, and riding trails.

The lake has miles of beaches and trails, and easy access to excellent boating and fishing. Anglers can fish year-round in the open tail waters of the dam. The area has a full-service marina. Summer regattas are held here.

Gavins Point National Fish Hatchery and Aquarium is located three miles west of Yankton on South Dakota 52, and is open April through December 31. For information, call 605-665-3352.

Gavins Point Dam and power house are five miles south of Crofton, Nebraska, where you can take a tour of the power plant. Tours are offered daily during the summer, and by appointment the rest of the year. For information, call 402-667-7873.

Canoeists can put in below Gavins Point Dam to float through Yankton, and continue all the way to Ponca State Park in Nebraska, 58 miles away. This segment has several large islands and many sandbars for camping and picnicking.

In August, attend the Riverboat Days held in Yankton, featuring an air show, water-ski show and competition, dancing and many other festivities. For information, contact the Yankton Riverboat Days, P.O. Box 483, Yankton, South Dakota 57078.

The Lewis and Clark Playhouse, located west of the entrance to the Yankton Unit of the recreation area, presents plays and musicals. For information, call 605-665-4711.

Equestrians have six miles of marked trails with two separate base camps available by reservation for groups.

During the winter, come to ice fish, cross-county ski, and snowmobile on miles of trails surrounding the lake. You can also enjoy bird watching since the Missouri River is on the traditional migratory pathway for Canadian geese and ducks.

Annual events include the Lewis and Clark Great Lake Escape in May, and the Lewis and Clark Heritage Days in July. A Pro-Am golf tournament, Yankton Riverboat Days, and Summer Arts Festival are held in August. The Lewis and Clark Lake Boat Parade and an Open Fiddler's Contest is in September, and Oktoberfest is held in October. For details, contact the Chamber of Commerce at 605-665-3636.

Incoming pilots can land at Chan Gurney Municipal located three miles north of Yankton. Rental cars are available.

INFORMATION
Lewis and Clark State Recreation Area
R. R. 1, Box 240
Yankton, South Dakota 57078
605-668-3435

NEWTON HILLS STATE PARK
15

LOCATION - The park is six miles south of Canton off U.S. 18 in the center of the Newton Hills.

FEATURES - Artifacts and burial mounds in the vicinity indicate the Woodland Indians occupied the area around 300 B.C. to A.D. 900. The park is in a wooded oasis at the southern tip of the Coteau des Prairie, Hills of the Prairie. Lake Lakota was named in honor of the Teton or Lakota Sioux.

Legends abound about the dark forest, telling of robbers hiding out, travelers being massacred, and a chief dying in the "quick mud" of Nehimi Springs. The remains of the cave and springs, both near the park, are still visible.

ACTIVITIES - Camp in the campground with 123 sites, 63 with electrical hookups, in the equestrian campground, or in one of the cabins heated during the winter. Go canoeing along the state's canoe trails. One is located on the Big Sioux River, and runs from Sioux Falls to this state park. Campsites are located along the canoe trail.

Go swimming and fishing in Lake Lakota. Only boating with electric motors and canoeing are allowed on the lake.

Hike the Coteau Trail and the Woodland Trail, a National Recreation Trail that winds through a hardwood forest. Equestrians have access to five miles of marked trails meandering through the woods and their own campground.

In early August, the Sioux River Folk Festival is held when you can hear a sampling of traditional, folk, bluegrass and Irish music.

During the winter, come to go cross-country skiing in the park or at Riverview near Canton. The area has 15 miles of tracked groomed trails, plus a heated ski shop with snacks and rentals. A multi-purpose shelter is open for year-round use.

Incoming pilots can land at Canton Municipal located one mile east of town. Rental cars are available.

INFORMATION
Newton Hills State Park
R. R. 1, Box 162
Canton, South Dakota 57013
605-987-2263

OAKWOOD LAKES STATE PARK
16

LOCATION - The park is ten miles north of Volga off U.S. 14, and 20 miles northwest of Brookings.

FEATURES - Oakwood Lakes State Park is located in the middle of eight glacial lakes formed in depressions left behind by the melting glacier. Breastworks Cabin, a historic cabin built in the 1860s, is located in the park. Recently ten prehistoric Indian burial mounds were excavated.

ACTIVITIES - Camp in the campground with 75 pads, 27 with electrical hookups, 10 tent sites, or stay in one of the camping cabins. Concessions and food service are available.

Go canoeing in the many coves found in the chain of lakes, fishing for pike and bullhead, boating from the boat launching ramp, and swimming from the beach. Come for one of their summer regattas, including annual canoe races in mid-July.

Hike the .75-mile Tetonkaha Trail on Scout Island. Tetonkaha means "home of the great summer lodge." Tour the visitor center to learn more about these early inhabitants. Interpretive programs are presented weekly.

In July, attend the annual Oakwood Old Style Canoe Races, or participate in the annual triathlon. During the annual Tetonkaha Rendezvous held in August, participants engage in muzzle-loading rifle shoots, tomahawk throws and wild game cookoffs.

During winter, come for the Frozen Foot Rendezvous, snowmobiling along six miles of trails, cross-country skiing, and warm up in the warming house.

Incoming pilots can land at Brookings Municipal located southwest of town. Rental cars are available.

INFORMATION
Oakwood Lakes State Park
R. R. 2, Box 10
Bruce, South Dakota 57220
605-627-5441

PALISADES STATE PARK
17

LOCATION - The park is four miles south of Garretson off South Dakota 11.

FEATURES - Split Rock Creek has carved deep gorges in the Sioux quartzite estimated to be 1,200 million years old. Red pipestone is found between the quartzite layers, and was used by the Indians to make pipe bowls and ornaments. This is one of the few areas in the nation where pipestone is found, and you can see depressions from when the Indians quarried the rock.

Jesse and Frank James were holed up in a cave on Split Rock Creek, and when Jesse was surprised by a posse searching for him, he reportedly jumped across the sheer walls of the riverbank. Today a footbridge spans the gap in Devil's Gulch, two miles north of the park.

ACTIVITIES - Camp in the campground with 38 sites, 16 with electrical hookups. Go canoeing, swimming and pan fishing in Split Rock Creek. Canoe in Split Rock Creek through the sheer walls of red quartzite. During high water in the spring, or after a heavy summer rain, the water becomes a challenge for white-water paddlers when some stretches become hazardous. The stream drops 130 feet in eight miles from an access point west of Garretson.

Hike the trails, attend weekly interpretive programs, or go rock climbing on the vertical cliffs in the canyon.

Beaver Creek Nature Area is located eight miles east of Sioux Falls, and has interpretive trails, beaver dams, an arboretum, and an original log cabin built in the 1870s. Each fall, Homesteader Day is held the second Sunday in September. Cross-country skiers come to ski the trails in the winter.

INFORMATION
Palisades State Park
R. R. 2, Box 244
Garretson, South Dakota 57030
605-594-3824

PELICAN LAKE STATE RECREATION AREA
18

LOCATION - The state recreation area is located on the lake's southwest side, seven miles southwest of Watertown off U.S. 212.

ACTIVITIES - Visitors come to go fishing, boating, swimming and water-skiing. Pelicans were once so numerous that the lake was called Pelican Lake. Many waterfowl still come through in the fall on their migration route.

Boat-launching facilities are available, and a sandy swimming beach runs the length of the .75-mile-long shoreline. The campground has six pads.

During the winter visitors come to go snowmobiling, cross-country skiing and ice fishing. A year-round shelter is available to warm up.

Incoming pilots can land at Watertown Municipal located two miles northwest of town. Rental cars are available.

INFORMATION
Pelican Lake State Recreation Area
400 West Kemp
Watertown, South Dakota 57201
605-886-4769

PICKEREL LAKE STATE RECREATION AREA
19

LOCATION - The park is ten miles north of Waubay.

FEATURES - The lake's name is Indian meaning "where you spear long fish." The summit near the south end of the lake was sacred to the early Indians who came here to pray, fast, and seek visions.

A state fish hatchery was originally built in 1929, and was replaced by a newer facility at nearby Blue Dog Lake.

ACTIVITIES - The lake is in the Glacial Lakes Region, and has two separate units, one on each side of the lake. The east unit has 17 pads with electrical hookups and four tent sites. The west unit has 44 pads with 41 providing electrical hookups, and access to excellent fishing. Go boating from the secluded marina on the east side of the lake, swimming from the beach, and hike the half-mile self-guided trail.

Regularly scheduled programs are presented during the summer season.

INFORMATION
Pickerel Lake State Park
400 West Kemp
Watertown, South Dakota 57201
605-886-4769

PLATTE CREEK STATE RECREATION AREA
20

LOCATION - The park is six miles south, and then seven miles west of Platte.

FEATURES - Lake Francis Case was one of four reservoirs created to harness the Missouri River, and is 107 miles long with a maximum depth of 140 feet. It has 540 miles of shoreline.

ACTIVITIES - Anglers can fish for walleye, pike and catfish. Go boating from the ramp where boat rentals are available.

Camp in the campground with 72 campsites, 16 with electrical hookups. A concession provides food, fishing supplies and fuel.

Randall Dam is a roosting area for one of the largest concentrations of eagles in the U.S. They're most commonly seen here during the winter.

Incoming pilots can land at Platte Municipal Airport located one mile northeast of town. Rental cars are available.

INFORMATION
Platte Creek State Recreation Area
Route 2, Box 113-1
Platte, South Dakota 57369
605-337-2587

RICHMOND LAKE STATE RECREATION AREA
21

LOCATION - The area is ten miles northwest of Aberdeen off U.S. 12.

ACTIVITIES - The South Unit has 24 campsites, 12 with electrical hookups. Go swimming, boating and water-skiing in Richmond Lake. Hike the Richmond Trail along the lake shore, or follow other trails over the hills and through the grasslands.

The Boat Ramp Unit has three launching lanes, and you can go water-skiing and fishing for walleye, pike, bass, perch and catfish.

The Forest Drive Unit has picnic facilities, hiking trails and a bridle trail.

During the winter, come to sled and toboggan on the hill, and warm up in the converted picnic shelter that becomes a warming house. Cross-country skiers can ski on groomed trails. Anglers come to go ice fishing.

Snowmobilers come to Forest Drive to ride along several miles of snowmobile trails, including the groomed Richmond Snowmobile Trail, or to follow the trails to Aberdeen or Mina Lake Recreation Area.

Incoming pilots can land at Aberdeen Regional located two miles east of town. Rental cars are available.

INFORMATION
Richmond Lake State Recreation Area
Route 2, Box 500
Aberdeen, South Dakota 57401
605-225-5325

ROY LAKE STATE PARK
22

LOCATION - The park is three miles southwest of Lake City off South Dakota 10.

FEATURES - The lake is in the glacial lakes region where evidence of a prehistoric Indian village has been uncovered, dating back to A.D. 900-1300.

ACTIVITIES - The park has two separate park areas. The West Unit has an aquarium, a swimming beach, boat-launching facilities, and a footbridge to Roy Island where you can hike a self-guiding trail. The East Unit has boating facilities and shore fishing for walleye, pike, bass and panfish.

Camp in one of the campgrounds. The East Unit has 36 pads and 13 tent sites, and the West Unit has 39 pads and six tent sites. Sixty-five of the sites have electrical hookups. Weekly campfire programs are presented during the summer.

If you prefer not to rough it, stay at the Roy Lake Resort located on the northwest shore off South Dakota 10. It has modern cabins, boat rentals, fishing, boating and a swimming beach. For information, call 605-448-5498 during the summer.

INFORMATION
Roy Lake State Park
R. R. 2, Box 51
Lake City, South Dakota 57247
605-448-5701

SHADEHILL STATE RECREATION AREA
23

LOCATION - The area is thirteen miles south of Lemmon in northwest South Dakota.

ACTIVITIES - Camp in one of the 48 campground sites, 20 with electrical hookups. Go fishing for pike, walleye, catfish and perch. Enjoy hiking, waterskiing, sailing, canoeing and swimming.

Rock hounds will notice many petrified trees around. To see more of them, visit the city of Lemmon's Petrified Wood Park and Museum at 500 Main Avenue from mid-May to mid-September. For information, call 605-374-5716.

Llewellyn John's State Recreation Area, 12 miles south of Lemmon, also has many park facilities constructed from petrified wood. While there, you can hike, picnic, camp or go fishing for stocked pike and bass.

Visit Slim Buttes 30 Battle Site located southwest of the park near Reva.

INFORMATION

Shadehill State Recreation Area
Box 63
Shadehill, South Dakota 57653
605-374-5114

SNAKE CREEK STATE RECREATION AREA
24

LOCATION - The area is sixteen miles west of Platte on South Dakota 44.

FEATURES - The park has oil-bearing shale, and sometimes lightning will strike it causing it to ignite. Red Rock is upriver from the park, and its large sandstone formation was a famous landmark used by the early steamboat captains.

ACTIVITIES - Most visitors come here to go walleye, catfish and bass fishing. Many anglers head for Landing Creek and Red Rock eight miles upriver.

Go boating with boat launches located on the northwest side of Lake Francis Case. The West Bridge launching ramp is on the opposite end of the bridge from the recreation area. Still another launch site is at Buryanek.

Camp in the campground with 96 sites, 50 with electrical hookups, or stay in the modern resort where you can replenish your camping supplies. You can swim from the beach, or go sailing, canoeing and water-skiing.

Incoming pilots can land at Platte Municipal one mile northeast of town. Rental cars are available.

INFORMATION

Snake Creek State Recreation Area
Route 2, Box 113-1
Platte, South Dakota 57369
605-337-2587

UNION COUNTY STATE PARK
25

LOCATION - The park is eleven miles south of Beresford off I-29, in southeastern South Dakota near the southern edge of the Coteau des Prairies.

FEATURES - The park is the site of the first homestead in the U.S., established under the Homestead Act of 1862, and is perched on a high hill overlooking the countryside.

ACTIVITIES - Camp in the campground with 24 campsites, 10 with electrical hookups, and six tent sites. An equestrian campground and trails are also available. Go fishing for catfish in the stream. Hike the trails, or attend interpretive programs that are presented on a variable schedule.

Tour the arboretum with its large collection of native and exotic trees and shrubs, particularly beautiful in the fall.

During the winter, come to go snowshoeing and cross-country skiing.

INFORMATION
Union County State Park
R. R. 1, Box 44
Beresford, South Dakota 57004
605-987-2263

WEST BEND STATE RECREATION AREA
26

LOCATION - The area is thirty-one miles east of Pierre on South Dakota 34.

FEATURES - Big Bend Dam was built across the Missouri River and created Lake Sharpe. The lake is 80 miles long, and has 200 miles of shoreline.

The original 24-mile loop in the river was a stopping place for early steamboat passengers traveling upstream in the 1800s. Passengers got off to hike the 1.5 miles across the neck of the river, reaching the west side in time to re-board the steamboat.

ACTIVITIES - Visitors come to go walleye fishing, particularly between Memorial Day and the end of July. You can camp in the campground with 128 sites, 68 with electrical hookups. You can also swim from the sandy beach, and go boating from the ramp in Lake Sharpe.

Besides the state recreation area, you can stay in one of the three lakeside areas: North Bend, Joe Creek and DeGrey. Each offers primitive camping, picnicking facilities, and boat-launching ramps.

Incoming pilots can land at Pierre Municipal three miles east of town. Rental cars are available.

INFORMATION
West Bend State Recreation Area
c/o Farm Island Recreation Area
Route 3, Box 111
Pierre, South Dakota 57501
605-875-3220

WEST WHITLOCK STATE RECREATION AREA
27

LOCATION - The area is twenty miles west of Gettysburg, on Lake Oahe.

FEATURES - Oahe Dam is 50 miles down river from the Whitlock area, and is one of the largest earthen dams in the world. With its construction, a lake 230 miles long was created.

The area was once a popular campsite for the Arikara and Mandan Indians, and a replica Arikara earth lodge is in the park.

Watch for Medicine Rock, an 18-foot boulder carved by early Indians with mosaics of human foot and hand prints. It's near the Gettysburg city limits.

ACTIVITIES - Visitors come here to fish for pike in the early spring, sometimes landing a 20-pound lunker. During the spring and summer, come fishing for walleye. For up-to-date information on the walleye fishing, call the walleye hotline at 605-845-2500.

You can also go swimming, boating, canoeing, sailing and water-skiing from the ramp. The campground has 103 campsites, 50 with electrical hookups. You can also stay in the lodge or cabins. Food service is available.

Tour the visitor center and nearby salmon spawning station to learn how a successful salmon fishery was created. You can also see a replica of an Arikara earth lodge.

Three commercial resorts are located near West Whitlock, and most provide cabin rentals, boats and concessions.

On the July 4th weekend, attend the Sitting Bull Stampede and Rodeo in Mobridge. For information, call 605-845-2387.

Incoming pilots can land at Gettysburg Municipal one mile south of town. Rental cars are available.

INFORMATION
West Whitlock State Recreation Area
Star Route 3, Box 73A
Gettysburg, South Dakota 57442
605-765-9410

*Covered bridges add a special charm to many Midwest locations,
including this one in Amnicon Falls State Park.*

WISCONSIN DIVISION OF TOURISM

WISCONSIN

Vacationers to Wisconsin will find countless scenic landscapes plus many recreational opportunities. Door County, Washington Island, Green Bay and Lake Michigan have good fishing, boating, and swimming. The northern lakes region features forest hiking trails, fishing, rafting and canoeing. For long-distance canoeing, check out the Saint Croix River and its tributary, the Namekagon.

Wisconsin is the site of the great Wisconsin glacier that retreated from the area approximately 10,000 years ago, leaving behind a large number of glacial features throughout the state. One of the best ways to learn more about what glaciers did to the landscape is to stop at some of the state parks located along the 1,000-mile-long Ice Age Trail.

Five state parks along the route include Horicon Marsh, Devil's Lake State Park, Interstate Park, Kettle Moraine State Forest–Northern Unit and Mill Bluff State Park. To get a map of the entire trail, contact Ice Age Trail, c/o Wisconsin Department of Natural Resources, P.O. Box 7921, Madison, Wisconsin 53707, 608-266-2181.

Wisconsin is also known for its many hiking and biking trails that lace the state. Some of these trails follow the Ice Age Trail or old railroad beds. Only a few of the trails are included in this book. For a copy of "Biking Wisconsin's State Park Trails," contact the Department of Natural Resources, Bureau of Parks and Recreation, P.O. Box 7921, Madison, Wisconsin 53707, or call them at 608-266-2181.

During the winter, the parks sponsor candlelight ski/walks. For information on dates, contact the Bureau of Parks and Recreation at 608-266-2181.

AMNICON FALLS STATE PARK
1

LOCATION - Amnicon Falls State Park is eight miles south of Superior on Wisconsin 2.

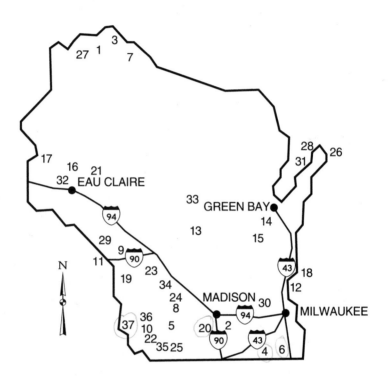

ACTIVITIES - The park has many cataracts and four waterfalls, with three of them almost 30 feet tall. Cross over the covered bridge to the nearby island. Enjoy picnicking, camping in one of 36 sites, and hiking the nature trail. The park usually opens the end of April and closes the first week of October.

Incoming pilots can land at Richard Bong Airport located three miles south of Superior. Rental cars are available.

INFORMATION
Amnicon Falls State Park
Box 435
Superior, Wisconsin 54880
715-399-8073

AZTALAN STATE PARK
2

LOCATION - The park is south of I-94 near Lake Mills on County Q, and approximately 50 miles from Milwaukee. Follow the signs in Lake Mills to East Lake Street. Turn left. Continue another two miles from town to Azatlan. Turn right on County Road Q. The park is up the hill from the intersection.

FEATURES - The park is one of the state's largest and most important archeological sites. It's the site of a 12th-century Indian village occupied from A.D. 900 to 1200 by an ancient Middle-Mississippi tribe. They built over 40 large, flat-topped pyramidal mounds and a stockade around the perimeter of their village. Portions of the stockade and two of the mounds have been reconstructed.

ACTIVITIES - For day-use only, the park is open from 7 a.m. until 9 p.m. April through November. Tour the nearby museum, which showcases its former pioneer village, a cabin built in the 1840s, and artifacts from the pioneer days. Enjoy a picnic, and go hiking along 3.5 miles of trails. Fishing is reportedly poor, but some pike, walleye and catfish have been caught. For camping, go to Lake Kegonsa State Park.

INFORMATION
Aztalan State Park
c/o Lake Kegonsa State Park
2405 Door Creek Road
Stoughton, Wisconsin 53589
608-873-9695 or 414-648-8774

BIG BAY STATE PARK
3

LOCATION - The Madeline Island park is available only by ferry from the mainland and is east of Bayfield. The ferry departs from the lake at the foot of

Washington Avenue. You can take your car aboard, or ride across without it, and walk or rent bikes in the park to get around.

FEATURES - The park features picturesque sandstone bluffs with caves carved out by Lake Superior.

ACTIVITIES - Camp in the campground with 17 campsites. Go hiking and explore the nature trails. Go swimming in Lake Superior from a beautiful 1.5-mile long sandy beach.

If you sail your own boat over to the island, you can dock at the Madeline Island Yacht Club that can accommodate three transient boats. It also has a charter office for sailboats and a ship store. Madeline Island has an historical museum located one block from the ferry dock, and four pioneer structures housing exhibits from the exploratory days of Wisconsin. To get a good look at the whole island, take the Madeline Island Nature Bus Tour, which begins from the dock, and lasts 1.5 hours.

In Bayfield, stop by the Apostle Islands National Lakeshore Headquarters at Washington and 4th Street to watch a slide show about the islands, and see their display highlighting some of their attractions.

INFORMATION
Big Bay State Park
Box 589
Bayfield, Wisconsin 54814
715-779-3346

BIG FOOT BEACH STATE PARK
4

LOCATION - The park is located 1.5 miles south of Lake Geneva on Wisconsin 120.

ACTIVITIES - The park has a 26-mile hiking trail that goes around the lake. Take a swim from the guarded sandy beach with 2,200 feet of frontage on Geneva Lake, and go camping in one of the 100 wooded campsites.

Picnic at nearby Ceylon Lagoon, built by one of the original owners to resemble a miniature Lake Geneva.

Every Thursday evening in July and August, enjoy outdoor "Concerts in the Park" at Flatiron Park on the lakeshore. Cruise the lake on one of the tours offered from May 1–October 31 at the Riviera Docks by the Geneva Lake Cruise Line. For information, call 800-558-5911 or 414-248-6206. If possible, time your visit to the lake to see one of the country's most unusual mail delivery techniques: by boat. You can even take a tour with the mail carrier.

A week-long balloon rally is held in Lake Geneva and Fontana in May. For specifics, call 414-248-4416.

Incoming pilots can land at Americana Airport located three miles northeast of Lake Geneva. Rental cars are available.

INFORMATION
Big Foot Beach State Park   414-248-2528
Route 3, Box 12
Lake Geneva, Wisconsin 53147

BLUE MOUND STATE PARK
5

LOCATION - Blue Mound State Park is on the highest point in southern Wisconsin, and is northwest of Blue Mounds from U.S. 18/151 via Blue Mound Road. It's also 25 miles west of Madison.

ACTIVITIES - Climb to the top of the observation tower from which you can see 40 miles on a clear day including the bluffs beside Devil's Lake State Park, and the state capitol dome in Madison.

The campground has 78 wooded campsites, with two providing electrical hookups. The campground is closed November through March, but the rest of the park is open year-round.

The Military Ridge Bike Trail feeds directly into this park. Bikers will love the park's pool for cooling off after a day's ride. It's open with life guards on duty from Memorial Day through Labor Day.

Hike the area's hiking trails or stroll along the 1.5-mile self-guided nature trail. Attend an evening program on Friday or Saturday evenings during the summer to learn more about the history of the area.

From late June through late July, attend the light operetta based on the life of Norwegian composer Edvard Grieg, presented in their outdoor theater. Information: 608-437-3038.

Go into town and tour Cave of the Mounds that is one of the largest limestone caves in the Midwest. It's open year-round, and hour-long tours leave every 15 minutes during the summer. For information, call 608-437-3038.

Incoming pilots can land at Dane County Regional-Truax Field at Madison. Rental cars are available.

INFORMATION
Blue Mound State Park   608-437-5711
Box 98
Blue Mounds, Wisconsin 53517

BONG STATE RECREATION AREA
6

LOCATION - The area is southwest of Milwaukee, and four miles south of Kansasville on Wisconsin 142, and eight miles east of Burlington.

ACTIVITIES - This state park offers just about every activity you can ask for: swimming from the sandy beach, fishing, picnicking, camping, riding horse-back, cross-country skiing, motorcycling, and hunting in season. It's open year-round, and has full-time naturalists who offer interpretive programs. It has special areas for sled dog training, hang gliding, flying ultra-lights, and hot air ballooning. Hike along 13 miles of trails, or their two self-guided nature trails.

Go into Burlington to explore a unique attraction: the Spinning Top Exploratory Museum. It has exhibits of over 600 modern and antique tops, and hands-on demonstrations are available if you make advance reservations. Call 414-763-3946 to arrange for your tour.

Flower lovers can browse through the St. Francis Friary and Retreat Center. They offer tours of their gardens, grottos and the facility from May through October by advance reservation. Call 414-763-3600.

Drama enthusiasts can check out the Haylofters Theater, Wisconsin's oldest community theater group. They present a series of dramatic presentations at the Malt House Theater at 109 North Main in Burlington. Call 414-763-9726 or 414-763-9873.

INFORMATION
Bong State Recreation Area
26313 Burlington Road
Kansasville, Wisconsin 53139
414-878-4416

COPPER FALLS STATE PARK
7

LOCATION - The park is four miles north of Mellen off Wisconsin 169.

ACTIVITIES - The park is open from mid-April through December 1.

Visitors enjoy coming here to see the deep 60- to 100-foot gorges cut by the Bad River. You can hike the trails passing through the hardwoods, cross the log footbridge that crosses the river to watch the falls, hike the self-guiding nature trail, or hike along the trail to Copper and Brownstone Falls where numerous vantage points are available for picture-taking.

Go for a swim from the sandy beach at Loon Lake, and fish for bass, pike, and trout in the Bad and Tyler Forks rivers.

Camp in the campground with 56 sites, 13 of them with electrical hookups, or backpack into another campsite. Food service is available in the park.

INFORMATION
Copper Falls State Park
Box 438
Mellen, Wisconsin 54546
715-274-5123

DEVIL'S LAKE STATE PARK
8

LOCATION - The park is south of Baraboo and the Wisconsin Dells. To reach it, from the Intersection of I-90/94, drive west for 13 miles on Wisconsin 33 to Wisconsin 123 where you continue south another four miles.

FEATURES - The park is one of nine units of the Ice Age National Scientific Reserve, and the lake is located between two glacially carved terminal moraines. It is now spring-fed, and its depth varies from 40 to 50 feet. The surrounding bluffs rise 500 feet above the lake.

ACTIVITIES - The park is open year-round; a naturalist is always on duty.

The campground has 415 campsites, 125 with electrical hookups. The campsites fill up on summer weekends, so reservations are recommended. Reservations cannot be made by phone, however, but must be made on their campsite reservation forms. These may be obtained at a state park office. For information, call 608-356-6618.

Concessions are available on both the north and south shores where you can rent fishing poles, snorkeling equipment, and rowboats. Scuba divers come here to dive, and wind surfers go to the North shore to wind surf.

Hiking some of the 15 miles of trails will bring you into close contact with the results of the glaciation that occurred here. If you follow the East Bluff Woods Trail, you get some wonderful overlooks of Devil's Lake, and intersect another short trail that takes you down to see potholes left behind by the melting glacial ice. Three other trails begin from the Steinke Basin parking area, and loop through the glaciated areas. During the winter, cross-country ski on 15.5 miles of trails.

To see some of the Indian Mounds located in the area, follow the Indian Mounds Nature Trail. Begin from the Nature Center to see effigy mounds of a mountain lion, a linear mound, and a bear effigy.

While in the area, be sure to stop by the Wisconsin Dells and take a riverboat tour. You can ride on both the Upper Dells and Lower Dells, a combination ride that takes four hours. The Upper Dells lasts 2 1/2 hours, and enables you to disembark and walk into two side canyons. At the second stop at Stand Rock, watch a daredevil dog leap across a five-foot gap between Stand Rock and an adjacent bluff. For information: 608-253-1561.

An unusual museum in Baraboo is the Circus World Museum, located on the Ringling Brothers' original winter quarters on the outskirts of town. You'll see over 170 circus wagons, and other circus memorabilia. During the summer, attend the Starlight Big Top Show. For information, call 608-356-0800, or 608-356-0800.

Incoming pilots can land at Baraboo-Wisconsin Dells Airport located four miles northwest of Baraboo. Rental cars are available.

INFORMATION
Devil's Lake State Park
S5975 Park Road
Route 4, Box 36
Baraboo, Wisconsin 53913

608-356-8301 or 608-356-6618 for
campsite information

ELROY-SPARTA STATE TRAIL
9

LOCATION - The trail runs between Elroy and Sparta.

ACTIVITIES - This newly developed biking/hiking trail is 32 miles long, and to avoid climbing some hills, the trail passes through three tunnels, one of them one mile long. The tunnels were built in 1873 by the Chicago and North Western Railroad, and still have their original wooden doors. Bike rentals, bicyclist pick-up service, and camping are available in Sparta.

If you ride through Kendall, you'll pass a restored railroad depot that's on the National Register of Historic Places. It serves as the main headquarters for the trail. Here you can see historic railroad photos and artifacts.

The Wilton Lions Club serves a pancake breakfast for bikers on Sundays from Memorial Day through Labor Day.

The state trail has six rest areas, and two rustic campgrounds with walk-in sites. Another campground is located in Elroy. If possible, ride the trail in the fall when the trees display their autumn foliage.

If you're in Elroy, stop by Duesenberg Motors to see reproductions of this famous car. The plant is open for tours. It's located at 1006 Academy Street, and is open daily Monday–Friday from 8:00 a.m. to 8:30 p.m. year-round. For information, call 608-462-8100.

For an additional ride, follow the Sparta-La Crosse bike path for another 23.5 miles. The bike path is open from May 1–October 31.

INFORMATION
Elroy-Sparta State Trail
Box 98
Ontario, Wisconsin 54651
608-337-4775

GOVERNOR DODGE STATE PARK
10

LOCATION - The park is three miles north of Dodgeville on Wisconsin 23, and 45 miles west of Madison.

FEATURES - The park has sandstone bluffs and deep valleys left untouched by the glaciers.

ACTIVITIES - The park is open year-round. Visitors can go swimming, fishing for panfish and muskie, and boating or canoeing in Cox Hollow or Twin Valley Lakes. Boats and canoes may be rented at the concession stand. The park also has horseback riding trails.

The park is the state's second largest. Its campground has 267 campsites, with 73 electrical hookups, and advance reservations are recommended. Stop at the visitor center to learn about naturalist-led nature walks which are offered from mid-June through August. Attend an evening program given twice a week during the summer.

Its 15-mile-long trail is utilized by hikers, bikers and cross-country skiers and snowmobiles. The trail connects with the Military Ridge Trail.

Nearby, check out Nature's Miracle Museum that has over 3,000 rocks, crystals, fluorescents and mineral specimens collected from all over the world. For information, call 608-935-5205.

If you happen to be in town on a Saturday, stop by the Folklore Village for their Saturday evening potluck and learn some new folk dances. It's on Highway BB, Route 3, and is open year-round. For information, call 608-924-4000.

Close by is the American Players' Theater located in the woods. You can attend performances with an emphasis on Shakespearean plays from June through October. For information, call 608-588-7401.

Incoming pilots can land at Dane County Regional-Truax Field, five miles northeast of Madison. Rental cars are available.

INFORMATION
Governor Dodge State Park   608-935-2315
Route 1, Box 42
Dodgeville, Wisconsin 53533

GREAT RIVER STATE TRAIL
11

See under LA CROSSE RIVER STATE TRAIL

HARRINGTON BEACH STATE PARK
12

LOCATION - The park is on the shore of Lake Michigan approximately 10 miles north of Port Washington. To reach it, take the Belgium-Lake Church exit off Wisconsin 143 and drive east one mile on Ozaukee County Highway D.

ACTIVITIES - The park is open from May 15–November 1, and is available for day-use only. If you arrive here on summer weekends or holidays, you'll need to park and take the shuttle to reach the activities' sites. Most people arrive here in late July or early August if they plan to swim, body surf, raft or go boating since an eastern wind is usually blowing by then. Hike the mile-long sandy beach along the lake shore.

INFORMATION

Harrington Beach State Park   414-285-3015
Box 75A
Belgium, Wisconsin 53004

HARTMAN CREEK STATE PARK
13

LOCATION - Hartman Creek is six miles west of Waupaca off Wisconsin 54.

FEATURES - Artifacts and effigy mounds indicate that the area was occupied around 9,000 years ago. There's evidence of their old trail systems and villages, and the Old Coach Bike Trail that crosses through the park was once part of a cross-country Indian trail, and later part of a stage coach line.

The west end of the park is part of the terminal moraine left behind by the Wisconsin glacier, and now has potholes, gullies and springs.

ACTIVITIES - The park has over 1,300 acres of woods, and features 10 miles of groomed cross-country ski trails for touring during the winter, and 17 miles of hiking trails during the summer. Enjoy swimming from the sandy beach, fishing, biking, boating or canoeing on the five lakes, going on guided hikes, or attending evening programs. Camp in one of 100 campsites open year-round.

Near the town of King, southwest of Waupaca, follow King Road east then County K south to the Old Red Mill and see the largest water wheel in the state. You'll also see a covered bridge, colonial shop and the Chapel in the Woods. It's open year-round. For information on the mill, call 715-258-7385.

Incoming pilots can land at Waupaca Municipal Airport located three miles southeast of Waupaca. Rental cars are available.

INFORMATION

Hartman Creek State Park   715-258-2372
N2480 Hartman Creek Road
Waupaca, Wisconsin 54981-9727

HERITAGE HILL STATE PARK
14

LOCATION - The park is at the intersection of Wisconsin 57 and 172, 2640 South Webster Avenue, in Green Bay. Green Bay is located in northeastern Wisconsin, at the junction of the Fox and East rivers which empty into the bay of Green Bay.

ACTIVITIES - The park re-creates the life and times of the Green Bay area from 1634 to the end of the 19th century, and has the state's oldest house constructed in 1776.

History buffs can take a guided tour of the over 20 furnished historical buildings dating from 1672 through 1905. The park's buildings are grouped into four themes: pioneer, military, small town and agricultural. Highlights include a restored Moravian church built in 1852, which has a working replica of the original 500 pipe organ. Check the schedule to see if you can hear it being played.

Get a copy of their special events including Civil War weekends, open air band and orchestra concerts featuring 19th-century music, old time country fairs and farm festivals. At Christmas, learn more about the "Spirit of Christmas Past," and find out how our holiday celebration grew from simple pioneer religious services to becoming the celebration we have today.

Living history presentations are offered daily. If you're lucky, perhaps you can also hear a spine-tingling account of what early surgery was like by the resident "surgeon" in the Fort Howard Hospital. The park is open daily spring and summer, and on selected weekdays and weekends at other times. For information, call 414-497-4368.

While in Green Bay, tour the Green Bay Packer Hall of Fame across from Lambeau Field at 855 Lombardi Avenue. Before strolling through the exhibits, watch a 27-minute show on the history of the team from 1919 to the present. Admission is charged. For information, call 414-499-4281.

Hazelwood is Green Bay's only public historic house, and is a good example of Greek revival architecture. It was built in 1837 on a hillside overlooking the Fox River, and is listed on the National Register of Historic Places. It's located at 1008 South Monroe Avenue. For information, call 414-437-0360.

For general information on Green Bay community events, call 414-494-1111, or for visitor information: 1-800-236-3976.

During the winter, Green Bay has several areas for cross-country skiing including Hilly Haven Ski Trail, 19 miles long, Reforestation Camp with 13.5 miles of groomed trails, and He-Nis-Ra Park with five miles of trails.

Incoming pilots can land at Austin Straubel International Airport located seven miles southwest of Green Bay. Rental cars are available.

INFORMATION
Heritage Hill State Park
2640 South Webster Avenue
Green Bay, Wisconsin 54301
414-448-5150

HIGH CLIFF STATE PARK
15

LOCATION - The park is three miles south of Sherwood off Wisconsin 55.

ACTIVITIES - The park is located on some limestone bluffs that overlook Lake Winnebago. History and geology enthusiasts will enjoy touring the park's museum to learn more about the effigy mound builders, effects of glaciation, and about the earlier quarry operations.

Park facilities include a 54-site campground. Boat from the marina, horseback along the riding trails, or go hiking, fishing for walleye, panfish, perch and bass, swimming, and purchase your necessities from the concession area.

Join a park naturalist on summer weekends for a guided hike, and attend an evening program to learn more about the park.

If you're in the area the last week in July and the first of August, go around the lake to Oshkosh to attend the EAA (Experimental Aircraft Association) fly-in. This annual event attracts thousands of airplane lovers and home-built plane builders, and features a daily airshow. The Concorde has visited the fly-in on three different occasions to offer rides up to Canada to break the sound barrier, and then return to Oshkosh. EAA members can camp across the road from the airfield in one of the largest campgrounds you've ever stayed in.

Also, tour the EAA Air Adventure Museum located on the field to see its collection of world-famous experimental aircraft. For information, call 414-426-4800.

INFORMATION

High Cliff State Park   414-989-1106
N7475 High Cliff Road
Menasha, Wisconsin 54952

HOFFMAN HILLS STATE RECREATION AREA
16

See under RED CEDAR STATE TRAIL

INTERSTATE STATE PARK
17

LOCATION - The park is located along the east side of the Dalles of the St. Croix River, and .5-mile south of St. Croix Falls on U.S. 8.

ACTIVITIES - See the Old Man of the Dalles rock formation, or hike the Potholes Trail to see some unusual holes carved by boulders that ground into the lava at the base of an ancient waterfall.

Stop by the interpretive center near the park entrance to watch their 20 minute film, "Night of the Sun." Attend naturalist programs offered evenings on Friday and Saturday from Memorial Day through Labor Day.

The park has 10 miles of hiking trails that include the Lake of the Dalles, a one-mile-long trail around the lake. Climb to Summit Rock to get a fantastic view of the rocky Dalles along the St. Croix River, or stroll among the ferns through the cooler valleys. The lake has a guarded beach for swimming during the summer, and you can camp in the campground with 85 sites.

Anglers can enjoy fishing either in the Lake O' the Dalles, or in the St. Croix River for pike, bass, crappie, walleye, catfish and sturgeon.

St. Croix Falls is headquarters for the St. Croix National Scenic Riverway that extends 252 miles. Its visitor center is located at the north end of St. Croix, and has exhibits on the logging and early settlers to the area plus a movie, "St. Croix Reflections," that is shown upon request. The naturalists will also assist you in planning canoe trips in the area. Imagine canoeing along the river during the fall when the hardwoods have taken on their fall hues.

INFORMATION

Interstate State Park	Superintendent
Box 703	St. Croix National Scenic Riverway
St. Croix Falls, Wisconsin 54024	Massachusetts and Hamilton Streets
715-232-1242	P.O. Box 708
	St. Croix Falls, Wisconsin 54024
	715-483-3284

KOHLER-ANDRAE STATE PARK
18

LOCATION - The park is south of Sheboygan, and is reached by going to Exit 48 off I-43 onto V Street. Drive east one mile on County Road V to County Road KK. Then continue south for another half-mile to the campground.

ACTIVITIES - This park has 1.5 miles of dunes and beach to explore with two self-guided nature trails. Tour the Sanderling Nature Center with its observation deck that overlooks Lake Michigan.

Camp in the campground with 105 sites, including 49 with electrical hookups. Go horseback riding along the trails, go swimming or fishing for trout in Lake Michigan, and attend naturalist programs.

Take a bicycle ride on the Sheboygan County Recreation Trail that is 36 miles long, and links Sheboygan to Fond du Lac. Ride out three miles from town to see Sheboygan Falls.

Incoming pilots can land at Sheboygan County Memorial Airport located three miles northwest of Sheboygan Falls. Rental cars are available.

INFORMATION
Kohler-Andrea State Park   414-452-3457
1520 Old Park Road
Sheboygan, Wisconsin 53081

LA CROSSE RIVER STATE TRAIL
GREAT RIVER STATE TRAIL
PERROT STATE PARK
19

LOCATION - The La Crosse Bike Trail begins in LaCrosse, and the Great River State Trail begins in Onalaska. Perrot State Park is one mile north of Trempealeau off Wisconsin 35.

ACTIVITIES - The GREAT RIVER STATE TRAIL follows the shore of the Mississippi River, and goes from Onalaska north through Trempealeau and Perrot State Park to the Trempealeau National Wildlife Refuge.

The LA CROSSE RIVER BIKE TRAIL goes 23.5 miles east along the La Crosse River into Sparta, and links the Great River and Elroy-Sparta State Trails. By combining these trails, the biker has almost 75 miles of recreational trails to ride, bike, hike, snowmobile and cross-country ski.

PERROT STATE PARK lies among the bluffs at the confluence of the Trempealeau and Mississippi rivers. From here, you can get some spectacular views of the Mississippi flowing 500 feet below you. The park is open year-round with camping from mid-April through mid-October, and the campground has 97 sites with 37 offering electrical hookups.

Climb 520-foot Brady's Bluff to the hiker's shelter to watch the barges maneuvering along the channel en route to Louisiana or to the Twin Cities.

The park has eight miles of hiking trails, including a self-guided nature trail, and a nature center attended seasonally by naturalists, who, on weekends, can teach you about the park's edible plants.

While you're in La Crosse, drive or bike up to Granddad Bluff to get a spectacular view of the Mississippi River from its 600-foot vantage point.

INFORMATION

Great River State Trail
c/o Perrot State Park
Route 1, Box 407
Trempealeau, Wisconsin 54661
608-534-6409

Perrot State Park
Route 1, Box 407
Trempealeau, Wisconsin 54661
608-534-6409

La Crosse River Bike Trail
c/o La Crosse Convention and
   Visitors Bureau
Riverside Park
Box 1895
La Crosse, Wisconsin 54602-1895
608-782-2366

LAKE KEGONSA STATE PARK
20

LOCATION - The park is in southern Wisconsin, 10 miles south of Madison, and five miles north of Stoughton where it's accessible from either I-90, exit 147, or from U.S. 51.

ACTIVITIES - Kegonsa means "lake of many fishes" in Winnebago, so it's not surprising that it's one of Wisconsin's most popular fishing sites where crappie, bluegill, perch, catfish and walleye are caught.

Hike the White Oak Nature Trail to see some of the mounds and watch for the large erratics or boulders scattered here by the retreating glacier that was also responsible for the formation of the large marsh in the park. Go boating from the ramp or dock, or swimming in the lake from the beach.

Camp in one of the 80 primitive campsites with no hookups. The park is open from April 1–October 31.

INFORMATION
Lake Kegonsa State Park
2405 Door Creek Road
Stoughton, Wisconsin 53589
608-873-9695

LAKE WISSOTA STATE PARK
21

LOCATION - The park is located five miles east of Chippewa Falls on Wisconsin 29. From the intersection of U.S. 124 and Wisconsin 29, continue north three miles on 124 until reaching County Road S. Continue northeast three more miles to County Road O, and then go east two more miles.

ACTIVITIES - This park is a haven for hikers—who are treated to 12 miles of trails along the lake's shoreline, through prairie land, woodland and marsh— and for people who love fishing for walleye, muskie, catfish, sturgeon and bass. The park has fish cribs along the lake bottom in front of the fishing pier that helps to attract walleye and bass.

You can also go boating or canoeing on the lake, horseback riding, and camping in the wooded campground with 81 sites, 16 of them with electrical hookups. Go water-skiing or swimming from the 300-foot guarded beach. Attend summer interpretive programs at the park's amphitheater, or join one of the naturalists for a guided hike.

Wintertime visitors come to cross-country ski along 13 miles of trails. Snowmobiles have 4.75 miles of trails within the park that connect with the county's trail system that spans 150 miles.

INFORMATION
Lake Wissota State Park
Box 360
Chippewa Falls, Wisconsin 54729
715-382-4574

MILITARY RIDGE STATE TRAIL
22

LOCATION - The 39.6-mile-long trail connects Dodgeville and Fitchburg, near Madison, Wisconsin. Parking lots are located at the intersection of Wisconsins 18/151 and PB east of Verona, and near Wisconsin YZ, .2-mile east of Wisconsin 23 near Dodgeville.

FEATURES - Much of the trail is along the old Chicago and North Western Railway line, so it has a very gentle grade ranging from two to five percent. Before the arrival of the railroad, the original path was an old military road built in 1835. The state trail goes to the top of Military Ridge, its highest point rising to 1,300 feet, and is located between Dodgeville and Mount Horeb. Mount Horeb is called the Troll Capital of the World, and is a Norwegian community that celebrates its heritage through its shops and activities. The trail's lowest point is at 930 feet in the Sugar River Valley.

ACTIVITIES - The trail is ideal for bicycling, hiking, running, plus snowmobiling and cross-country skiing during the winter. Bikers need to purchase a permit before riding the trail, and these are available in the towns along the route.

Camping along the trail is not allowed, but you can camp at Blue Mound State Park. Bicyclists can camp at Governor Dodge State Park. Both parks accept advance reservations.

If you begin your trek near Verona, you'll see a branch of the Ice Age Trail intersecting the bike path a short distance from its start. This 1,000-mile-long trail was designed to follow the entire length of the moraines left behind by the glacier, marking its furthest advance. To date, only 160 miles of this trail have been certified by the National Park Service. For additional information on the completed trail segments passing through Wisconsin, contact the Wisconsin Department of Natural Resources, Box 7921, Madison, Wisconsin 53707, or the Ice Age Trail Council, 2302 Lakeland Avenue, Madison, Wisconsin 53704.

Incoming pilots can land at Dane County Regional-Truax Field located five miles northeast of Madison. Rental cars are available.

INFORMATION
Military Ridge State Trail   608-935-2315
Route 1, Box 42
Highway 23 North
Dodgeville, Wisconsin 53533

MILL BLUFF STATE PARK
23

LOCATION - The park is four miles northwest of Camp Douglas and may be reached from Wisconsin 12 and 16 that parallels I-90/94. Exits are located at Oakdale, five miles northwest of the park, or at Camp Douglas, two miles southeast.

FEATURES - The park is famous for its 100-foot sandstone bluffs and petroglyphs (rock carvings), shaped like bird tracks, and are believed to date back to the Upper Mississippi Indian culture.

ACTIVITIES - Enjoy rustic camping in one of their 21 sites from Memorial Day through Labor Day, and swimming from the beach. The park is part of the Ice Age National Scientific Reserve. Hike the trail leading to the top of Mill Bluff.

Tomah is a good place to stop at one of the local cheese shops to sample their wares. Ask for a taste of their cheeses.

INFORMATION
Mill Bluff State Park
Highway 33E
Ontario, Wisconsin 54651
608-337-4775

MIRROR LAKE STATE PARK
24

LOCATION - The park is near Lake Delton and the Wisconsin Dells. To reach it, at the intersection of I-90/94 go south for .5-mile on Wisconsin 12 to Fern Dell Road, and then west for another 1.5 miles.

ACTIVITIES - Camp in the campground with 144 sites, with 27 of them offering electrical hookups. This campground is usually booked throughout the summer, so advance reservations, particularly on the weekend, are suggested. Only nine campsites in Cliffwood, and 18 campsites in Sandstone Campground have electrical outlets.

The lake has sandstone cliffs that rise up to 50 feet, and also has 9.75 miles of beautiful hiking trails where you can explore the results of the glacier that was here from 10–20 thousand years ago.

Go fishing for 20-inch bass, crappie, perch, and northerns from the shore or in the lake, canoeing or boating in no-wake craft, or go swimming from the sandy beach.

Watch for the pileated woodpecker, the largest woodpecker in North America. They dig large rectangular-shaped holes in the trees, and the males display a brilliant red crest.

During the winter, ice-anglers compete in the annual Pickerel Slough Fisharee. Cross-country skiers have access to 3.5 miles of trails. Snowmobiles have access to nine miles of trails.

While you're in the area, take a tour on one of the riverboats on either the Upper or Lower Dells. The Upper cruise makes three stops so you can get a closer look at the towering rock canyons on the sides of the river. One stop is at Stand Rock where a trained dog leaps from Stand Rock to a nearby bluff top. Boat tours go from mid-April through late October. For information, call 608-253-1561.

Incoming pilots can land at Baraboo-Wisconsin Dells Airport located four miles northwest of Baraboo. Rental cars are available.

INFORMATION
Mirror Lake State Park   608-254-2333
Route 1, Box 283
Baraboo, Wisconsin 53913

NEW GLARUS STATE PARK
25

See under SUGAR RIVER BIKE TRAIL

NEWPORT STATE PARK
26

LOCATION - The park is five miles from the Village of Ellison Bay in Door County, and north of Sturgeon Bay. To reach it, go north and then east from Ellison Bay on Wisconsin 42 and Newport Road.

FEATURES - Since the park is mostly wooded, a remnant of the old hardwood forest is set aside as the Newport Conifer-Hardwoods Scientific Area.

ACTIVITIES - This semi-wilderness area provides the visitor with opportunities for hiking on 28 miles of trails with an overall elevation gain of only 50 feet. Go swimming from the 3,000-foot beach, and backpack camping along a wild beach that extends 11 miles beside Lake Michigan. The backpacking units are scattered throughout the park, and are located an average of 1.5 to 3.5 miles from the trailheads.

Incoming pilots can land at Door County-Cherryland Airport located two miles west of Sturgeon Bay. Rental cars are available.

For activities in Sturgeon Bay, see Whitefish Dune State Park.

INFORMATION
Newport State Park   414-854-2500
475 South Newport Lane
Ellison Bay, Wisconsin 54210

PATTISON STATE PARK
27

LOCATION - The park is ten miles south of Superior on Wisconsin 35.

ACTIVITIES - Be sure to see Big Manitou Falls, the state's highest waterfall, which drops 165 feet into the steep-walled gorge carved by the Black River. You'll also see Little Manitou Falls, and can camp in the campground with 59 sites, 18 with electrical hookups. Go hiking, trout fishing, and swimming in Interfalls Lake. The park is open year-round.

Go into town and take a harbor sightseeing cruise from Barker's Island Dock. For information on departures from May to mid-October, call 715-394-6846.

Incoming pilots can land at Richard Bong Airport located three miles south of Superior. Rental cars are available.

INFORMATION
Pattison State Park
Route 2, Box 435
Superior, Wisconsin 54880
715-399-8073.

PENINSULA STATE PARK
28

LOCATION - To reach the park, follow Wisconsin 57 north out of Green Bay to Wisconsin 42, and continue north to the park entrance located in the village of Fish Creek on the "thumb" that extends northeast into Lake Michigan. The park occupies the entire peninsula between Ephraim and Fish Creek on the Green Bay side of Wisconsin 42.

ACTIVITIES - Enjoy camping on the beach, or in one of the park's four campgrounds that accommodate 473 camping units, 100 of them with electrical hookups. The park is heavily used during the summer and on fall weekends, so reservations are advised.

Go hiking along 17 miles of trails, climb the 110 stairs into the lighthouse built in 1868 at Eagle Bluff where you can see the surrounding islands of northern Green Bay, Peninsula State Park, Upper Michigan and even part of Lake Michigan, and watch the ships passing below your feet.

Play golf on the 18-hole park course, fish for trout and bass, or go sailing on the bay from the harbor at Horseshoe Island that guards the entrance to Nicolet Bay.

Bicyclists can ride five-mile Sunset Trail, part of the park's designated bikeway. You can rent sailboats, paddle boats, wind surfers, canoes and bikes from Nicoleg Beach or from Bike Rentals located in the park.

Go for a drive along the scenic roads of the park's 20 miles of shoreline.

Incoming pilots can land at Door County-Cherryland Airport located two miles west of Sturgeon Bay. Rental cars are available.

INFORMATION
Peninsula State Park
Route 42
Fish Creek, Wisconsin 54212
414-868-3258

PERROT STATE PARK
29

See under LA CROSSE RIVER STATE TRAIL

PIKE LAKE STATE PARK
30

LOCATION - The park is west of Milwaukee, and is two miles east of Hartford on Wisconsin 60.

ACTIVITIES - Campers love coming here because of the panoramic views they can get from the summit of 1,350-foot high Powder Hill. The campground opens in mid-April, and closes the end of October, and has 32 sites with no hookups. It's located in the Kettle Moraine area, and the Ice Age Trail passes through the park. Many glacial features may be seen along the Pike Lake Trail section.

Fish either during the summer, or go ice fishing in the winter for walleye, northerns, perch and bluegill. Swim, water-ski and canoe on the lake.

One of the most popular times to visit here is in the fall when you can hike in the hardwood forest and mushroom hunt, pick berries, and gather nuts along the way.

Incoming pilots can land at Hartford Municipal Airport located two miles northwest of Hartford. Rental cars are available.

INFORMATION
Pike Lake State Park
3340 Kettle Moraine Road
Hartford, Wisconsin 53027
414-644-5248

POTAWATOMI STATE PARK
31

LOCATION - The park is 2.5 miles northwest of Sturgeon Bay. It's directly across Green Bay from Sawyer Harbor, and west of Sturgeon Bay on Wisconsin C.

ACTIVITIES - Go out onto its observation platform from which you can see Marinette across the bay, and Chambers Island, 20 miles to the northeast.

Enjoy boating from the ramp, camping in the campground with 125 wooded campsites, 23 of them with electrical hookups. Have a picnic, and go swimming from the beach beside Sturgeon Bay. Hike the 20-mile shoreline that's dotted with granite boulders or erratics left behind by the glacier

The park has nine other miles of hiking trails through the hardwoods. This would be beautiful during the fall. Hike the .5-mile-long "Ancient Shores" nature trail along the shoreline of the two glacially carved lakes, Algonquin and Nipissing, to see ancient shorelines located 20 to 60 feet above the present water level.

Go fishing for chinook salmon, brown trout, perch, bass, walleye and northern pike. Anglers gather here in the fall when the chinook salmon spawning run occurs. Sometimes these fish reach 20–40 pounds.

Bike or hike the Ahnapee State Trail that begins on the southern end of Sturgeon Bay, and goes down to the north side of Algoma. Its 15.3 miles follow an abandoned railroad grade, and the trail is another section of the 1,000-mile-long Ice Age National Scenic Trail. Information on the trail may be obtained through the Potawatomi State Park.

Nearby attractions include the Door County Museum and the Sturgeon Bay Marine Museum where you can learn the history of shipbuilding and commercial fishing. You'll see sailboats from the turn-of-the-century, and artifacts collected from sunken ships. Since Sturgeon Bay is one of the biggest shipbuilding ports on the Great Lakes, you can watch ships, boats and yachts being constructed here.

If you visit Sturgeon Bay in late May, you'll be in time to see one of Wisconsin's most extensive cherry orchards in full bloom.

Incoming pilots can land at Door County-Cherryland Airport located two miles west of Sturgeon Bay. Rental cars are available.

INFORMATION
Potawatomi State Park
3740 Park Drive
Sturgeon Bay, Wisconsin 54235
414-743-8869 or 8860

RED CEDAR STATE TRAIL
HOFFMAN HILLS STATE RECREATION AREA
32

LOCATION - The bike path borders the Red Cedar River beginning at a former rail freight depot on the west side of Menomonie and traveling south to the Chippewa River. The state park is nine miles northeast of town.

ACTIVITIES - The state trail runs miles along the Red Cedar River through the Dunnville Wildlife Area. As you ride, you'll pass through woods, prairies, and below sandstone cliffs, and cross the 846-foot former railroad bridge. It's open year-round, and is also groomed for cross-country skiing during the winter months.

For a change of pace, try canoeing down the Red Cedar River that parallels the trail, and then returning by bicycle.

Several miles south of Irvington, stop to see the rock landmark called "The Pinnacle" where legend holds that French soldiers hid a treasure of gold somewhere on the west bank of the river when they had to escape an Indian attack. At mile 4.5, go fishing for smallmouth bass. Near Downsville at mile 5, watch for bald eagles and osprey during the late summer and early fall.

If you're in town during the summer on Tuesday evening, go by the Wilson Park bandstand at 8 p.m. to hear the Ludington Guard Band perform.

Antique hunters should be sure to stop by the Chamber of Commerce office to get a map of all the area's antique shops.

INFORMATION

Red Cedar State Trail   715-232-1242
Route 6, Box 1
Menomonie, Wisconsin 54751

Hoffman Hills State Recreation Area   715-232-1242
Route 6, Box 1
Menonomie, Wisconsin 54751

RIB MOUNTAIN STATE PARK
33

LOCATION - The park is four miles southwest of Wausau on County Road NN.

FEATURES - Rib Mountain is one of the oldest geological formations on earth, and is estimated to be around a billion years old.

ACTIVITIES - Go up the 60-foot observation tower to get an unforgettable view of the Wisconsin River Valley. Enjoy picnicking, hiking, and camping in the campground with 30 sites, open from May 1–October 31.

Drive to the top of the mountain on a road maintained year-round.

Each June, Wausau is the site of the annual World Kayaking Championships and "Logjam" festival. For details, call the Wausau Area Convention and Visitors Council at 715-845-6231 or 800-236-WSAU.

Attend a performance in the Grand Theater on 4th Street that has been restored to its original Greco-Revival splendor. Special tours may be arranged. For information, call 715-842-0988.

Incoming pilots can land at Wausau Municipal Airport located south of Wausau. Rental cars are available.

INFORMATION
Rib Mountain State Park
5301 Rib Mountain Drive
Wausau, Wisconsin 54401
715-359-4522

ROCKY ARBOR STATE PARK
34

LOCATION - From Wisconsin Dells, go northwest for one mile on U.S. 12.

ACTIVITIES - Because of its proximity to the Wisconsin Dells, this campground is generally booked up during the summer months, so reservations are suggested. The park has 89 wooded campsites with 18 electrical hookups, and is open Memorial Day–Labor Day.

Hike the one-mile Green Deer Nature Trail to get a flavor of the picturesque area noted for its rock formations.

While in the area, don't miss taking a boat ride on the Wisconsin Dells. The 15-mile ride upstream takes you past towering sandstone cliffs and deep canyons carved by the melting waters of the Wisconsin River, and scoured out by the glaciers that once filled the area. The Upper Dells trip takes 2.5 hours, and enables you to get off the boat to take three side trips to explore some of the side canyons. At one of the stops, watch a fearless dog leap from Standing Rock Formation to an adjoining rock over five feet away and 46 feet above the ground. The Lower Dells trip takes an hour and is non-stop.

Incoming pilots can land at Baraboo-Wisconsin Dells Airport located four miles northwest of Baraboo. Rental cars are available.

INFORMATION
Rocky Arbor State Park
c/o E10320 Fern Del Road
Baraboo, Wisconsin 53913
808-254-2333

SUGAR RIVER BIKE TRAIL
NEW GLARUS STATE PARK
35

LOCATION - The northern end of this trail begins in New Glarus and ends by Brodhead.

FEATURES - The entire trail is part of the 1,000-mile-long Ice Age National Scenic Trail. New Glarus is referred to as Wisconsin's "Little Switzerland."

ACTIVITIES - This 23-mile-long bike trail was built along an abandoned railroad bed, and is popular among bicyclists because of its relatively level grade. You can rent bicycles at the trail's headquarters. Bicycle campers can overnight at the New Glarus Woods State Park that caters to bicyclists, and has 18 gravel sites.

If you're in the town of New Glarus the last full weekend in June, attend the Heidi Festival, or the Volksfest the first Sunday in August, or the Wilhelm Tell Pageant presented on Labor Day weekend.

INFORMATION
Sugar River Bike Trail
Box 805
New Glarus, Wisconsin 53574
608-527-2334 (summer)
608-325-4844 (winter)

New Glarus State Park
New Glarus, Wisconsin 53574
608-527-2335

TOWER HILL STATE PARK
36

LOCATION - From Spring Green, drive south 2.5 miles on Wisconsin 23 to CR-C, then continue east for one more mile.

ACTIVITIES - The park is open from May through October when you can camp in one of the 15 sites in the wooded campground. Enjoy fishing for catfish, and go boating from the ramp.

A restored Civil War shot tower is here, and visitors can see a film and displays on lead shot made here during the 1800s for use in the developing Wisconsin territory. The park provides access to the Wisconsin River, and canoers often stop here to camp overnight.

Many tourists come to this area to see The House on the Rock that is located nine miles south of town on Wisconsin 23. This amazing attraction was built as a retreat house on a rock outcrop. Gradually other buildings were added with mechanical musical devices, animated figures, and the world's largest carousel. Allow at least two to three hours for the tour. It's open from April through October from 8 a.m. until dusk. For information, call 608-935-3639, extension 15.

From late June through mid-October, see Shakespeare performed under the stars at the American Players' Theater. For information, call 608-588-7401.

INFORMATION
Tower Hill State Park
Route 3
Spring Green, Wisconsin 54651
608-588-2116

WYALUSING STATE PARK
37

LOCATION - The park is seven miles southeast of Prairie Du Chien on U.S. 18 and Wisconsin 35, and then five more miles west on County C.

ACTIVITIES - The park lies on the spot where Marquette and Joliet discovered the Mississippi River. This beautiful campground is located on a bluff above the confluence of the Wisconsin and Mississippi rivers, and has two family campgrounds with a total of 132 sites. Wisconsin Ridge campground has 32 sites with electrical outlets, and is open year-round.

Hiking in the dense forest affords some wonderful overlooks of the river. Several trails follow a ledge located above the river. Trail maps for the 15 miles of trails are available at the ranger station. Indian mounds line the Sentinel Ridge Walk, one of the self-guided nature walks. The Point Lookout hike was once used by the early Indian sentries who kept watch on all activity on the river below.

From Memorial Day through Labor Day, park naturalists give talks, guided hikes, and evening programs.

Swimmers should go to the Wyalusing Recreation Area, two miles south of the park on Wisconsin X.

Take a guided tour of Villa Louis, a mansion built over a century ago by the state's first millionaire. It's in Prairie Du Chien one mile northwest of town at 521 Villa Louis Road on St. Feriole Island. The tour takes 1.5 hours. For information, call 608-326-2721.

Incoming pilots can land at Prairie De Chien Municipal Airport located two miles south of town. Rental cars are available.

INFORMATION
Wyalusing State Park
13342 County Highway C
Bagley, Wisconsin 53801
608-996-2261

State Park Index

KEY TO THE INDEX

CG = Campground   **FS** = Fishing   **HK** = Hiking   **CO** = Concessions
VC = Visitor's Center   **WA** = Water Activities   **PG** = Page

Park Name	CG	FS	HK	CO	VC	WA	PG
Jubilee College	•	•	•			•	22
Kankakee River	•	•	•	•		•	22
Kickapoo	•	•	•	•		•	23
Lake Le-Aqua-Na	•	•	•	•		•	24
Lincoln Trail Homestead			•		•	•	25
Lincoln Trail	•	•	•	•		•	25
Lincoln's New Salem	•	•	•		•		26
Lowden	•	•				•	27
Miathiessen			•	•			27
Mississippi Palisades	•	•	•	•	•	•	27
Moraine Hills		•	•	•		•	28
Moraine View	•	•	•	•		•	29
Mt. Pulaski Courthouse							29
Murphysboro	•	•	•	•		•	30
Nauvoo	•	•	•			•	30
Pere Marquette	•	•	•	•	•	•	30
Postville Courthouse							32
Pyramid	•	•	•			•	32
Railsplitter				•			32
Ramsey Lake	•	•	•	•		•	34
Red Hills	•	•	•	•		•	34
Sand Ridge	•	•					35
Sangchris Lake	•	•	•			•	36
Shabbona Lake	•	•	•	•		•	36
Silver Springs	•	•	•				37
South Shore	•	•				•	37
Starved Rock	•	•	•	•	•	•	38
Stephen A. Forbes	•	•	•			•	38
Trail of Tears	•	•					38
W. G. Stratton			•	•		•	39
Wayne Fitzgerrell	•	•	•			•	39
Weinberg-King	•	•	•				40
Weldon Springs	•	•	•	•		•	40
White Pines Forest	•	•	•	•			41
Wolf Creek	•	•	•			•	42

INDIANA

Park Name	CG	FS	HK	CO	VC	WA	PG
Bass Lake	•	•				•	47
Brown County	•	•	•	•	•		47
Chain O'Lakes	•	•	•		•	•	48
Clifty Falls	•			•	•		49
Harmonie	•	•	•			•	50
Indiana Dunes	•	•	•			•	50
Lincoln	•	•	•		•	•	51
McCormick's Creek	•	•	•		•	•	53
Mounds	•	•	•			•	53
Ouabache	•	•	•			•	54
Patoka Lake	•	•	•			•	55
Potato Creek	•	•	•	•		•	56
Shades	•	•	•			•	56

Park Name	CG	FS	HK	CO	VC	WA	PG
Crawford State Fishing Pit	•	•		•		•	91
Eisenhower	•	•	•	•		•	92
El Dorado	•	•	•	•		•	93
Elk City	•	•	•			•	93
Fall River	•	•		•		•	94
Glen Elder	•	•	•		•	•	95
Kanopolis	•	•	•	•		•	96
Keith Sebelius	•	•	•	•		•	97
Lake Scott	•	•	•	•		•	97
Lovewell	•	•				•	97
Meade	•	•				•	98
Melvern Reservoir	•	•	•	•		•	92
Milford	•	•		•		•	98
Mushroom Rock	•	•	•	•		•	99
Perry	•			•		•	99
Pomona	•	•			•	•	100
Prairie Dog	•	•			•	•	100
Sand Hills				•			101
Toronto	•	•	•			•	102
Tuttle Creek	•	•	•	•		•	102
Waconda Lake	•	•	•		•	•	95
Webster	•	•	•			•	103

MICHIGAN

Park Name	CG	FS	HK	CO	VC	WA	PG
Algonac	•	•				•	107
Bald Mountain		•	•	•		•	107
Baraga		•	•	•		•	108
Bay City		•	•	•	•	•	109
Bewabic		•	•	•		•	110
Brighton		•	•	•	•	•	110
Brimley		•	•	•		•	111
Cheboygan		•	•	•		•	112
Clear Lake		•	•			•	112
Colonial Michilimackinac							113
Fayette		•	•	•	•	•	114
Fisherman's Island		•	•	•		•	115
Fort Custer		•	•	•		•	116
Fort Wilkins		•	•	•	•	•	116
Grand Haven	•	•	•	•			117
Hartwick Pines	•	•	•	•	•	•	118
Highland	•	•	•	•		•	119
Hoffmaster	•	•	•	•	•	•	120
Holland	•	•	•	•		•	120
Holly	•	•	•	•		•	121
Indian Lake	•	•	•		•	•	122
Interlochen	•	•	•	•		•	123
Island Lake	•	•	•	•		•	124
J. W. Wells	•	•	•			•	125
Lake Gogebic	•	•	•			•	125
Leelanau	•	•	•			•	126

MISSOURI

Park Name	CG	FS	HK	CO	VC	WA	PG
Crowder	•	•	•			•	203
Cuivre River	•	•	•			•	204
Dr. Edmund A. Babler Memorial	•		•	•			205
Elephant Rocks				•			206
Finger Lakes	•	•				•	206
First Missouri State Capitol							207
Ha Ha Tonka			•	•			208
Harry S. Truman	•	•	•			•	209
Hawn	•	•	•				210
Johnson's Shut-ins	•	•	•				211
Knob Noster	•	•	•			•	212
Lake of the Ozarks	•	•	•		•	•	212
Lake Wappapello	•	•	•	•		•	213
Lewis and Clark	•	•				•	214
Long Branch	•	•				•	214
Mark Twain Birthplace	•	•	•			•	215
Meramec	•	•	•	•		•	216
Missouri River				•			217
Montauk	•	•	•	•		•	217
Onondaga Cave	•	•	•	•		•	218
Pershing	•	•	•			•	219
Pomme de Terre	•	•	•			•	219
Prairie				•			220
Roaring River	•	•	•	•	•		220
Rock Bridge Memorial			•	•			221
Sam A. Baker	•	•	•	•	•	•	222
St. Francois	•	•	•			•	222
St. Joe	•	•	•			•	223
Stockton	•	•	•		•	•	224
Table Rock	•	•	•		•	•	224
Thousand Hills	•	•	•	•		•	225
Trail of Tears	•	•	•			•	226
Wallace	•	•	•			•	227
Washington	•	•	•	•	•	•	227
Watkins Mill	•	•	•			•	228

NEBRASKA

Park Name	CG	FS	HK	CO	VC	WA	PG
Arbor Lodge				•			231
Ash Hollow Cave	•			•		•	233
Branched Oak	•	•			•	•	234
Brownville	•	•				•	234
Buffalo Bill							235
Burchard Lake	•	•	•				236
Calamus Reservoir	•	•				•	236
Chadron	•	•	•	•	•	•	237
Enders Reservoir	•	•		•		•	238
Eugene T. Mahoney	•	•		•		•	238
Fort Atkinson				•			239
Fort Kearny	•	•	•		•	•	239
Fort Robinson				•			241

Park Name	CG	FS	HK	CO	VC	WA	PG
Fremont Lakes	•	•				•	242
Indian Cave	•	•	•				243
Johnson Lake	•	•				•	244
Keller Lake	•	•	•				245
Lake McConaughy	•	•				•	245
Lewis and Clark	•	•			•	•	246
Louisville	•	•				•	247
Medicine Creek Reservoir	•	•		•		•	247
Memphis Lake	•	•					248
Merritt Reservoir	•	•	•			•	248
Mormon Island	•	•				•	249
Niobrara	•	•	•			•	250
Pawnee Lake	•	•	•	•		•	250
Pelican Point	•	•				•	251
Platte River	•	•	•	•	•	•	252
Ponca	•	•	•			•	253
Red Willow	•	•		•		•	254
Rock Creek Station	•			•	•		254
Schramm Park				•			255
Sherman Reservoir			•				255
Summit Lake	•	•					256
Swanson Reservoir	•	•				•	256
Two Rivers	•	•	•	•		•	256
Victoria Springs	•	•				•	257
Wildcat Hills	•			•			258
Windmill	•	•				•	258

NORTH DAKOTA

Park Name	CG	FS	HK	CO	VC	WA	PG
Beaver Lake	•	•	•			•	263
Black Tiger Bay		•				•	263
Cross Ranch	•	•	•		•	•	263
Devils Lake State Park		•	•			•	265
Fort Abraham Lincoln	•	•	•			•	267
Fort Ransom	•	•	•				268
Fort Stevenson	•	•	•	•		•	269
Graham's Island	•	•	•			•	270
Icelandic	•	•	•		•	•	270
Lake Metigoshe	•	•	•			•	271
Lake Sakakawea	•	•	•	•		•	272
Lewis and Clark	•	•	•	•		•	273
Little Missouri Bay	•		•				273
Narrows						•	274
Shelver's Grove	•					•	274
Sully Creek	•				•	•	274
Turtle River	•	•	•			•	275

OHIO

Park Name	CG	FS	HK	CO	VC	WA	PG
A. W. Marion	•	•	•	•		•	277
Alum Creek	•	•	•	•		•	279

About the Author

Vici DeHann was an elementary schoolteacher in the Boulder Valley Schools for 31 years where she has taught grades K–6. She is the author of eight other books: *Bicycling the Colorado Rockies*, *Hiking Trails of the Boulder Mountain Parks and Plains*, *Moving Through the Ratings: Passing from Private to Professional Pilot*, *The Runner's Guide to Boulder County*, *Bike Rides of the Colorado Front Range*, *Pilot's Cross-Country Guide to National Parks and Historical Monuments*, *The Pilot's Cross-Country Guide to National Parks*, and *State Parks of the West*.

Vici DeHaan is an avid outdoors person who has hiked in the Colorado Rockies all her life. She also plays handball with the Boulder Valley Retired Teachers. She's been singing actively for 40 years, and also plays the piano as time permits.

Vici holds a private pilot's license and a ground instructor's rating. She and her husband, Warren, have flown their light plane all over the United States, Canada and Mexico. The live in Boulder, Colorado, and have five children and two grandchildren.